godless

How an Evangelical Preacher Became
One of America's Leading Atheists

DAN BARKER
Foreword by Richard Dawkins

Ulysses Press

Published in the U.S. by
ULYSSES PRESS
P.O. Box 3440
Berkeley, CA 94703
www.ulyssespress.com

ISBN13: 978-1-56975-677-5
Library of Congress Control Number 2008904135

Acquisitions Editor: Nick Denton-Brown
Managing Editor: Claire Chun
Editor: Scott McRae
Editorial Associates: Juana Castro, Lauren Harrison,
Abby Reser, Emma Silvers
Indexer: Sayre Van Young
Cover design: Double R Design
Interior design and production: what!design @ whatweb.com

Printed in the U.S. by Bang Printing

4 6 8 10 9 7 5 3

Distributed by Publishers Group West

Advance Praise for *Godless*

"I think *Godless* is fabulous. It came on Friday, and I
spent much of the weekend reading it. It was a revelation to me.
Others have made the journey ('faith to reason,' childhood to
adulthood, fantasy to reality, intoxication to sobriety—however
one likes to put it), but I don't think anyone can match the
(devastating!) clarity, intensity, and honesty which Dan Barker
brings to the telling. And the tone is right all the way through—
not belligerent or confrontational (as is the case with so much, too
much, of the literature on this subject—on both sides).
I think *Godless* may well become a classic in its genre."
—OLIVER SACKS
author of *Musicophilia: Tales of Music and the Brain*

"Atheists are the last of the minorities in America
to come out of the closet, and like other civil rights movements
this one began with leaders like Dan Barker and his Freedom
from Religion Foundation defending the civil liberties of godless
Americans, who deserve equal protection under the Constitution.
In his new book, *Godless*, Barker recounts his journey from
evangelical preacher to atheist activist, and along the way
explains precisely why it is not only okay to be an atheist,
it is something of which to be proud."
—MICHAEL SHERMER
publisher of *Skeptic* magazine, monthly columnist for
Scientific American, author of *How We Believe*,
Why Darwin Matters, and *The Mind of the Market*

"Conversions on the road to Damascus are for those
who hear voices and fall prey to delusions and who would be better
off seeking professional help. Much more valuable in the human
story are the reflections of intelligent and ethical people who listen
to the voice of reason and who allow it to vanquish bigotry and
superstition. This book is a classic example of the latter."
—CHRISTOPHER HITCHENS
author of *God Is Not Great: How Religion Poisons Everything*

"My kids are in the process of learning about literature, and a rule of thumb they've picked up concerns how to recognize the protagonist of a story: It's the character who undergoes the greatest transformation. This makes sense, because one of the hardest things we confront is the need to change. By this criterion, in the enormous story of what we all do with our lives, Dan Barker is one of the most interesting and brave protagonists I know. *Godless* is a fascinating memoir, a tour of one distressing extreme of religiosity, a handbook for debunking theism. But most of all, it is a moving testimonial to one man's emotional and intellectual rigor in acclaiming critical thinking."

—ROBERT SAPOLSKY
author of *Why Zebras Don't Get Ulcers:*
An Updated Guide to Stress, Stress-Related Diseases and Coping

"Dan Barker's esteemed reputation is richly deserved. I recommend getting three copies. You will need one as a source of evidence to which you will frequently refer. There will be miles and miles of underlining as you mark the pages of special interest to you. You will need your second to lend to others. You will be enthusiastic about this book, and you will want to share its wisdom with family and friends. Others will likewise want to share it, and the book will never be returned to you. Finally, you will want a third copy to be in pristine condition on your bookshelf, since Dan Barker has created a volume which will only grow in its historical significance."

—DAVID MILLS
author of *Atheist Universe*

"This book profoundly affected me. It's funny, and poignant, and most importantly, true! You must read this book."

—JULIA SWEENEY
comedian, actress, Saturday Night Live alum

For bonnie Annie Laurie

TABLE OF CONTENTS

Foreword

It isn't difficult to work out that religious fundamentalists are deluded—those people who think the entire universe began after the agricultural revolution; people who believe literally that a snake, presumably in fluent Hebrew, beguiled into sin a man fashioned from clay and a woman grown from him as a cutting: people who find it self-evident that the origin myth that happened to dominate their own childhood trumps the thousands of alternative myths sprung from all the dreamtimes of the world. It is one thing to know that these faith-heads are wrong. My mistake has been naively to think I can remove their delusion simply by talking to them in a quiet, sensible voice and laying out the evidence, clear for all to see. It isn't as easy as that. Before we can talk to them, we must struggle to understand them; struggle to enter their seized minds and empathize. What is it really like to be so indoctrinated that you can honestly and sincerely believe obvious nonsense—believe it with every fiber of your being?

Just as Helen Keller was able to tell us from the inside what it was like to be blind and deaf, so there are rare individuals who have broken the bonds of fundamentalist indoctrination and are also gifted with the articulate intelligence to tell the rest of us what it was like. Some of these memoirs promise much but end up disappointing. Ed Husain's *The Islamist* gives a good picture of what it is like to be a decent young man gradually sucked in, step by step, to the mental snake pit of radical Islamism. But Husain doesn't give us a feeling for what it is really like, on the inside, to believe passionately in arbitrary nonsense. And even at the end of the story, when he has escaped from jihadism, it is only the political extremism that he abjures: he seems even now not to have shaken off his childhood belief in Islam itself. Faith still lurks, and one fears for the author that he remains vulnerable. Ayaan Hirsi Ali's *Infidel* is a fascinating and moving account of her escape from the singular oppression that is a woman's lot under Islam (and "under" is the right word), including the unspeakable barbarism of genital mutilation. But even at her most devout, she was never the kind of zealot who goes around preaching and actively seeking victims to convert. Again, her book doesn't really help the reader to understand mental possession by religious delusion. The most eloquent witness of internal delusion that I know—a triumphantly smiling refugee from the zany, surreal world of American fundamentalist Protestantism—is Dan Barker.

Barker is now one of American secularism's most talented and effective spokespeople—together with his delightful partner (in all senses of the word) Annie Laurie Gaylor. Dan, to put it mildly, was not always thus. He has a truly remarkable tale to tell of his personal history and breakout from the badlands of religious fundamentalism. He was in it right from the start, up to his ears. Dan was not just a preacher, he was the kind of preacher that "you would not want to sit next to on a bus." He was the kind of preacher who would march up to perfect strangers in the street and ask them if they were saved: the kind of door-stepper on whom you might be tempted to set the dogs. Dan knows deeply what it is like to be a wingnut, a faith-head, a fully paid-up nutjob, an all singing, all glossolaling religious fruit bat. He can take us—simultaneously laughing and appalled—into that bat-belfry world and even make us sympathize. But he also knows what it is like to stumble upon the unaccustomed pleasure of thinking for oneself, without help from anybody else, right in the teeth of opposition from what was then his entire social world. The socially unacceptable habit of *thinking* led him directly to realize that his entire life so far had been a time-wasting delusion. All by himself, he came to his senses—in a big way. Unusually, he has the verbal skills and the intelligence and the sensitivity to tell us the whole story, step by painful—and yet exhilarating—step.

His account of his early indoctrination into his parents' fundamentalist sect, his unquestioning faith in the literal truth of every word of it, his disturbingly easy facility in "saving" souls, his successful career as a preacher and musician and composer for Jesus, is riveting. Even more fascinating is the process by which the doubts set in and gradually multiplied in that intelligent but naive young mind. Then there is the pathos with which he tells of the interregnum period when he was already a convinced atheist, but could not quite bring himself to leave the church of which he was a minister—mostly because this was the only life he knew, and he found it hard to face the world outside, or confront his family with the truth. As so often where there is pathos, comedy is not far behind, and there is a sort of dismal comedy in the responses of Dan's religious friends when he finally announced his atheism. In all the many letters he received, not one offered any kind of *reason* why atheistic beliefs might actually be wrong. Perhaps the funniest example is that of the Rev. Milton Barfoot, who said to Dan's brother, in apparently honest bafflement, "But, isn't Dan afraid of hell?" No, Reverend, Dan doesn't believe in hell anymore, that's one of the things about being an atheist, you see.

Dan's delay, after he became an atheist and before he resigned from the ministry, carries the likely implication that there are lots more clergymen out there who have ridden the same course as Dan but shied at the final fence: reverend atheists who dare not jump from the only way they know to make a living, dare not lose their ticket to respect in the limited society in which they move—their big fish-hood in a very small pond. How hard must that be to give up? Fascinatingly, since the publication of his previous book, *Losing Faith in Faith*, Dan Barker himself has become a kind of secret rallying post for large numbers of now faith-free but still pusillanimous clerics. Like a kind of atheistic father confessor, Dan is a magnet for the disillusioned clergy. As a good confessor, he will not betray their confidence as individuals, but there is nothing to stop him from telling their story in a general way and, once again, there's comedy mixed in with the pathos.

Dan Barker's own confessor is each reader of this book, and it is hard not to revel in the role. It is hard to disavow the exultation as Dan breaks the shackles, and even more so when he is later joined in unbelief by the parents who had been responsible for his original religious fervor, and by one of his two brothers. It wasn't that he turned his preaching skills on his family in reverse, and worked hard to deconvert them. Rather, it simply had never *occurred* to any of the family that being an atheist was even an option. As soon as they had the example of Dan before them, to show that a decent and good person could be a non-believer, they started thinking for themselves about the real issues and it didn't take them long to reach the obvious conclusion. In his mother's case, it only took her a few weeks to conclude that "religion is a bunch of baloney" and a little later she was able to add, happily, "I don't have to hate anymore." Dan's father and one of his two brothers followed a similar course. The other brother remains a born again Christian. Perhaps one day he too will see the light.

Deconversion stories occupy only the opening chapters of this book. Just as Dan's religiously doped youth gave way to a more fulfilled maturity, so later chapters of his book move on, and give us the generous reflections of a mature atheist. Dan Barker's road from Damascus will, I predict, become well trodden by many others in the future, and this book is destined to become a classic of its kind.

—Richard Dawkins

The Richard Dawkins Foundation For Reason & Science
www.RichardDawkinsFoundation.org

The Official Richard Dawkins Website
www.RichardDawkins.net

Introduction

The first time I *ever* spoke publicly about my atheism was on Oprah Winfrey's *AM Chicago* television show. That was in 1984 and less than nine months earlier I had been preaching the gospel to appreciative audiences. Now here I was, about to attack everything I had once professed. I was nervous. I had been on television before as a Christian musician, but this was entirely different.

Anne and Annie Laurie Gaylor of the Freedom From Religion Foundation (the first atheist friends I had ever knowingly met) handled the first segment of the show, discussing atheism. After the commercial, the camera pointed to me and the lights came up.

"Joining me now," said Oprah, "is a former ordained minister of 17 years who gave up his religion: Dan Barker. So, tell me your story, Dan, the *ex*-reverend."

"I was one of those guys who would walk up to you on the street and tell you about Jesus Christ," I began, "and would convince you to say the sinner's prayer, would convince you that you were a sinner deserving of damnation, tell you about Jesus' love, read the bible to you and pray with people like yourself. I was an evangelist and I loved the gospel, the calling of the ministry—and I've changed my mind."

"What made you change your mind, Dan?"

"I could give a little levity," I said. "In 30 years of going to church and being a preacher, I never got to sleep in on Sunday mornings." [laughter]

"Well, Dan, for goodness sake! Sleep in on Saturday!" Oprah quipped. "But what is the real reason? You woke up one morning and you said—what?"

"No, for me it was a five-year struggle. I was always in love with reason, and intelligence, and truth. I thought Christianity had the truth. I really believed it. I dedicated my life to it."

"When did you become a Christian?" Oprah interrupted. "When you were a little boy?"

"I was raised in church, but at the age of 15 I dedicated my life to Jesus Christ. I accepted a calling of God on my life to be a minister, to be an evangelist, and at that age I went out and started sharing. I went to the mountains and jungles of Mexico to share my faith for years. I traveled the United States, standing in parks and on street corners, telling people about Jesus' love. A 15-year-old evangelist."

"I know," Oprah said. "I did it in the third grade. I understand."

"And I really haven't changed. I'm still searching for intelligence and reason and values, and I still love the truth. I'm still the same person, the same minister who wants to know what is real and what is true, and I have decided that the evidences for Christianity are not solid evidences. The bible is an unreliable document, and it is a very uninspiring document. My heart cannot accept what my mind rejects."

"And you have decided what? There is no God?"

"I am an atheist."

"You went for 17 years as a minister to not believing in God! What does that say about you?"

"That I was wrong," I replied.

The word "godless" is defined in the *American Heritage Dictionary* as "1. Recognizing or worshiping no god. 2. Wicked, impious, immoral." This equating of atheists with evil no doubt stems from the bible: "The fool hath said in his heart, There is no God. They are corrupt, they have done abominable works, there is none that doeth good...they are all gone aside, they are all together become filthy: there is none that doeth good, no, not one." (Psalm 14:1-3)

It's hard to believe that I used to preach that sermon. I now know that the bible and the dictionary are wrong. Atheists are not filthy, corrupt fools. Millions of good people live moral, happy, loving, meaningful lives without believing in a god.

Oprah said it was 17 years, but it was actually 19 years between my first sermon at the age of 15 and my last sermon at the age of 34. Part 1 of *Godless*, Rejecting God, tells the story of how I moved from devout preacher to atheist and beyond.

Part 2, Why I Am an Atheist, presents my philosophical reasons for unbelief. While Refuting God gives simple, thumbnail responses to most theistic arguments, Cosmological Kalamity (which you are welcome to skim if philosophy is not your cup of tea) shows how I deal in depth with one of those arguments.

Part 3, What's Wrong With Christianity, critiques the bible (its reliability as well as its morality) and the historical evidence for Jesus. Biblical Contradictions gives a brief list of discrepancies, but Understanding Discrepancy takes one of these into greater depth, showing that we skeptics are not simply rattling off shallow lists.

Part 4, Life is Good!, comes back to my personal story, taking a case to the United States Supreme Court, dealing with personal trauma and experiencing the excitement of Adventures in Atheism.

This is a great time to be an atheist. The polls show that "nonreligion" is the fastest growing religious identification in the United States. In Europe, after centuries of religious strife, most of the people are secular and the ornate churches are empty. That seems to be happening on this continent, too. The corner is slowly being turned. College students, as a group, are the least religious demographic in the nation. Hundreds of secular freethinking campus organizations are sprouting up as evidence of this impending—and I say welcome—change. The phenomenal success of atheist books such as Sam Harris' *The End of Faith*, Daniel Dennett's *Breaking the Spell*, Christopher Hitchens' *God is Not Great*, Ayaan Hirsi Ali's *Infidel* and Richard Dawkins' international blockbuster, *The God Delusion*, shows that there is a hunger for reason, science and true human morality.

I am convinced there is also restlessness among the clergy and in the pews. (See the many former ministers and priests I talk about in Chapter 18.) My story is one example of what can happen when the superstitions of the past are put under the bright light of reason. I hope *Godless* will be helpful to atheists and agnostics who are looking for ways to talk with religious friends and relatives, but my real desire is that a Christian reader will finish this book and join us.

—**Dan Barker**

Freedom From Religion Foundation
ffrf.org

A NOTE ON WORD USAGE
The style of this book is not to capitalize "bible" unless it is a specific bible, such as the King James Bible, or when it appears capitalized in a quote by a believer.

PART 1

Rejecting God

Chapter One
The Call

When I was 15 I received a "call to the ministry." It happened one evening in late 1964 during a week of revival meetings at Anaheim Christian Center in Anaheim, California. This was during the start of the Charismatic Movement—a slightly more respectable and less frenetic Pentecostalism within mainline churches that today sports hundreds of independent churches and loose associations of congregations around the world, but at that time appeared as a wild, exciting, uncrystallized phenomenon that woke up a lot of dull congregations. My parents, after years of mostly fundamentalist Christianity, had gotten involved with the Charismatic Movement because they were attracted to the "living Gospel," where the presence of God seemed more real, immediate and powerful than in traditional worship services.

The meetings at that "spirit-filled" church were intense, bursting with rousing music and emotional sermons. Believers did not sit passively praying in pews. Weeping worshippers waved their arms to heaven. Some fell prostrate to the floor, in submission to the Creator. People stood to speak in tongues, and others translated the "heavenly language" into English. Some practiced faith healing, prophecy, discernment (diagnosis of problems, such as "evil spirits") and other "gifts of the spirit" that accompany being "baptized in the Holy Spirit." It was a night that changed my life.

I had already been "saved." My parents were Christian, but belonging to a Christian family does not make you a Christian any more than having a baker for a father makes you a loaf of bread. Each person has to make his or her own decision. According to the teachings of the New Testament, I had confessed to God that I was a sinner deserving eternal torment and I had accepted the death of Jesus on the cross as payment for my sin. I humbly asked Christ to come into my heart and make me a new creature, and I became "born again," by faith. I had been baptized and I knew I was going to heaven, but I didn't know what to do with the rest of my life—what little might remain before Jesus returned—until that evening in Anaheim.

Sitting in that meeting, I felt an intense desire to sing, pray and worship and I experienced strong inner sensations that I could only describe as "spiritual." I was convinced I was communicating with God and that He was talking to me through His Spirit. I had never had these feelings in any other context, and since the "spirit-filled" environment triggered them, I knew that I had confirmation of the reality of God. Today, I would say "assumed," but back then I "knew." It felt real, and good. I had been taught, and I believed, that spiritual sensations are not necessary to the Christian life because it is faith alone that saves you, but it was affirming to feel something that wonderful, supplementing my faith. God was not just an idea, He was a reality. I had a personal relationship with Jesus, and he had something to say to me as one of his close friends and servants.

I listened to a sermon about how the end of the world was near, and about how Jesus was returning "any moment" to claim his followers and judge the earth. I heard preachments from the bible about Jesus' mandate to "Go ye into all the world, and preach the gospel to every creature." Millions of people still needed to be saved, and the time was short. I knew God was talking directly to me, and I knew right then how to live the rest of my life. I accepted the call. I would spend my life bringing lost people into the kingdom of heaven.

I couldn't understand or articulate it at the time, but as a teenage boy I was probably starting to wonder about my future and a career. Whether it was "spiritual" or "psychological," it must have made sense to settle the question of what I wanted to do with my life, making an end run around the important but difficult struggle that so many young people experience. Accepting the "call" to become a minister made everything clear. I wanted the rest of the world to share in the gospel, to be saved, to know Jesus personally, to have meaning in life, to go to heaven, and to create a better world in the short time we had left. It felt right. Satisfying.

Beginning that night in Anaheim, my life had a purpose.

My Dad had done the same thing 15 years earlier. He had been a "worldly" professional musician in the 1940s. He played all over California for the USO during World War II. He was a member of the

Teenagers, a band that accompanied Hoagy Carmichael on his weekly *Something New* radio show. You can see Dad playing a trombone solo in the 1948 Irving Berlin movie *Easter Parade* when Judy Garland sings her first song, her hand resting on Dad's shoulder. But after he got married (he met Mom in a dance band) and started having children, he became a religious conservative, renounced his dance-band life, threw away his worldly albums and enrolled in Pacific Bible College in order to become a preacher. But he was unable to continue due to the financial pressures of raising three little boys, so he dropped out and got a job, eventually becoming an Anaheim police officer. I didn't think I was fulfilling my Dad's dreams—I was certain that God was calling *me,* personally—but looking back on it, I'm sure there must have been some influence from my parents. Mom taught Sunday School and Dad did some lay preaching over the years, so a life of ministry was not an unusual choice. Both of my younger brothers were heavily involved in Christian ministries, though neither of them became ordained or worked as full-time ministers.

For a couple of years, starting when I was 13, my family formed a musical group that would perform in various churches in southern California. My Dad played trombone and preached. My mother was a beautiful singer and always brought the congregation to tears with her rendition of "His Eye Is On the Sparrow." My brother Tom played trombone and my brother Darrell played trumpet, while I played piano. We sang those simple yet powerful gospel harmonies that "stir the soul." I suppose it was no surprise that I felt the "call" to continue a life of ministry.

I remember thinking that night in Anaheim, when I was called to be a preacher, that I didn't need to wait to graduate from a seminary or became ordained. I was "born again" and "filled with the spirit." I had the bible, the word of God, to speak for itself. What else did I need? Since God is powerful, there was no reason he couldn't start using a 15-year-old preacher right away. "Out of the mouth of babes" and all that. Besides, Jesus was coming soon! I didn't think the world would last long enough for me to go to college or get married or raise a family.

I started carrying my bible to school and talking to friends about Jesus. I joined up with evangelistic youth teams that took weekend missionary trips to poor villages in Mexico, just below the California border, where I preached my first sermon at the age of 15 alongside the dusty bank of an irrigation canal in the tiny village of Ejido Morelia. During the summer, I went on week-long and month-long trips into Mexico and the Southwest, with such groups as YUGO (which means "yoke" in Spanish but stands for Youth Unlimited Gospel Outreach) and the Frank Gonzales Evangelistic Association. Anticipating that I might become a missionary to Mexico, I devoted myself to mastering Spanish.

I'll never forget my first soul-winning experience. One Friday evening in June, near my 16th birthday, while I was wondering how I was going to spend the summer vacation of 1965, I received a phone call from someone at YUGO asking if I would fill a vacated leadership spot on a traveling gospel team. My parents said, "Go for it!"

Early the next morning, traveling from Los Angeles to Texas with 10 other young people in an eight-door stretch car that kept breaking down, I discovered that I had been appointed captain of one of the outreach groups. My responsibilities were to include supervising a team of three girls (all older than me), two weeks of preaching in two San Antonio Hispanic churches, and directing a Vacation Bible School for children. I was also told that I would be training local teenagers in the techniques of soul winning. I had never done any of these things before, but it was assumed I was capable since they had heard I was an "on fire" young Christian. My faith was so strong that I was willing to do anything for Jesus, trusting that he would give me the strength and the words.

I'm sure my nightly sermons were not great, but no one complained. I let the girls handle the day activities for children while I prepared for the soul-winning workshop on Saturday—which worried me considerably, since I had never before won anyone to Christ.

When the day arrived, we "California evangelists" gathered the inexperienced local teenagers from the churches for some preliminary training. I taught them how to share the basic plan of salvation and how to get a person to the point of conversion. When it was time to go out into a park and put it into practice, the kids expressed some hesitation, but I assured them that nothing was too hard for God. And besides, they were going to learn some lessons about faith and obedience. They didn't know it was my first time as well!

As I moved out into the park, entourage trailing, I remember thinking: "What am I doing? What if I fail? I want to go home!" Yet at the same time I was thinking: "This is exciting! This is God's work—and I'm part of it!"

I spotted a young man, perhaps 17 years old, slowly pedaling a bicycle. "Hi!" I said. "I'm from California and I came here to talk to you about Jesus." He stopped and gave us a cautious look.

"Are you a Christian?" I asked.

"No," he said, "I'm a Catholic."

He stayed on his bike, spinning the pedal with his foot.

"Great! Then you know about the plan of salvation?"

"No. I'm a Catholic," he repeated.

"Then let me ask you a question. If you died right now, would you go to heaven or hell?"

He hesitated, glancing around the park. "I don't know," he answered. "I hope I would go to heaven."

"Well, if you don't know if you're saved, then you're definitely not saved," I said. "The bible says you can know for certain that you have been redeemed." I continued with the plan of salvation, explaining that we are all sinners worthy of eternal damnation, which he already knew. I described the need to confess sin, repent and accept Jesus into his heart and his life, letting the blood of the cross wash away all guilt and shame. Listening politely and shyly, as did the rest of the team, he indicated he understood all I was saying.

"Then, would you like to be born again?" I asked.

"Sure," he said.

"You would?" I asked, trying to swallow my astonishment. It couldn't be this easy. "What do I do now?" I thought. "Well, then, uh...let's pray," I said.

"Here?" he asked. "In the park?"

"Sure. This park is part of God's sanctuary of creation. He can talk to your heart right here, right now."

We bowed our heads and I prompted the fellow to repeat the "Sinner's Prayer" after me. Actually, I had to make it up, digging the words from my memory of past revival meetings. He prayed with me, out loud. When we were finished I said, "Now, do you know you are saved?"

"I think so," he responded.

"Great. Now be sure to read the bible and pray every day, go to church and find some Christian friends."

We let him ride off and never saw him again. But the group became quite enthused, spreading out to share the good news of the gospel with the poor lost souls who had come to spend a nice summer afternoon in the park.

For me it was an exciting moment. I had won a soul to Christ; I had a star in my crown. It was like earning my wings, or getting the first notch on my six-shooter. Of course, I gave all the credit to the Holy Spirit, but I accepted it as an authentication of my calling to the ministry. It was a heady moment. I was a real evangelist, an active participant in God's holy cause, a soldier of the cross. It was like the first taste of blood, and I wanted more.

Back in California, as a teenager singing in the Anaheim Christian Center choir, I had accepted the small but important ministry of choir librarian, organizing the music, proudly carrying it all home in the basket of my bicycle, and neatly arranging everything for the next rehearsal or performance. I had started doing this even before I was called to preach.

When Kathryn Kuhlman started coming to Los Angeles for her regular faith-healing services at the Shrine Auditorium, our choir formed the initial nucleus of her stage choir. I was there for her first regular visit in the mid '60s and for two years I hardly missed a meeting, remaining choir librarian as the group grew in size, eventually incorporating singers from dozens of charismatic churches in Southern California.

It was the sound of the organ, more than anything else, that established the mood of the place. With its dramatic sweeps and heady crescendos flooding the huge vaulted building, we felt engulfed by the presence of God's Holy Spirit, breathing in, breathing out, laughing and crying for joy and worship. Here and there a woman was standing, arms reaching upward, eyes closed, praying in an unknown tongue. Wheelchairs and crutches littered the aisles. Hopeful candidates pressed to find a seat as close to the front as possible; the balconies were standing-room-only.

My responsibilities as librarian did not inhibit me from sensing the intense hopefulness of the occasion. Before Kathryn walked out on stage the building radiated that strange, eager beauty of an orchestra tuning up before a symphony. I would often watch her as she stood backstage, nervous yet determined, possessing a holy mixture of humility and pride, like a Roman or Greek goddess in her flowing gown. The audience was anxious. The Spirit was restless.

The organ crescendo reached a glorious peak as Kathryn regally walked out on stage. Those who could rose to their feet, praising God, weeping, praying. It was electrifying and intensely euphoric. I felt proud to be a witness to such a heavenly visitation.

Kathryn would often deny that she was conducting "healing meetings." She stated that her only responsibility was obedience to God's moving; it was *His* business to heal people, and it didn't need to happen in every meeting. Of course, the people had come for miracles, and would not be disappointed. She often seemed uncertain how to start. She would pray, talk a little, preach somewhat freely, or just stand silently crying, waiting for God to move. He always moved, of course—but the audience couldn't stand it, this delay of climax. (It was like the anticipation on Christmas mornings, waiting for Dad to finish reading the biblical nativity story before we could open the presents.)

In those early months, before local ministers began sitting on the stage in front of the choir, we singers were placed directly behind Kathryn in folding chairs. I always sat in the front row, right behind her, about six or eight feet from her center microphone, peering past her down into the sea of eager faces in the audience—the faces of people who had come to be blessed. The choir would often sing quietly behind the healings, "He touched me, yes, he touched me! And, oh, the joy that floods my soul! Something happened and now I know; he touched me and made me whole!" It was rapturous. Ecstatic.

After 20 or 30 preliminary minutes, which included a few choir numbers, the healings would begin. People would be ushered up to Kathryn, one at a time, some sitting in wheelchairs, to receive a "touch from God." She would face the candidate, touching the forehead, and would either ask the problem or directly discern the need. Often the supplicants were "slain in the spirit," meaning they fell backwards to the floor under God's presence, often with arms raised in surrender. I sometimes had to pick up my feet when they fell in my direction. Kathryn had a "catcher," a short, stocky, redheaded former police officer who would move behind the people and soften the fall. He was often quite busy. People would be dropping all over the stage, even choir members and ushers. He rushed back and forth like a character in a video game, never missing, though it was sometimes quite close.

It didn't matter that the healings were visually unimpressive. We were in God's presence and a miracle is a miracle. Sometimes an individual would discard crutches or push Kathryn around the stage in the unneeded wheelchair, things like that. But the healings were usually internal things: "Praise God! The cancer is *completely* gone!"

One very common cure was deafness. Kathryn would tell the person to cover the good ear (!) and ask if she could be heard. "Can you hear me now? Can you hear me now?" she would ask, speaking louder and louder until the person nodded. Then she would dramatically move away and speak softly to the person, who would jump and say, "I can hear you! I can hear you! Praise God!" The place would fall apart, people screaming and hopping. Miracles do that to people. It was an incredible feeling, an ecstasy beyond description. We felt embraced by the presence of a higher strength, participating in a group worship (hysteria), floating on the omnipresent surges of the organ music, joining in song with heavenly voices.

In one service Kathryn replied to the criticism that some of her healings were purely psychosomatic by saying, "But what if they *are* merely psychosomatic? Is that not also a miracle? Doctors will tell you that the hardest illnesses to cure are the psychosomatic ones." God works in mysterious ways.

As I look back on it now, I can see that most of the "miracles" were pretty boring. The excitement was in our minds. I saw people walk up to the side of the stage in search of a healing, before being told by an usher to sit in a wheelchair to be rolled up to Kathryn. When Kathryn quietly told the person to "stand up and walk the rest of the way," the crowd went wild, assuming that the person couldn't walk in the first place. I never witnessed any organic healings, restored body parts or levitations. A few crutches and medicine bottles littered the aisles, but no prosthetic devices or glass eyes. The bulk of the "cures" were older women with cancer, arthritis, heart problems, diabetes, "unspoken problems," etc. There was an occasional exorcism (mental illness?), too. We had come to be blessed and we were not to be cheated, taking the slightest cue to yell, sing and praise God. I think, in retrospect, the organist was the real star of the show, working with Kathryn to manipulate the moods. We were so malleable.

Experiences like that were tremendously affirming. When I was "seeing miracles," it seemed so real, so powerful, that I wondered who in the world could be so blind to deny the reality of the presence of God. Nonbelievers must be stupid or crazy! Anyone who deliberately doubted such proof certainly deserved hell.

I used to pray and "sing in the spirit" all the time. Riding my bike around Anaheim, I would quietly speak in tongues, exulting in the emotions of talking with Christ and communing with the Holy Spirit. If you have never done it, it is hard to understand what is happening when people speak in tongues. I actually got goose bumps from the joy, my heart and mind transported to another realm. It's a kind of natural high that I interpreted as a supernatural encounter. I'm certain there are chemicals released to the brain during the experience. (I know this is true of music and the cerebellum, but has anyone studied the brain during glossolalia?) While some of my friends may have been sneaking out behind the proverbial barn to experiment with this or that, I was having a love affair with Jesus. I didn't think I was "crazy"—I was quite functional and could snap out of it at any moment, like taking off headphones—but I did feel that what I had was special, above the world.

Jesus said that "My kingdom is not of this world," and I felt like my physical body was just a visitor to planet earth while my soul was getting messages "from home." It gave me a sense of overwhelming peace and joy, of integration with God and the universe, of being wrapped in the loving arms of my creator. It caused everything to "make sense." I'm not sure why, but it did. I simply knew from direct personal experience that God was real, and no one at the time would have been able to convince me that I was delusional. I would simply say, "You don't know." I had seen miracles. I had talked with God. I knew the truth and the world did not.

My third- and fourth-year Spanish teacher at Anaheim High School was James Edwards, the head of the Anaheim School District foreign language department. He was a great teacher, but I had heard that he was an agnostic, or unbeliever, or something bad. This was not long after the 1963 U.S. Supreme Court's *Schempp* decision that removed prayer and bible reading from the public schools, so we Christians were quite recently wounded and sensitive about the issue of religion on our campus. Anaheim High School was forced to end the tradition of opening each day with a morning bible reading broadcast to the classrooms. But I figured that I possessed a calling from a higher level than the Supreme Court, and I proudly took my bible to school, being careful to place it on top of my other books so that everyone would notice.

I often took two bibles to school: the King James Version and another in Spanish. When Mr. Edwards would give us some free time to read Spanish literature, I would open my Reina-Valera bible and kill three birds with one stone: learn Spanish, worship God and prepare myself for my missionary career. I noticed that Mr. Edwards noticed.

One day as I was leaving the class, Mr. Edwards called me over to his desk and told me that he wanted to talk with me after school. I was pretty sure he wanted to talk about my bible in the classroom—the bible hardly qualifies as Spanish literature, I thought—so I prayed all day long. After gymnastics I steadied my nerve and walked into his classroom. He shut the door and went back to his desk, where I was standing.

"Dan," he said, "I notice that you have been bringing your bible to class."

"Yes," I said, swallowing hard.

"And I notice that you have been reading your bible during class time."

"That's right," I answered, ready to do battle with Satan. I was his top student, so I didn't fear any academic lecture.

"Well, then," he continued, hesitating, "maybe you are the one who can help me."

"Help you, Mr. Edwards?" I asked, anticipating some kind of trick.

"Yes. Maybe you can help me make sense of spiritual things." His whole manner changed, and he started talking like a humbled man, friend to friend, hurting. I was surprised to see him like this. He told me that he was an agnostic, but that he was starting to think that there might be something "out there." He had read some articles about ESP and other psychic phenomena, and was deciding that a strictly materialistic view of life was unrealistic and unsatisfying.

"Dan, you seem so confident and happy. Tell me what you believe."

So, I told him that I believed in God, that God was revealed in the bible, that we were all sinners, that God sent his son, Jesus, to die for our sins, that Jesus rose from the grave to conquer death, that we could confess our sins and accept Jesus as our personal savior and be born again, becoming "new creatures" without guilt and with a joy and purpose in life to know God, praise God and do his will. I took advantage of the opportunity, telling him everything I believed. He listened quietly, and as our meeting ended he thanked me and told me he wanted to hear more.

We met every day or so after that, with me mostly talking and him listening. I kept stressing the reality of God, and the moral difference between believers and nonbelievers. We became friends. Sometimes during break between classes he would stop me in the hallway and ask about a verse in the bible. I felt self-conscious, knowing that some of my classmates were watching and wondering.

Early one day Mr. Edwards found me in the hallway and excitedly pulled me over. He was grinning. "Dan, I had to tell you. I did it!"

"What happened?" I asked, still able to be surprised that the important head of the district language department was treating me like a buddy.

"I accepted Jesus as my personal savior. This morning as I was getting out of my car in the parking lot, it hit me. What you were saying about making a conscious, deliberate decision to accept Jesus made perfect sense. I prayed right there in the parking lot and it happened! My sins are forgiven and I am now a child of God."

After that, he and I became "brothers" in Jesus, spending much time discussing the bible. In spite of the recent court decision about religion in the schools, we started a prayer and bible-study group on campus. We called it an "advanced Spanish literature and discussion" group (something like that), and the first and only piece of Spanish literature we discussed was the bible. (This was a front, folks.) Some other Christians heard what was happening, and this group became a focal point for devout students, including a couple of other high school evangelists like myself. We dropped the Spanish pretense and quickly turned it into a Christian club.

James Edwards came to my church a couple of times and introduced himself as "Dan Barker's son," meaning that I was his spiritual father, which embarrassed me a little, though it was quite affirming to a young preacher. I was called to the ministry in that church and I was now "bringing in the sheaves," so to speak. After I graduated from high school, I would occasionally return to speak to the expanding

Christian group we had started, which had to be moved to the choir room because it had grown too big for a classroom. They all wanted to learn about my missionary and evangelistic adventures, and to meet the guy who started it all. I heard that James Edwards was still holding those Christian meetings on that campus 25 years later!

Experiences like these helped to affirm and cement my commitment to my "calling from God." I was effective. I had proof. I was encouraged and appreciated. I felt like I was set apart for a special ministry, and I devoted every day to it. I got involved with several local ministries, including the gentle Peralta Brothers—Eli (who had been my first-year Spanish teacher), Abraham, Aaron and Benjamin. They were second-generation Mexicans who sang Spanish gospel music to the Hispanic churches in southern California and northern Mexico, and for whom I played piano and occasionally filled in for an absent voice.

I eventually spent a total of about two years as a missionary in Mexico, trying to convert Catholics into Christians. (Looking back on it, I am embarrassed at the arrogance and ignorance of American Protestant evangelists, thinking we should convert an entire "lost dark country" to Jesus.) Besides the ministry, being in Mexico was an eye-opening cultural experience. During one of the first visits across the border, I was in a church with no glass in the windows. As we were sweeping the cement floor before the evening meeting little children were climbing through the windows, jumping from pew to pew, playing and laughing. In a misguided moment of saintly solemnity, I yelled to one of the boys: "Don't you know this is a church? You should not be playing here! And you should wear shoes when you come into the House of God." He looked up at me and said, "I don't have any shoes."

During another early missionary trip below Tijuana, I walked up to a group of young men and in not-yet-perfect Spanish said, "God has sent us here to talk to you about Jesus. Do you know Jesus?" One of the guys pointed down the street and said, "Yes. He lives down around the corner beside the pharmacy."

In a little town on the Sea of Cortez, in 1965, I met Manuel Bonilla, a diminutive but exuberant Christian singer and guitarist whose immense talent made him seem larger than life. His ministry was beginning to be noticed throughout Latin America, and when he came up to Los Angeles in 1966 to record his songs he asked me to produce one of his first projects. I was 16 when I arranged and recorded an entire album for Manuel, including the song "Me Ha Tocado" ("He Touched Me"), the same song we sang at the Kathryn Kuhlman meetings. That simple recording, which I arranged for piano, marimba, guitar and a trio of background voices, became a big hit in the Spanish-speaking Christian world and is still selling today. It was exciting to hear myself, a high school student, playing piano on Spanish radio stations in southern California and Mexico. Manuel went on to become the leading Spanish Christian recording artist in the world, selling in more than a dozen countries. He used me to arrange and produce many of his California recordings from those early years. There were about a dozen albums through the 1970s, which grew in sophistication as we both learned the ropes of the recording industry.

I did not view my music production and performance as a career during those years of ministry. I was reluctant to charge money for what I considered an honor and a duty. I was serving God. Looking back on it, I realize I *should* have charged more, especially later when I was married and we started raising children, but of course the world was going to end at any moment so why plan for the future? The bible teaches: "Take no thought for tomorrow. Tomorrow will take thought of the things of itself."

One day I walked into the mayor's office of a small city in Mexico and told him that God had sent us there to preach to his town and that he was going to allow us to use the large kiosk in the downtown park, for free, as a stage for our performance. Without hesitating, he said, "Bueno." He even made sure we had police protection. Dozens of people came up to the kiosk that evening to pray, confess their sins, and ask Jesus to come into their hearts.

Right after high school, in 1967, before going to bible college, I spent a year with the Frank Gonzales Evangelistic Association, a cross-country gospel team. Frank, a graduate of Bob Jones University, was a flashy Mexican-American trumpet player who preached bilingual, hell-fire sermons. I spent that year singing, playing the piano, preaching, doing house-to-house witnessing and getting doors slammed in my face, but winning converts.

I was playing the accordion standing on picnic tables in the park... singing about Jesus in restaurants and inviting the rest of the customers to join us...holding weeklong revival services in large and small churches across the continent.

I once drove non-stop from one side of the continent to the other—from Riverside, New Jersey, to Riverside, California—and later even further, straight through from Norfolk, Virginia, to Los Angeles. Among my other experiences:

Driving through freezing blizzards and blinding desert sandstorms.

Approaching members of the Hell's Demons motorcycle gang in Phoenix to invite them to hear a sermon about the love of Jesus.

Holding drug awareness musical rallies in complicit public high schools—rallies that were just a front for us to invite the students to an evening evangelistic rally (we didn't know the *first* thing about preventing drug use).

Playing soccer and basketball in countless prisons across Mexico and the United States so that we could witness for Jesus during halftime.

Rounding up hundreds of barefoot children in Mexican towns and villages so that we could sing Protestant choruses to them and tell them about *Jesús*—counting all the hands that were raised when we asked who wanted to be saved and reporting back to American churches how many *thousands* of souls we had converted.

Sleeping on church pews, church roofs and once on top of a Volkswagen van.

Hiking up and down mountainsides and ravines to remote villages that required an additional interpreter since the Indians there didn't know Spanish. (I tried to learn some Mayo, but all I can remember now is "Dios ta enchianía"—God bless you.)

Inviting ourselves to local TV and radio stations, with some success, so that we could get the gospel to as many people as possible.

During those years, I was the kind of guy you would not want to sit next to on a bus. After a few minutes of chitchat, I would turn and say, "I can see that you are going through some real struggles right now. (*How does he know?*) I can tell that you are experiencing some problems with a relationship in your life. (*How does he know?*) You are wondering what it is all about. You don't know what is the purpose of life. (*How DOES he know?*) I used to feel the same way, and God has sent me to tell you that Jesus is the answer."

You would be surprised at how often this crude technique actually worked. I was more often respected than resisted. There seems to be a general feeling that if someone claims to be speaking for God, then he must be telling the truth—or at least it is safer not to challenge such a person. If it is religious, it must be good. After all, who has any answers? Our lives *do* have problems and mysteries. A preacher must be on to something; otherwise, we wouldn't need preachers. It is easy to proselytize. I don't understand all the psychology behind preaching, but I know that it works. Otherwise, we would not see the growth of movements such as early Christianity and Islam, or modern Evangelicalism, Pentecostalism and Mormonism. Most people are uncertain and susceptible, vulnerable to someone else's confidence and certainty. If you want to be a preacher, then "just do it." Do it with confidence and style. It works. (Just like anyone in sales will tell you.)

But with religion, most people are uncritical. Never once in 19 years of preaching did anyone ever come up to me after a service and ask, "Rev. Barker, what were the sources for your sermon?" I was accorded an immense amount of unearned respect, simply for being a minister. Where were the skeptics, atheists, agnostics and humanists? (Well, why should I expect them to be in church?) Why did anyone rarely challenge my asserted "authority" to speak for God? I do remember a few slammed doors. I recall only two or three times during all those years when someone on the street would reject what I was saying, and it was a huge surprise to me when they simply walked away. Now, I don't blame them; but at the time, I was perplexed at how someone could be so lost that they would run from God.

I traveled with the Frank Gonzales ministry every summer for many years as Frank's accompanist and as a preaching leader of my own team, and they were hectic summers. (I suspect that my problem with kidney stones originated with that experience. I spent days driving through blistering heat, drinking little, pushing the team, stopping to visit the bathroom only when absolutely necessary.) During the summer of 1967, I dehydrated and spent three days in Guaymas, Mexico, on my back in a burlap hammock being fed glucose through an intravenous needle, eating nothing, sucking on ice cubes. That was the same summer I got mangled by a dirty German Shepherd in the town of Zacapu, in the mountains of Michoacán between Mexico City and Guadalajara, after I hopped over the adobe wall behind a church into the next yard to retrieve a volleyball. I didn't get rabies, but I went into some kind of nervous shock and slept for more than two days after being medicated at a local clinic. I know that kind of living is reckless, but at the time

I figured it was justified. The world was going to end any day, and I had given my life and body to Jesus as a "living sacrifice."

From 1968 to 1972, I attended Azusa Pacific College, an interdenominational state-accredited Christian school in California, and majored in religion. Looking back, I can see that most of the religion courses (with a couple of notable exceptions) were simply glorified Sunday School classes and I don't remember that we delved very deeply into the evidences or arguments for or against Christianity. It wouldn't have mattered anyway, since I wanted to be out in the streets preaching the gospel, not stuck in a classroom chewing over pointless history and philosophy. After all, the world was ending soon. My attitude was that it is not necessary to know how an automobile works in order to drive one, nor is it imperative to become a biblical scholar or theologian in order to save souls from damnation. All of those "Christian evidences" could be left to the experts who, I believed, had already figured it all out and who could provide the historical, documentary and archeological evidences if anyone ever asked. (No one ever did.)

I believed that my education was secondary to my calling. I was pretty successful at winning souls, probably much more so than my professors, and although I got good grades, I didn't see what difference it made. I coasted through college, spending almost every evening and weekend out somewhere preaching, singing, playing the piano and doing the *real* work of the ministry.

Most of my memories at Azusa Pacific College are ministry-related. I sang and played piano for the Dynamics Chorale, which toured the state promoting the college and Jesus. I often played piano for daily chapel services. One year I was elected Christian Life Director of the student body government and brought in dynamic Christian speakers and performers such as Andrae Crouch ("It Won't Be Long") and Audrey Mieir ("His Name is Wonderful"). We listened to end-time author Hal Lindsey (*The Late, Great Planet Earth*) assure us that the second coming of Jesus would be no later than the mid 1980s. That late?

For many years, Azusa Pacific College sent hundreds of students down to Mexico to learn something about mission work, and because of my experience I was involved as organizer, performer, preacher and interpreter. We took teams of young American students into many of the dusty villages below Mexicali to sing and preach in churches at night, and during the day to play games and tell stories to children in order to bring them to Jesus. I ushered the Azusa Pacific soccer team into the overcrowded Mexicali jail to challenge the prison team and, win or lose, preach to them. (We mostly lost. Those inmates have a lot of time to practice.) After a while, the prison officials and guards came to know me, so I was the perfect liaison for such ministries. Flattering the ego of the main warden, I even managed to gain entry for a film crew (whose nervous cameraman was told, "Don't shoot the guards!") that was making a documentary film about Christian youth ministries. This time it was basketball and we lost again, but I would love to find that film if I could remember who made it.

One December I took about 20 college students all the way down to Mexico City, traveling by Tres Estrellas de Oro buses, to spread the "good news" that we were sure few had heard. Four of us young men formed a gospel quartet, and we used to trade off preaching. It was before one of our meetings, as we were preparing and praying, when Gary, who sang bass in the quartet and whose turn it was to preach that night, whispered to us that he had lost his voice and was unable to sing or talk. We gathered in a circle around Gary and laid our hands on his shoulders, and I prayed out loud for God to heal Gary's voice, ending with the words: "Gary, in the name of Jesus, be healed!"

Gary looked up and yelled, "Praise the Lord!" in a strong voice. He went on to sing and preach that night. If experiences like that don't cement your faith, nothing will! Gary is the same fellow who threw away his Coke-bottle-thick eyeglasses one day in Mexico, convinced that God had healed his vision. A few weeks later he stumbled into an optometrist's office in California to buy a new pair. (He also wrote that song, "It's a Happy Day," which was a popular Christian chorus for a few years.)

I was in college, and getting decent grades, but I wasn't sure why I was there, when there was so little time left to live on this late, great planet. I was dismissive of ordination or degrees. I figured I didn't need a piece of paper bestowed by humans to tell me what I already knew: that God personally called me to the ministry of the Gospel. After four full-time years, I fell nine elective units short of graduation and never went back to finish. (In 1988, Azusa Pacific University allowed me to transfer some creative writing units from the University of Wisconsin and mailed me my degree in religion.)

I like languages and enjoyed the two years of New Testament (koine) Greek at Azusa, which I still find useful. It added a certain credibility to my sermons to be able to throw in an occasional word from the original text of the New Testament (so I thought), though I don't think the listeners cared. "Paul called himself a slave of Christ," I would preach, "and the word 'slave' in the Greek is *doulos*." I would announce this with solemn authority, hesitating slightly before the final word. No one asked why it was important to point that out. They must have thought I was on to something.

At Azusa Pacific I met a singer (again paralleling my dad's life). The world had not ended yet, so Carol and I were married in 1970, when I was barely 21. We have four children: Becky (1973), Kristi (1975), Andrea (1977), and Danny (1979).

Over time, I was an associate pastor in three churches in California. My first full-time post was in 1972, right out of college, at Arcadia Friends Church in my wife's denomination. (They didn't care that I didn't have a degree or wasn't formally ordained.) The Friends are the modern Quakers, and in California they are more evangelical than their eastern forbears. (Richard Nixon was from that denomination.) I directed the choir, often preached from the pulpit and led Wednesday night bible study and worship. Joy Berry, who later became a well-known children's author, was minister of Children's Education at the same church at that time and also ran the Christian Day School there. (As a pleasant coincidence, Joy later came out as an agnostic, broke her ties with Christian publishers and today we remain freethinking friends with similar stories. More than 80 million copies of Joy's books have sold worldwide.)

The Quaker/Friends tradition abjures the sacraments (except for marriage, I think, which they probably don't call a sacrament), because of the Protestant break with the formalism of Catholicism. Worship is supposed to be directly with God, with no intermediaries, saints, priests or rituals. I remember how absurd this became one Wednesday evening during a social potluck, when Pastor Ted Cummins made a few remarks before praying for the meal and happened to mention some of the words from the Last Supper in the bible. A few days later he was called to task by the denomination for conducting the sacrament of Communion.

We are all heretics!

I have mixed memories of Pastor Ted, a genuinely friendly, gentle and approachable person with a smart and beautiful wife and four darling children. He was not a hell-fire preacher. He was a friend and a peer. One evening I happened to enter the sanctuary to find Ted alone, kneeling in prayer at the front pew. After a moment, with no words said, I walked over and placed my hand on his shoulder and silently prayed for God to bless him. He looked up and smiled. The following Sunday he told me that that was the first and only time during his entire Christian life that he ever felt anything. He said he had always taken things by faith alone, but until that moment he had never known that anyone could feel the spirit of God. Years later, an alcoholic, he left the ministry and went into seclusion, ruining his family and his life. He died too young in 2006, and although his final tragic years clouded the memorial, no one forgot the truly loving, vibrant man he used to be.

After more than a year at Arcadia Friends Church, I was "called by God" to move to Glengrove Assembly of God, in La Puente, California. The Assemblies of God are Pentecostal, more in line with my own Charismatic upbringing than my wife's calmer Quaker heritage. I'm glad I worked at that church for a year and a half. It gave me a direct experience of that animated slice of Christian life. There was a lot of speaking in tongues, faith healing, fiery hanky-waving sermons by sweaty evangelists, women on their backs on the floor with arms raised in tearful prayer, hand-clapping gospel choirs and "Jesus movement" music. I even saw a few exorcisms, or "casting out of spirits" as we called it. I took the youth choir on tour around California and Mexico. I preached from the main pulpit at least once a month and led bible study and worked with the youth minister on evangelical outreach.

Directing the adult choir was more of a ministry than an art, since there was only a handful of truly good singers. I had to compensate for the quality of talent with an increase in rhythm and volume—we were worshipping after all, not performing at Carnegie Hall. One evening, as I was rehearsing the adult choir, I stumbled into one of those horribly embarrassing moments I wish I could forget. (So why am I telling it here?) In an amateur church choir you are apt to have members who are not very confident, sometimes waiting to join in after they hear everyone else start to sing, in order not to make a mistake. But as a director, I wanted the first note to be as strong as the rest of the line, with a solid, loud entrance. We were rehearsing

"Happiness Is the Lord" but the first note was sounding weak and tentative because some of the men were not coming in with everyone else. Exasperated, I turned and said, "The first word of the song is 'happiness,' but I don't hear the first syllable. You tenors are coming in with 'piness'," I emphasized loudly, not realizing what word I had just pronounced. Two older ladies gasped and others turned their red faces away, trying not to look shocked or laugh. When it dawned on me what had just happened, seeing the glaring looks from the men in the back row, I turned around and faced the sanctuary, making things worse. Today I would chuckle with everyone else at such a hilarious moment, but this was church, God's work, a holy endeavor that was not to be sullied by profanity. My wife later told me that some of the women were having a good laugh behind my back, and I eventually took it in stride, although I did consider it odd for church members to be making fun of a "man of god." (At least I did not call two bears from the forest to tear them to pieces. See II Kings 2:23–24.)

The people at Glengrove Assembly were sincere and sweet, but I quickly found them to be a bit noisy for my tastes. My wife must have been even more uncomfortable, coming from a non-Pentecostal background.

So I got another "call from God," this time to the Standard Christian Center in the central California town of Standard, a former logging town near Sonora in the Gold Rush mother lode foothills north of Yosemite. (It's interesting how God always seemed to "call" me exactly where I wanted to go.) That congregation was much more in line with the Charismatic Movement that I had experienced at Anaheim Christian Center where I was first called to the ministry. And what's more, it was a renegade full-gospel split from the Christian Church (in the Disciples of Christ tradition that also spawned the Church of Christ), the same denomination that my dad grew up in and which founded Pacific Bible College where Dad had studied to be a minister. (Looking back on all the "coincidences" with my dad, I wonder how much free will I really have.) The motto of the Disciples tradition was, "Where the bible speaks, we speak; where the bible is silent, we are silent." Of course, it is impossible to reconcile that principle with the Charismatic Movement, but we tried.

When I submitted my letter of resignation to Glengrove Assembly, the pastoral staff and deacons were not convinced that I had truly received a "call from God" to move on. We got along well and it seemed to them that I was abandoning a well-developed ministry. Dave Gustaveson, the youth pastor and a good friend, told me he had struggled in prayer to know if my decision was truly right for me and the church. One day in the men's room, while he was "talking with the Lord," he noticed the word "Standard" on the urinal. He took it as a sign and announced to the congregation that it was truly God's will for me to move on to Standard, California, with their blessing. (Thanks, Dave.)

The pay at Standard Christian Center was not great, but it provided a minimum of financial security for a growing family. We lived in a small mobile home in the oak-dotted foothills south of Sonora. Although I did a lot of preaching to the congregation, filling in for the main pastor, calling on members, directing the choir, running Wednesday night bible study, organizing activities for the youth group and helping out in the church-affiliated Christian bookstore, I never was the senior pastor, and never wanted to be. I always considered myself first an evangelist. After a few years of working in local churches, directing choirs with admirable dedication and hopeful musicianship, counseling people with problems that I hadn't the faintest idea how to approach (except with bible verses and prayer), and working on sermons that I fancied were insightful but bounced off the listeners like rain off an umbrella, I found myself getting restless to hit the road again. I could only stick it out in each church for about 18 months before feeling the "call" to move on.

I felt bad leaving the Standard Christian Center. The people were gracious and we had a good program going there, but it was a dead end for my evangelistic calling. I asked church leaders if they would consider being my home base, sending me out as their cross-country "missionary" to the world. They reluctantly agreed, but not before the main pastor, Bob Wright, convinced me that for my ministry to be more credible I would have to become ordained. I respected Bob and yielded to the pressure to make it official. One Sunday morning in May 1975, the church held an ordination service, directed by Pastor Bob, in which I was asked questions about my calling, the bible and theology, and then was unanimously ordained. The deacons and pastors stood around me in a circle, placing their hands on my shoulders and head, invoking God's blessing on my ministry. They presented me with an ordination certificate, which no one ever asked to see during all my years of ministry (though I did have to show it to the State of California in 2002 when, as an atheist "minister," I performed a secular wedding for a nonreligious couple).

For the next eight years my wife and I lived "by faith" as touring musical evangelists, still expecting Jesus to return at any moment, "like a thief in the night." The expression "living by faith" is more than a profession of belief. It is an adventure and a risk, putting your life in the hands of God. Neither of us had a job. We had no regular income, no health insurance, and of course no retirement plan since we would never need it in the short time remaining before the rapture. All our belongings were in storage for the first year and we lived on the road, accepting housing from church members, friends and relatives. When Carol was pregnant with our second child, we booked a national evangelistic itinerary, hopped in our yellow Chevy Nova with about $100 cash, and bounced around the country from church to church, not charging for the ministry but accepting freewill "love offerings," trusting that we would get enough money from each service to allow us to make it to the next. I remember many hopeful, prayerful moments sitting in the car after the service, opening the envelope to see if there was enough cash to make it to the next church. We normally got between $50 and $100 per meeting, sometimes nothing at all. It was easy to book Sunday meetings; it was difficult to keep busy the rest of the week.

In 1976, when my wife was pregnant with our third child, we rented a small house in Pomona, and she decided to stay home from the extended trips, tending to the family, joining me mainly when I ministered in the Southern California area. When that house was carted away in 1977 to make room for a Mormon temple, we moved to a house in Ontario, California.

Our ministry was a mix of music and message. We sang duets and solos, and I preached the gospel, varying the message to relate to each audience as I felt prompted by the Holy Spirit. It was all bible-based, stressing the importance of obedience to God and the joy of possessing a personal relationship with Jesus, and of course, the need to be a faithful servant who is ready and waiting for Christ's return. We were sincere. I indeed felt that I was talking with God and that Jesus was my Lord and friend. During service, people would often come down to the altar to confess their sins and accept Jesus as their savior. It seemed so right to be doing something so powerful. My work and music was constantly affirmed by the testimony of others and by the testimony of the Spirit, or what I thought and sincerely believed was the Spirit giving witness to my heart and mind. I had no doubts that it was all real.

In the summer of 1975, during our first cross-country tour, we heard from our contacts in Canton, Ohio, that the week of meetings had been cancelled. I told them we had no choice but to pass through Ohio since our itinerary took us further east the following weeks. If nothing else we would have to sit out the days. When we got to Ohio I managed to book a couple of small last-minute meetings, but otherwise we just sat around in these people's nice home watching the clock tick. A framed sign next to the clock said simply, "Do the next thing." That motto has stayed with me to this day, a very useful bit of obvious advice. Not able to sit still, I went down to the basement piano and wrote a musical for children based on an idea that my wife had when she directed a Sunday School Christmas program with puppets the year before. I figured maybe we could use the musical if we ever went back into local church work.

That fall, back in southern California, I did some transcription for a friend who wrote children's songs and I played part of my new musical for her. She liked it and told me that she had heard that Manna Music, the respected gospel publisher, was looking for a new children's musical for Christmas, and she gave them a call. Carl Farrer invited me in to play it, so I drove to Burbank with my penciled manuscript and a prayer.

I was a little nervous when I sat down at the piano at Manna Music. As I was halfway through the introduction to the first song, Carl grabbed my arm and said, "Stop. Don't play any more." He took a deep breath and said, "I can tell you right now that we will publish this musical."

"But you haven't heard anything," I said.

"I've heard enough to promise that even though [owner of the company] Hal Spencer hasn't heard this yet, he will love it, and this will be a hit for us." I was stunned. "Now go ahead. Let's hear the whole thing." Carl was the first person to hear it all the way through, and ever since that quiet morning with just the two of us at the piano, he and I have been close friends. We have drifted apart, of course, since my deconversion to atheism in the 1980s—different circles—but we have never lost that connection, and talk on the phone from time to time. In November 2007 I visited the 80-something Carl at his home in Austin, Texas, and it was as if no time had passed. Some friendships are truly transcendent.

I came back to Manna Music a couple days later and played the musical for Hal Spencer and other staff. They all loved it! "We have been searching for a new Christmas musical for children," Hal said, "and you walk in the door and hand it to us. This is an answer to our prayers." They made few suggestions, no real edits, and in 1976 *Mary Had a Little Lamb* was published and recorded. (Get it? Mary was the mother of Jesus and Jesus was the Lamb of God.) It was Manna's bestseller for a couple of years, and it remained near the top of the list for many years. I'm still getting royalties from that musical to this day.

Suddenly, I was a published composer. This gave my ministry a broader scope. I wrote a sequel, an Easter musical called *His Fleece Was White as Snow*, as well as some additional songs, and started getting invitations to appear in churches as a national Christian songwriter. The musicals were performed by churches and Christian schools, and are still being presented to a lesser degree decades later. *Mary Had a Little Lamb* was translated into Spanish and German, and has been performed around the world at Christmas. At a Christian Booksellers Association convention, Hal introduced me to Dale Evans (wife of Roy Rogers) who told me that her grandchildren loved *Mary Had a Little Lamb*.

The second musical, *His Fleece Was White as Snow*, is based on the fact that Jewish law required an offering of an unblemished animal, and that Jesus was supposedly the final, sinless Passover sacrifice. Although I have always been happy with the artistic quality of this work (which includes a flamenco I still play), the lyrics and the story now embarrass me. I actually kill off the star of the show, a cute, unspotted lamb named Snowy!

A couple of years later I started working on a third musical for Manna Music, *Everywhere That Mary Went*, that was based on the handful of New Testament references to the mother of Jesus, noticing that her appearances in the story always point to her son's ministry—a not-so-subtle rebuke to Catholics. I did not finish that work before my views started to change, so the world was spared those great insights.

I was once invited to a church in East Los Angeles to be guest conductor of *Mary Had a Little Lamb*. Instead of using children, this congregation used the adult choir. Its members dressed up like camels, sheep, pigs and donkeys, and it was quite amusing. But what I remember most was the huge painted sign hanging above the pulpit saying "Jesus Is Coming Soon!" The sign needed to be repainted and cleaned, and I saw cobwebs around the back. I now wish I had had a camera! Of course, at the time I thought the message of the sign was right-on, and the irony of the cobwebs was tucked in the back of my mind.

One of my adult octavos published by Manna Music, "There is One," was sung by Robert Schuller's Hour of Power choir on national television, though as a street evangelist renouncing wealth, I didn't think much of Schuller's glitzy Christianity. I was still involved with Manuel Bonilla, who preached and sang to the common people, and with many of the California Hispanic churches, which were not wealthy.

With my new contacts in the recording industry I was able to produce, arrange and play piano on at least a dozen more of Manuel's albums, including some innovative children's records in Spanish that became immensely popular. (If you happen to spot one of Manuel Bonilla's animated children's videos on the Internet, you will know that those are my arrangements and that I played piano and directed the kids' choir.) We were able to hire top-rate Hollywood studio musicians, including my regular drummer and percussionist Fred Petry (a busy studio player who had toured with Stan Kenton) and guitarist Grant Geissman. Since I spoke Spanish and identified with Manuel's life and ministry, I became a good interface with the Los Angeles recording industry for those projects. On subsequent trips to Mexico we would hear the people singing the arrangements exactly as we had recorded them, which they had learned from the radio. One of the songs Manuel and I co-wrote is a beguine called "No Vengo Del Mono" (translated, that means "I don't come from a monkey"), mocking evolution. Another song I produced for Manuel, with a college-age choir in the background, was "Pronto, Sí Muy Pronto, Veremos Al Señor" ("Soon and Very Soon, We Will See the Lord"), which truly expressed our end-time expectations.

Besides working in evangelism, as a preacher or as an invited Christian songwriter, I made a supplemental income with record production in the Los Angeles area for various clients, mostly Christian, in addition to Manuel Bonilla. I never produced any big-time albums, but I did work on a lot of "B" projects: a pastor and wife singing duets, a junior high school choir going on tour, songwriters needing demos or records for their touring ministry, various Christian vocalists in English and

Spanish who needed music to sell at their rallies and services, and literally hundreds of children's songs for Christian publishing companies and curriculum houses. I once did a marathon recording session of more than 100 songs in one week for Gospel Light Publications, a leading publisher of Sunday School and Vacation Bible School (VBS) curriculums. (At the end of that fun but grueling week, Fred Petry quipped, "I hate to play 128 songs and run, but I have to go now.")

I wrote much of the music and produced many of the early recordings for Joy Berry's company, Living Skills Press, which then was connected with the educational division of Word Books, the largest Christian publisher. Some of the character singing on Joy's albums was done by Hal Smith, the voice actor who played Otis on *The Andy Griffith Show* and who did Goofy for Disney and the Owl in *Winnie the Pooh*. (He was a genuine pleasure to work with, though I have no idea what his religious views were.) Word published a collection of my religious children's songs written for Joy's *Ready, Set, Grow!* series of books, with accompanying music that I produced for them. I played piano with Paul Mickelson, Billy Graham's organist, on a piano/organ album of Christian hymns. I produced a Christian aerobic exercise album called *Body and Soul*, with some of *The Lawrence Welk Show* singers performing disco arrangements of well-known hymns such as "Leaning On The Everlasting Arms." (That was hilarious!) I got to hire Thurl Ravenscroft (the voice of Tony the Tiger), who sang a very deep bass line for the *High On Christmas* album I arranged and produced in a pop style for Parade Records in the early 80s.

I worked in more than a dozen studios in Hollywood and southern California. I didn't pretend to be the best producer in town, but I was dependable, sincere, on schedule, never over budget and I communicated well with the religious clients. I was also cheap. I sometimes proudly worked for nothing, happy to be a part of the cause. I actually lost money on the *High on Christmas* project, due to a sloppy contractual agreement, and had to borrow money to pay off the debts. I figured that recording Christian music was part of my evangelistic calling, since it was spreading the word through music. In retrospect, I now realize that if I hadn't been such a blinkered believer, if I hadn't been convinced that Jesus was coming back "any day now," I might have had a decent career as a music producer, doing something I was good at and loved. I now know it was negligent, as a parent of young children, to sell myself so cheaply, allowing the clients to reap the profits while my family very often struggled to eat. But like the idealistic starving holder of a lottery ticket who is waiting for news from the sweepstakes office, I knew Jesus was coming soon to take us all to heaven.

I played the piano for Pat Boone in 1972 to a crowd of more than 10,000 in Phoenix. We met briefly backstage—yes, he was wearing white patent-leather shoes—where we talked over some tunes, keys and tempos, and then I sat at a grand piano beside him on stage as he talked about Jesus and sang Christian songs.

Jimmy Roberts (of *The Lawrence Welk Show*) used me as his accompanist on a two-week cross-country tour in the early 1970s. I played in a Christian rock band called Mobetta for many years, performing mainly at public high-school assemblies in gymnasiums with horrible acoustics. For about 10 years, starting in college, I directed a singing group called The King's Children, ministering in southern California churches, and also served a very brief term as musical host for Dr. Gene Scott's TV show on Channel 30 in Glendale. It was for The King's Children that I wrote my first song: "I'm Tellin' the Whole Wide World About Jesus."

I sometimes took a team of ministry to the Union Rescue Mission in the skid row section of Los Angeles, preaching to the winos and other down-and-outers who wanted something to eat and a place to sleep but had to sit through a religious service first. We would sing our gospel songs and one of us would preach, looking out at the rows of unshaven, bored, hungover and sleeping men who were forced to endure our wisdom before the doors to the dining room were opened. We truly thought we were helping these men, offering them hope in place of despair. Once in a while one of them would shout "Amen!" but that might have meant "enough" instead of "bravo."

For several years I wrote and produced Gospel Light's VBS Mini-Musicales, short, easy-to-perform cantatas with three or four songs. Gospel Light Publications is one of the leading Sunday School and children's curriculum publishers in the world. I enjoyed working with Christian outreach groups, children's ministries, singers, publishers, missionaries, evangelists—anyone who was doing the work of the Lord. This was not a career for me. It was a ministry.

I used to think that everything that happened to me had a spiritual significance. If I was looking for a parking space and a car pulled out of a space right near where I wanted to be, then I would say, "Thank you, Jesus, for giving me a place to park." If I had to park six blocks away, I would say, "Thank you, Jesus, for teaching me patience." The bible says "All things work together for good to them that love God." I viewed all income as an undeserved gift from heaven. I tried to interpret every news event as fitting into God's plan for the world. If something bad happened then I would say, "There is the price for evil." If something good happened then I would say, "There is a sign of God's blessing." Any news from the Middle East was a sign that God was focusing attention on the site of the arena for the last days, which was just around the corner. Nothing in my life was accidental. Every occurrence was a lesson to be learned, or a part of divine purpose, or a temptation from the Devil. Behind the visible world was a very real spiritual world inhabited by angels, demons, spirits and saints, all fighting to win my soul and demolish the other side. As you might imagine, this made my life very interesting.

One day I was driving home through the foothills east of Modesto, California. I was thinking about my ministry and praying that God would teach me how to follow his direction. I really wanted to obey God, to be a faithful servant, and to recognize His "true voice" in my spiritual ear. As I was traveling down the highway I "heard" my mind say, "Turn right." I figured this had to be the voice of God, and if I was ever to learn how to obey I had better do what I was told. I turned right. The little road led off into farmland and I just kept driving, waiting for another signal. After a while I heard the voice again: "Turn left." So I turned left. This kept up, turning here and there, and I was beginning to feel excited about what God might have in store for me when I got to wherever he was leading me. Maybe, I thought, there would be some lost, godless person who was desperate to hear the gospel. Or, maybe I would find a generous donor to my ministry.

I kept driving until I came to a dirt road out in the middle of nowhere, and I heard, "Turn here." I turned and drove about a half-mile to a dead end in the middle of a cornfield. I stopped my car and turned off the engine, looking around for whatever it was that God had in mind. I really expected someone to come walking out of the corn, or something like that. After about 15 minutes I began to feel rather stupid. Then a few minutes later I realized that there must have been some other reason why God would bring me out to the dead-end of a dirt road. It finally dawned on me: God was testing my faithfulness! With a warm feeling all over my body I felt the Spirit say, "I am proud of you, Dan. You are an obedient child. You can go now."

Since I have become an atheist I often hear from believers who tell me that I could not possibly have been a true Christian or I would never have left Christianity. If I had truly known Jesus personally, like they do, then I would never have denied him. I must have been merely pretending to convince myself that God was real, they insist. Well, yes, I know exactly what they are saying. I used to preach that sermon. I preached it, believed it, knew it and felt it. If I did not have an authentic relationship with God, then why not? Why would God reveal himself to *them*, and not to me? I read the same bible, prayed with an open, humble spirit, and received inner confirmation of a "presence" witnessing to the truth of what I believed. If what I felt was phony, why would a good God allow me to be so deceived? (And how does anyone else know they are not being deceived as well?)

I had no doubts at all that what I experienced was authentic, not until near the end of my ministry. I sometimes ask these people, "Who are *you* to decide who is a true Christian?" Jesus said, "Ye shall know them by their fruits" and my life exhibited the "fruits of the spirit." Paul wrote that "the fruit of the Spirit is love, joy, peace, longsuffering, gentleness, goodness, faith, meekness, temperance: against such there is no law." I was not perfect—nobody is—but judging by the bible, no one else can make a stronger claim to being a Christian. I had been "born again" and believed it and announced it. I had been "filled with the spirit" and lived it. I had dedicated myself to a life of ministry. I was a "doer of the Word, not a hearer only." I had lived by faith, putting my life, health and future on the line—how many "true believers" have done that? I prayed, spoke in tongues and "sang in the spirit." I searched the scriptures for guidance. I knew that Jesus was my friend, lord and savior, and I had a daily inner dialogue with him, asking for help and praising him for his blessings. I had brought people to faith in Jesus and had seen many converts. I had heard countless testimonies of believers who told me they felt the "spirit of God" on my ministry (unless they were not true Christians either). There are people in the ministry today who credit me with helping to inspire them to preach and become ministers. I was invited and re-invited to minister in hundreds of Christian churches. How many "true Christians" can say they have done as much? The reason I rejected Christianity was not because I did not understand or experience it. It wasn't because I despised God or hated the Christian life. I loved what I was doing and never imagined throwing it away.

If I was not a true Christian, then nobody is.

Chapter Two
The Fall

It was 1979 and Jesus had not returned.

I was invited to speak at an American Baptist Church in Ontario, California, and before the meeting the pastor and I were talking in his office. I was surprised to hear him say, "We have a couple of members of our church who do not believe Adam and Eve were historical people."

"What?" I thought. "And you let them remain members?"

"Don't get me wrong," he said. "I believe Adam and Eve were historical people, because the bible does not tell lies. But these members think the story may have been metaphor. Since they are great Christians, I don't think this small disagreement is enough to matter."

The pastor continued by saying that some people consider parts of the bible that *appear* historical to be simply stories with a moral lesson. They believe that when Jesus told the Parable of the Prodigal Son, he did not intend us to think that there existed an actual prodigal son person with an address and Social Security number. It is not the historical fact of the tale that is important—it is the underlying message that counts. If Jesus can make up stories, why can't other biblical writers? Some people think the story of Adam and Eve was a Hebrew parable created by the ancient Israelites to explain the origin of the sinful human race, and the moral lesson is what is important, not the physical existence of two protohumans, with or without navels.

I was shocked by this kind of talk. Liberal talk. The fundamentalist mindset does not allow this latitude. To the fundamentalist there is no gray area. Everything is black or white, true or false, right or wrong. Jesus reportedly said: "I wish that you were cold or hot. So because you are lukewarm, and neither hot nor cold, I will spit you out of my mouth." (Revelation 3:15-16, and not a very nice image.) As a fundamentalist, I used to dislike liberals more than atheists, because with atheists, you at least knew where they stood. (This was a principle only: I didn't actually know any atheists—well, I probably did, but I didn't know that I knew any atheists. That ought to tell us something right there.) Atheists are cold and true Christians are hot, but liberals are lukewarm. Liberals have "a form of godliness, but denying the power thereof" and offer more of a temptation away from devout faith than any atheist could pose. I felt that attempting to learn what a liberal Christian believes was like trying to nail Jell-O to a tree.

The next time you talk with an extreme fundamentalist, beware. If you use gray talk—relativistic, situational, provisional, tentative—that will translate to black. That is why the issue of Adam and Eve was so distressing to me. I'm embarrassed to admit this now, but it was a big deal back then, and still is to bible literalists. (Yes, even fundamentalists know there is metaphor in the bible. When Jesus said "I am the door" we did not think he had hinges or a doorknob. But in the absence of any indication or justification for treating the plain words of the text figuratively, we had to take it at face value.)

In order to maintain a fellowship with Christians who had a slightly different view, I made this little shift in my mind, a move that to most readers would seem simple enough, but to me was a huge and danger-ous leap. I did not jettison the historical Adam and Eve—that would have been too much and impossible at the time. What I did was say, "Okay, I believe Adam and Eve were historical, of course, because the bible does not indicate Genesis is a parable or metaphor, but that should not stop me from fellowshipping with believers who might feel differently about it." Those Christians who had a tiny variance from my theology were not bad people. They worshipped God and promoted Christianity. They were not going to hell for a sincere difference of opinion. I could still call them brothers or sisters in Christ. That was a little nudge in the direction of tolerance, but a gargantuan spiritual (and psychological) concession to make. I discovered that I could live with a small amount of gray. Not that I liked it, but I could do it.

That was the first of many little steps over the next few years. Those initial and timid movements away from fundamentalism were psychologically more traumatic than the intellectual flying leaps that came later. When you are raised to believe that every word in the bible is God-inspired and inerrant, you can't lightly moderate your views on scripture.

I was about 30 years old when I started to have these early questions about Christianity. Not doubts, just questions. I was working on two more musicals for Manna Music—*Everywhere That Mary Went* and *Penny*, about the one lost lamb that was missing from the fold of 100—which I never finished because my views were changing as I was trying to write. The continental plates were shifting imperceptibly. I didn't have any problems at that time with Christianity. I loved my Christian life, I believed in what I was doing, and it felt right. However, my mind must have been restless to move beyond the simplicities of fundamentalism. I had been so involved with fundamentalist and evangelical matters that I had been ignoring a part of myself that was beginning to ask for attention. It was as if there were this little knock on my skull and something was saying, "Hello! Anybody home?" I was starving and didn't know it, like when you are working hard on a project and you forget to eat and you don't know you are hungry until you are *really* hungry. I had been reading the Christian writers (Francis Schaeffer, Josh McDowell, C. S. Lewis, etc.) and really had not read much of anything else besides the bible for years. So, not with any real purpose in mind, I began to scratch this intellectual itch. I read some science magazines, some philosophy, psychology and daily newspapers (!), and began to catch up on the true liberal arts education I would have had years before if I had gone to a real college. This triggered what later became a ravenous appetite to learn, and produced a slow but steady migration across the theological spectrum that took about four or five years.

I was not aiming for doubt or atheism. I thought each little move was the last one. "Ah, I'm growing more mature in my beliefs," I told myself. I originally thought my faith was being strengthened by this additional information, when it was actually my knowledge that was being strengthened. I had no sudden, eye-opening experience. When you are raised like I was, you don't just wake up one morning, snap your fingers and say, "Oh, silly me! There's no God." It was a slow, sometimes wrenching, halting, circuitous process.

Since I had become an independent evangelist, with no local congregation to answer to (the church in Standard did not end up functioning as a home base), I perhaps felt freer to experiment intellectually and to investigate what other Christians believed. I didn't study nonbelief (how would I know how to do that?), I studied other believers. As I visited different congregations that represented many varieties of faith, it slowly dawned on me that there is no single Christianity—there are thousands of Christianities. (There may be as many Christianities as there are Christians.) There are many hundreds of denominations and sects, and each one of them can open the bible and prove that *theirs* is the correct interpretation and the others are all off in some way, either slightly aberrant or grossly wrong. They can all do that.

Paul wrote that "God is not the author of confusion," but can you think of a book that has caused more confusion than the bible?

Jesus still had not returned, obviously, and I began to realize that it was not going to happen. Every generation of Christians, including the first, has thought they were living in the "end times." Jesus is reported as telling his disciples, "There be some standing here, which shall not taste of death, till they see the Son of man coming in his kingdom." (Matthew 16:28) He promised, "Behold I come quickly." (Revelation 3:11) But 2,000 years is not "quickly." It slowly dawned on me—duh—that something was very wrong with what I believed. "Oh," I thought. "I guess I am growing up here."

Gradually, I began to swing across the theological continuum, becoming less and less fundamentalist and more of a moderate evangelical. I was accepting invitations to preach and sing in a variety of churches, mostly evangelical, but also in some moderate and liberal congregations that had performed my music. My sermons began to have less hell and more love. I talked less about the afterlife and more about living *this* life. (I was raising four growing kids by now.) I was still a strong, committed believer, but preaching less evangelism and more "Christian walk."

I vividly remember driving the freeways of southern California and running all of this through my mind, talking with "God," talking with myself, arguing, rebutting, weighing emotion against reason, asking what it was all about. One thought kept rising to the surface, as if spoken from somewhere else: "Something is wrong." I couldn't figure it out. I couldn't really articulate the questions properly, but a voice in my mind kept saying, "Something is wrong. Admit it." I think that was the voice of honesty—I knew it was not the voice of God.

I think it was at this point that I made the leap, not to atheism, but to the commitment to follow reason and evidence wherever they might lead, even if it meant taking me away from my cherished beliefs.

As the months passed, that voice kept getting louder: "Something is wrong."

After a couple of years of this process of reevaluation, I had migrated into a more moderate position, where I still held the basic theological beliefs but discarded many lesser doctrines as either nonessential or untrue. I remember the way I was thinking then: every Christian has a particular hierarchy of doctrines and practices, and most Christians arrange their hierarchy in roughly the same manner. The existence of God is at the top, the deity of Jesus just below that, and so on down to the bottom of the list, where you find issues like whether women should wear jewelry or makeup in church. What distinguishes many brands of Christianity is where they draw their line between what is essential and what is not. Extreme fundamentalists draw the line way down at the bottom of the list, making all doctrines above it equally necessary. Moderates draw the line somewhere up in the middle of the list. Liberals draw the line way up at the top, not caring if the bible is inerrant or if Jesus existed historically, but holding on to the existence of God, however he or she is defined, maintaining the general usefulness of religion, and valuing rituals to give structure or meaning to life.

As I traveled across the spectrum, I kept drawing my line higher and higher. I read some liberal and neo-conservative theologians, such as Tillich and Bultmann. These authors, though perhaps flawed in this or that area, appeared to be intelligent and caring human beings who were using their minds and doing their best to come to an understanding of truth. They were not evil servants of Satan attempting to distract believers from the literal truth of the bible. I came to respect these thinkers and even to admire some of their views, without necessarily embracing the whole package. After a couple more years of evolving theology, I became one of these hated liberals, in my own mind, though few people suspected it. God did not spit me out of his mouth.

Interestingly, during this waning of faith, I could still "talk with God." I prayed and spoke in tongues and it felt the same as always. I was not an atheist yet, but since I was doubting everything else, I began to wonder if I should question my own inner experience. After all, followers of other religions report mystical and spiritual trances, so maybe I should not trust my own subjective emotions. Maybe I should put *myself* under the microscope. If everyone else could be wrong, then so could I. My religious experiences did not get weaker. They did not start to feel hollow or empty. (In fact, I can still reproduce those feelings today, just as strong.) What happened is that another part of my mind—the rational mind—started looking at the emotional part of my mind as if from a distance. I became my own test subject. "Look at that! I'm talking with God. It sure feels real, but it must be a trick of the brain." It *had* to be a trick of the brain, since it was beginning to look like a personal god probably did not exist. What a strange and wonderful thing to realize.

At that time in my migration, with my theology trying to keep pace with my intellectual and rational maturing, I still believed in a god but had no idea how to define it. All the while, I was still getting invitations to preach and sing in various churches, many of which were fundamentalist and conservative evangelical. Long before then I had stopped my direct "soul winning" sermons and tailored my message to be palatable to just about any church. This was easy since most of the churches that invited me at that time were interested in my published music, so I could simply perform a number of songs with brief inspirational introductions and keep the preaching to a minimum. I was able to adjust to the expectations of the audience, becoming more or less evangelistic according to the flavor of each church. Even then, I felt somewhat hypocritical, often hearing myself mouth words about which I was no longer sure, but words that the audience wanted to hear.

In my secret life of private reading I was impressed with enlightened writers in science magazines. In particular, an article by Ben Bova about "Creationist's Equal Time" in *OMNI* magazine turned the lens around so that I was gazing back at the fundamentalist mindset. The article laid bare the dishonesty of the "equal time for creationism in the science class" argument by asking how many Christians would welcome a chapter about evolution inserted between Genesis and Exodus. I became more and more embarrassed at what I used to believe, and more attracted to rational thought. Like an ancient bone that slowly fossilizes, the bible became less and less reliable as a source of truth and reason slowly took its place. I found myself asking heretical questions.

Where did we get the idea that words on a page speak truth? Shouldn't truth be the result of investigation and analysis?

If I think it is so easy for millions of people to be misled into a false religion because of a tendency to believe error, what makes me exempt?

If the Prodigal Son is a parable and Adam and Eve are a metaphor, then why is God himself not one huge figure of speech?

I kept moving and moving, picking up the pace, enjoying the scary feeling of "growing up" and learning. My mind felt like it was waking up. In my thirst for knowledge I did not limit myself to Christian authors since I also wanted to understand the reasoning behind non-Christian thinking. I figured the only way to truly grasp a subject was to look at it from all sides. If I had limited myself to Christian books I would probably still be a Christian today. I read philosophy, theology, science and psychology. I studied evolution and natural history. At first I laughed at these worldly thinkers, but I eventually started discovering some disturbing facts—facts that discredited Christianity. I tried to ignore these facts because they did not integrate with my religious worldview.

During those years of migration, I went through an intense inner conflict. On the one hand I was happy with the direction and fulfillment of my Christian life; on the other hand, my intellectual doubts were sprouting all over. Faith and reason began a war within me. And it kept escalating. I would cry out to God for answers, and none would come. Like the lonely heart who keeps waiting for the phone to ring, I kept trusting that God would someday come through. He never did.

The only proposed answer was *faith,* and I gradually grew to dislike the smell of that word. I finally realized that faith is a cop-out, a defeat—an admission that the truths of religion are unknowable through evidence and reason. It is only indemonstrable assertions that require the suspension of reason, and weak ideas that require faith. Biblical contradictions became more and more discrepant, and apologist arguments became more and more absurd. When I finally discarded faith, things became more and more clear.

But don't imagine that this was an easy process. It was like tearing my whole frame of reality to pieces, ripping to shreds the fabric of meaning and hope, betraying the values of existence. It hurt badly. It was like spitting on my mother, or like throwing one of my children out a window. It was sacrilege. All of my bases for thinking and values had to be restructured. Adding to that inner conflict was the outer conflict of reputation. Did I really want to discard the respect I had so carefully built over so many years with so many important people? But even so, I couldn't be distracted from the questions that had come to the forefront. Finally, at the far end of my theological migration, I was forced to admit that there is no basis for believing that a god exists, except faith, and faith was not satisfactory to me.

I did not lose my faith—I gave it up purposely. The motivation that drove me into the ministry—to know and speak the truth—is the same that drove me out.

I lost faith in faith.

I was forced to admit that the bible is not a reliable source of truth: it is unscientific, irrational, contradictory, absurd, unhistorical, uninspiring and morally unsatisfying. (I talk about this in later chapters.) Beliefs that used to be so precious were melting away, one by one. It was like peeling back the layers of an onion, eliminating the nonessential doctrines to see what was at the core, and I just kept peeling and peeling until there was nothing left. The line that I was drawing under essential doctrines kept rising until it popped right off the top of the list. I threw out all the bath water and discovered there was no baby there!

Opening my eyes to the real world, stripped of dogma, faith and loyalty to tradition, I could finally see clearly that there was no evidence for a god, no coherent definition of a god, no good argument for the existence of a god, no agreement among believers as to the nature or moral principles of "God," and no good answers to the positive arguments against the existence of a god, such as the problem of evil. And beyond all that, there is no need for a god. Millions of good people live happy, productive, moral lives without believing in a god.

People sometimes ask me, "What was the one thing that caused you to change your mind?" I guess they are thinking that if they can "fix" that one thing, then I will go back to faith. But there was no "one thing." It was a gradual process. It would be like asking, "When did you grow up?" We can all point to a general period in our lives, but not to a specific moment. (I once asked that question during a talk at a Unitarian Church in Michigan and a woman spoke up and said, "I remember the exact moment, but I forget his name.") It is good that there was no "one thing." I do remember a number of poignant moments of realization, but these were the result of my skepticism, not the cause.

It was during the summer of 1983 when I told myself that I was an atheist. Nobody else knew this for about four or five lonely months.

Maybe a couple of my friends, and my wife, were suspecting something was askew, but since I still had a pretty successful ministry the outward appearance was as if little had changed. As far as I was concerned, I was the only atheist in the world. I knew there must be other atheists out there, but that was irrelevant. I did not become an atheist because I wanted to join a club. I was not converted by the "atheist movement." I saw no atheist evangelist on TV who persuaded me to change my views. I came to it all on my own, and that's how it should be. Almost every other atheist and agnostic I have met since then, who was raised religious, tells the same story: it is a private, independent process of free thinking. That is what gives it strength. It makes my conclusions my very own, valued because of the precious process of being forged and proved in my own mind.

Between the summer and Christmas of 1983 I went through an awful period of hypocrisy. (Can an atheist make a confession? I suppose I am now asking forgiveness from other freethinkers. What should my penance be?) I was still preaching, and I hated myself. I was living with the momentum of a lifetime of Christian service, still receiving invitations to minister, still feeding my family with honoraria from ministry and singing engagements in churches and Christian schools. I knew I should have just cut it off cleanly, but I didn't have the courage or clear-sighted vision to know how to do that. In preparation for some vague need for what might lie ahead, I took some classes in computer programming, telling my wife that I enjoyed computers and that perhaps I could supplement our income with this skill. Right away I got a job as a part-time programmer of 68000 Assembly Language for a company that makes monitoring systems for the petroleum industry. This eventually turned into a full-time job. (A year later, as an open atheist, I worked as a programmer/analyst designing and coding dispatching systems for the railroads, and I got to do a lot of fun, onsite installation and testing of a real-time multi-tasking system for N&W and Burlington Northern in the Midwest.) This provided me with the perfect transitional job—a way to ease out of ministry. I was still preaching on the weekends and doing some occasional record production at night, but in my mind I was letting go of the ministry. I had no choice.

In November, still a hypocrite, I accepted an invitation to preach in Mexicali, a Mexican city on the California border. I like that town. Even though I no longer believed what I was preaching, I still enjoyed the travel and the many friends I had south of the border. The night after a service in an adobe mission in the Mexicali Valley south of town, I went to bed on a burlap cot in a Sunday School room that doubled as a guest room for visiting preachers. I didn't sleep much that night. I could see some stars out the window, and I remember staring up at the ceiling as if I were gazing right up into outer space, contemplating my place in the universe. It was at that moment that I experienced the startling reality that I was alone. Completely and utterly alone. There was no supernatural realm, no God, no Devil, no demons, no angels helping me from the other side. No big eyeball judging my thoughts and actions. I am a biological organism in a natural environment, and that is all there is. The stars ingest and recycle matter and energy, and I saw myself as a little, low-wattage star, glowing faintly in the dark universe, destined to burn out like a sun after it has spent its fuel. It was simultaneously a frightening and liberating experience. Maybe first-time skydivers or space walkers have a similar sensation. I just knew that everything had come to rest, that the struggle was over, that I had truly shed the cocoon and I was, for the first time in my life, that "new creature" of which the bible so ignorantly speaks. I had at last graduated from the childish need to look outside myself to decide who I was as a person. This was no mystical experience, but it was uplifting. It was like learning that the charges against me had been dropped for a crime of which I had been falsely accused. I was free to put the matter aside and get on with life.

I was right at the point of figuring out how to end the charade and come out to the world as an atheist, but in a sense, I am glad I went through those months of hypocrisy. I learned something important from that strange vantage point. I remember standing in the pulpit, hearing myself speak words that I no longer believed, seeing the audience react as before. After one service, a woman came up to me with tears in her eyes and said, "Reverend Barker, your sermon was so meaningful. I want you to know that I felt the spirit of God on your ministry tonight!" And I thought, "You did? What does that tell us about the game we are playing?" Of course, I would have said (as many do) that it doesn't matter who speaks the word of God, and that even though I was a nonbeliever, the message is the same. But this woman told me that she "felt the spirit" on my ministry. I realized that the whole sermon/worship setup is a huge drama that we are all acting out, not just the person in the pulpit, but the audience as self-selected participants without whom there could be no preaching. We were all playing along with the illusionary meaningfulness of it all.

The last time I stood before a congregation as a minister was the following month, during the Christmas week of 1983. I had flown up to San Jose for meetings in one church, and after that I drove a rental car over to Auburn, northeast of Sacramento, to do a Christmas concert for a young, growing congregation meeting in a public school building. The arrangement was for the Auburn church to provide my plane ticket back to Southern California. They had made a hoopla of the occasion, and as I entered the building I saw that the church was packed with townsfolk.

Before the meeting, I met in a side room with the pastors and other leaders of the church, and we all held hands in a circle and prayed for God's blessing on the evening, a very familiar but now strangely foreign ritual. They were especially excited because there was a man in the audience who was in church for the very first time. The man's name was Harry, and he was the town atheist! Everybody liked Harry. He was a respected businessman who would give you the shirt off his back, but he wasn't a Christian. Harry had recently remarried, and his new wife had become born-again and had convinced him to attend church with her for the Christmas concert. Harry came because he loved music and wouldn't be just sitting through a sermon. They were all praying that my ministry would influence Harry that evening, and that Harry would turn his life over to Jesus Christ. They laid hands on me and prayed loudly that God would instill a very special blessing on my ministry so that Harry would be saved.

I was dreading the concert, hating myself with every ounce of disdain. As I walked up to the grand piano that was sitting under the spotlight, I tried to scan for Harry, though I had no idea what he looked like. Everyone was seated in near darkness, as if I was singing to a faceless congregation. So, in my mind I was singing to Harry, and to Harry alone. I went through the motions and performed my songs, thinking how utterly stupid they were and how ridiculous I must be sounding to Harry. Between songs I did my patter, tiny sermonettes that tied things together. It was one of the most difficult things I have ever had to do in my life. It took a tremendous effort just to get the words out, words that I no longer believed. It can still make me cry to think back on that moment. At a couple of points I just stopped talking, deadly silent, blank as a new sheet of paper. The audience must have thought that the Holy Spirit was moving in my soul. I somehow managed to fall back on showmanship and willed myself to continue. At one point near the end of the concert I almost lost it. I was singing some of my particularly dumb lyrics and almost stopped right in the middle of the song to say, "This is crap." I wanted to turn to the audience and say, "Harry! You are right. I'm sorry. There is no God, and this is mumbo-jumbo nonsense." But I avoided that dramatic possibility and somehow, like Pagliacci, got through the performance. Besides, they hadn't yet given me my plane ticket back home.

Afterward, certain people were invited over to the pastor's home for Christmas refreshments. Harry and his wife showed up. I guessed that this was supposed to be my opportunity to "lay it on" to Harry and convert him to Jesus, but I didn't talk to Harry at all that night, except maybe to shake his hand. I was so ashamed of myself, so embarrassed at how we were treating this man, singling him out like he had a social disease. I sat near the Christmas tree, Harry sat across the room in an armchair, and I avoided eye contact. How I was wishing everything were different, that I was really free and grown up and that he and I could just get together and talk. I don't know if I would have liked Harry or not. I don't know if he would have had anything profound to say, or if he would have even cared about my dilemma. But I respected the man immensely. He had the courage to be different. Sometime during the little party the pastor spoke up and said something about how nice it was for all of us to get together to celebrate the birth of the Savior, and Harry in a loud voice immediately said, "Not all of us." He was fearless. He seemed proud to be identified as an atheist, and happy to be an independent thinker. The sermons and songs of the thousands of dedicated Christians I had ever known did not measure up to that one simple and brave comment spoken by an unbeliever.

I never preached another sermon. I never accepted another invitation to perform a religious concert. To be fair to myself and to everyone else, I knew that I had to cut it off quickly and cleanly. In January 1984 I wrote a letter to everyone I could think of—ministers, friends, relatives, publishing companies, Christian recording artists, fellow missionaries—breaking it off for good, telling them that I was no longer a Christian, that I was an atheist or agnostic (I didn't have the distinction clear in my mind then), that I would no longer accept invitations to preach or perform Christian music, and that I hoped we could keep a dialogue open. I remember that moment, hesitating for a few seconds at the mailbox beside Chaffey High School in Ontario, California, holding those dozens of envelopes in my hand and thinking, "This is it." Dropping those letters into the slot was a million times more satisfying than any religious experience. It was real.

Chapter Three
The Fallout

My letters were mailed, every important person in my life would soon know that I was no longer a Christian—and I walked away from that mailbox a free person. I knew there would be strong responses, but I was not afraid. I had made my own free choice, and no believer in the world would deny me that freedom. You can't believe if you don't have the freedom not to believe. Here is the letter I mailed, dated January 16, 1984, to more than 50 colleagues, friends and family members:

> *Dear friend,*
>
> *You probably already know that I have gone through some significant changes regarding spiritual things. The past five or six years has been a time of deep reevaluation for me, and during the last couple of years I have decided that I can no longer honestly call myself a Christian. You can probably imagine that it has been an agonizing process for me. I was raised in a good Christian home, served in missions and evangelism, went to a Christian college, became ordained and ministered in three churches as Assistant Pastor. During those years I was 100 percent convinced of my faith, and now I am just about 100 percent unconvinced.*
>
> *The purpose of this letter is not to present my case. Yet I will point out that my studies have brought me through many important areas, most notably: the authenticity of the bible, faith vs. reason, church history—and a bunch of other fun subjects like evolution, physics, psychology, self-esteem, philosophy, parapsychology, pseudo-science, mathematics, etc.*

I'm not sure what the purpose of this letter is, except to serve as a point of information to a friend or relative whom I consider to be important in my life, and with whom I could not bear to be dishonest. I have not thrown the baby out with the bath water. I still basically maintain the same Christian values of kindness, love, giving, temperance and respect that I was raised with. Christianity has much good. Yet I feel I can demonstrate an alternate, rational basis for those values outside of a system of faith and authority. Of course, I admit, those values cannot save me from the fires of hell—but it is irrational to hold a fear of something which is nonexistent, and to allow that fear to dominate one's philosophy and way of life.

If the bible is true I will run to it willingly. If there is a God, I would be silly to deny Him. In fact, the little child in me still sometimes wishes to regain the comforts and reassurances of my former beliefs. I am a human being with the same fears and feelings we all share. The bible says those who seek will find. You know me. I am constantly seeking. And I have not found. Right now I am somewhere between the agnostic and the atheist, although I spend a great deal of time in both camps.

There is much more to say, and I would greatly appreciate any input you can offer. I would suggest, though, that before we attempt any meaningful dialogue, we should understand as much as possible about each other's thoughts. If you wish, I will send you any of various papers I am preparing, including: The Bible, Faith vs. Reason...

Finally, I am not your enemy. Our enemy is the one who doesn't care about these subjects—who thinks that you and I are silly to be concerned with life and values. I intend no disrespect to you, or anyone who

*is genuinely interested in religion and philosophy. It
is the non-thinker who bothers me and with whom
meaningful interaction is impossible.*

Dan Barker

Today, I would write a completely different letter, but that's where I was at the time, in the process of changing one worldview for another. Today, I would point out that the "Christian values" I found to be praiseworthy are simply human values, and that not all Christian values are good—in fact, no values that are exclusively Christian are admirable. The "little child" nostalgia lasted about a year, and has been replaced with embarrassment that I ever believed or missed my belief. The definitions of agnosticism and atheism have been clarified. But that letter is a perfect snapshot of who I was, and reading it again brings back many of those old feelings.

It wasn't long until the reactions started coming in, and they were all across the board. Some were predictable, but others surprised me.

"Sorry to hear about your recent commitment to be uncommitted to the Lamb of God that you so beautifully had written about and put to music in such a successful way," wrote Assembly of God pastor Mark Griffo. Mark was one of the kids in the choir I directed at Glengrove Assembly. I had encouraged him to enter the ministry over the objections of his family, and we had served as missionaries together in Mexico.

"I realize you're not my enemy, as you stated, but Satan is! He's out to rob, kill and destroy life... My heart tears within me trying to figure out the answer you'll give [children] when they ask you, 'Dan, can you write more songs so my future children can know the source of love, Jesus Christ, like you do?' I'm praying for you always and looking forward to your resurrection."

To Mark, I am dead.

Mark's wife, Debbie, was less charitable: "Meaningful interaction you want? There is nothing meaningful about the beliefs that you have chosen... I am sorry that the Lamb you once wrote about is no longer Lord of your life. To really know the almighty God, Saviour, King, all knowing, all powerful, all loving creator of you and I, is to *never* leave

Him... Humble yourself in the sight of the Lord." There's that recurrent theme: I was faking my Christian life, but she wasn't.

David Gustaveson, director of Youth With a Mission's Pacific & Asia Christian University in Hawaii and one-time pastor at Glengrove Assembly, wrote: "I was somewhat shocked by your letter... I guess I'll just have to pray harder... I believe an acid test is to simply cry out to God (whether you believe or not) and ask Him to radically and ruthlessly correct you if you are wrong. It would be better for God to use 'any means' to show you the truth, than for one to find out he had been misled too late. I have read your papers and, of course, they present a good case. I wouldn't expect anything else from someone as brilliant as you. I think the contradictions in the bible show the beauty of God speaking through frail humanity, and yet keeping the main message of the bible intact."

I sent Dave an exhaustive response, telling him that I had indeed prayed exactly as he suggested, and congratulating him for the surprising and honest acknowledgment that there are truly contradictions in the bible. He replied by sending me a box of 14 cassette tapes from a theologian.

I had penned a note at the bottom of my letter to Gospel Light Publications, telling everyone there that I would understand if they decided not to continue working with me. We were in the middle of another VBS Mini-Musicale project. Wes Haystead wrote: "Thanks for honestly sharing your journey with me. I promise not to start bombarding you with tracts and Josh McDowell books. As to our continuing to work together, I vote aye. Provided of course that you can get me three songs for Sunrise Island real quick. Sort of sounds like schedule takes precedence over principles, eh? Actually, I value highly your talent, your sensitivity, your flexibility and your friendship. Therefore, I hope we can continue working together until one of us converts the other or you feel the goals of our projects are incompatible with your directions."

I reluctantly agreed to finish the project, feeling it would have been unprofessional to back out of a business agreement, but asked if I could use a pseudonym to save us both the embarrassment. So, if you ever see the *Sunrise Island* Vacation Bible School musical written by "Edwin Daniels," you will know that an atheist composed it. Writing those songs, I confess, was a strange experience. I felt like a total hypocrite.

To the defense of Gospel Light, Wes did tell me that they thought I was merely going through a stage, a spiritual crisis, and that he was certain I would come back to Christ. We cannot accuse Gospel Light of knowingly hiring a nonbeliever because everyone there thought I was a Christian when we started the project. Regardless, I can testify that the creation of such music, which the religious publisher accepted and was performed by believers in churches and Christian schools around the country, was purely artistic craftsmanship and not "inspired" by faith. (Stephen Foster did a similar thing when he composed Sunday school hymns while not a believer.)

Hal Spencer, president of Manna Music, wrote: "My immediate response is that this can't be true and that you are only going through a doubting time of your life. However, knowing you, I'm afraid that there is more to it than that. I will be asking the Lord to guide me also if there is something that I can say which might influence your feelings."

Hal and I met for lunch a couple of months later and I got to hear what "the Lord" guided him to say. Although he is quite knowledgeable about the music industry, he had not given much thought to theology or philosophy. He kept pointing to a leaf in a flower arrangement next to our table, saying, "How did that leaf get here?" After I pointed out the problems with the traditional design and first-cause arguments, he turned back to the leaf and said, "But I just can't imagine how that leaf got here without a Creator." (Richard Dawkins calls this the Argument from Incredulity.) We later bumped into each other in Nashville, when I was there for my first public debate and Hal was attending a country/gospel music awards ceremony. The chance meeting was so surprising that he quipped, "See, this proves there is a God!" Manna kept selling my musicals for many years, and Hal continued to treat me professionally.

Eli Peralta was my ninth-grade Spanish teacher and a member of the Peralta Brothers Quartet, with whom I had ministered during high school. He wrote: "Thank you for letting us know the status of your life change. Rest assured that the pureness and clarity of your communication is being accepted in a spirit of love and consideration. It is significant that in the days prior to your letter arriving, I was reminiscing about our fellowship and friendship of years gone by and wishing that we could visit sometime. My brothers and I still think of you with many fond memories and (think of the) fun times we had together. I have informed them regarding your journey from faith to reason, and even though it has made a significant emotional impact on us, I for one feel a deep sense of calm and still consider ourselves friends!" Eli never had an unkind cell in his body. This is true friendship.

Jill Johnson, wife of the music minister at the Auburn, California, church where I did my final Christian concert and preaching, sent me a surprisingly tolerant letter: "I totally support your sincere desire to seek out the truth in love. I feel for you because in a certain sense the decision you've made has got to be a cataclysmic event not only for you and those you love (I keep thinking of your dad for some reason), but also to so many outside your home sphere. But I believe in honesty and since you believe with all of your being in what you espouse, I'm sure it's a necessity for you to continue following this path. When you 'break the rules' there are always those who will have a desire or a need to punish or judge or condemn...and I just hope and pray most people will be gentle with you even though you and they are not in agreement. I am so happy that I was able to hear you in concert and I have no doubt that you will continue to create beauty in spheres other than the Christian one." I guess I was a good showman: Jill had heard that final performance and suspected nothing. But neither did I suspect she would be so understanding, which may be a signal that not all fundamentalists are as intolerant as their God.

Loren McBain, pastor of the First Baptist Church of Ontario, California, which my family was attending and where I had briefly served as interim Music Director, wrote: "I'd really like to stay in touch with you if only for lunch once in a while. I'd especially be happy to play chess when you want, the odds now clearly in my favor since God will be on my side!" Perhaps with patience running thin, the same man wrote a less friendly letter 10 months later: "You and I both know Dan that you have heard, and you fully understand 'God's rules for living,' and that you are now living by your own rules. I understand them as simple disobedience." I later heard that he felt bad about that second letter, which effectively shut the door on our friendship.

A co-worker in Christian music and children's books, Scoti Domeij, wrote: "Does this mean that we won't be seeing each other at MusiCalifornia [a Christian conference] (Ha! Ha!). I am not offended or the least bit surprised by your journey from faith to reason. Your questioning has surfaced in many different ways when we have been together. I do feel some sadness and wonder what hurt and deep disappointments have precipitated your journey from faith to reason."

That is another theme I heard a lot: "How were you hurt?" Although my deconversion to atheism was intellectual, not emotional, I suppose it is true that I suffered some "deep disappointments." I was initially saddened, for example, to learn that the bible is not as reliable as I had been taught to believe it was. So, yes, it hurt to know that I had been deceived, deliberately or innocently, by people whom I had trusted. But my problem was not with those people: it was with the truth of the claims of Christianity.

Shirley and Verlin Cox had regularly helped me arrange meetings in Indiana. "I must admit to a bit of a shock," Shirley wrote. "At first I wanted to write a 'preachy' letter to you but after much reflection and prayer I realize you know more 'bible' than I and Verlin will ever know. We haven't been through college the way you have... Yes, we are broken hearted that you've rejected our Lord but we have hope and our prayers will continue. While in Florida last year we were delighted to see your '*Mary Had a Little Lamb*,' and churches in Indiana in our area still present it. Oh yes, '*Mary Had*' was a puppet show on TV."

I received a letter from Sister Tammy Schinhofen, of whom I had no memory: "About eight years ago you were instrumental in my accepting Jesus as my *personal Savior*. I thank God that I am a jewel placed in your crown. Don't let the enemy take away or tarnish your crown." She was referring to the belief that Christians will someday rule the universe alongside God; hence, we will all be wearing a kingly (or queenly) crown. But doesn't this make it a status symbol? "My crown has more jewels than yours!"

One of my best friends was a man who was largely responsible for the promotional success of my musicals, a strong Christian who had little need for organized religion. It was not easy for him, being gay in a fundamentalist community. He wrote: "I don't know if I can say I 'enjoyed' your letter—there must be a better word. I know how you feel. I've surely been there myself (may still be there). What struck me so forcefully was the realization that 'the Christians' react to your questioning as they do, *not* because you have lost *your* faith, but because you have lost *theirs*!" That's a great line! It would have been just as bad if I had converted to Islam or Mormonism. But he was wrong. I *had* actually lost faith, not just someone else's faith, but the very concept of faith as a valid tool of knowledge. Well, no, I had not lost faith: I had discarded it, thrown it away, rejected its value. I wouldn't say, "I lost my cancer," or that an illness is something to be missed. However, I am certain that to this friend, my commitment to rationality was a kind of "faith," or substitute for faith, and in that context his remarks were meaningful.

I heard from many people to whom I had not mailed my letter, so the gossip must have been flying. Many of the letters were sincere, but without content. "I don't have any answers," wrote one friend. "It's not a matter of logic or intelligence," wrote another. "Human intellectual ability and capacities, no matter how great, are not sufficient," wrote a woman faith healer.

Many of the letters contained *ad hominem* arguments. One co-worker told me that I had "given in to the desires of self life" (What other kind of life is there?), and a neighbor wrote that I must be "hurt and bitter." Another tried to get me to admit my "deep wounds." A woman preacher announced that "sometime along the way you became angry with God." (If true, why is that *my* problem?) A former co-pastor told me that "you are on a selfish journey at the expense of your own integrity." How does he define integrity?

Roxanne Olson, the high school-aged daughter of one of my close Christian friends, living in a missionary compound, wrote: "I can't say I pray for you every day because I don't. Right now in school we are learning biology from a teacher who only knows about philosophy, medieval history and English literature. How do you think we got on this planet?" I wrote to her and her mother, who were living in a community operated by the charismatic evangelistic organization Youth With A Mission in Kona, Hawaii, and I challenged the school to a debate on the issues. I never heard a thing from them about that.

A few weeks after my letter was sent out, I received a call from the vice president and dean of academic instruction at Azusa Pacific University, Dr. Don Grant. He and the director of alumni affairs met with me for lunch one afternoon to see what had gone wrong with one of their emissaries. Don had been the director of the Dynamics Chorale, for which I played piano and sang on scholarship during my years at Azusa Pacific. It was an amicable lunch, but they nevertheless were fishing for some way to get me back in the fold. The conversation was at a more articulate level than most, but when I offered rebuttals that they had never heard, they fell back on the same old *ad hominem* responses, psychological guesswork, and so on. As we were walking back to our cars I thanked them for their time and willingness to discuss the issues, and I made them a challenge. I told them that I would be willing to participate in a debate at Azusa Pacific against any one of their professors on the question of the existence of God. I never heard from them again.

A few months earlier, before he received my letter, Manuel Bonilla had told me that he just "knew" the spirit of God was in my life, especially since I had recorded an unusually "inspired" arrangement on one of his albums that year, playing the piano with conviction and "spirit" behind his singing. We talked on the phone after he received my letter and I asked Manuel if he would be surprised to know that while I was performing that song I was a secret atheist and that my inspiration was musical, not spiritual. He didn't say a word. When I talked with Manuel again in 1985, he was friendly, but told me that he would be willing to offer me some counseling to help me get through my struggles. The only thing I could think of was to say that I was happy, and to thank him for his friendship.

Manuel and I met again in Tucson in 2003 and talked about the possibility of my producing a secular children's album for him that could be sold in schools, but it never happened. The thought of it becoming known that he was working with an atheist must have been too much. I do receive a nice seasonal greeting card from Manuel and Anita every year, and I still consider them to be gentle friends.

Shortly after my letter was sent out I met for lunch with Bob and Myrna Wright, two very close friends at the time. Bob was the pastor who conducted my ordination ceremony. They told me that they wanted to apologize to me. They were sorry they had not sensed my inner struggles leading up to my rejection of Christianity. If they had known, they said, perhaps they could have helped me avoid the discouragement and disappointment that led to my change of views. This was a difficult meeting because I loved and respected these people and I knew that they were sincere. I told them that my deconversion had nothing to do with any personal problems, that it had to do with the nature and content of the Christian message itself. I told them that "inner struggles" are good, and I tried to explain that *ad hominem* counseling was beside the point. They didn't get it.

"What would happen to me," I asked, "if I were to die right now?" They were silent. "Bob, you're an ordained minister. You know your bible. What happens to unbelievers?"

"Well, the bible says they go to hell," he responded.

"You know me," I continued. "I'm not a bad person. I'm honest. If I walk out of this restaurant and get killed by a truck, will I go straight to hell?" They didn't want to answer that question, squirming in their seats. "Well, do you believe the bible?" I pressed.

"Of course," Myrna said.

"Then will I go to hell?"

"Yes," they finally answered, but not without a great deal of discomfort. Perhaps it was not the best lunch topic or the most diplomatic way to treat friends, but I wanted to make the brutality of Christianity real to them. I knew it would be hard for them to imagine their God punishing someone like me. I later heard that they were perturbed with me for having coerced them to say I was going to hell. It forced them to acknowledge that, as much as we wanted to be friends, their religion considers me the enemy.

The letters I received and the conversations that followed my "coming out" displayed love, hatred, and everything in between. Many friendships were lost, others transformed, and still others strengthened. Of all of the attempts to get me back in the fold, not a single one had any intellectual impact. Although I was saddened at having discontinued some relationships, I found I did not miss them. I didn't think I was smarter than these people were; we just chose different priorities and grew apart. I suppose it was somewhat like a divorce—even though there were good times and happy memories, once it's over, it's over.

I'll tell you, this is a great way to test your friendships. Imagine doing this yourself. If you are an atheist, try telling your friends that you have become a born-again preacher. If you are a lifelong Republican, announce that you have switched parties. How many of your "friends" would stay your friends? Some undoubtedly would, because your friendship is a true horizontal peer relationship of unconditional admiration and enjoyment of each other's person. But some of them would not, because you (and they) would learn that the arrangement was contingent on something external to the relationship, such as belonging to the same club, faction, philosophy or religion. As soon as that external link disappears, so does the artificial bond that brings you together. That's when the friendship loses its point. But this is good, because then you know who your friends are. If they were true friends, they would have gladly accommodated your freedom of choice even if it made them uncomfortable. You can't lose something that was not there in the first place.

Few of the letters offered any defense of bible contradictions. No one presented any documentary evidences from the first century or offered a single rational argument for the existence of a god beyond the where-did-we-come-from garden variety. (I know there are stronger arguments, and I'll deal with them later.) Most of the negative responses centered on things like humility, shame, attitude, prayer—in short, "spiritual" intimidation.

I never heard from Rev. Milton Barfoot, the pastor at Glengrove Assembly of God, but my brother, Darrell, told me he had spoken briefly with him about me, and all he could say was, "But isn't Dan afraid of hell?" That's it. Of all the things this learned, ordained minister could utter in response to honest intellectual searching, the first thing he thought of was hell. Oh, gosh, now I see it! I should stop questioning and just be afraid.

Dave Gustaveson's challenge to "cry out to God" was nothing less than intellectual dishonesty. One of my friends asked me simply to "pretend that Jesus is real and he will make himself real to you." Had either of them ever "cried out to Buddha" or "pretended that Allah is real" as an acid test of their existence? These people were asking me to lie to myself. They should have known better. They should have known that I had already "cried out to God," that I had frequently prayed and "felt the spirit" within me. It is easy to produce or coax inner feelings, and it happens in all religions. They didn't seem to realize that I was not seeking inner confirmation—I was seeking objective, external evidence. And isn't "pretending Jesus is real" simply begging the question? Even if I had managed to fake it by pretending to pray to a being in whom I do not believe, would an omniscient god not know this? And why should I have had to ask in the first place? Why doesn't God simply reveal himself to everyone? And even faking it, as they must have imagined I was doing (or could do), why did God not respond? Their challenge actually backfired: "Thanks. I tried it and it failed. There is no God."

The almost universal tone of the letters and conversations was that I was the one with the problem. None acknowledged that my change of mind might be an indictment of Christianity itself. Some of them formerly had come to me for counseling, but now they no longer wanted to learn from me. (I don't think they should have to.) They all assumed that the challenge then at hand was to get me back. Even the few who did ask to read my papers never commented on them, except superficially. Although I expected this, it was a strange feeling to be demoted from a respected authority to a problem child. I suppose if I had learned less, or stopped learning altogether, I would still have had the trappings of clerical credibility. But no thanks. Here is one emperor who did not want the clothes, or want to be emperor at all.

I don't know if any of these people have since moderated their views, but I do know that none of them remained the same. You can't avoid being affected when one of your colleagues challenges the very core of your beliefs. Although the long-term fallout from my friends and co-workers is hard to know, the effect on my family was much more dramatic.

My parents had moved to Arizona, and when they got my letter they were shocked. They had been proud of their son's work as an ordained minister and evangelist, and of my reputation as a Christian songwriter. Not knowing anything about my gradual inner change, the announcement came as a total surprise. My sweet mother, a Sunday School teacher in Apache Junction, immediately hopped on a bus, traveling from Phoenix to my home in California, to see firsthand what had happened to her son. We had a long, emotional discussion into the early morning hours. I don't remember much of what was said that night, but Mom later reminded me that we opened the bible and read some of the horrible stories about the petty and cruel God of scripture, and I had said, "Mom, you are a good person. Do you really want to teach this awfulness to children? The God of the bible is a monster. You are nicer than that!" She would never be the same, but it wasn't until much later that I learned the long-term effects of that visit. At the time, I did not want to become a reverse evangelist to my own parents, so after that meeting I refrained from pressuring them to change their opinions. A family is a family, after all.

My mother tells me that after that meeting she was stunned by the dissonance. Backing off to get some perspective, she stopped going to church. In a *Wisconsin Magazine* article (July 28, 1991), journalist Bill Lueders quotes my mother, Pat Barker, as she recalled our late-night meeting: "The answers he gave me impressed my heart and mind. I had so much love for my son that I knew in some way he was right."

One morning as she was watering her desert garden, Mom saw a dead bird on the ground, and she thought, "How sad!" As she looked closer she saw that its flesh was being attacked by a mob of ants. How horrible! That pretty little songbird had come to a gruesome fate. Then she remembered all those years she had sung "His Eye Is On the Sparrow," praising God for his watchfulness: "I sing because I'm happy. I sing because I'm free. His eye is on the sparrow, and I know He watches me." Here on the ground was evidence that God's eye was not on the sparrow at all. If there were a God, his eye was at that moment on the ants and microbes feasting on the bird's misfortune. But, then, everything in nature could be someone else's breakfast, so the only "eye" is the impersonal eye of natural selection, which is a process of survival, not the result of cosmic parental care. On her own, she came to the same realization that I had come to on that cot in Mexicali—the realization that we are simply naturally evolved biological organisms in an amoral material environment, and that if there is any caring to be done, we are the ones to do it. All those years she was singing "His Eye Is On the Sparrow," it was actually *her* eye that was on me and my brothers. She was a wonderful mother.

Within weeks Mom concluded that religion was "just a bunch of baloney," as she told the reporter. She felt a "tremendously great disappointment in God." She began to do some reading and thinking of her own, and eventually started calling herself an atheist. "I don't have to hate anymore," she said happily.

One fact that surprised my mother was that no one in her church ever seemed to care about her departure. She had been a member of the Assembly of God for years, had performed in the choir, had sung solos regularly in services, was faithfully teaching Sunday School and had participated in many other functions. The only incident out of the ordinary, after leaving the church, was an embarrassing moment when she was grabbed at the supermarket by an older woman who was shaking, speaking in tongues and praying to cast the Devil out of my mother. This only confirmed my mother's newfound opinion that religion is "baloney."

It took my dad a little longer. When he got my letter he ran down to the church altar and poured out his heart to God. He enlisted the assistance of church members to pray for me. The pastor laid hands on Dad, asking God for a special blessing during this trial of faith. At first Dad, the bible school alumnus, tried to argue with me in a friendly and fatherly way, and mailed me many pages of correspondence on the issues, which I answered promptly. Eventually he relented, due probably more to Mom and Darrell's influence than to mine. He began to read the "other side," and eventually came to respect the reasoning of freethinkers, philosophers and scientists.

The same *Wisconsin Magazine* article quotes my father, Norman, discussing how he dealt with his son's change of views: "I tried to straighten him out. It worked the other way around." After Dad stopped believing in God, he was amazed at how quickly his Christian friends turned on him. "I used to think it was a tough thing to be a Christian in this big, bad world. You want to see something interesting, try not being one." He reports, "I'm much happier now. To be free from superstition and fear and guilt and the sin complex, to be able to think freely and objectively, is a tremendous relief."

One of the immediate benefits to my dad was his reclamation of music. Back in the 1950s, when he and Mom became "born again," Dad abandoned his musical career, threw away his collection of swing recordings, turned his back on his "sinful" life and played his trombone only in church. He had come to view popular, worldly music as a threat to spiritual health and godly morality. Dance bands encouraged a carnal lifestyle. When he finally gave up religion, he was free to come back home to his talent. But this didn't happen in one clean break. Before completely leaving the church, Dad began to play his trombone in big bands in the Phoenix area, reconnecting with the delicious life he had abandoned almost 40 years earlier. He didn't tell anyone at church because he knew they would disapprove: "Resist the temptations of the world!" One Fourth of July, when Dad was playing at a party, a TV crew showed up to cover the event. The next day the pastor's wife called my dad to ask, "Norman, did I see you on TV last night?" Ha! The all-seeing eye of God!

Dad would not continue this double life for long. One evening, he drove to church, took his trombone case out of the car and walked toward the building. He could hear the praying, singing and preaching. When he got to the door it struck him that he did not belong in that alien world any more. Hoping that no one would notice, he quickly turned around, got back in the car and drove home, never to return. He traded "Onward, Christian Soldiers" for "Don't Get Around Much Any More."

I suppose it was implicit, but I never suggested to my parents that they should become atheists. They did their own thinking. They decided to investigate the issues for themselves. It is exciting to see what happened in their lives. I don't think it is possible to pull someone out of religion if they don't want to go.

My parents later admitted that they made some mistakes in raising their three boys in a fundamentalist household. My mother says that their motivation was to do "the right thing." In spite of the religious overkill, I had a very enjoyable childhood. Sure, we were indoctrinated with an illegitimate and intolerant worldview, but my parents were decent, caring people in spite of their faith. They raised me with good principles. One thing they taught me by example is that you should never be ashamed to speak what you think is the truth. That lesson has stayed with me my entire life.

When Darrell got my letter he was shocked at first, but then he got excited. Darrell had been an almost-skeptic for many years, not knowing exactly what he believed but covering the bases. I had always thought he was a borderline Christian. His whole attitude to Christianity, he later told me, was, "Exactly how much sin can I commit and still get to heaven?" I did not convert my brother to atheism; in reality, his big toe was already across the line. Darrell said that when he heard his big brother—his ordained-minister, Christian-songwriter big brother—articulate criticisms of Christianity, it suddenly legitimized and crystallized all of those unspoken and unformed questions he had been carrying around for years. It made it okay to doubt. "If *Dan* can say it, then so can I!" When I gave him a book on humanism, he said, "That's what I am! I never knew it until now, but I am a humanist."

For a while, though, Darrell was uncomfortable with the word "atheist." He once asked to accompany me to a meeting of atheists in Los Angeles, then almost changed his mind before coming in. A year or two later Darrell became one of the chapter directors of that group, Atheists United. He went on to complain about violations of state/church separation in Redlands and San Bernardino. He became a plaintiff in a successful lawsuit protesting county ownership and maintenance of a Christian theme park on public property. Darrell is a successful salesman and he has learned to put his considerable skills of persuasion to good use. My folks told me that Darrell was a solid support for them when they were going through their initial disillusionment with religion. It is helpful to have someone to talk to during times like this, and Darrell called them regularly to compare notes and cheer them up in their journey out of faith. Today, with more fervor and skill than he ever exhibited as a Christian, Darrell is a walking, driving advertisement for freedom of thought. (He often plays freethought music and initiates skeptical conversations with passengers on the airport shuttle van he owns.)

The change in my parents and in Darrell was tremendously heartening. I never would have predicted such an outcome. My parents had been fervent disciples of Jesus for years, and Darrell had been a street preacher with Christians in Action (CIA), a missionary/evangelism organization. (He confesses now that he joined that group mainly to wrangle an early discharge from the Marine Reserves on a "ministerial" basis—he did *not* want to fight in Viet Nam.) I should have known that in a family built around true love and acceptance, there is nothing to fear. The fact that these born-again, door-to-door preachers were open to change gives me hope. Some values are truly transcendent (in the natural sense), rising above religious walls. Human love, kindness and intelligence are better than belief, and superior to superstition.

My other brother, Tom, is still a born-again Christian. He gave his life to Jesus at a Billy Graham crusade in the early 1960s, and after some rocky high school and college years (including a shockingly bad semester at Oral Roberts University), he rededicated his life to God. He is a good man, a loving father, hard working and conscientious, now a retired high-school principal, still living in California. He and his wife make occasional missionary trips to Mexico in support of their faith. Although Tom and I have never been very close, we enjoy seeing each other and the subject of religion rarely comes up. I sometimes refer to Tom as the "white sheep" of the family.

My maternal grandmother, "Grams," was an uneducated, lovingly eccentric and generous woman whose views on religion fluctuated according to her medication. She and I were very close. When she received my letter she must have been torn apart with the issue, writing: "I won't give in to the Devil." Later, Grams wrote me again, in a more characteristic mood: "You sure don't have to defend yourself to me. You are a good man, one of the best I have ever seen, and I am thankful for that. I just stay open minded and try to live a good life. That's all I can do." A few years later Grams told me that she had scared off some Jehovah's Witnesses at her front door, growling, "Get out of here! I'm an atheist!" I don't think she really was an atheist, because at other times she spoke about God and Jesus in her life. But at least she became more broad-minded. To a large degree this was due to the change in my parents.

My dad's mother was living in Oklahoma. After Granddad died in 1986, she and I worked on a four-year project, publishing *Paradise Remembered*, a book of Granddad's collected stories of life as a Delaware (Lenape) Indian boy in Indian Territory before Oklahoma became a state. She was a member of the Christian Church her entire life. When she happened to see one of my appearances as an atheist on *The Oprah Winfrey Show*, she wrote me a postcard saying, "I saw you on TV. That is not *our* Danny." In spite of that understandable awkwardness, we got along wonderfully.

My uncle Keith, Dad's younger brother, was a recovering alcoholic who credited his sobriety to his deep faith in God. He had arranged for me to be hired in my first job as a computer programmer, designing monitoring systems for tank farms, and he was excited to be working not only with a family member, but with another strong Christian (he thought) as well. The job started in 1983, just when I had given up my faith, but he did not know it because I was still hypocritically preaching on the weekends. When he received my letter, he did not reply. We continued to work together as if nothing had happened, and I left it at that. One day as we were driving back to southern California from a computer show in Las Vegas, he pointed to a huge rock formation in the landscape and said, "Isn't that beautiful!" I looked at it for a moment and said, "Yes, it is beautiful. You can see how the multicolored ancient sedimentary sea beds were thrust upward after millions of years of tectonic pressure and are now tilted at an improbable angle." He turned to me and snapped, "Do you have to ruin everything?"

I appreciated and respected Uncle Keith immeasurably. Dad's two other brothers responded in a friendly and civil manner to the drastic change in our views, but Keith ended up ostracizing both of us, refusing to answer letters. I went on to another programming job and never saw Keith again. After I mailed him a copy of *Paradise Remembered* (his own dad's memoirs), which was received with excitement and gratitude by the rest of the family, he sent it back to me without explanation. I can only assume (as he once implied to Dad on the phone before breaking it off with us) that he was unwilling to associate with his "unclean" nephew.

My Christian marriage did not last either. When I told Carol that I was writing this book, she asked me not to say anything about her. I suggested that it would seem strange, even insulting, if I cut her completely out of the story. So she asked me to keep it to a minimum. Carol had always wanted to be married to a minister, and although she tried to adapt as much as possible to my change, she could only bend so far without breaking. She was ultimately unwilling to be disloyal to her faith. From her point of view, the bible commands Christians to "be ye not unequally yoked together with unbelievers." From my point of view, having become aware of feminism, egalitarianism and freedom of opinion, I could no longer imagine a marriage in which the man is the "head" of the wife, as the bible sets it up. Divorce is always painful, but we were fortunate that it was not too messy. We did not have much property to fight about, and neither of us wanted to fight anyway. She remains a faithful believer and is now married to a Baptist minister, as she continues to see that as her role in life.

Around this same time, I read Annie Laurie Gaylor's book, *Woe To The Women: The Bible Tells Me So*, published by the Freedom From Religion Foundation, which details the harm to women that stems directly from biblical teachings, and I wrote her a letter of thanks, telling her a little of my story. Three years later we were married, and it is one of "our little stories" that she never responded to that first letter. She lost it. But her mother, Anne Gaylor, who was president of the Foundation, found the letter and sent me a nice note asking me if I would write an article for *Freethought Today* about my deconversion. That article, "I Just Lost Faith in Faith," ran in the summer of 1984.

A few months later Anne and Annie Laurie were invited to be guests on Oprah Winfrey's *AM Chicago* show, at about the time Oprah was beginning to be noticed nationally. She was doing a show about atheism and asked Anne if she knew of any other atheists with good stories to tell, so Anne told her about this former minister in California. The producers called me and I jumped on a plane to Chicago to be one of the guests on the show. Not only was that the first time I publicly spoke about my atheism—on television, no less—but that was also the first time I had knowingly talked with any other atheists. I was nervous, not because of being on TV—I had done a lot of Christian television—but because this was the first time I would be speaking to an audience that was not supportive, and might even be hostile.

I met Anne and Annie Laurie before the show that morning, talked briefly with Oprah in the green room, and then went out before the cameras. We actually have videotape of the day we met! On the tape, you can see that we are checking each other out. They were a little worried about me, wondering if I would falter or be too soft in my atheism, and I was a little apprehensive about exactly what kind of people these outspoken atheists would be. During the show you can see us all relax as we all realized that we were among friends.

Computer programming became the perfect transitional job for me until I was able to go to work with the Freedom From Religion Foundation. In 1985, the company I was working with moved me to the midwest to be close to the railroad dispatching systems we were installing in Indiana and Illinois. That job was fun! We moved real trains on real tracks, using a custom real-time multitasking system, one of the tasks which I designed myself. I lived in hotels most of that year, and was able to drive up to the Freedom From Religion Foundation in Madison, Wisconsin, on weekends and rare days off, and gradually started volunteering there. In 1986, as the railroad systems were needing less maintenance, I decided to stay in Madison and work on a contract basis for the Foundation, designing and installing its first computer system.

In May 1987, Annie Laurie and I were married. The freethought-feminist wedding, a "match not made in heaven," took place in Sauk City, Wisconsin, at historic Freethought Hall. A woman judge wearing purple shoes with her judicial robe conducted the ceremony, announcing at the critical time, "You may now kiss the groom." The next month

I was hired full-time as public relations director for the Foundation. That's one way to get a job: marry the boss's daughter.

In 2004, Annie Laurie and I were elected co-presidents of the Freedom From Religion Foundation, which is today the largest organization of atheists and agnostics in the country.

Our daughter Sabrina was born in 1989, a fourth-generation freethinker on her mother's side of the family and, in spite of her red hair and light complexion, a full member of the Delaware (Lenape) Tribe of American Indians. I am a member from my dad's side of the family. We also have some Chiricahua Apache blood, from my mother's great-grandmother, who was in the Arizona tribe from which Geronimo came. (Geronimo's clan fought the intrusion of the Spanish missionaries.) We have not indoctrinated Sabrina into atheism, as if that were even possible. The last thing a freethinking family will do is coerce thought. We did not take her to Atheist Sunday school (is there such a thing?) or force her to memorize Bertrand Russell. But, of course, she has heard Annie Laurie and me talking about our work and she has attended many of the speeches and events at the Foundation's annual conventions, which amounts to a kind of "freethought education," I suppose. In the end, she is her own person, and she knows that she is free to make her own philosophical and political decisions. When I sometimes remind her that she is free to become a born-again Christian or anything she wants, she just snickers and says, "Oh, Dad."

My four kids from my first marriage are grown now and the daughters are raising their own children. They have always been very good about the whole controversy. Unless they bring it up, or unless it happens to arise in the course of normal conversation, we do not discuss religion. When they visited Wisconsin as children, I offered to escort them to the church of their choice, but they never took me up on it. Two or three times during her high school years my daughter, Becky, sent me a letter urging me to "come back to God," so I know she struggled with the issue. But I have repeatedly told all my children that my love for them is not contingent on what they believe. They can be Christians if they want, as long as they are good people and don't hurt others. They went to church with their mother, who worked at a Christian school, and their stepfather, a youth director at a Baptist church and later a pastor. They know what I think. I have never wanted them to be forced into a position of having to choose between parents. They are smart kids, and I have to trust that they have the ability to sift fact from fiction, and right from wrong. Danny now calls himself an agnostic. As far as I know, the girls, who may harbor some nominal or liberal beliefs, don't seem to go to church regularly. When they were young, I dedicated *Just Pretend: A Freethought Book for Children* to them, which says:

> No one can tell you what to think.
> Not your teachers.
> Not your parents.
> Not your minister, priest, or rabbi.
> Not your friends or relatives.
> Not this book.
> You are the boss of your own mind.
> If you have used your own mind to find out what is true,
> then you should be proud!
> Your thoughts are free.

And like my dad, I have also found a new joy in music. When I moved to Madison I started playing jazz piano, averaging more than 100 gigs a year since then. This might sound like a Sunday-evening church testimony, but I have to say that life has been much richer and happier since I was healed of the religious delusion. As the lyrics to one of my songs say: "The superstitious monkey is off my back. I'm thinking for myself, and I am back on track. And I can tell you: life is good!"

Jesus has still not returned, and never will. But who needs him?

Chapter Four
The New Call

The motivation that drove me into the pulpit is the same one that drove me out. I was a minister because I wanted to know and speak the truth, and I am an atheist for the same reason. I have not changed; my conclusions have changed. When I learned that Christianity is not true, I had to decide: "Do I want God, or do I want truth?" You can't have both.

Though I remain the same person I've always been, I have grown in learning—which is supposed to happen to all of us. I say "supposed" because there are some to whom growth and progress represent a threat. Religious conservatives do not want to move on. Religious conservatives have consistently resisted progress, preferring to maintain tradition for the sake of tradition alone, even if the tradition is bad. Some of us have a different priority. We prefer truth to tradition, progress to precedent, learning to loyalty. When I was a minister, I was convinced that I was preaching truth. It didn't matter then, and doesn't matter now, that what I was preaching happened to be tradition. What matters is whether it is true. When I decided to follow truth and jettison God, I did not lose a thing. I simply gained a new perspective.

Still, once a preacher always a preacher (in my case, at least), so the question now was, "Should I preach atheism?" Or, would it be better to simply back away from a life of proselytizing and get a real job? Most atheists and agnostics are not preachers. Most are happy to live and let live. When was the last time an atheist knocked on your front door? Has an agnostic ever handed you literature on a street corner?

When all is said and done, we can't help being who we are. I had developed certain habits and skills in the ministry and still wanted to change the world for the better. That's why some people will tell me: "You're still a preacher!" And I reply, "Is that bad?" Some accuse me of replacing one ideology for another. "You have turned 180 degrees.

You thought you were right before, and you think you are right now." Well, yes. I do think I am right now, and I am zealous about it. If zealousness is a fault, then all preachers are guilty. If advocacy is good, it is good for all of us. "You were wrong before, maybe you are wrong now." If that is true, I will admit it and apologize, like I have already shown I know how to do. "If there is no God," they say, "why do you care? Why be obsessed with something that does not exist?" (In other words, why not shut up?)

I am not "obsessed" in a manic sense—I do have a life; *they* are the ones who seem to be obsessed—but yes, I am very concerned about our species' preoccupation with superstition and irrationality and confident that if someone like me can be healed of such delusions, so can others.

So when I started working with the Freedom From Religion Foundation, I felt like I had come home. Even before then I was speaking out, but now I could actually continue my life as a "professional evangelist," devoting my time to promoting reason, science and humanistic morality. Not unlike the cross-country evangelist I was before, I now get to travel the continent and the world, speaking, performing at freethought concerts and debating theists. What a blast! I get to do all this as a part of my job!

As I write this, I have participated in 64 formal public debates. I have also done hundreds of informal debates, mainly on the radio, television and as part of panel discussions, but when it comes to the number of timed, moderated debates before an audience, I think I now hold the record for an atheist. There are dozens of good, qualified atheist debaters in the world, and many of us are in touch with each other, comparing notes, discussing strategies and recommending books, so I can't pretend that my ideas are all original. The most common debate I do is "Does God exist?" I also debate:

- "Can we be good without God?"

- "Did Jesus rise from the dead?"

- "Should state and church be separate?"

- "Is the bible reliable?

- "Evolution vs. Creationism (or Intelligent Design)"

- "Is Christianity true (or worthwhile)?"

My first debate was in February 1985 in Nashville, Tennessee, on the historicity of Jesus, with Dr. Rubel Shelly, author and well-known pastor of Woodmont Hills Church of Christ. He and I have done five debates over the years. One of them, focusing on the "problem of evil," took place in his large church with more than 1,500 people in the audience, on April 21, 1999, the day after the Columbine school shootings. (We had done the first half of the debate at Vanderbilt University the day before.) There were two armed policemen standing in the back of the church that night, apparently because the city was worried that a large gathering with lots of young people might become a target for copycat shootings (and perhaps because there was an atheist in town.) The only thing unusual that happened was that someone stole my box of books and literature from beneath the display table in the lobby, in spite of the presence of law enforcement. The thief may have been a Christian who did not think such literature should be read by impressionable minds.

During preliminary remarks, I said I would have liked to perform a song, but since this was the non-instrumental denomination of the Church of Christ, there was no piano in the building. (No kidding! This sect believes it is wrong to use any musical instruments in worship. There was also a split by a related Christian Church faction that does not think the communion cup should have a handle.) During questions from the audience that night, a young man came to the microphone to thank me for my remarks because, after hearing the debate, "My faith has been strengthened." I thanked *him* for the compliment! If his faith was strengthened, then his pastor lost the debate. Faith is what you need when you don't have certainty. The more you learn, the less you need to believe.

I debated Doug Wilson twice, once at the University of Delaware and again in his hometown of Moscow, Idaho. He is the author of *Letter from a Christian Citizen* (a response to Sam Harris's *Letter to a Christian Nation*) and a presuppositionalist Calvinist pastor. During our first debate, he claimed that without the bible there is no basis for morality, so I read him Psalm 137:9, which says, "Happy shall he be, that taketh and dasheth thy little ones against the stones." I then asked, "Is it moral to throw little babies against rocks?" With little hesitation, he replied, "Yes, it is." (I'm paraphrasing from memory.) There was audible gasping from members of the audience, including many Christians.

According to Wilson, we mortals are incapable of making moral judgments on our own and must submit to the superior wisdom of God. If the bible says we should be happy (or "blessed," as some translations render it) to kill the innocent children of those who worship other gods, then it would be immoral not to do it.

I then switched to the Christian scriptures and read from Luke 12:47-48 where Jesus demonstrated his compassion by advising us that there are some slaves who should not be beat as hard as other slaves because they didn't know any better: "That slave who knew what his master wanted, but did not prepare himself or do what was wanted, will receive a severe beating. But the one who did not know and did what deserved a beating will receive a light beating." (NRSV) I asked Doug, in front of that stunned audience, "Is it a good idea to beat your slaves?" He replied, "Yes, it is." Another gasp from the audience.

I was expecting Wilson to be a compassionate Christian and attempt to apply a modern interpretation, claiming context or metaphor or insist that Jesus was simply giving an example of what does happen, not what should be done. But there is no need to defend the bible when all we have to do is blindly obey it. In Wilson's mind, slavery is not a bad idea, since the bible commands it and Jesus not only never condemns it, but also incorporates it into his teachings as if it were the most natural order (which it was to the authors of the bible). At least Wilson is consistent, I'll give him that. Consistently awful. During our second debate, attended by many Calvinist ministers, I told the horrible story of how John Calvin had co-reformer Michael Servetus burned at the stake for the "crime" of questioning his scriptural interpretations. Not only did Wilson not join me in denouncing Calvin, he came to his defense! Well, how could he not, being a Calvinist pastor? "Anyone who holds John Calvin in high regard," I told that audience, "is morally bankrupt."

Christian philosopher Peter Payne, during our "Does ethics require God?" debate at the University of Wisconsin in Stevens Point in 2005, made a similar argument, though I think he is generally more compassionate than Doug Wilson. During cross-examination, I asked Payne, "If God told you to kill me, would you do it?" He was (thankfully) hesitant to answer, and said something about being certain God would never ask him to do such a thing. I repeated the question, stressing the first word: "*If* God told you to kill me, would you do it?" He was still reluctant to respond, but finally admitted that if he were certain God were telling him to do it, he would "have to consider it." After the debate, the organizers collected response cards from the audience, one of which was from a student named Kerri with this message penned at the bottom: "I love (heart-shape) Dan Barker, but if God told me to kill him, I would. (smiley face)."

I have a debate tactic on hand that I rarely get to use, but is very effective when it happens. Dr. Shelly was one of the victims, at our debate in Birmingham, Alabama. I felt bad because he is a kind and gentle person and his public embarrassment was obvious. I guess by telling this tactic, I'll never get to use it again. Here's what you do: If the theist brings up the second law of thermodynamics, ask if he or she knows how many laws of thermodynamics there are. If the answer is "no," this is a good indicator that the person you are debating is superficially informed about the topic, probably recycling an argument from a creationist book, and has no real understanding of the science.

Michael Horner was my first victim of this tactic, at a debate at the University of Northern Iowa in 1992. He had included the second law of thermodynamics in his opening statement, claiming that since entropy (or "disorder") increases in a closed system, evolution or the emergence of an ordered universe is impossible, requiring an outside creator. During cross examination, I said to Mike: "You mentioned the second law of thermodynamics. Do you know how many laws of thermodynamics there are?" He stammered a bit, searched for words, and then smiled and said, "There are at least two." That earned him a good laugh, which probably included some deserved sympathy.

An argument is not bad simply because you don't know the whole science, so if I had left it at that, I might be accused of an *ad hominem* attack. Showing that your opponent's grasp of a topic is not as deep as he or she might make it appear can remind the audience that your opponent has something to learn (we all do), but the argument still needs to be rebutted on its merits. (Hint: Never bring up an issue during a debate that you are not prepared to defend in depth.) It is easy to point out that the earth, bombarded by energy from the sun, is not a closed system, and though our observed universe is probably indeed a "closed system" (if that means anything), the second law of thermodynamics applies only to the energy of particles, which did not exist at the earliest stage of the Big Bang. The second law of thermodynamics is irrelevant to the topic, and useless as a theistic argument.

There are four laws of thermodynamics numbered Zero through Three.[1] If my opponent doesn't know this, I have scored an easy rhetorical point, but in order to be fair, it is important to follow quickly with the more relevant question: "Since you obviously imagine that the Second Law, which is derived from *within* the universe, applies to the universe as a whole, does the First Law also apply? Since the First Law states that energy/matter cannot be created, doesn't that rule out the creation of the universe?"

Some debate opponents have made comments that are just plain nutty. At Arizona State University, Bob Siegel, a former Jew who is now a Christian minister and radio talk show host, claimed that one of the evidences for the existence of God is that God talks to him personally.

"God talks to you?" I asked.

"Yes, he does."

"What does his voice sound like? Is God a tenor or a baritone?"

"He's a baritone," Bob replied. (Audience gasps.) The voice of God sounds very much like the voice of Bob Siegel.

I was debating a local Christian minister in Colorado Springs who used the last three minutes of his opening statement to play a Christian song on a tape machine. "Close your eyes and listen to this music," he said, "and you will feel the spirit of God." So we listened, though I noticed that not all of the freethinkers in the audience had their eyes

---

1   The four laws of thermodynamics have precise mathematical expressions, but informally, Law Zero states that if each of two systems is in thermal equilibrium with a third, they are in thermal equilibrium with each other. Law One states that energy cannot be created or destroyed. Law Two states that the entropy of a closed system tends to increase to its maximum value (entropy is the amount of energy not available for work, sometimes informally referred to as "disorder" or "chaos"). Law Three reduces to the conclusion that Absolute Zero can never be reached in a finite amount of time. There are also some tentative candidates for Law Four (the fifth law), so the number might change.

closed. When I stood up to make my statement, I started by saying that I indeed felt something while listening to that music. I heard a repetitive cadence between the dominant seventh and the major tonic with an occasional suspended fourth on the five chord, a composing tactic that is designed to evoke a trance-like effect. I did feel the emotion, but not the Holy Spirit.

In March 2006, I debated Todd Friel, a popular Christian radio talk show host, at the University of Minnesota. Todd is a funny guy, a former stand-up comic with lots of punchy one-liners. When he was introduced, there was a huge response of cheering and applause from the audience, and I could see how happy he was to be among his friends and admirers. Then, when I was introduced, there was an even louder burst of applause and cheering, for just as long, from the atheist and agnostic students who were not about to be outdone by the believers. You should have seen the look on Todd's face when he realized, "This is not my crowd." The debate was quite lively, if not terribly deep, and I would have thought Todd would want to forget his performance. But to my surprise, he chose to put it on the Internet as an example of how to deal with nonbelievers. I have heard from people who say it had the opposite effect.

Many debate opponents have been much better than that. Pastor and Christian author Greg Boyd and I did two debates, one on the historicity of Jesus and another on the resurrection. He is articulate and friendly, and since he plays drums, we joked that we might scrap the debate and just play music all evening. Although he is a bible-believing conservative, he has come under a lot of flak from other Christians for his advocacy of "openness theology" (which puts limits on God's omniscience) and a strict separation of church and state.

Some debaters, of course, are expert in their field and I am forced to deal with sophisticated scientific and philosophical arguments that are not always easy to dismiss.

I debated Oxford philosopher Richard Swinburne at University College in Dublin, Ireland, in 2007 on the existence of God. Our disagreement hinged on the concepts of complexity and simplicity. He feels that the fact that every electron behaves exactly the same is evidence for an external control, or designer, otherwise they would all veer randomly and chaotically and no life would be possible. I pointed out, as most atheists do, that the design argument for God fails since it attempts to account for complexity by simply adding more complexity (God), which assumes the existence of the very thing you are trying to explain. "God is defined as a personal being, and a personal being is not simple," I told Swinburne. He turned to me and countered that God is the most simple person possible, since his characteristics are defined in infinite terms and mathematicians know that zero and infinity are the simplest concepts. (Huh?) It seems to me Swinburne is equivocating, making zero equal to its reciprocal, turning infinitely complex into infinitely simple. In any event, zero is not "simple." Zero is nothing. If the "simplicity" of the infinite complexity of God (sounds like an oxymoron) is like zero, then God is like nothing.

In my debate with Phil Fernandes in 2000 (during which he accused me of not being open-minded), I brought up the fact that theistic claims are not falsifiable. In order for a statement to be true, there must be other statements that can be made which, if true, would make the original statement false. The failure to prove those other statements actually strengthens the original statement. The statement "all polar bears are white" is falsifiable because the statement "there exists a black polar bear" would prove it wrong. The fact that we have not yet found a black polar bear strengthens our claim about white polar bears. If you can't find such statements that would (but not necessarily do) prove you wrong, then you can't say your proposition is true or false. I don't think Fernandes grasped the point of falsifiability in principle. During cross-examination, I asked him to tell us how a person could, in principle, win a debate against him:

"Give me an example of a statement which, if true, would make your hypothesis false."

Fernandes replied: "I think that if you could show that the beginning of the universe, that atheism explains that more adequately than theism does. If you could explain—"

"But what, specifically? Make a statement."

"I am making a statement. Give me some good evidence to believe that no God exists. I mean, the Big Bang cosmology—Robert Jastrow, who himself was an agnostic, admits that Big Bang cosmology, he refers to it in his book *God and the Astronomers* as 'scientists climbing the highest mountain and when they got to the top they found a band of theologians waiting there for centuries,' which shows that the universe had an absolute beginning, the beginning of space, matter and time."

"So, what you're saying, then, is that someday if scientists do answer that question, you will reject your belief in a god?"

"That's only one of the things. I've listed several reasons."

"Okay, but if scientists do close that gap, and we say, 'Aha! Now we know,' you will reject your belief in a god? Will you be honest enough to say that your statement is falsifiable?"

"You're—basically, at this point, I want to say something... How much evidence would it take for Phil Fernandes to reject the existence of his brother? Hey, I met the dude. Personally. I knew him. I walked with him."

"So it is not falsifiable to you..."

"How do you falsify—I think you could present good evidence that could maybe possibly refute me in a debate or whatever, but how can you prove to someone that another person doesn't exist when they've had a personal encounter and a personal relationship with that person?"

"So, Jesus talks to you, and that's why you believe in him? He talks to you and you have a—"

"No, I believed in him before I heard him talking to me."

"But he does talk to you?"

"I believe that God communicates to us in his Word, through circumstances, through prayer, and things of that sort. And, by the way, Thomas Aquinas did too, and he wasn't an idiot, so I don't think I should be pushed into that category." (Audience laughter)

"...What if I were to be so silly as to say to you that 'I know in my heart of hearts—I have a personal experience—that atheism is real, and I know there is no way you're going to talk me out of it.' What would you say to my attitude?"

"Oh, I would say—and I don't mean this in a negative way—but I would say basically you're a person who is close-minded, in the sense that they're not open to the other options. (Audience laughter, applause.) However, I am close-minded. You can't prove to me that my brother doesn't exist, because I know him personally and I walk with him."

Falsifiability cuts both ways, of course. I am often asked what would cause me to change my mind. "What would you accept as proof that there is a God?" I can think of dozens of examples. If you were to tell me that God predicted to you that next March 14 at 2:27 a.m. a meteorite composed of 82 percent iron, 13 percent nickel and 3 percent iridium, approaching from the southwest and hitting the Earth at an angle of 82 degrees, would strike your house (not mine, of course), penetrating the building, punching a hole through your Navajo rug upstairs and the arm of the couch downstairs, ending up 17.4 inches below the basement floor and weighing 13.5 ounces, and if that happened as predicted, I would take that as serious evidence that atheism is falsified. If Jesus would materialize in front of a debate audience, captured on videotape, and if he were to tell us exactly where to dig in Israel to find the ark of the covenant containing the original stone tablets given to Moses—well, you get the idea. Atheism is exquisitely vulnerable to disproof. Theism is not.

Cross-examination is the most enjoyable part of a debate. It is the time when the audience gets to see the participants talk to each other, vulnerable, thinking on their feet. For that reason, some debaters decline cross-examination. In my debate with Christian apologist Norman Geisler, he refused to agree to the cross-examination, preferring to read his entire presentation from a prepared text. (To be fair, some people are better writers than speakers.) In fact, he read his *rebuttals* from a text that he prepared *before* the debate without knowing what I was going to say. After I asked Dr. Shelly about the number of laws of thermodynamics, he declined to do any more cross-examinations. Of course, something similar to cross-examination happens during questions from the audience after the formal presentations, which is always more spontaneous than the prepared remarks, and I think more fun, since it engages the audience.

I have sometimes been caught off guard during these unscripted moments, so I understand the hesitation. After the formal questions during my first debate with Doug Wilson, when I was really tired from hours of talking, a man came up with a question. I thought I had heard everything, but this guy asked: "Mr. Barker, are you a *practicing* homosexual?" That was so out-of-the-blue that I laughed and was speechless for a few seconds. I didn't want to seem eager to distance myself from homosexuals, as if there were something wrong with being gay, but I also did not want to give the man any reason to think he had figured me out. I mumbled something like, "I am not a homosexual, but if I were I would not be ashamed of who I am, and besides, this has no relevance to the topic of the debate." I later realized why he was asking the question. In his mind, atheism is the refusal to conform to moral standards, so I must be wrestling with sexual temptations (like he was, presumably), and since his church is apparently teaching him that homosexuality is an evil unleashed on the world, *that* must be the reason I don't believe in God, not all those phony reasons I carefully explained during the debate. I later came up with the perfect response, the answer I'll be ready to give the next time I get asked that question: "No, I am not a homosexual—but now that I have met *you...*"

In more than 20 years of atheist advocacy, I have rarely been harassed or threatened. Most public audiences are respectful, even the most philosophically "hostile" crowds. But on occasion someone will lose his or her cool. I once spoke before a large audience at Kansas State University, in Manhattan, Kansas, and right in the middle of my talk a skinny Baptist preacher in the center of the room, wearing white shirt and thin black tie, stood up and started yelling, "Blasphemy!" He kept talking louder and louder, berating me for my apostasy. I listened for a minute and then tried to say something, but he would not stop. When he noticed the student security approaching from both sides, asking him to leave the room, he quickly sat down. "Do you really think I committed blasphemy?" I asked. "Thank you for the compliment!"

That's a good tactic, thanking people for what they think is an insult. If someone tells me I am going to hell, I say, "Thank you! All the great people are in hell. Elizabeth Cady Stanton, Mark Twain, Johannes Brahms, George Gershwin, Albert Einstein, Bertrand Russell, Margaret Sanger... I was afraid you were going to tell me to 'go to heaven' and spend eternity with Jerry Falwell." Mark Twain said the same thing better: "Heaven for climate; hell for society."

I was giving a talk at Iowa State University in 2004, during First Amendment Week, led by students and by my friend Hector Avalos (an atheist professor of religion). Each day of the week was devoted to a different one of the five freedoms spelled out in the Constitution. I was there to talk about religious freedom. Right in the middle of my talk, my microphone went dead and I had to raise my voice to be heard. Someone went backstage to the amplifier and noticed that the volume on my channel had been turned down to zero. My channel only. When I was told what happened, I said, "Wow! That's great! It's not often you say something so provocative that you need to be censored—especially during Free Speech Week. Thank you for the compliment."

In 2007, at the University of California at Monterey Bay, a woman disrupted the meeting, yelling, "This man is a liar! Don't believe him!" She was trying to warn the students not to be misled by Satan. We let her talk for a minute or so, and then I tried to thank her for her comments but she would not stop. She came walking up to the front of the room and turned to the audience and said, over and over, "This man is a liar! This man is a liar!" At that point we realized she was truly irrational, and we asked her to leave. I reminded her—or I tried to remind her, as she would not stop yelling—that she was now breaking the law, and I quoted the verse that tells Christians to "be subject to every ordinance of man." She still would not stop. It was the only time the police ever had to remove someone from the room when I was speaking.

One of the least threatening, most enjoyable and interesting debates was with Hassanain Rajabali, a Muslim scholar, in January 2003 at the Islamic Center in Queens, New York. (We also met again the following year in Dearborn, Michigan, for a team debate with me and Richard Carrier against Rajabali and Michael Corey.) We originally had agreed to debate the topic "Does God exist?" But after the Muslim organizers discussed it, they told me that that wording starts from the assumption that God does not exist, which is insulting to Allah, and they wanted to know if I would agree to change it to "Does God not exist?" I agreed, pointing out that as a consequence, I should take the first opening statement, since I would be arguing the affirmative. I would be saying, "Yes, God does not exist," and Rajabali would be responding, "No, God does not not exist." Since a double negative is a positive, it amounts to the same thing, except that I got to go first and set the tone for the event. The audience was advised to split into females on one side of the room and males on the other. Most of my left field of vision was women in dark clothing with scarves, shawls and veils, and on the other side were men dressed as they pleased. Although someone had warned me that whenever the name of Allah is spoken, the people would respond with something in Arabic, it was still a little amusing to hear the crowd "interrupting" me from time to time.

I was happy to do this debate because to this point I had been only minimally acquainted with Islam. I learned a little of the life of

Muhammad and read through the Koran. Since I was debating a true follower of Allah, I was anxious to read the 23rd Sura from the Koran that is called "The Believers," and was surprised to learn that in order to be a good Muslim, you must be humble in prayer, avoid vain talk, be active in charity, and limit your sexual intercourse to your wives and your slaves. (I didn't bring this up during the debate because I assumed that American Muslims would not own slaves.)

Rajabali's main arguments were morality and existence. I had trouble following his reasoning, but he basically insisted that the existence of contingent beings like us requires a higher context within which our identities make sense. The Anthropic Universe exists within a frame of reference, and that reference is God, who needs no frame of reference because he is infinite. When I asked him for evidence of the existence of God, he replied by saying, "The fact that you and I exist."

During the debate, Rajabali said that Allah is a "just" God, as well as an "infinitely merciful" God, so I jumped at the rare opportunity to positively disprove the existence of God, as so defined. Justice means that punishment is administered with the exact amount of severity that is deserved for the crime that is committed. We don't put children in prison for stealing cookies, and we don't merely fine a murderer $50. Mercy, on the other hand, means that punishment is administered with *less* severity than deserved. When the police officer lets you off with a warning instead of a ticket for breaking the speed limit, that is mercy.

If God is infinitely merciful, he can never be just. If God is ever just (not to mention infinitely just), then he cannot be infinitely merciful. A God who is both infinitely merciful and just not only does not exist, he *cannot* exist. This is one of the positive arguments for the nonexistence of God based on incompatible properties (or incoherency). If God is defined as a married bachelor, we don't need to discuss evidence or argument; we can simply claim a logical impossibility. (See Chapter 7 for more incoherency arguments.) In response, Rajabali chided me for failing to think in multiple dimensions at the same time. "When Qur'an says God is Merciful, and God is Just," he went on, "these simultaneous characteristics cannot be compartmentalized, we must understand them holistically." I guess that explains it.

By the way, I also pointed out that if God is infinitely merciful, then I cannot go to hell. It wouldn't matter how I lived or what I thought, infinite mercy would absolve me of any crime, no matter how great, including the crime of refusing to believe in God, accept his authority or admit that I had done anything wrong.

The Islamic Center in Queens is huge, occupying at least one entire city block, with many meeting rooms and classrooms. It also has a mosque. I had never seen a mosque in person, and before the debate I asked Ali Khalfan, the organizer who was my main contact, if I could see it. He took me around to the other side of the block where we entered the mosque and saw carpets on the floor and a number of people kneeling and praying to the opposite wall. It was smaller than I thought, but very pretty. Since I had been reading about Islam, I knew about the qibla wall, which orients the worshipper toward Mecca, and I pointed east to the niche or alcove and whispered to Ali, "Is that the direction to Mecca?" He nodded his head. "But that's not right," I replied. I pointed my finger down at an angle into the earth and said, "*That* is the shortest distance to Mecca." He didn't smile. Pointing back to the east, I said, "If you pray in that direction, your prayers will go straight out into space at a tangent and miss Mecca." He still did not smile, so I whispered, "What do you expect when you invite an atheist?"

I suppose it is possible that prayers are affected by gravity and bend around the planet, so I couldn't press the point. To his credit, Ali continued to be friendly and took my heresy in stride. But I wonder if he thought about the fact that the *qibla* (a directional prayer wall) is a flat-earth concept. And why does it matter which direction you pray? If God is everywhere, how can you turn and face him?

After the debate I told Ali that I was really impressed with the kindness and generosity of the people. They gave me gifts and fed me wonderful food. They were gentle, thoughtful, humorous and articulate. "You people are so nice," I told him. "Well, Dan," he replied, "Allah commands me to be nice to you." I was stunned. *Allah commands me to be nice to you.* I didn't say a word, but I was thinking, "So—you don't really want to be nice to me on your own? You actually want to be cruel, but you are restraining yourself? You don't find in me any qualities that merit your admiration? You are forcing yourself to pretend to be my friend in order to please your God? I'm supposed to be impressed with that?"

I'm sure he did not realize the insult of his comment. Or the lack of morality. "If Allah commands you, will you be mean to me? Where is the friendship in that?" I left those thoughts unspoken because I think people should be judged by their actions, not by their beliefs, and his actions were truly gentle and admirable.

Another fun moment happened during one of my debates with John Morehead in Sacramento, California, on the resurrection of Jesus. At one point, he mentioned that he had a list of more than 20 qualified bible scholars who supported his position that Jesus historically rose from the dead. I was ready for him. "I don't think it is appropriate to argue from authority," I replied. "But since you do, and since you offer your list of scholars, I counter with a list of my own." I held up a list of 75 highly qualified bible scholars, most of them believing Christians with at least one Ph.D. in biblical languages and related subjects, and showing the universities and institutions where they teach. Each of the scholars is convinced that the resurrection of Jesus is legend or myth.

The idea that truth should be democratic is a common theme among many believers. If that were true, we would have to treat women as second-class citizens because if we polled the entire planet we would find sexism rampant. The same is true with racism. Some say that the sheer numbers of Christians must trump dissent—so too bad, atheists, you lose. Some claim that there were more atrocities committed by atheistic Stalin and Mao than by the Christian Crusaders and Inquisitors, as if the approach to truth is simply a matter of piling up the bodies and picking the smaller stack. (Why should Christianity have a stack of bodies at all?) Michael Horner is fond of saying "the consensus among scholars" during debates (as if the scholars of the world had actually been polled), when he probably means "the consensus of the scholars that I choose to read." Of course, it is important to give weight to informed experts, but we should not turn authority into dogma. We should take every claim and argument on its own merits. Every decent scholar in the world would expect us to independently test their conclusions, not simply take their word for it. The question should not be "Is Christianity popular?" or "Is Christianity useful?" The important question should be "Is Christianity true?"

In April 2008, I debated Dinesh D'Souza, author of *What's So Great About Christianity*, in Memorial Chapel at Harvard University. Sponsored by the Humanist Chaplaincy at Harvard and the Secular Student Alliance, the topic was "Christianity vs. Atheism." The debate was driven by questions from Divinity School students. Dinesh is a likable speaker with a broad knowledge of history but a shallow knowledge of the bible. He actually claims that the Western concept of universal equality originated with Christianity, quoting Galatians 3:28: "There is neither Jew nor Greek, bond nor free, male nor female: for ye are all one in Christ." If D'Souza had done the barest minimum of bible study—for example, reading Paul's entire brief epistle to the Galatians—he would know that this verse applies only to baptized Christians, and only in regards to the specific issue of circumcision. (That's right—they were wrestling with the important question of whether new converts should be bodily mutilated.) Even worse, Paul goes on to state that the descendants of Ishmael, the Arabs (today, the Muslims), should be "cast out." This is hardly universal equality!

Displaying an even weaker understanding of philosophy and science, D'Souza claimed that since there are laws of nature, there must be a lawgiver. I pointed out that this is an equivocation. Most Philosophy 101 students know that there is a difference between prescriptive laws (like the highway speed limit) and descriptive laws (like the inverse-square law of gravitational attraction). D'Souza is comparing apples and oranges, hoping to confuse gullible believers, although I was told that many in that Harvard audience immediately saw right through his slippery tactic.

John Allen Paulos, in his book *Irreligion*, gives a wonderful original example of this dishonest trick, using the definition of the word "is." "It's not hard to equivocally move back and forth between these meanings of 'is' to arrive at quite dubious conclusions. For example, from 'God is love,' 'Love is blind,' and 'My father's brother is blind,' we might conclude, 'There is a God, and he is my uncle.'" Many theistic debaters make exactly this kind of mistake.

Jesus is quoted as saying that he came to uphold the old theocratic laws—which are, presumably, prescriptive laws—not to overthrow or improve them. (Matthew 5:17) We freethinkers want to do the opposite. That's why I love debates, and my new "calling."

PART 2

Why I Am an Atheist

Chapter Five
Why I Am an Atheist

If there is anything that is obvious, it is that the existence of God is not obvious. There would be no "Does God Exist?" debates if the question were one of evidence. By now someone would have won the Nobel Prize for demonstrating the existence of a hitherto unknown force in the cosmos. Any scientist in the world would jump at the chance to be the one who finally proved that God is real. Of course, some philosophers and theologians feel that this can never happen because a supernatural being, by definition, is beyond the reach of science, which can only examine the natural world.

Nevertheless, most non-philosophers do feel that there is a wealth of evidence for a god. Miracles, changed lives, fulfilled prophecies, biblical revelation, the resurrection of Jesus, unsolved scientific questions (which they mistake for evidence), coincidences they say could not have happened by chance, inner experience, selfless acts of kindness and so on all prove to the believer that God exists. Some offer attempts at rational arguments (examined in the next chapter). Since many of these believers cannot imagine *themselves* as nonbelievers, they try to detect some ulterior motive for atheism. Rather than accept the straightforward statement that there is no evidence for a god, which allows the implication that their worldview might be wrong, many Christians have claimed to guess the "true" cause of unbelief. Here are some of the *ad hominem* arguments I have heard:

- "You resent moral guidelines and want to be free to live a life of sin and selfishness."

- "You dislike authority."

- "You want to be different and stir up trouble."

- "You are arrogant and hate God and want to be higher than God, like Lucifer (Satan)."

- "Your heart is in the wrong place."

- "You have been hurt by Christians, or offended by certain nonrepresentative immoralities and crimes in the Church."

- "You are impatient and disappointed that not all your prayers are answered."

- "You feel let down by God, who didn't answer your prayers the way you wanted."

- "You are cold, empty and pessimistic."

- "You are an angry person."

- "You are too stupid, blind, limited or afraid to see what is obvious to everyone else."

- "You have been seduced by scientists into refusing to accept the possibility of miracles."

- "You are an atheist because you don't know the true meaning of love."

None of these accusations is true. None is relevant. A strong clue that a person is arguing from a position of weakness is when they attack character rather than arguments and facts. Bertrand Russell pointed out that *ad hominem* is a last-ditch defense of the losing side. My atheism has nothing to do with any of this. Even if it did, how would it add to the evidence for a god?

By the way, an *ad hominem* argument is not the same as a character attack. *Ad hominem* is when you use the character of your opponent to dismiss his or her argument. It would not be *ad hominem* to say that "My opponent is a thief," but it *would* be to say that "My opponent's conclusion is wrong because my opponent is a thief." My opponent might be a horrible person with ulterior motives, but that would not make his or her reasoning or conclusion wrong.

The only times the opponent's character is relevant in a debate are when the specific topic is morality, when it is fair to examine possible hypocrisy, or when eye-witness evidence is being offered and a history of dishonesty might weaken credibility. In those cases attacking character is not *ad hominem*. If the Catholic Church, for example, claims that believing in Christ makes you a better person, then it is not unfair to point to the clergy sexual abuse scandal as evidence against that claim. (Who should be more representative of the religion than the priests?) It would be *ad hominem* and inappropriate, however, if I were to say, "Don't believe anything the Church teaches because their leaders are pedophiles."

When Peter (if the story is true) told his friends that he saw the resurrected Jesus, the fact that he had recently lied by denying that he knew Jesus lowers the credibility of his testimony. It is not *ad hominem* to point this out because it is not part of a logical argument; it is an assessment of the reliability of a witness.

The claim that I am an atheist because I don't understand "love" is particularly ironic. I do understand what love is, and that is one of the reasons I can never again be a Christian. Love is not self-denial. Love is not blood and suffering. Love is not murdering your son to appease your own vanity. Love is not hatred or wrath, consigning billions of people to eternal torture because they have offended your fragile ego or disobeyed your rules. Love is not obedience, conformity or submission. It is a counterfeit love that is contingent upon authority, punishment or reward. True love is respect and admiration, compassion and kindness, freely given by a healthy, unafraid human being.

The argument about "anger" is equally intriguing. There is nothing wrong with anger if it is not expressed destructively. Paul said believers should get angry (Ephesians 4:26). Jesus got angry (Mark 3:5). Christians get angry often. I am rarely angry, certainly never when I am discussing atheism with believers, but many Christians project their own feelings back toward me and claim that I am angry when I quote horrible bible verses or level criticisms of Christianity that make *them* angry. What if I were to say, "The reason you are a Christian is because you are an angry person"? Many atheists, as well as believers, are often justifiably angry at the way religion clouds judgment and leads to dangerous behavior, but that is a *result* of reason and ethics, not a cause of it.

The word "atheist" is not a label; it is merely a description. (Although, of course, any word can be made into a label for PR reasons.) Since I do not believe in a god, I am by default described as an atheist. If there *is* evidence for a hypothesis, then I will gladly look at the data. If the claim itself is illogical, however, or if it is based on something other than honest investigation, it can be dismissed as wishful thinking, misunderstanding or a lie. Theists do not have a god: they have a belief. Atheism is the lack of theism, the lack of *belief* in god(s). I am an atheist because there is no reason to believe.

Some theists say this is absurd. Just because a few atheists are unconvinced is no reason to discard the wealth of evidence accepted by the rest of the world, they insist. These believers would ask me to say: "I am an atheist because there is no evidence *that I accept* for the existence of God." Well, of course that's true. I am the one being asked to judge and I have to use my reason. But if they are suggesting that I must agree that it is okay for *them* to accept the so-called evidences, I can't do that. None of the "evidences" proves a supernatural being, so those who continue to believe are acting irrationally. If they want me to believe, too, they have to convince *me*, not just themselves.

To play the same game, I could argue that even though few adults believe in Santa Claus, there is plenty of evidence for his existence. A real Santa cannot be completely ignored, I might say, because he is revealed somewhere in the millions of youthful testimonials, song lyrics, stories and holiday displays, and is a time-tested cultural tradition. (My children actually heard reindeer hooves on the roof and sleigh bells ringing. It was years later when I told them that it was just me, their dad, playing with their imaginations.) Does all the evidence for Santa disappear just because you are skeptical? I am free to believe in Santa Claus if I want. The evidence for Santa remains, I might say, regardless of your doubt.

Actually, the *facts* remain—but they are not evidence for a real Santa Claus. They are evidence for something else: culture, history and the charming imaginations of children. They are evidence for consumerism and goodwill, tale spinning and song writing, game playing, community stories and children's literature. But they are not evidence for an actual Santa Claus. We know this because each of the so-called proofs for Santa can be explained in natural terms and understood as part of a myth-making process. The fact that most adults believe in God is no more reason for me or anyone else to believe than the fact that most children believe in Santa. The possibility that the belief in God is useful is no reason to believe, either. Many claim that their behavior is improved by their belief in God, but so is the behavior of millions of children during the middle weeks of December. Most of us have matured into "A-Santa-ists," and some of us have matured into "A-theists." We have grown up and we are satisfied with natural explanations for the myth.

Of course, even the staunchest skeptic admits that one natural explanation does not completely rule out other possibilities. Perhaps there is a higher level of understanding that allows Santa to exist even though we are unable to prove it yet. The fact that kids have creative imaginations does not necessarily indicate that everything they imagine must be false. Even so, I can still claim that if there are adequate natural explanations that account for all the facts, then there is no driving need to search for supernatural explanations. This is just common sense. Without such a rational limit there would be no end to the fanciful layers that could be added to any hypothesis. (This is usually referred to as Occam's Razor, the principle that suggests we should normally accept the explanation that requires the fewest assumptions.) The skeptic, slavishly honoring all the possibilities, could be forced to spend a lifetime running around trying to disprove an infinite number of fantastic theories.

For example, maybe Santa is an ambassador from a distant planetary outpost populated with red-and-white creatures who monitor the activities of specially chosen short people (elves and children?), seeking "conducive" humans as psychic vehicles for messages to holy reindeer that levitate when children dream during the winter solstice, with most adults being too hardened to believe. Can anyone prove that this scenario is untrue? (You read it here first.) Since I don't have the means or the inclination to disprove such an idea, is this paragraph now allowed to count as evidence for such a theory?

A rational person would give the preceding paragraph an exceedingly low probability (virtually zero). However, if some natural explanation arises for the existence of the paragraph (such as an admission that I just made it up), then the probability can be safely dropped to zero point zero and the discussion shifts from the reaches of outer space to the reaches of my inner brain.

Perhaps in a court of law it is more relaxed. In a trial any object or testimony that might have a relevance to the case may be considered "evidence" before there is a verdict. In science it is the other way around: a fact is admitted as evidence only *after* the connection has been made. I may insist something is evidence, but that does not make it so. There must be a connection and it must be clear.

Theists think the connection is clear. They have traditionally presented a large number of evidences for their faith, and at first glance those evidences appear overwhelming. For a skeptic to attack this plethora of widely accepted "proofs" might look like David confronting Goliath! After all, atheists are a minority. How can so many good believers be so wrong? How can all of these facts be ignored?

They are not ignored. Remember that David defeated Goliath (in the story, not in history). Many have closely examined these "proofs" for a deity and have found them wanting. They are addressed in the following chapters in more detail. The main reason I am an atheist is because these claims can be shown to have perfectly natural explanations and, as with Santa Claus, the probability for the existence of a supernatural being can be safely dropped to zero.

In the name of honesty, it *must* be dropped to zero.

I have often heard Christians say we must "start with God." (That happened in my debates with Rajabali, mentioned in Chapter 4.) Isn't that interesting? Would they say we must "start with unicorns" or must "start with UFOs?" We can only start where we both agree, and proceed from there. We both agree that there is a natural universe—no argument there. It is the religious persons who maintain additional "supernatural" or transcendent assertions that go beyond what we both accept. It is unreasonable and unfair for them simply to fold their arms and demand that I disprove their allegations. Any impartial investigator will agree that we should start with what we *do* know, and then proceed from there. We should start with nature. We should start with the nonexistence of God and then the believer should argue *for* God's existence, not demand that atheists argue *against* it. The burden of proof in any argument is on the shoulders of the one who makes the affirmative claim, not the one who doubts it.

Someone once objected to my criticisms as attempts to "explain away" the proofs for a god. I am not trying to explain them away; I am trying to explain them. The success of this rational approach hinges on something that in theory everyone advocates, but in practice is quite elusive: a complete impartiality on both sides. I am willing to change my mind, but I don't see many believers admitting even the possibility that they might be wrong—that *they* are the ones with the problem. Believers are usually only concerned with winning me to their views. Impartiality, which is adequate for mundane matters, seems always to cave in to loyalty when religious matters are discussed. Since most believers' religious views are something of an extension (or sometimes a replacement) of their personality, when you question their beliefs you are often perceived as attacking *them* personally—their identity within their religious culture and their meaning in life, moral code, honor, intelligence, judgment and everything they are as individuals. ("How dare you tell me that my loving grandmother lived her entire life believing a lie!") Most of them have invested a lot of time, energy and money in their faith, and they aren't apt to back off or "lose face." They would rather earn devotion points within their co-believing community than give any credibility to some Lone Ranger atheist.

Of course, none of this proves or disproves either position. If it did, that would be *ad hominem*. Christians may be loyal and dishonest, but they still may be correct. Atheists might be rational and honest, but they might be wrong. The lack of impartiality of most believers merely underlines the difficulty of dialogue with atheists. One question I often ask of religionists is, "I will happily change my mind if I am proved wrong. Will you?" Most of them proudly say, "No way!"

Bible criticism is not necessary to atheism—God might be Brahma instead of Yahweh—but can be useful in order to answer those Christians who offer "scriptural proof" for God. Some believers claim that it is unfair to reject Christianity until the bible has been completely studied and correctly interpreted in the context of history and the "total unified message of Scripture." If we doubters just had a better understanding, they say, if we would just hold off a little longer, if we could read it in the original Greek and Hebrew, if we would study under the right teachers, if we would take a course in hermeneutics, if we would earn a Ph.D. in history or theology or philosophy, and so on. They demand that we be "qualified" before making a final decision.

But is this a fair request? There are millions of unqualified Christians who have only the slightest familiarity with the bible, yet their decision to believe is considered praiseworthy. Church pews are packed with biblically illiterate worshippers. If it is necessary to have a degree in theology before making an informed decision, then millions of Christians will have to be ushered out of church. Even the least educated atheist knows enough about the bible to judge its reliability or relevance. How many Christians know that much about the Koran? Yet they all feel qualified to discard the religion of Islam that is followed by millions of devoted Muslims. Is a Baptist rejection of Hinduism based on an exhaustive analysis of the Vedas? Is it fair for a Catholic to dismiss Judaism before memorizing the Talmud in the original Hebrew? How many Lutherans or Pentecostals can quote even one passage from the Book of Mormon?

How many atheist books has the average Christian read?

Everyone knows that the bible contains accounts of miracles, and that is reason enough to conclude that there may be better uses of one's time than studying Scripture. (And, no, this is not an *a priori* dismissal of the supernatural. It is the same criterion of natural regularity that Christians use in evaluating other religions. How many Baptists believe that ancient Roman amulets cured diseases?) Most believers are addicted through repetition to the idea that their bible is the greatest, most important, most inspired book in the world, and therefore the miracle accounts must be true—really good people can make themselves believe them. But the rest of us are under no obligation to feel that way. I was taught, and sincerely preached, that Scripture is the ultimate measure of truth, never imagining during all those years that the bible itself might come under a higher measure of truth, under the scrutiny of reason.

Of course, isn't this the problem? The issue is not so much *what* we think, but *how* we think. Epistemology. Scientists and rationalists gain knowledge by applying limits. Believers do the opposite, as faith has no borders. Without limits anything is possible. I could claim, for example, that this book was not written in the normal manner: I just concentrated intently and it materialized before me on the table in an instant of time, complete, typeset and ready for the printer. Who would believe such an absurd claim? But if you don't, why believe the even more absurd claims of the bible? We all know there are limits to what can be true. The scientist and historian—anyone in pursuit of verifiable knowledge—applies specific criteria in a uniform manner across time to help determine what is true or false.

Most religionists, who are normally quite capable of analyzing everyone else's ideas with careful precision, suspend the rational process when they approach their own beliefs. Suddenly, everything is possible, even probable. "The bible says it, I believe it," some say. We who doubt are accused of an "*a priori* bias" against miracles or a "prejudiced denial" of the supernatural, when we are merely following the process that all humans use to learn anything. If I say that I possess an honest inductive conclusion that all ravens are black or that people do not resurrect from the dead, based on careful observation of the world around me, then is it fair to say that such views are based on an *a priori* dismissal of any and all possibilities?

When ministers who are untrained in science make cosmological pronouncements that contradict science, why are they granted more credibility than professional physicists, mathematicians or biologists? This certainly is not because they are qualified—it is because, like quacks, they are *believed* qualified. Some ministers may know something about science or have specialized knowledge on certain subjects, but they have no special edge. I know. I used to be one, and I have met more than 1,000 ministers personally. There is nothing there. No advantage, no inside track, no superior abilities or sublime knowledge. Ministers are only successful if people want them to be. There are no preachers alive who could succeed without a following, without gullible people willing to call them "Pastor," "Reverend" or "Father."

Many ministers have earned respect as decent human beings working to lessen violence and improve humanity, and their contributions to the betterment of the world are applauded by all of us, believers and atheists alike. But this could be said about anybody. Ministers have no corner on compassion, no corner on charity. There are thousands of exemplary atheists who do not turn their good deeds into an excuse to pastor (shepherd) other human beings, or to stand up weekly before their "flock" and pontificate, or to advertise to the world how great their (non)religion is. Many atheists walked shoulder-to-shoulder with Baptists and Methodists in the civil rights marches. Most atheists I know contribute to charity and work for social causes. Ministers, priests and rabbis are not automatically better people.

When I was an ordained minister I was considered an authority on the bible and Christianity. I never pretended to be the greatest theologian or bible scholar in the world (I was a soul winner), but no one ever objected to the "wisdom" of my sermons and my ministry was quite fruitful. My credentials were never challenged. Since I was a "man of God," I automatically got respect. But now that I am an atheist, all of this seems to count for nothing in the eyes of believers. My opinions are now "foolishness," they say. It appears that Christians are not honest when they ask unbelievers to give the bible a chance. I gave it all the attention it could possibly require, more than most of them have done. Many atheists know far more about the bible than most Christians. Many of us have given Christianity (or Islam or Judaism) more than a fair shake and have done all the work that, if we were believers, should have earned us the respect granted so easily to others. But the only thing that would impress most believers is an attitude of belief. I was considered a leader, but only as long as I led people where *they* wanted to go (which was heaven). If I were to walk back into one of those churches, would they listen to my preaching now? Would they want to hear what I have learned about the bible?

I used to be one of those true believers, and I know that my motives were well intended. I wasn't trying to deceive deliberately, or to avoid truth. I was a victim myself. Many Christians are fine people who want the best in life. They are trying to do what is right as best as they know how. When I preached the gospel I was not knowingly spreading deception. I was just caught up in an erroneous way of thinking, seeing only what I was allowed to see and forcing facts to fit a preconceived (ill-conceived) worldview.

People are invariably surprised to hear me say I am both an atheist and an agnostic, as if this somehow weakens my certainty. I usually reply with a question like, "Well, are you a Republican or an American?" The two words serve different concepts and are not mutually exclusive. Agnosticism addresses knowledge; atheism addresses belief. The agnostic says, "I don't have a knowledge that God exists." The atheist says, "I don't have a belief that God exists." You can say both things at the same time. Some agnostics are atheistic and some are theistic.

Agnosticism is the refusal to take as a fact any statement for which there is insufficient evidence. It may be applied to any area of life, whether science, UFOs, politics or history, though it is most commonly invoked in a religious context as it was first used. The word *agnostic* was coined by Thomas Huxley, who attached the prefix *a-* (not, without) to *gnostic*, which is from the Greek *gnosis* (knowledge). One common fallacy about agnosticism is that it is a halfway house between theism and atheism—but that cannot be since it performs in a different arena. If you answer the question "Do you have a belief in a god?" with a "yes" (by any definition of "god"), then you are a theist. If you cannot answer "yes" you are an atheist—you are without a belief in a god.

Another fallacy is that agnostics claim to know nothing, making them equal to skeptics (à la Hume) who claim that nothing can be known to exist outside the mind. Although there may be a few who continue to push philosophy to this extreme, most contemporary agnostics do claim to know many things that are supported by evidence. They may possess strong opinions and even take tentative stands on fuzzy issues, but they will not claim as a fact something for which data is lacking or something which data contradicts. Agnosticism is sensible.

It turns out that *atheism* means much less than I had thought. It is merely the lack of theism. It is not a philosophy of life and it offers no values. It predicts nothing of morality or motives. In my case, *becoming* an atheist was a positive move—the removal of the negative baggage of religious fallacy—and that is rather like having a large debt canceled. It has brought me up to zero, to where my mind is free to think. Those atheists who want to go beyond zero, who want to actually put some money in the bank—and most of them do, I think—will embrace a positive philosophy such as humanism, feminism or another naturalistic ethical system. Or, they will promote charity, philanthropy, learning, science, beauty, art—all those human activities that enhance life. But to be an atheist, you don't need any positive philosophy at all or need to be a good person. You are an atheist if you lack a belief in a god.

Basic atheism is not a belief. There is a difference between not believing there is a god and believing there is no god—one is the absence of belief and the other is the presence of belief. Both are atheistic (absence of theism), though popular usage ("Everybody believes in something") has ignored the former. George Smith, in *Atheism: The Case Against God,* calls it the difference between "implicit" and "explicit" (or "critical") atheism. Michael Martin, in *Atheism: A Philosophical Justification,* calls it "negative atheism" versus "positive atheism." Others describe it as "soft" versus "hard" atheism. I like to call it lower-case "atheism" versus upper-case "Atheism." Although there is certainly a subset of hard Atheists within the set of atheists, basic atheism is the *absence of belief* in a god or gods, whether that absence is due to a critical rejection of theistic assertions, to unfamiliarity with the subject (as with a baby or with a nontheistic culture), or to noncommittal agnostic/skeptic principles.

Atheism and nontheism are the same, though, of course, they may carry a different stigma in today's society. Smith suggests the term *anti-theists* for "Atheists," the subset of atheists who positively deny the existence of a god. Of course, most atheists will sometimes speak of "denying" god or informally state that "there is no god." It may not be unjustifiable to think of a "lack of belief in god" as a relaxed "belief that there is no god" when repeated attempts to prove theism continually fail. However, even the atheists who "deny" the existence of a god (which I often do in casual conversation) will have to back off when pressed against the philosophical wall, and admit that a lack of belief is not a belief.

In the western world, "God" is the Judeo-Christian deity and "god" is any of the others. Give me a definition of a god and I'll tell you whether I am a theist, atheist or Atheist (anti-theist). I am definitely anti-Yahweh-ist and anti-Zoroaster-ist since these creatures are self-contradictory and absurd, and since there exist natural explanations for the origins of those myths. If you define "god" as a natural species of superior extraterrestrials orbiting Proxima Centauri then I am an atheist (soft, negative atheist), via agnosticism. I have no present basis for belief in such things, though I am open to evidence. If you want to identify "god" merely as the principle of "love" (or some other semantic twist of fuzzy liberal theology), then I guess you could call me a "theist" by that limp, impersonal definition—though I would avoid the word because it would be meaningless and confusing. When you speak the word, "god" and "God" sound the same. Naming a natural phenomenon "god" is ambiguous since it traditionally implies a superior being or transcendent mind. If "god" is just a synonym for some other natural concept for which we already have a good label, then it can be—should be—thrown away.

There are some who avoid the word *atheist* because of the popular stigma attached to it. In a context where they might be labeled and possibly misunderstood, they prefer to be called rationalists, agnostics or nontheists. I am not opposed to this. I think there can be some very good reasons for keeping views private, such as family harmony or job security. Some atheists join the Unitarian-Universalist Church for that reason. (Unitarianism, a creedless religion, can make a great cover, especially if you are running for public office.) Some people just have a distaste for *any* label. On the other hand, there are atheists like myself who view the stigma as an advantage, as a chance to be on the cutting edge. If you are discussing religion and you are an atheist, why not say so? Some of us atheists figure that the word has suffered from bad press and it is time to correct the image. That's why I wrote the song "Friendly, Neighborhood Atheist."

Although "atheism" is a negatively constructed word—"not theism"—this does not mean it is a negative concept. It is a double negative. Consider other positive ideas that are constructed as negative words: nonviolence, independence, antidote, antibiotics. Since a belief in a god is irrational and potentially dangerous, atheism—the lack of such belief—is positive.

Since leaving fundamentalism I have noticed that contrary to what I used to preach, most atheists seem to be deeply concerned with human values. Why is this? Perhaps it is because any person who has the impulse (and the courage) to be identified as an atheist in today's society must be deeply motivated by something. Maybe it is:

- Anger at religious immorality

- Disgust with superstitious anti-intellectualism

- Fear of the dangers of Christian intolerance

- Dissatisfaction with the way religious divisiveness interferes with true compassion

- Empathy for the victims of sectarian bigotry

- Outrage at the hypocrisy of believers

- Impatience with the churches that actively retard social progress

Whatever the moral motivation may be it likely originates in a mind that is deeply concerned with fairness and compassion, love for real human beings and concern for *this* world, not merely a rational approach to truth that rejects arguments for a supernatural being. My own rejection of religious morality (if that is not a contradiction in terms) is a by-product of the drive to discover a better system of ethical principles (not code of rules) for my species and me.

"Have atheists ever built any hospitals?" I am sometimes asked. Yes, they have. The obvious example is the Soviet Union, with an officially atheistic government, where hundreds of hospitals were constructed. In the United States, university hospitals (such as the one in my city of Madison, Wisconsin) are entirely secular, built with tax dollars from all citizens, atheists as well as theists. Atheists tend not to flaunt their views like many denominations that name their institutions "Baptist Hospital" or "Saint Mary's Clinic." Of course, most of these religious hospitals receive public money, and they all charge the same high rates so there is very little "charity" offered. The religion gets the credit but the taxpayers get the bill. Until religious bigotry is lessened, how many believers would choose to go to First Atheist Hospital?

Two nonbelieving brothers from Baraboo, Wisconsin, who wisely used their name rather than their religious opinions to identify their work, built the famous Ochsner Clinic in New Orleans. University College Hospital in London was founded by people who were disappointed with the way sectarian hospitals were giving preferential treatment to members. (Atheist philosopher Jeremy Bentham was involved in the early planning stage.) One of the members of the Freedom From Religion Foundation, Dr. Edward Gordon, was an atheist physician who donated his time and money to bring free medical care to poor villagers in the mountains of the Philippines. He climbed those hills and tended to those people, working alongside Catholic doctors who often charged for their services, never thinking he would receive any other reward than the satisfaction of helping others.

What about faith? Some believers agree with us atheists that the evidence for God is weak, even nonexistent. Many concur that the arguments for God are ultimately unconvincing unless you are predisposed to believe. It all comes down to faith, they say. Faith would be unnecessary, they remind us, if God's existence were proved to be a blunt fact of reality. There would be no way to separate the (good) believers from the (bad) unbelievers. Since faith is a virtue, proof of God's existence would deny us the opportunity to impress God with our character. If belief were easy, it would count for little in demonstrating our loyalty and trust of our Father.

But this is a huge cop out. If the only way you can accept an assertion is by faith, then you are admitting that the assertion can't be taken on its own merits. If something is true, we don't invoke faith. Instead, we use reason to prove it. Faith is intellectual bankruptcy. With faith, you don't have to put any work into proving your case or overcoming objections. You can "just believe."

Truth does not ask to be believed. It asks to be tested. Scientists do not join hands every Saturday or Sunday and sing, "Yes, gravity is real! I know gravity is real! I will have faith! I will be strong! I believe in my heart that what goes up, up, up must come down, down, down. Amen!" If they did, we would think they were pretty insecure about the concept.

Faith is actually agnosticism. Faith is what you use when you don't have knowledge. When someone says, "The meeting is at 7:30, I believe," they are expressing some doubt. When you tack "I believe" onto a comment, does that make it stronger?

If faith is valid, then anything goes. Muslims believe in Allah by faith, so they must be right. The Hindus are right. The Greeks and Romans were right. More people claim to have seen or been healed by Elvis Presley than ever claimed to have seen the resurrected Jesus. With faith, *everybody* is right. Suppose an atheist, refusing to look at any religious claims, were to say, "You must have faith that there is no God. If you believe in your heart that nothing transcends nature and that humanity is the highest judge of morality, then you will know that atheism is true. That will make you a better person." Wouldn't the Christians snicker?

Hebrews 11:1 says, "Faith is the substance of things hoped for, the evidence of things not seen." In other words, faith is the evidence of non-evidence. It is a free lunch, a perpetual motion machine. It's a way to get there by not doing any work. Hebrews 11:6 says, "Without faith it is impossible to please him: for he that cometh to God must believe that he is." Even the bible admits that you can't know if God exists. You have to "believe that he is." Abracadabra.

Jesus reportedly said, "If ye have faith as a grain of mustard seed, ye shall say unto this mountain, Remove hence to yonder place; and it shall remove; and nothing shall be impossible." How many faith-peddlers could pass this straightforward test? If Christians are not doing stupendous acts (that can't be done naturally), then how do they know their faith in God is valid at all? How do they know they are even saved at all? Paul says, "For by grace are ye saved through faith...not of works, lest any man should boast." But James says, "Ye see then how that by works a man is justified, and not by faith only." Are believers saved by works, or aren't they?

Religionists sometimes accuse nonbelievers of having faith. Every time you flip a light switch you exercise faith, they say. But this is not faith; it is a rational expectation based on experience and knowledge of electricity. If the light fails to turn on, my worldview is not shattered. I expect that the light will sometimes fail due to a burnt-out bulb, blown circuit or other natural cause. This is the opposite of religious faith. The light does not turn on because of my expectation. Rather, my expectation is based on experience. If lights were to begin failing most of the time, I would have to adjust my expectations. (Or adjust my electrical system.) But religious faith is not adjustable. It remains strong in spite of a lack of evidence, or in spite of contrary evidence.

Sometimes we nonbelievers might express faith, but when we do it we are not pretending that our faith makes the statement true. We often assert trust or confidence in something that is not known 100 percent. For example, I respect my dad tremendously, from what I know of him. I have "faith" and trust in his character. But this does not mean I know everything, nor does it mean I can't be wrong about him. It is possible that my dad is actually a serial murderer who has not been caught yet, though I doubt it. (I hope he smiles when he reads this.) The point is that although I do often express sentiments with near absolute confidence, I am open to the possibility that I might be wrong, admitting that my faith claim is not a knowledge claim. My dad has earned my respect. God has not. Scientists do something similar when they claim that a "fact" can be asserted when the evidence passes a certain threshold, such as the common 95 percent level. In fact, I think all knowledge is like this: we probably can't say we know a thing with 100 percent certainty, except maybe "I think, therefore I am," and even that has its critics. But scientific confidence is not faith—it is a tentative acceptance of the truth of a hypothesis that has been repeatedly tested, and it is subject to being overturned in the light of new evidence. The data and methods of testing are publicized, peer reviewed and open to any of us for examination. This is nothing at all like religious faith, which makes a leap from possibility to fact. Or, often, from impossibility to fact.

Some believers say it is just a matter of degree. If scientists are allowed to make a leap from 95 percent to fact, they reason, then believers are allowed to make a similar leap from *any* probability to fact. Even if this is true, after examining all the evidence and reasoning, I am convinced that the probability of the existence of God is way below 50 percent, way below even 5 percent. If we are going to allow any leaps, then they should round off in both directions: anything over 50 percent can round off to "true" and anything under 50 percent to "false." If theists can say "God exists" with less than 100 percent certainty, they should let me say, even if I admit less than 100 percent uncertainty, that "God does not exist."

The bible says that the "*ungodly* are like chaff which the wind blows away." (Psalms 1:4) That's fine with me. I prefer the winds of freethought to the chains of orthodoxy.

Chapter Six
Refuting God

Theists claim that there is a god; atheists do not. Religionists often challenge atheists to prove that there is no god, but this misses the point. In general, atheists claim that god is unproved, not disproved. In any argument, the burden of proof is on the one making the claim. Of course, if a specific god is defined incoherently, with mutually incompatible properties, then such a being by definition is logically proved not to exist. (See the next chapter.) Some atheists feel the entire debate is pointless until the term "god" is made understandable. Words like "spirit" and "supernatural" have no referent in reality, so why discuss a meaningless concept?

Some theists first try to argue for a general, undefined god or for the reasonableness of the god concept, trying to establish the existence or likelihood of *some* kind of creator or intelligent designer before moving on to argue for *their* particular choice (usually one of the traditional gods). This is a legitimate debate—"Is there a god?" as opposed to "Does God exist?"—but let's not make the mistake of thinking it is a balanced controversy between two equally likely positions: "yes" for the theist, "no" for the atheist. The burden of proof is always on the shoulders of the affirmative, not the negative—innocent until proven guilty. If a person claims that an antigravity device exists, it is not incumbent on others to prove that it doesn't. The proponent must make a case beyond a reasonable doubt. Everyone else is justified in withholding belief until evidence is produced and substantiated.

Many theists have tried over the centuries to prove a god exists. There are many lines of theistic reasoning and volumes have been written on each. Many of these arguments are reduced to a "god of the gaps" strategy. At most, the theists might prove the existence of a current gap in human knowledge, but this does not justify filling the gap with their god. After all, what happens when the gap closes someday? The gaps are actually what drive science—if we had all the answers there would be no more science. The following paragraphs briefly summarize some of the most common theistic arguments and the refutations. (Deeper discussions of some of these arguments are elsewhere in the book.) Atheism is the default position that remains when all theistic claims are dismissed.

"How can you explain the complex order of the universe? I can't believe the beauty of nature just happened by accident. Design requires a designer."

This is probably the most common argument for a god, but it merely assumes what it wishes to prove. Any attempt to "explain" anything requires a higher context within which it can be understood. To ask for an explanation of the natural universe is simply to demand a higher universe, effortlessly conjuring up the answer to the question. The universe (or the cosmos) is "all there is." It is not a *thing*. A god would certainly be a part of "all there is," and if the universe requires an explanation, then god requires a god, *ad infinitum*. If by "universe" we mean only our own local observable universe within the larger cosmos of multiple universes, perhaps we might call it a "thing." Then, however, its context would be natural not supernatural and the designer, if it existed, would be natural, and the question shifts to the explanation of the complexity of the entire cosmos, with the same problem.

The mind of a designer would be at least as complex and orderly as the nature it created and would be subject to the same question: "Who made god?" Richard Dawkins calls this god the Ultimate Boeing 747, playing off the complaint that a windstorm blowing through a junkyard would not likely produce a complicated jet airplane. He notes that a designer of such a machine must be *more* complex than the machine itself. However, if functional complexity requires a designer, then the mind of the designer, being even more functionally complex than its creation, also requires a designer. If it doesn't, then the argument is dishonest. You can't require that everything except what you are arguing for needs a designer. That brings your desired conclusion into your premise. This is known as "begging the question" and is illogical. (It reminds me of the cartoon of the witch doctor coming down from the smoking volcano and announcing to the people, "God told me that his wrath will be appeased by the sacrifice of somebody other than myself.")

There is design *in* the universe, but to speak of design *of* the universe is just theistic semantics. The design that we do see in nature (as opposed to the deliberate design of human artifacts) is not intelligent. Living organisms are the result of the mindless, uncaring reality of natural selection that builds complexity in extremely tiny increments over vast periods of time by keeping survival advantages through the blunt process of weeding out failures, which are denied the opportunity to reproduce by being eaten, starved, frozen, killed in competition or accidents, or beat to mating opportunities, or not being chosen as a mate, and so on.

The only genes that get passed on are the genes from successful parents, for whatever reason their environment allowed reproduction to happen, and those genes have a better chance of becoming the "fittest to survive" if the environment doesn't change too much in the next generation. (Extinction is the ultimate weeding out, though this can make room for other species. We humans owe a lot to the elimination of other species, such as the dinosaurs.) Evolution explains how complexity can arise from simplicity. Creationism can't do that: it tries to explain complexity with *more* complexity, and so explains nothing.

Many theists accept the fact of evolution—how could they not, with all the evidence and reasoning supporting natural selection?—but they remind us that the initial appearance of self-replicating molecules has not yet been explained. They are right. Although there are many good hypotheses, we still don't know how this happened. But this does not allow theists to fold their arms and say, "See—you don't know. We have an answer and you don't. We're smarter than the scientists!" That argument for God is based on ignorance, not facts. It is a "god of the gaps" argument. Failure to solve a natural riddle at this time does not mean there is no answer. For millennia humans have created mythical answers to "mysteries" such as thunder and fertility, but the more we learn, the fewer gods we need. God belief is just answering a mystery with a mystery, and therefore answers nothing.

"The universe appears to be fine-tuned for life. The odds against all the various constants randomly falling into the narrow range required for life to exist are so astronomically high that it is virtually impossible for it to have happened by chance. There must have been a 'fine tuner' of the universe."

The phrase "fine tuning" appears to beg the question because it implies a "tuner," but if we treat it metaphorically to mean "appearance of fine tuning," as we do with "appearance of design," then we can proceed with the argument. Still, it suffers from various defects. First, how do we know if any of those constants could have been different from what they are, and if they could, by how much? The only way to compute odds is to divide one number by another. So, if the constants could have been different, what is the ratio between the range of possible values and the range of life-allowing values? Until these numbers are known, there is no way to assign a probability. We only say that it seems unlikely from what we know.

Second, life as we know it is not the only type of life that might arise in a universe. The likelihood against any one particular life might indeed be something we would not bet on, but the likelihood of *some* kind of life might be very high or even probable. Until we know how many kinds of life are possible, there is no way to produce two numbers to divide.

Third, how many chances are there? If there is only one shot at a universe, a single opportunity to "tune" the constants, then the odds indeed seem high against life forming. But if there are many opportunities, such as many Big Bangs occurring, then that raises the numerator in the fraction, upping the odds for life. How do we know how many universes, or Big Bangs, there might be? That number is greater than zero, since it happened at least once. If it can be *only* one attempt, how do we know that? What law or principle would limit the number of universes to exactly one? After all, theists believe we should not impoverish our imaginations regarding the possibility of an eternal, omnipotent being, so why should we place limits on the cosmos?

Most cosmologists now use the word "cosmos" to talk about "all there is" and the word "universe" to talk about a particular observable universe such as our own within the larger cosmos. Many or most cosmologists are now convinced that some kind of multiverse is likely. A multiverse is a collection of universes, and there are many scenarios. Physicist Paul Davies said that "some kind of limited multiverse" is probable, although I wonder what that limit would be. (He probably means it is not infinite.) He says we have hit the "cosmic jackpot," which is just another way of saying that we happen to be in one of those universes that allow life, obviously. Some multiverses are spatial, assuming the immense inflation of the early universe, meaning that the cosmos is so unimaginably huge that there is room for trillions and trillions of "bubble universes," ours being just one bubble in the huge champagne glass. Others propose a string of Big Bangs, one after the other in an oscillating universe in which ours is the current n^{th} iteration. (This seems to be less likely, though, now that we see the acceleration of the expansion of the universe.) Others propose multi-dimensions, or billions of universes concurrently existing side-by-side. Still others suggest that there are splitting universes in alternate realities, with each instant of time following every possible path. This would put us in one of those paths while our "alternate selves" would be in other paths, and everyone thinking they are the only one. There are other multiverse scenarios, too.

We have not proved such a multiverse of universes yet. All we know is that they are plausible, and that there is at least one. The important point here is that if there is more than one, then the numerator of the fraction that determines probability rises, making the "fine tuning" of the constants (if they vary) to allow for life by random chance more likely. In fact, some think the numerator is much larger than the denominator, meaning it would be a true miracle if life never appeared anywhere in the cosmos. Some even think that the number is so inconceivably huge that universes must repeat themselves, and you (or someone identical to you) have already read this book.

My brother, Darrell, asked me to explain this principle—the law of large numbers and probability—which our brains did not evolve to intuitively grasp. So, I asked him to imagine the following:

I have a box with 12 unique coins in it: a penny, nickel, dime, quarter, half-dollar and dollar in both U.S. and Canadian currency. I give the box one shake to produce an arrangement of heads and tails. Then, I give an identical box to him and ask him to give it a shake. Would he bet that he got the same result? Darrell said, "No, of course not, it would be very unlikely." Next, I asked him to imagine 1,000 people, each with an identical box of 12 coins, each giving their box one shake. What would he think then? In that case, Darrell said, he would bet there was a match. What if instead of any of those boxes matching my box, they just had to match another box in the bunch? Or, what if each box was shaken 1,000 times? And so on. In those cases, Darrell agreed we would have a sure winner.

But those numbers are small in comparison to the universe. In most multiverse scenarios, there are trillions upon trillions to a high power of universes, each being shaken. In some scenarios the number is infinite—if God can be thought infinite, why can't the cosmos? Most of those universes will be stillborn, producing nothing that would resemble life. But many of them will not. Many of them will happen to match the universe we are in.

Theists might point out that we have no direct evidence of such a multiverse, but then neither do we have evidence of a god.

"The universe is governed by natural laws. Laws require a lawgiver. There must be a divine governor."

The universe is not "governed" by anything, nor is it "obeying" anything. There is a difference between prescriptive laws and descriptive laws. Natural laws are merely human definitions of the way things normally behave, not prescriptive mandates, as with societal laws. When I let go of a pencil, it does not think, "Oh, the force is released and I am free to move. I better move toward the center of the earth or I am in deep trouble with my designer." A photon does not restrain itself by saying, "Go easy on the gas pedal. I don't want to get a ticket for traveling faster than the speed of light." The laws of nature, unlike the laws of traffic, describe what does happen, not what we would like to happen. Using these laws allows us to make predictions so that when matter "behaves" according to natural regularity, it *seems* as if it is conforming to what our minds are expecting to happen. ("You are a very obedient raindrop. You are accelerating just like you are supposed to according to the laws of gravity, and you are also obeying the laws of friction by letting air resistance slow you to a constant velocity. Good raindrop!") Besides, if this argument were valid, the mind of a god, not being a random jumble of synapses, would equally be "governed" by some laws of order itself, thus requiring a higher lawgiver.

"It is improbable that the complexity of life occurred by accident. The second law of thermodynamics, which states that all systems tend to disorder, makes evolution impossible. There must have been a creator."

No biologist claims that an organism suddenly appeared in one random arrangement of atoms or that any particular species was inevitable. Life as we know it—humans, for example—did not *have* to evolve. Any of megatrillions of viable possibilities might have adapted, making it quite likely that something would survive the ruthlessness of natural selection. It was not aiming at us.

Using probability after the fact is like a lottery winner saying, "It was highly unlikely that out of the millions of entrants I could have picked the right ticket, therefore someone must have caused me to win." It is indeed highly unlikely that any particular person can be predicted to be the winner—which is exactly what each contestant is trying to do when he or she obtains a ticket. But it is not at all unlikely that one person will win. In fact, we would consider it a true miracle if no one ever won a lottery. In some lotteries a winner is guaranteed, so there is no mystery at all. In the gargantuan lottery of natural selection, we should not be surprised that something like us became "winners."

People who are impressed with the design argument are like the guy who is amazed at all the rivers that were made to flow along state borders. How did they do that? It must have been a massive, expensive feat of engineering to divert all that water. Additionally, many rivers are made to flow conveniently to the major cities, right to us! There is no other explanation, he thinks, other than intelligent design. But this is backward, hindsight design—our minds imposing a pattern after the fact. It was not inevitable that a river would be used as a state border (most are not), nor was it inevitable that our life, or any life, would have arisen. We can't press the analogy too far, however, because even though evolution and rivers both have branches, the "flow" is in opposite directions. But we can understand how people might look at the natural, winding, unbroken line of descent from ancestral life forms to their parents, compare that with a river taking the path of least resistance and wonder, "How did this happen? How did I get here? It must have been designed!"

Creationists usually misquote the second law of thermodynamics, which states that disorder increases in a closed system. The earth is currently part of an *open* system, getting energy from the sun. Driven by the immense input of solar energy, complexity routinely increases, as with the growth of an embryo or crystal or storm system. Ultimately, of course, the sun will cool and life on earth will disappear.

"Millions of people personally know God through an inner spiritual experience."

Many theists claim their particular god can be known directly, through meditation, prayer or mystical experiences. I used to feel it so I understand, but such experiences point to nothing outside the mind. Mysticism can be explained psychologically. It is not necessary to complicate our understanding of the universe with fanciful assumptions. We do know that many humans habitually invent myths, hear voices, hallucinate and talk with imaginary friends. We do not know there is a god.

There are millions of people who claim to know a deity, but this is a statement about humanity, not about the reality of their gods. Truth is not attained by vote. Religions differ radically and appeals to inner experience only worsen the conflict. Believers in one particular god have no trouble dismissing the "personal experiences" of the believers of other gods, so they must agree with me that the human race possesses an immense propensity to subjectively "know" things that are wrong. What makes *them* exempt from such error crafting?

Besides, if I were to say that I have an inner personal knowledge that there is no god, would they take my word for it? (See Chapter 19 for more on personal experiences.)

"Why would so many people believe in a god if he doesn't exist? What is the explanation for such belief? If our brains have a receiver, doesn't that suggest a transmitter?"

Religions arose for various natural reasons, including dealing with death, illness, invaders, dreams and fear of the unknown. Also, there is the usefulness of a tribal story to unite the people, the need to assume agency in nature (a useful "assume the worst" error that confers an automatic survival advantage over those without such a strategy), the need for our prematurely born (compared to other species) infants to submit to the authority of the father figure until they are mature enough to think for themselves, and so on. Religions can be powerful mechanisms for giving a feeling of meaning to life and personal/cultural identity. But in addition to religion, we also possess nearly universal urges toward sexism and racism, and although these attitudes may have been useful to some of our tribal ancestors in a brutal evolutionary way, no one would think we are obligated to maintain the truth of such beliefs in the light of modern science and morality. The receiver-transmitter argument could be used to prove the existence of dead ancestors or anything else we dream about. (See Chapter 19 for more on this topic.)

"Atheists lack spiritual insight and can hardly criticize the theistic experience of God. That would be like a blind person denying the existence of color."

Is faith a "sixth sense" that perceives another world? If so, then why don't we all have it? The blindness analogy is inapt because blind people do not deny the sense of sight built into an organism, or that color exists. Blind people know that they have eyes and neural pathways to vision centers in the brain, and they also know that their lack of sight is due to a malfunction of part of this machinery. The blind and the sighted live in the same world, and both can grasp the natural principles involved. The spectrum of frequencies of electromagnetic radiation that we call "light" can be experienced independently of vision. A machine could be built that emits a different sound frequency corresponding to a light frequency, and the blind person could hear it, examine it and test it. The existence of color need not be taken by faith. If we atheists are lacking a "spiritual sense," then where is it, how does it function and what exactly is not working right?

The theist gives no independent means of testing "spiritual" insight, so it must be doubted. The skeptic does not deny the reality of subjective religious experience, but knows it can be psychologically explained without reference to a supposed transcendent realm. Dreams, for example, can seem real, but few people imagine they are in touch with another world when they are asleep.

One of the indications that mentally ill people are getting healthy is when their obsession with religion decreases. When they stop saying they are talking to Moses, or that they *are* Moses, we take it as a good sign. Those of us who do not talk with a god are not the ones with the problem. The charge that atheists are handicapped and that theists are the truly "complete" human beings is unfounded and arrogant.

"We all have a feeling of right and wrong, a conscience which puts us under a higher law. This universal moral urge points outside of human-ity. It is consistent that God, a nonphysical being, would relate to us by such sublime means."

Here is another argument based on ignorance. Ethical systems are based on the worth humans have assigned to life: "good" is that which enhances life and "evil" is that which threatens it. We do not need a deity to tell us it is wrong to kill, lie or steal. Humans have always had the potential to use their minds to determine what is kind and reasonable.

There is no "universal moral urge" and not all ethical systems agree. Polygamy, human sacrifice, infanticide, cannibalism (Eucharist), wife beating, self-mutilation, foot binding, preemptive war, torture of prisoners, circumcision, female genital mutilation, racism, sexism, punitive amputation, castration and incest are perfectly "moral" in certain cultures. Is god confused?

To call god a "nonphysical being" is contradictory. A *being* must exist as some form of mass in space and time. But even if such a being existed, what authenticity could its opinions hold regarding us physical creatures? Values reside within physical brains, so if morality points to "god" then we are it. The god concept is just a projection of human ideals. (See Chapter 12 for more on morality.)

"If there is no absolute moral standard then there is no ultimate right or wrong. Without God there is no ethical basis, and social order would disintegrate. Our laws are based on scripture."

This is an argument for *belief* in a god, not for the existence of a god. The demand for "absolute" morality comes only from insecure religionists who don't trust (or have been told not to trust) their own moral reasoning. (Voltaire quipped: "If god did not exist, it would be necessary to invent him.") Mature people are comfortable with the relativism of humanism since it provides a consistent, rational and flexible framework for ethical *human* behavior—without a deity.

American laws are based on a secular constitution, not the bible. Any scriptures that might support a good law do so only because they have met the test of human values, which long predate the ineffective Ten Commandments.

There is no evidence that theists are more moral than atheists. In fact, the contrary seems to be true, as portrayed by centuries of religious violence. Most atheists are happy, productive and moral. There have been some wonderful Christians and wonderful atheists. There have been horrible Christians and horrible atheists. Stalin was a horrible atheist. Hitler was a horrible Christian. People should be judged by their actions, not by their beliefs. (See Chapter 10 and Chapter 12 for a deeper analysis of moral questions.)

"Everything had a cause, and every cause is the effect of a previous cause. Something must have started it all. God, who exists outside of time

and space, is the eternal first cause, the unmoved mover, the creator and sustainer of the universe."

The major premise of this argument, "everything had a cause," is contradicted by the conclusion that "God did not have a cause." You can't have it both ways. If *everything* had to have a cause, then there could not be a first cause. If it is possible to think of a god as uncaused, then it is possible to think the same of the universe.

Some theists, observing that all "effects" need a cause, assert that God is a cause but not an effect. But no one has ever observed an uncaused cause and simply inventing one merely assumes what the argument wishes to prove. If a god can be thought eternal, then so can the universe. The word "cause" is a transitive verb. Causality requires temporality. If God exists outside of time, he cannot cause anything. (See Chapter 8 for more on this subject.)

"God can't be proved. But if God exists, the believer gains everything (goes to heaven) and the unbeliever loses everything (goes to hell). If God doesn't exist, the believer loses nothing and the unbeliever gains nothing. There is therefore everything to gain and nothing to lose by believing in God."

Pascal's Wager, first formulated by French philosopher Blaise Pascal, is not an argument at all. It is sheer intimidation. It is not a case for a god's existence; it is an argument for belief, based on a threat of violence. "If you don't believe, you will be tortured." With this kind of reasoning we should simply pick the religion with the worst hell. The Islamic hell might be hotter than the Christian hell, so Christians, "What if you are wrong?"

It is not true that the believer loses nothing. We diminish this life by preferring the myth of an afterlife. We sacrifice honesty to the maintenance of a lie. Religion demands time, energy and money, draining valuable human resources from the improvement of *this* world. Religious conformity, a tool of tyrants, is a threat to freedom.

Nor is it true that the unbeliever gains nothing. Rejecting religion can be a positive and liberating experience that allows you to gain perspective and freedom of inquiry. Freethinkers have always been in the forefront of social and moral progress. Nonbelievers have more time! Since they are not wasting money or resources on the nonexistent supernatural world, nonbelievers have more ability to make *this* world a better place.

(How do poor churchgoers explain to their hungry children that God needs the milk money more than they do?)

What kind of person would eternally torment an honest doubter? If their god is so unjust, then theists are in as much danger as atheists. Perhaps God will get a perverted thrill from changing his mind and damning everyone, believers and unbelievers alike.

Pascal was a Catholic and assumed that the existence of a god meant the Christian God. However, the Islamic Allah might be the true god, which turns Pascal's Wager into a riskier gamble than intended.

I have my own bet: Barker's Wager. Suppose there is a god, but he is only going to reward those people who have enough courage *not* to believe in him. This god is no less likely than Pascal's. By believing in a god, Christians are risking eternal torture! When they die, they will be very surprised (so will we atheists).

In any case, basing belief in a deity on fear does not produce admiration. It does not follow that such a being deserves to be worshipped.

"God is a being than which no greater being can be conceived. If God does not exist in actuality, then he can be conceived to be greater than he is. Therefore, God exists."

There are dozens of varieties of the ontological argument, but St. Anselm was the first to articulate it in this manner. The flaw in this reasoning is to treat existence as an attribute. Existence is a *given*. Nothing can be great or perfect that does not first exist, so the argument is backwards.

A good way to expose this reasoning is to replace "being" and "God" with some other words. ("Paradise Isle is an island...") You could prove the existence of a perfect "void," which would mean nothing exists!

The argument squashes itself because God can be conceived to have infinite mass, which is disproved empirically. And it is comparing apples and oranges to assume that existence in conception can somehow be related to existence in actuality. Even if the comparison holds, why is existence in actuality "greater" (whatever that means) than existence in conception? Perhaps it is the other way around.

No wonder Bertrand Russell said all ontological arguments are a case of bad grammar!

"The bible is historically reliable. There is no reason to doubt the trustworthy testimonies that would hold up in court. God exists because He has revealed Himself through scriptures."

The bible reflects the culture of its time. Though much of its setting is historical, much is not. For example, there is no contemporary support for the Jesus story outside the Gospels, which were anonymously written 30 to 80 years after the supposed crucifixion (depending on which scholar you consult—see Chapter 15.) Many accounts, like the creation stories, conflict with science. The stories of the bible are just that: stories.

The bible is contradictory. A glaring example is the discrepancy between the genealogies of Jesus given by Matthew and Luke. The story of the resurrection of Jesus, told by at least five different writers, is hopelessly irreconcilable. Scholars have noted hundreds of biblical errors that have not been satisfactorily addressed by apologists. (See Chapter 13 and Chapter 16.)

The bible, like other religious writings, can be accounted for in purely natural terms. There is no reason to demand it be either entirely true or false. Christianity is filled with parallels from pagan myths, and its emergence as a second century messiah cult stems from its Jewish sectarian origins. The Gospel authors admit they are writing religious propaganda (John 20:31), which is a clue that it should be taken with a grain of salt.

Thomas Paine, in *The Age Of Reason,* pointed out that scripture cannot be revelation. Revelation (if it exists) is a divine message communicated *directly* to some person. As soon as that person reports it, it becomes second-hand hearsay. No one is obliged to believe it, especially if it is fantastic. It is much more likely that reports of the miraculous are due to honest error, deceit or zealous theological interpretations of perfectly natural events.

Outrageous claims require outrageous proof. A criterion of critical history is the assumption of natural regularity over time. This precludes miracles, which by definition "override" natural law. If we allow for miracles, then all documents, including the bible, become worthless as history. (See Part 3, "What's Wrong With Christianity," for more on the bible.)

"There are many scientists who believe in God. If many of the world's most intelligent people are theists, then belief in God must be sensible."

This is just an appeal to authority, which atheists could do equally well or better. Academics as a group are much less religious than the general population, and scientists as a group are the least religious of academics. Though it is easy to find token scientists who believe, none of them can scientifically demonstrate their faith. Belief is usually a cultural or personal matter separate from occupation and no one, not even a scientist, is immune from the irrational seductions of religion.

"The new science of quantum physics is showing that reality is uncertain and less concrete. There is now room for miracles. A theistic world view is not inconsistent with science."

A miracle is supposed to be a suspension of natural law that points to a transcendent realm. If the new science makes miracles naturally possible (a self-contradictory concept), then there is no supernatural realm and no God.

In quantum physics, the term "uncertainty" does not apply to reality, but to our *knowledge* of reality. There is disagreement about "indeterminacy"—some think it is only in our minds, and others think nature is intractably indeterminate—but the only thing that can be "uncertain" is a mind.

Theism implies a supernatural realm. Science limits itself to the natural world. So theism can *never* be consistent with science, by definition (unless the god is defined as a natural being, which it rarely is).

"Belief in God is not intellectual. Reason is limited. The truth of God is only known by a leap of faith, which transcends but does not contradict reason."

This is no argument. Admitting that something is nonintellectual removes it from the realm of discussion. Yes, reason *is* limited—it is limited to the facts. If you ignore the facts you are left with nothing but hypotheses or wishful thinking.

Faith is the acceptance of the truth of a statement in spite of insufficient or contradictory evidence, and has never been consistent with reason. Faith, by its very invocation, is a transparent admission that religious claims cannot stand on their own two feet.

Sartre said that to believe is to know you believe; to know you believe is to not believe.

Even if theism were a consistent hypothesis (which it is not), it would still need to be proved. This is why most theists downplay *proof* and *reason* and emphasize *faith*, sometimes ludicrously claiming that science requires faith or that atheism is a religion.

"There is strong evidence of psychic powers, reincarnation and such. You have to admit there is something out there!"

Most scientists disagree that there is strong evidence for "parascientific" claims. When carefully examined with rigid controls, these claims are generally exposed as misinterpretations or outright fraud. Even if they were legitimate, mysterious phenomena could have perfectly natural explanations. And even if they didn't, they wouldn't necessarily point to a god. In such cases, skeptics prefer to withhold judgment rather than jump to superstitious conclusions.

It should be noted that even if the theistic arguments I've covered here were valid, they would not establish the creator as a singular entity nor would they establish a creator that is personal, perfect or currently alive.

Also, none of these theistic arguments address the presence of chaos, ugliness and pain in the world, which make an omnipotent deity responsible for evil.

Since by careful examination all theistic arguments are faulty, atheism remains the only rational position.

DEFINITIONS:

Religion: System of thought or practice that claims to transcend our natural world and which demands conformity to a creed, bible or savior.

God: A being who created and/or governs the universe. It is usually defined with personal aspects like intelligence, will, wisdom, love and hatred; and with superhuman aspects like omnipotence, omniscience, immortality, omnibenevolence and omnipresence. It is most often pictured interacting with humanity, but is sometimes held to be an impersonal "force" or nature itself.

Theism: Belief in a personal god (or gods).

Deism: Belief in an impersonal god (or gods), or a god who may no longer exist or who is absent and irrelevant.

Atheism: Absence of belief in any god.

Agnosticism: Refusal to accept the truth of a proposition for which there is insufficient evidence or logical justification. Most agnostics suspend belief in a god.

Freethought: The practice of forming opinions about religion on the basis of reason, without reference to authority, tradition or established belief.

Rationalism: The idea that all beliefs should be subject to the proven methods of rational inquiry. Special treatments like *faith* or *authority*, which are not allowed in other disciplines, are not acceptable for analyzing religion.

Truth: The degree to which a statement corresponds with reality and logic.

Reality: That which is directly perceivable through our natural senses, or indirectly ascertained through the careful use of reason.

Reason: A tool of critical thought that limits the truth of a proposition by the tests of **verification** (what evidence or observations confirm it?), **repeatability** (can anyone else replicate the results?), **falsifiability** (what, in theory, would disprove it, and have all such attempts failed?), **parsimony** (is it the simplest explanation, requiring the fewest assumptions?) and **logic** (is it free of contradictions and *non sequiturs*?).

Humanism: Secular humanism is a rationalistic, natural outlook that makes humanity the measure of values.

All of these words have suffered from multiple definitions. The definitions of *religion* and *god*, of course, can vary with the believer. Most atheists consider themselves to be freethinkers, rationalists, agnostics and humanists since they are not mutually exclusive labels. *Agnosticism* is here defined by Huxley's original intention, though current popular usage wrongly views it as a halfway house between theism and atheism.

Any person, for whatever reason, who cannot say the words "I have a belief in a god" is an atheist.

Chapter Seven
Omni-Aqueous

I am a lower-case atheist—lacking a belief—when it comes to the general question of the existence of god(s). There are certainly some definitions of a god that I have not examined, and I suppose the number of possibilities is infinite. I can invent many myself, and so can you. Formally, I can't say that I know or believe that all of those hypothetical as-yet-undefined beings do not exist. It would take more than a lifetime of painstaking analysis to rule them all out, so I simply decline to believe in any of them.

Informally, I think it is justifiable to say that God does not exist since the lack of evidence for such a creature makes it seem extremely unlikely. Those believers who introduce their inner feelings of "knowing God" as partial evidence for their claims will certainly permit me to do the same when I state that in addition to all the rational arguments for atheism, it is also my gut feeling that "there are no gods."

Being a lower-case atheist on the general question, however, does not mean that I am not an upper-case Atheist—possessing a belief or knowledge—regarding a specific definition of a god. There are some gods—such as the God of the bible—that I claim to *know* do not exist because, like the married bachelor, they cannot exist. Many definitions of "God" are incoherent. They contain mutually incompatible properties that are impossible to reconcile; therefore, they do not exist. This is not dogma—it is simple logic.

Religious doctrines are most vulnerable when expressed in absolute terms. Terms such as "all," "always," "never" and "infinitely" should raise some red flags. I already mentioned the impossibility of a being that is both infinitely merciful and (infinitely) just. Superlative characteristics also include the cardinal doctrines about the nature of the Christian God: omniscience, omnipotence, omnipresence and omnibenevolence.

According to Christianity, God is omniscient—"all-knowing." Although this doctrine is fundamental, it is rarely defined or examined. It is simply a given. (Could a proper god be anything less?) If we scratch beneath the surface, however, we see that omniscience—knowing everything in the past, present and future—is impossible. The concept loops back on itself and creates an infinite hurdle that not even a deity can leap. (If believers can mix superlatives, I can mix metaphors.)

To "know" is to contain a true image or idea within a mind. A being that knows *everything* must also know itself. Therefore, the mind of an omniscient being must contain an image of itself within itself. It would also have to contain an image of the image of itself, and an image of that image, and so on. It would have to know that it contains those images, and also contain an image of itself knowing that it contains not only those images but the image of knowing that it contains the knowledge of such images—well, you see where this is going. Mathematicians know that something is wrong with their equations when infinities pop up. Computer programmers try to safeguard against infinite loops, which can "blow the stack" and hang up the system. (When your computer crashes, that is often the reason.) An omniscient being blows the stack. It cannot function.

Suppose you wanted to make a perfect map of the earth. This map would be so precise that it would include not only the oceans, continents, cities, roads and landmarks, but blades of grass, roof shingles and bubbles behind a whale surfacing in the Pacific—everything. Such a map would have to be updated regularly. The map would have to be very large to admit a useful resolution, much larger than you could hang on an easel. You could start with a gigantic map a few square miles in size, placed out in the desert where it does not obscure too much of the surface that it has to represent. To be perfect and up-to-date, such a map would have to include itself. So, on the map would be a tiny drawing of the map itself. And to be perfect, the tiny drawing would include the little details on the map, including a tiny drawing of the tiny drawing—and so on and so on. It becomes clear that such a map is impossible. The necessary degree of resolution would require that the map be at least as large as the Earth itself, obscuring the earth totally, and at that point it would make no sense to have a copy of what we can look at directly. We could throw it away and simply acknowledge that reality is its own map.

Now imagine that the map is not just a two-dimensional geographical drawing, but a four-dimensional space-time image of the entire universe. Imagine, too, that the map is being constantly updated, like what our brains try to do as we live our daily lives, although this map would be perfect and encompass everything within the event horizon of our expanding universe. This virtual reality map could be made digital, to be updated more efficiently at nearly the speed of light on a massive super computer. Visualize a galaxy-wide automated representation of the universe, somewhere out in deep space. Since the computer is part of the universe, it must contain a representation of itself. To be perfect, it would need to keep track of itself keeping track of itself. This would add to its size. It would take so much time and energy "tracking itself tracking itself tracking itself" that it would get caught in an infinite loop, draining its resources and accomplishing no useful work. (Some computer viruses work like this.) Or it would blow the stack and stop working.

If there is a God, maybe he could accomplish this relatively simple (to him) task of keeping track of the universe by existing somehow "outside" the universe in an unimaginably huge dimension, looking "down" (or "across" or "into") our cosmos. (This hypothesis seems to have coherency problems of its own, which I deal with elsewhere.) But that is not the problem. The problem is God himself. In order for God to know everything, he has to know not only about all the unknown galaxies and extrasolar planetary systems and where all the undiscovered diamond mines and my missing socks are located, he also has to know everything about *himself*. He has to know what he is going to think next. He has to anticipate that he is going to need to know what he is going to think next, and after that into the infinite future. Like the computer virus, an omniscient God gets caught in an infinite loop keeping track of itself and cannot have a single thought. (Maybe that's why the God of the Old Testament blows his stack so much.) It doesn't matter what method God uses to store and retrieve data in his super mind, he has to have *some* kind of internal representation. If theists argue that the intelligence of God is something altogether different from human or computer intelligence, then they are admitting that the idea of omniscience is meaningless. If "all-knowing" does not compare with "knowing," then the phrase lacks relevance to human understanding and we may as well say that "God is mmpfghrmpf" instead of "God is omniscient."

Some theologians admit these and other problems and tinker with the definition of omniscience. Some, such as Greg Boyd, claim that God has a "limited omniscience," that he knows everything that is knowable but that not everything is knowable, not even to God. Others suggest that "all-knowing" means "knowing more than anyone else" or "super knowing." Maybe God knows *soooo* much more than we do that it amounts to the same thing. Fair enough, but this underscores the fact that omniscience—total omniscience—is incoherent. Perhaps a lesser god exists, but a god who is truly omniscient cannot exist. It therefore does not exist.

The Christian God cannot be both omniscient and omnibenevolent. If God were omniscient, then he knew when he created Adam that Adam would sin. He *knew* human beings would suffer. Regardless of whether the existence of evil can be theologically explicated, an all-knowing Creator deliberately placed humans in its path. This is at least criminal negligence, if not malice. Those who invoke "free will" forget that we all act according to a human nature that was supposedly created by God himself. You can argue all around the bushes on this point, but you can't get away from the fact that Adam did not create his own nature. At the moment of creation, an omniscient deity would have been picturing the suffering and damnation of most of his creation. This is mean-spirited. God should have had an abortion rather than bring a child into such misery. Perhaps a lesser (or malevolent) god exists, but the problem of evil gives the lie to the claim that a god can be both all-good and all-powerful.

What do believers mean when they say their god is all-powerful? (Let's ignore the fact that the biblical God is weaker than chariots of iron, according to Judges 1:19.) "Power" can be taken two ways: ability or authority. The word "omnipotent" contains "potent," relating more to force than to command, although Christians claim that their God possesses both strength and leadership. Power is the ability to do a certain amount of work in a certain amount of time. Power (or energy) is a physical force, at least, and if God, at minimum, is not materially mighty, then he is not God. An omnipotent God must be able to counteract the greatest possible force that could exist in the universe. Imagine a black hole created by all the mass of the universe collapsing in one place. God must possess a physical energy at least as great as this. And if he is omnipotent he can potentially outweigh the combined energy of any multiple number of universes such as ours. He must be, in principle, infinitely powerful.

The universe (or more properly the cosmos) encompasses all the mass/energy available anywhere. If God possesses energy that not only created but also interacts with the material world, then, by definition, he is part of the natural universe or the universe is part of him, which is the same thing. Whatever God's source of energy might be, it exists *somewhere*, adding to the size of the cosmos. Supernatural does not mean unnatural. An omnipotent God would make the cosmos infinitely massive, a fact that is contradicted by the expansion of the universe (or, if God is outside our own pocket universe, by the uniformity of such expansion), or by the fact that we are not all instantly compressed by the gravity of infinite matter or incinerated with heat by being in the presence of such a grotesquely massive black hole out there.

Some argue that it is provincial for us locals to picture God as a huge physical being with infinite mass. God works from a "spiritual" dimension, they say—whatever that means—and therefore does not add to the material world. Somehow, God can manipulate the existing mass/energy in the universe without adding to it, and without sucking everything into himself. But if "omnipotence" is meaningful, it has to indicate something to us humans who do not transcend nature. By definition a "spirit" is nonphysical, so a "spiritual god" should have no power—no real power—at all. According to believers, however, whenever God proves his power it is manifested as a physical act in the tangible world: an earthquake, flood, moving star, sun standing still, plague of locust, a sea opening up to let people cross, a voice from a burning bush that Moses could hear, footballs changing their trajectories, and so on.

If God is "directing" nature from outside, he is still required to do so in a way that causes ordinary matter to react. There needs to be an energy/mass nexus, or connection, for any work to be done. (Of course, claiming that god is "energy" is to deny that he is "spirit.") If "all-powerful" does not relate to "powerful," as we humans understand the word, then the phrase is incoherent. We may as well say that "God is rrrghphrrth" instead of "God is omnipotent." Since we know that an actual infinite mass (not the mathematical "infinite mass" some posit for black holes) would make all life, indeed all existence, impossible, we know that an all-powerful God does not exist, cannot exist. The very idea of existence requires limited power, limited mass, limited energy. Since "spirit" has no power, a powerful spiritual being cannot exist.

Those who would claim that God does not have to be infinitely powerful to counteract the largest possible force in the universe are forgetting that God supposedly *created* the universe out of himself. The argument of limited omnipotence (sufficient power to do anything that would ever need to be done) implies that God has a restriction on how large a universe he could create. Could he have created a universe 20 times more massive than the current one? Five thousand times more massive? If not, he is not omnipotent. The old riddle is not entirely inapt: can God create a stone so large that he can't lift it? Either way, God emerges short of omnipotence. Avoiding the question by claiming that God would never want to do such a thing implies that God's power has bounds, and that he is a slave to his own character.

Why should God need power, anyway? Power is what you utilize when you have a problem, a hurdle to jump, a need in your life. If God is able to manipulate matter and energy with some spiritual magic, then what good is power? To admit that God uses power is to concede that God has problems, needs and physical challenges. Why drown the human race with a flood? Why not just make them disappear? Why make the earth split open to swallow the followers of Korah? (Numbers 16) Why not just whisper to Moses to expel them from the tribe? (One answer is that maybe God gets a kick out of seeing people tortured in horrible ways—"That'll show you not to question the authority of Moses!" That certainly weakens the claim of omnibenevolence.)

The combination of omnipotence, omniscience and omnibenevolence is what makes the Problem of Evil such a thorn to traditional theists. Although technically the Problem of Evil is not an incoherency argument—the existence of evil is positive empirical evidence against the existence of an all-good deity—it is the "omni" in omnibenevolence that makes it incompatible with omniscience. If God knows in advance that there will be evil as a direct or indirect result of his actions, then he is not all good. He is at least partly responsible for the harm. Since God has the desire and the power to eliminate evil, why doesn't he?

If God truly is all-knowing and all-powerful, then he is not omnibenevolent when he does not stop unnecessary harm. This is especially true when he is asked to do so by his children, who claim to love him (and he them) and who pray for his protection, believing he meant it when he said that "All things whatsoever you shall ask in prayer believing, you shall receive." Since the success of such praying is no better than random chance, we have empirical evidence that God, if he exists, does not care. He cannot possibly be all three "omnis" at once. How could he have created an angel named Lucifer who possessed some quirk in his character that would cause him to go wrong? If this were deliberate, then God is an accessory to evil. If it were accidental, then God is not omnipotent.

Omnipotence contradicts omniscience. To be omniscient means that all future facts are known to the person who is all-knowing. This means that the set of knowable facts is fixed and unchangeable. If facts cannot be changed, then this limits the power of God. If God knows what will happen tomorrow, then he is impotent to change it. If he changes it anyway, then he was not omniscient.

And this brings us to FANG, my Freewill Argument for the Nonexistence of God. (I was not the first to think of this, but I claim the acronym.) Whether theists think God is all-powerful, or merely very powerful, or even self-limiting in his power, they must think that God is at least free to exercise whatever power he has. Whether humans have free will or not is a good question—atheists as well as theists disagree about that. But there are very few believers, if any, who think God himself does not have free will. God is usually defined as a person, after all, and we normally think of a person as having the ability to make decisions, which requires some concept of freedom, whether real or illusory. Since God, according to theists, is not illusory and is the perfect person, then he has perfect freedom, or so you would think. Otherwise, Christians are worshipping a robot.

In order to make a freely chosen decision you have to have at least two options, each of which can be avoided while the other (or "another," if there are more than two) is selected. To be able to freely choose, there has to be a period of uncertainty or indeterminacy during which the options remain open and during which you could change your mind before it is too late. Free will, if it exists, requires that you not know the future. However, if you are omniscient, you already know all of your future choices and you are not free to change what you know in advance. You cannot make decisions. You do not have a period of uncertainty and flexibility before selecting. You do not have free will. If you do change what you thought you knew in advance, exercising the prerogative of omnipotence, then you were not omniscient in the first place. You can't have both free will and omniscience. If God is defined as having free will and knowing the future, then God does not exist.

By the way, this contributes to my compatibilist position on human free will. (Not all atheists agree with me.) I am a determinist, which means that I don't think complete libertarian free will exists. Since we don't know the future—and it is probably good that we don't because it is the attempt to anticipate the future that makes our survival-machine minds what they are—we have the *illusion* of free will, which to me is what "free will" actually means.

I admit that my definition of free will is subject to debate. To me, acting as if we have it while openly admitting that we don't is a good strategy for getting through life and making moral judgments based on "freely" chosen motives, which also provides for accountability. In any event, if we knew the future we would not be arguing whether free will exists. It shouldn't bother us that we don't have actual free will because neither does God, if he is omniscient.

Omnipresence is also a problem. To be "present" means for matter and/or energy to occupy space-time at some spatial coordinates at a particular point in time. Technology extends our senses with machines, allowing viewers, for example, to be "present" at a televised event, but even this requires a physical connection: camera, microphone, sensor, receiver, speaker. God is not "present" at every location in the universe, not in any ordinary sense. To say that God is present in a "spiritual" sense is meaningless until "spirit" is defined. Since spirit is normally described as something "immaterial" or "transcendent" (which merely identify what it is *not*, not what it *is*), this means that being present spiritually is not to be present at all. We may as well say that "God is sshhffhgtyrh" rather than "God is omnipresent." Those theists who argue that God exists "outside of time" make it even worse. If you live "outside" of temporal coordinates, then you cannot be present "inside" space-time. You are non-present rather than omnipresent. If God is defined as a nonmaterial or nontemporal being who is omnipresent—occupying physical reality—then God does not exist.

John 7:38 reports: "He that believeth on me, as the scripture hath said, out of his belly shall flow rivers of living water." I take this to mean that those who believe in an omnipresent, totally free, all-knowing, all-good and all-powerful god are omni-aqueous: all-wet.

Chapter Eight:
Cosmological Kalamity

"Daddy, if God made everything, who made God?" My daughter, Kristi, asked me this when she was five years old.

"Good question," I replied. Even a child sees the problem with the traditional cosmological argument.

The old cosmological argument claimed that since everything has a cause, there must be a first cause, an "unmoved first mover." Today no theistic philosophers defend that primitive line because if *everything* needs a cause, so does God. The only way they can deal with my kindergartner's question is if they can first get God off the hook.

One approach has been to claim that only *effects* need a cause. Since a first cause is not an effect, it is exempt from causation. Another attempt conceives of a contingent cause of the universe, resting at the top of a pyramid of relationships rather than at the beginning of a chain of temporal events. But this *a priori* tactic of exempting the conclusion (a creator) from the causality required of everything else—with no evidence that any special "causeless" or "noncontingent" objects actually exist—makes the creator a part of the definition of the premise, which is circular reasoning. These versions fail to get God off the hook.

Today, a more sophisticated version of the cosmological argument is being propounded that connects early Islamic theology with current Big Bang cosmology. According to the Kalam Cosmological Argument—a medieval Islamic argument dealing with the beginning and cause of the universe—infinity is just a concept. An actual infinity does not exist in reality. If the series of temporal events is infinite, we never could have traversed it to arrive at the current moment. Yet we *have* reached this moment; therefore, the series of events must have had a beginning. Today, cosmologists almost universally confirm that our observable universe began at a Big Bang, a singularity[1] that brought into existence not only matter and energy, but space and time as well.

Building on this, Christian philosophers such as William Lane Craig are promoting an up-to-date version of the cosmological argument that they think avoids the problems of earlier attempts:

1. Everything that begins to exist has a cause.

2. The universe began to exist.

3. Therefore, the universe has a cause.

This may be seductive to those who already believe in a god. To me, it seems suspicious. The clause "Everything that begins to exist" sounds artificial. It is not a phrase we hear outside the context of theistic philosophy. It appears to be an *ad hoc* construction designed to smooth over earlier apologetic efforts.

DOES KALAM BEG THE QUESTION?

The curious clause "Everything that begins to exist" implies that reality can be divided into two sets: items that begin to exist (BE), and those that do not (NBE). In order for this cosmological argument to work, NBE (if such a set is meaningful) cannot be empty[2], but more important, it must accommodate *more than one item* to avoid being simply a synonym for God. If God is the only object allowed in NBE, then BE is merely a mask for the creator and the premise "everything that begins to exist has a cause" is equivalent to "everything except God has a cause." As with the earlier failures, this puts God into the definition of the premise of the argument that is supposed to prove God's existence, and we are in fact begging the question.

---

1   The Big Bang is not an "event." An event takes place in time and space: it needs a context. Since time and space are a part of the universe itself, calling the Big Bang an "event" would place it in a context beyond itself, which amounts to a presumption of transcendence.

2   An empty set can be significant. It can be quite meaningful to say, "I have no friends." But we know what defines a set of friends, and we can point to non-zero examples of this set in real life. A null set is significant only if it could possibly be non-null, and that can only happen if we know what constitutes an item in that set. In the case of NBE, we have no examples, so a null set would be equal to no set at all.

Where do theists obtain the idea in the first place that there is such a set as NBE? By what observations or arguments is the possibility of beginningless objects warranted? Certainly not via the cosmological argument, which simply assumes NBE. And not from science, which observes nothing of the sort. If theists get their initial idea from a religious document or from "inner experience," their argument may be more presuppositionalist than evidentialist.[3]

To say that NBE must accommodate more than one item is not to say that it must contain more than one item. The set might actually contain only one of the eligible candidates. The cosmological argument could be made successful if it could be shown that NBE contains exactly one item from a plural set of possibilities, and if the winning candidate turns out to be a personal creator. The question of accommodation is not whether the set *does not* contain more or less than one item; it's whether it *cannot* contain other than one. If it *cannot*, then the argument is circular. It would be like a dictator staging an election that permits no other candidates but himself: it's rigged from the start. (I am indebted to Michael Martin for insights on this matter via personal e-mail correspondence.)

Additionally, if the only candidate for NBE were God, then the second premise, "The universe began to exist," would reduce to "The universe is not God." If NBE is synonymous with God, the argument looks like this:

1. Everything except God has a cause.

2. The universe is not God.

3. Therefore, the universe has a cause.

This is logical, if not very useful. The circular reasoning is revealed when theists build from this point. Based on the above "universe has a cause" conclusion, Craig argues for a personal creator:

---

3   I'm not accusing theists of special pleading. It is not impossible to *conceive* of beginninglessness: Stephen Hawking's recent 2D-time model is an intriguing example and some atheists have suggested that the universe is eternal. But these ideas come *after* the cosmological argument, and since they are normally rejected by theists, they can hardly be considered a basis for the original justification of NBE. Besides, the idea of the beginning of the universe *itself* deals with "all of reality," not with any item.

"We know that this first event must have been caused. The question is: How can a first event come to exist if the cause of that event exists changelessly and eternally? Why isn't the effect as co-eternal as the cause? It seems that there is only one way out of this dilemma, and that is to infer that the cause of the universe is a personal agent who chooses to create a universe in time. Philosophers call this type of causation 'agent causation,' and because the agent is free, he can initiate new effects by freely bringing about conditions which were not previously present." [4]

This appeal to a personal creator depends on the premise that "we know this first event must have been caused." However, as we have shown, if God is the only item allowed in NBE, the argument effectively (if not intentionally) begs the question. In order to avoid begging the question, theists must produce one or more real or hypothetical candidates other than God for NBE.

We have no experience of any NBE objects in the natural universe (how could we?), nor can we propose anything hypothetical that does not begin to exist as a real item in the natural universe. [5] We can't have such a thing within the natural universe if "begin" means "begin in time" because time itself is a result of the Big Bang. No item in the natural universe transcends time, so it cannot "not" begin to exist. Assuming that current Big Bang cosmology is correct, it would be incoherent to say that something happened "before" time began.

But perhaps there could be something outside [6] the natural universe that would be accommodated by NBE, besides God. (Craig seems to allow this ontological possibility when he "infers" [7] that the external cause of the universe is an "agent causation," implying that it might be otherwise.) NBE might be open to an impersonal force as well as a personal force—or a number of impersonal and personal forces. This

---

4   W. L. Craig, *Reasonable Faith: Christian Truth And Apologetics,* (Wheaton, Illinois: Crossway Books, 1994) p. 117.

5   In the conceptual world, of course, there are things with no beginning, such as the set of negative numbers. But the thrust of Kalam is that infinities do not exist in the real world.

6   This might still amount to begging the question, because the existence of the supernatural is part of the package that theists want to prove.

7   How can an inference be drawn from observations within the natural universe that applies *outside* that universe?

would not necessarily lead to polytheism, deism or violate the principle of economy—it might be true that *only* the personal agency actually exists from the set of possibilities.

If theists, however, allow the theoretical possibility of an impersonal transcendent object in NBE—and it seems they must allow this, or some other nontheistic hypothesis—and if they have not convincingly eliminated it (or them) from the set of actual items in NBE, then they must remain open to the possibility that the origin of the universe could be explained in a purely naturalistic manner.

Transcendent does not equal supernatural.

Have theists successfully eliminated all but one candidate for NBE? By what criteria have they concluded that an impersonal force cannot cause a universe? After all, experience within the universe shows us that many impersonal causes "create" many natural effects.

Craig appears to be justifying the hypothesis of a personal external force via the fact that the natural universe contains complex intelligence and free personal agency—humans, for example—and a creator must be at least as complex as the thing it created[8]. Otherwise, the creation would have been greater than the creator, which is impossible.

But is it impossible? What exactly does "greater" mean? Flowing water created the Grand Canyon. Which is greater? Loose pebbles start avalanches. We build machines that are "greater" than ourselves: forklifts, jet airplanes. We create machines that "think" better than we do—witness the defeat of world chess champion Garry Kasparov to IBM's Deep Blue. A man and a woman who are both of average intelligence can produce a child who is a genius. Nature abounds with examples of complexity arising from simplicity.

If this is true in the natural world then why would it not be equally true in a transcendent or supernatural world, if such a world exists? If we are allowed to draw an inference, as Craig does, from one world to the other, then we cannot rule out the possibility of the universe (or God) having arisen from simpler causes. There is no way to dismiss

---

8   This, by the way, is one way of refuting teleological arguments. If functional complexity requires a designer, then the designer also needs a designer because the designer must be at least as complex as the thing it designed. A creator God, if he existed, would possess a functionally complex, wonderful, organized, purposeful mind...but that is a different argument.

the option that impersonal forces created the right situation for the universe to arise.

This principle holds in biology. The overwhelming consensus among biologists is that we evolved from simpler ancestors, and so did our ancestors. Theists who agree that the universe originated in a Big Bang about 15 billion years ago should not be uncomfortable with the observation that life evolved over that vast period of time. (Those few theists who accept cosmology but reject biology may be picking their experts based on theology rather than science.) If theists such as Craig think we can infer anything from natural observation about the characteristics of a transcendent creator, then we naturalists could be justified in playing the same game. We might "infer" that the creator (if it exists) evolved from a less complex, non-personal source.

Some theists dismiss biological evolution from simpler origins (some discard only macroevolution, and some only the evolution of DNA), but even if they are right this would not help them. Complex/simple does not necessarily translate to personal/impersonal. Who is to say that personality could not have arisen from an impersonal cause? The impersonal might be more complex. If this is impossible, theists must explain why.

Even if it is wrong (in spite of a wealth of evidence) that complexity arises from simplicity, in order for the cosmological argument to hold, theists must at least acknowledge the possibility of one or more transcendent forces that is not personal. They must ontologically contend with something else "out there" that is not God. They must define it, and then eliminate it, in order to avoid being accused of begging the question.

Theists who get the point might mention that the "something else," even if clearly defined, would be merely theoretical. True, but so is God.[9] If they had evidence for God they wouldn't need the Cosmological Argument at all.

IS KALAM SELF-REFUTING?
If an actual infinity cannot be a part of reality, then God, if he is actually infinite, cannot exist.

---

9   Stephen Hawking, in his introduction to *Before The Beginning* by Martin Rees, calls God a "theoretical construct."

To get around this problem, some theists insist that God is not a part of "actual" (natural) reality. They regularly talk about a place "beyond" the universe, a transcendent realm where God exists "outside of time." Craig rapturizes that "*the universe has a cause.* This conclusion ought to stagger us, to fill us with awe, for it means that the universe was brought into existence by *something* which is greater than and beyond it."[10] [emphasis in original]

Of course, if you live "outside of time," whatever that means, then you don't need a beginning in time. A transcendent being, living "beyond" nature, is conveniently exempt from the limitations of natural law. And all complaints that God must have had a cause or a designer (using the same natural reasoning that tries to call for his existence) can be dismissed by theists who insist that God is outside the loop, unaffected by natural causality and beyond time.

Yet theists continue to describe this "timeless" being in temporal terms. Phrases such as "God decided to create the universe" are taken by us mere mortals to be analogous to such natural phrases as "Annie Laurie decided to bake a pie." If such phrases are not equal or analogous to normal human language, and if they are not redefined coherently, then they are useless. We may as well say "God blopwaddled to scrumpwitch the universe."

The word "create" is a transitive verb. We have no experience of transitive verbs operating outside of time (how could we?), so when we hear such a word we must picture it the only way we can: a subject acts on an object. Considering the point at which an action is committed, there must be an antecedent state "during" which the action is not committed, and this would be true either in or out of time.

To say that "God created time" is not comprehensible to us. But if he did it anyway, in spite of our lack of imagination, then it couldn't have happened "after" the decision to commit it because there was no "before." We might still, however, imagine the act of creation as "following" the decision to create. Or to avoid temporal terms, the creating succeeds the deciding in the logical order. In logic we say that a conclusion "follows," though we do not mean this happens in space or time. It doesn't "happen" at all. Craig agrees that "the origin of the universe is causally prior to the Big Bang, though not temporally

---

10   Craig, *Reasonable Faith*, p. 116.

prior to the Big Bang,"[11] but doesn't seem to realize that causality requires temporality.

Either in or out of time, the decision of a personal agency to commit an action happens antecedent to the action itself. Even if the deciding and the acting happened simultaneously[12], it would still not be true that the acting was antecedent to the deciding. Imagine God saying, "Oh, look! I just created a universe. Now I'd better decide to do it."

This means that a series of antecedent causal events must exist in the mind of a time-transcendent creator, if such a being exists. Since the Kalam argument claims that "an actual infinity cannot exist in reality," it shoots itself in the foot. Although Kalam deals with temporal succession, the same logic applies to non-temporal antecedent events, if such things are a part of reality. If the series were infinite, then God never could have traversed the totality of his own antecedent mental causes to arrive at his decision to say "Let there be light." Therefore, sticking with Kalam, there must have been a "first antecedent" in the mind of an actual God, which means that God "began" to exist. (This means "began causally," but theists have conceded the appropriateness of expressing non-temporal actions in temporal language.)

If theists counter that the Kalam argument applies only to the impossibility of an actual mathematical infinity within the material universe and that the transcendent, timeless domain of the creator is an entirely different kind of "infinity" that is not subject to the same laws, then they are begging the question, again. Exempting the conclusion, by definition, from the premises by excluding the supernatural (the very thing theists are trying to prove) is circular reasoning. If it is true that an "actual infinity cannot exist in reality," then a being that is actually infinite cannot be a part of reality. In other words, the Kalam *disproves* the reality of a beginning-less God. If infinity is just a concept, as Kalam insists, then an infinite God is just a concept.

---

11 Craig, W. L. (1992). "The Origin and Creation of the Universe: A Reply to Adolf Grunbaum," *British Journal for the Philosophy of Science* 43. (As quoted in "Some Comments on William Craig's 'Creation and Big Bang Cosmology' " [http://www.infidels.org/library/modern/adolf_grunbaum/comments.html] (1994) by Adolf Grunbaum.

12 Simultaneous creation is not only non-intuitive, but also problematic. Without temporal succession, there is no way to determine the order of cause and effect. If creation happened simultaneously, we cannot eliminate the possibility that the universe created God. (Don't some atheists say that "God" is a human creation?)

If we take Kalam seriously, there is no escaping the fact that God (if he exists) had a beginning, either in or out of time.[13] Since this is true, the phrase "Everything that begins to exist..." includes God. Sticking with the cosmological argument, it follows that God has a cause.

We are back to my kindergartner's question.

By the way, I have never heard a coherent definition of what it means for a god to exist "outside of time." This seems to be an equivocation, a hand-waving dodge of the issue. To "exist" (as an object) means to occupy space and time. Things that exist are measurable.

St. Augustine was philosophically and scientifically naive when he suggested that God exists outside of time. There is no way to be "outside" of time, as if there were an edge or border to it. Augustine and many modern Christians are still thinking like flat-earthers. Time is a dimension, not a thing. Like all dimensions, it has no existence of its own, and it has no beginning, ending or edge. If you want to measure something, say the height of the page of this book, you start at one point, which you label zero, and then count the number of centimeters from that point to the other side along a dimension. It makes sense to say the page is so many centimeters tall, but what about the dimension itself? How long is the dimension? The zero point was chosen arbitrarily along the dimension. Does it make sense to ask of the beginning of the dimension, or the end? It does make sense to ask about the edge of the book, but where is the edge of the dimension? It is nowhere. Time is a dimension of space-time. Things that exist can be measured along that dimension. We can meaningfully talk about "the beginning of the Civil War," but we cannot make any sense of the phrase "beginning of time" as if it were just a very long ruler. That would be like measuring the very concept of measuring, which is jumping up one logical sphere.

We have read about the hypothetical ant crawling on the surface of a huge beach ball. Like flat-earthers wondering where the edge of the world was, no matter where the ant moves, it will never get to the end, to the edge. Every point on that surface is the same, so we might just say that every point is the beginning and every point is the end. The same is true with the dimension of time. Every instant is now. Every

---

13 The Book of Genesis portrays the Hebrew deity creating the world in time: "On the first day, second day, etc." To the biblical literalist, God's actions are indeed temporal, and therefore under the jurisdiction of Kalam.

point in time is the "beginning" and every point in time is the "end." It is meaningless to ask "When did time start?" or "What happened before time started?" In fact, scientists insist that the dimension of time is simply a by-product of objects moving in space. Before there was matter, there was no before.

If God is outside of time, then is time outside of God? If so, there is something else besides God in the cosmos.

To say that God does not exist within space-time is to say that God does not exist. And even if it is true that God does exist "outside of time," despite our failure to intuitively grasp what appears to be an impossibility, then how can he possibly interact with us mere temporals? It would be similar to an author trying to interact with one of the fictional characters in his or her novel—you can't get there from here.

At this point, the theist might remind us that we do have scientific knowledge of the beginning of the universe, but we have no such evidence regarding God. That is true, but it is self-incriminating. Yes, science is a material endeavor—it is impossible to probe the supernatural (whatever that is) with the tools of the natural world—but to say that we have no evidence that God had a beginning is to underscore the fact that we have no evidence about God at all. The Kalam argument was being propounded a millennium before scientists embraced the Big Bang, and its merits were then, as now, nonscientific.

DOES KALAM COMPARE APPLES AND ORANGES?

Another way to show that the Kalam argument may be mere wordplay is to identify the supernaturalistic assumption hidden in the second premise. Here is the argument again:

1. Everything that begins to exist has a cause.

2. The universe began to exist.

3. Therefore, the universe has a cause.

Notice how the words "everything" and "universe" are paired. In this syllogism, the two terms are considered to be of the same essence, at the same logical level. As an analogy, consider the following faulty argument:

1. All apples that fall from trees become bruised.

2. This orange fell from a tree.

3. Therefore, this orange is bruised.

This argument is wrong because...well, because we are comparing apples and oranges. An orange is not a member of the set of apples.

"The universe," to philosophers (or "the cosmos," to cosmologists), is the set of all things. A set is a collection of items. A set can be a member or subset of another set, and it can be considered a subset of itself, but a set cannot meaningfully be a member of itself.[14] Yet the cosmological argument treats the universe as if it were an item in its own set. The first premise refers to every "thing," and the second premise treats the "universe" as if it were a member of the set of "things." But since a set should not be considered a member of itself, the cosmological argument is comparing apples and oranges.

You can't draw an inference or law from the relationships between items in a set that applies to the set as a whole. The fact that each member of an orchestra plays in harmony with all other members of that orchestra does not mean that all orchestras play in harmony with each other. The fact that a distance of two separates each number in the set of even numbers from its immediate neighbors does not mean that the set of even numbers is separated from *its* neighbors by a distance of two. Such thinking inaptly transfers a truth from one level to another. When you say that "Everything that begins to exist has a cause," you can't pull yourself up by your bootstraps and say that the set of all these things (the universe), even if it *did* have a beginning of sorts, must follow the same rules or maintain the same relationships as the items that it contains.

---

14   I know there are some theoretical attempts to treat sets as members of themselves—the "set of all sets" ought to include itself, or the "set of concepts," being a concept, ought to include itself—but I think these are examples of mixing logical spheres, producing confusing semantics. A set-as-collection has a different referent from a set-as-concept. (All sets-as-concept probably have the same referent.) To be useful, a concept should boil down to its lowest level of referent and avoid paradoxes: the "set of sets of sets of sets, etc." is obviously artificial, lacking any useful referent. The "catalog of all catalogs that does not list itself" is paradoxical, therefore impossible. In any event, "the universe" is a collection of material things (lowest referent), not a "collection of concepts." (Thanks to Doug Krueger and Alan Gold for insights on this matter.)

To illustrate, consider a faulty argument that uses the word "began":

1. Every nation began with a revolution.

2. The Alliance of All Nations began 10 years ago.

3. Therefore, there was a revolution 10 years ago.

This is illogical because the Alliance of All Nations is not an individual nation, and the word "began" means something entirely different when it is applied to the set as a whole. Likewise, in the cosmological argument, the clause "begins to exist" should not mean the same thing when applied to "the universe" that it means when applied to individual "things" within the universe.

Explaining the Kalam cosmological argument, Craig writes:

"The logic of the argument is valid and very simple; the argument has the same logical structure as the argument: All men are mortal; Socrates is a man; therefore, Socrates is mortal. So the question is, are there good reasons to believe that each of the steps is true? I think there are."[15]

But this is not right. The "all men are mortal" argument does not have the same logical structure as the Kalam. Socrates is a man, but the universe is not a "thing." The argument would have the same logical structure as the Kalam if it said: All men are mortal; the human race is made of men; therefore, the human race is mortal. It is easy to spot the illogic when phrased in this manner.

Bertrand Russell, in his 1948 debate with Fr. Frederick Copleston, touched on the matter:

"I should say that the universe is just there, and that's all... I can illustrate what seems to me your fallacy. Every man who exists has a mother, and it seems to me your argument is that therefore the human race must have a mother, but obviously the human race hasn't a mother—that's a different logical sphere."[16]

What does "everything" mean? Standing alone, it is synonymous with the universe (or cosmos). But in the cosmological argument,

---

15   Craig, *Reasonable Faith,* p. 72.

16   In *Bertrand Russell on God and Religion,* ed. Al Seckel, (New York: Prometheus Books, 1986), p. 131.

"everything" does not refer to "all things that exist" because it is followed by the limiting clause "that begins to exist." This implies (as we have seen) that there are some things (NBE) that are not a part of this particular set. "Everything" is understood, in this context, as two separate words—every thing—referring to each individual item within BE. This is supported by the fact that "begins to exist" is singular, referring to one "thing" in the set BE. (Craig uses the word "whatever," which means "whatever thing.")

A "thing" is an object or system that is distinct in some manner from other objects or systems. *Webster's New World Dictionary of the American Language* defines *thing* as: "anything conceived of or referred to as existing as an individual, distinguishable entity; *specif.*, a) any single entity distinguished from all others [each thing in the universe]..." (The same dictionary also defines *thing* as an abstract concept, but we can assume that theists consider God and the universe to be real objects.)

A "thing" is something distinguishable, and to be distinguishable is to be limited. To say that I ate a strawberry is to say that what I ate was not a watermelon or a peach. To say that my daughter is a redhead signifies that she is not a blonde or a brunette. To say that my friend is from New York means that he is not from Chicago, Paris or any other city. In order to be considered a "thing," an object must be a part of a larger context within which and by which it can be limited. The object must be able to be "pulled away" from other objects.

Is the universe a "thing"? When the cosmological argument moves to its second premise—the universe began to exist—we are being forced to view the universe as a particular item in the set of "things." But is the "set of all things" a "thing" itself? How is the set of all things distinguished from other things or other sets? In what context does the universe exist within which it can be identified as a distinct object?

If we even *suggest* that the universe (cosmos) is a discrete "thing" (not just a concept), we are implying a realm above and beyond the universe within which it is contained, limited and defined. This amounts to assuming transcendence. Theistic philosophers hope no one will notice that the language they are using effortlessly conjures the existence of a realm beyond nature, portraying "the universe" from a distance as if "it" had an environment. It is easier for nontheists, who are not tempted to mix logical spheres to avoid such question begging.[17]

Copleston, responding to Russell, asked: "But are you going to say that we can't, or we shouldn't, even raise the question of the existence of the whole of this sorry scheme of things—of the whole universe?"

"Yes," Russell replied. "I don't think there's any meaning in it at all. I think the word 'universe' is a handy word in some connections, but I don't think it stands for anything that has a meaning."[18] (Today, cosmologists would substitute the word "cosmos" for "universe," which is what Russell was talking about: the entirety of existence.)

What statements can we make about the universe that show us what it is not? The Grand Canyon is not in New Jersey, the Egyptian pyramids were not built in the 20th century and baseballs are not made of jellybeans. Where does the universe not exist? Of what is it not made? How does it differ from a non-universe?[19] Such questions are meaningless when asked of the "set of all things."

In summary, in order for the Kalam Cosmological Argument to be salvaged, theists must answer these questions, at least:

1. Is God the only object accommodated by the set of things that do not begin to exist? If yes, then why is the cosmological argument not begging the question? If no, then what are the other candidates for the cause of the universe and how have they been eliminated?

2. Does the logic of Kalam apply only to temporal antecedents in the real world? If yes, this assumes the existence of nontemporal antecedents in the real world, so why is this not begging the question? If no, then why doesn't the impossibility of an actual infinity disprove the existence of an actually infinite God?

---

17 Atheists are sometimes accused of having a "bias against the supernatural," but it could be countered that theists have a "bias against the natural."

18 In *Bertrand Russell on God and Religion*, p. 129.

19 We could say that "The universe is not composed entirely of pork chops," but this does not distinguish the universe from any other set. We will never stumble upon a "set of all things" made entirely of pork chops, and say, "Oops, this is not the universe." (If we thought we did, we would have to admit that it is only a subset of all things that exist—a part of the universe, not another universe.) We *can* find rivers in New Jersey, pyramids built in the 20th century and jellybeans in various shapes, and we would agree that their existence contributes to the set of all things that those other things are not.

3. Is the universe (cosmos) a member of itself? If not, then how can its "beginning" be compared with other beginnings?

In the absence of good answers to these questions, we must dismiss the Kalam Cosmological Argument for the existence of a god.

Chapter Nine
Dear Theologian

Dear Theologian,

I have a few questions and I thought you would be the right person to ask. It gets tough sometimes, sitting up here in heaven with no one to talk to...I mean, really talk to. I can always converse with the angels, of course, but since they don't have free will and since I created every thought in their submissive minds, they are not very stimulating conversationalists.

Of course, I can talk with my son, Jesus, and with the "third person" of our holy trinity, the Holy Spirit, but since we are all the same there is nothing we can learn from each other. There are no well-placed repartees in the Godhead. We all know what the others know. We can't exactly play chess. Jesus sometimes calls me "Father" and that feels good, but since he and I are the same age and have the same powers, it doesn't mean much.

You are educated. You have examined philosophy and world religions. You have a degree that makes you qualified to carry on a discussion with someone at my level—not that I can't talk with anyone, even with the uneducated believers who fill the churches and flatter me with endless petitions, but you know how it is. Sometimes we all crave interaction with a respected colleague. You have read the scholars. You have written papers and published books about me, and you know me better than anyone else.

It might surprise you to think that I have some questions. No, not rhetorical questions aimed at teaching spiritual lessons, but some real, honest-to-God inquiries. This should not shock you because, after all, I created you in my image. Your inquisitiveness is an inheritance from me. You would say that love, for example, is a reflection of my nature within yourself, wouldn't you? Since questioning is healthy, it also comes from me.

Somebody once said that we should prove all things and hold fast that which is good. My first question is this:

Where did I come from?

As I sit up here in heaven and look around, I notice that there is nothing else here besides the objects that I have created and me. I don't see any other creatures competing with me, nor do I notice anything above me that might have created me, unless it is playing hide-and-seek. In any event, as far as I know (and I supposedly know everything), there is nothing else but me in-three-persons and my creations. I have always existed, you say. I did not create myself because if I did, then I would be greater than myself.

So where did I come from?

I know how you approach that question regarding your own existence. You notice that nature, especially the human mind, displays evidence of intricate design. You have never observed such design apart from a designer. You argue that human beings must have had a creator, and you will find no disagreement from me.

Then, what about me? Like you, I observe that my mind is complex and intricate. It is much more complex than your mind; otherwise, I couldn't have created your mind. My personality displays evidence of organization and purpose. Sometimes I surprise myself at how wise I am. If you think your existence is evidence of a designer, then what do you think about my existence? Am I not wonderful? Do I not function in an orderly manner? My mind is not a random jumble of disconnected thoughts—it displays what you would call evidence of design. If you need a designer, then why don't I?

You might think such a question is blasphemy, but to me there is no such crime. I can ask any question I want, and I think this is a fair one. If you say that everything needs a designer and then say that not everything (Me) needs a designer, aren't you contradicting yourself? By excluding me from the argument, aren't you bringing your conclusion into your argument? Isn't that circular reasoning? I am not saying I disagree with your conclusion. How could I? I'm just wondering why it is proper for you to infer a designer while it is not proper for me.

If you are saying that I don't need to ask where I came from because I am perfect and omniscient while humans are fallible, then you don't need the design argument at all, do you? You have already assumed that I exist. You can make such an assumption, of course, and I would not deny you the freedom. Such *a priori* and circular reasoning might be helpful or comforting to you, but it does me little good. It doesn't help me figure out where I came from.

You say that I am eternally existent and I might not object to that—if I knew what it meant. It is hard for me to conceive of eternal existence. I just can't remember back that far. It would take me an eternity to remember back to eternity, leaving me no time to do anything else, so it is impossible for me to confirm if I existed forever. And even if it is true, why is eternal greater than temporal? Is a long sermon greater than a short sermon? What does "greater" mean? Are fat people greater than thin people, or old people greater than the young?

You think it is important that I have always existed. I'll take your word for it, for now. My question is not with the duration of my existence, but with the origin of my existence. I don't see how being eternal solves the problem. I still want to know where I came from.

I can only imagine one possible answer, and I would appreciate your reaction. I know that I exist. I know that I could not have created myself. I also know that there is no higher God who could have created me. Since I can't look above myself, then perhaps I should look below myself for a creator. Perhaps—this is speculative, so bear with me—perhaps you created me.

Don't be shocked. I mean to flatter you. Since I contain evidence of design, and since I see no other place where such design could originate, I am forced to look for a designer, or designers, in nature itself. You are a part of nature. You are intelligent—that is what your readers say. Why should I not find the answer to my question in you? Help me out on this.

Of course, if you made me, then I could not have made you. The reason that I think I made you is because you made me to think I made you. You have often said that a Creator can put thoughts in your mind. Isn't it possible that you have put thoughts in my mind, and now here we are, both of us wondering where we came from?

Some of you have said that the answer to this whole question is just a mystery that only God understands. Well, thanks a lot. The buck stops here. On the one hand you use logic to try to prove my existence. On the other hand, when logic hits a dead end you abandon it and invoke "faith" and "mystery." Those words might be useful to you as placeholders for facts or truth, but they don't translate to anything meaningful as far as I am concerned. You can pretend that "mystery" signifies something terribly important, but to me it simply means you don't know.

Some of you assert that I did not "come" from anywhere—that I just exist. I have also heard you say, however, that nothing comes from nothing. You can't have it both ways. I either exist or I don't. What was it that caused me to exist, as opposed to not existing at all? If I don't need a cause, then why do you? Since I am not happy to say that this is a mystery, I must accept the only explanation that makes sense. You created me.

Is that such a terrible idea? I know that you think humans created many other gods: Zeus, Thor, Mercury, Elvis. You recognize that such deities originate in human desire, need or fear. If the blessed beliefs of those billions of individuals can be dismissed as products of culture, then why can't yours? The Persians created Mithra, the Jews created Yahweh and you created me. If I am wrong about this, please straighten me out.

My next question is this:

What's it all about?

Maybe I made myself, maybe some other god made me or maybe you made me—but let's put that aside for now. I'm here...but why am I here? Many of you look up to me for purpose in life, and I have often stated that your purpose in life is to please me. (Revelation 4:11) If your purpose is to please me, what is my purpose? To please myself? Is that all there is to life?

If I exist for my own pleasure, then this is selfish. It makes it look as if I created you merely to have some living toys to play with. Isn't there some principle that I can look up to? Something to admire, adore and worship? Am I consigned for eternity to sit here and amuse myself with the worship of others? Or, to worship myself? What's the point?

I have read your writings on the meaning of life and they make sense in the theological context of human religious goals, even if they don't have much practicality in the real world. Many of you feel that your purpose in life is to achieve perfection. Since you humans fall way short of perfection, by your own admission (and I agree), then self-improvement provides you with a quest. It gives you something to do.

Someday you hope to be as perfect as you think I am. But since I am already perfect, by definition, then I don't need such a purpose. I'm just sort of hanging out, I guess.

Yet I still wonder why I'm here. It feels good to exist. It feels great to be perfect. But it gives me nothing to do. I created the universe with all kinds of natural laws that govern everything from quarks to galactic clusters, and it runs okay on its own. I had to make these laws, otherwise I would be involved with a lot of repetitive busy work such as pulling light rays through space, yanking falling objects down to earth, sticking atoms together to build molecules and a trillion other boring tasks more worthy of a slave than a master. You have discovered most of those laws and might be on the verge of putting the whole picture together. Once you have done that you will know what I know: that there is nothing in the universe for me to do. It's boring up here.

I could create more universes and more laws, but what's the point? I've already done universes. Creation is like sneezing or writing short stories; it just comes out of me. I could go on an orgy of creation. Create, create, create. After a while a person can get sick of the same thing, like when you eat a whole box of chocolates and discover that the last piece doesn't taste as good as the first. Once you have had 10 children, do you need 20? (I'm asking you, not the pope.) If more is better, then I am obligated to continue until I have fathered an infinite number of children and an endless number of universes. If I must compel myself, then I am a slave.

Many of you assert that it is inappropriate to seek purpose within yourself, that it must come from outside. I feel the same way. I can't merely assign purpose to myself. If I did, then I would have to look for my reasons. I would have to come up with an account of why I chose one purpose over another, and if such reasons came from within myself I would be caught in a loop of self-justified rationalizations. Since I have no Higher Power of my own, then I have no purpose. Nothing to live for. It is all meaningless.

Sure, I can bestow meaning on you—pleasing me, achieving perfection, whatever—and perhaps that is all that concerns you. But doesn't it bother you, just a little, that the source of meaning for your life has no source of its own? And if this is true, then isn't it also true that ultimately you have no meaning for yourself either? If it makes you happy to demand an external reference point on which to hang your meaningfulness, why would you deny the same to me? I also want to be happy, and I want to find that happiness in something other than myself. Is that a sin?

On the other hand, if you think I have the right and the freedom to find happiness in myself and in the things I created, then why should you not have the same right? You, whom I created in my image?

I know that some of you have proposed a solution to this problem. You call it "love." You think I am lonely up here and that I created humans to satisfy my longing for a relationship with something that is not myself. Of course, this will never work because it is impossible for me to create something that is not part of myself, but let's say that I try anyway. Let's say that I create this mechanism called "free will," which imparts to humans a choice. If I give you the freedom (though this is stretching the word because there is nothing outside of my power) not to love me, then if some of you, a few of you, even one of you chooses to love me, I have gained something I might not have had. I have gained a relationship with someone who could have chosen otherwise. This is called love, you say.

This is a great idea, on paper. In real life, however, it turns out that billions of people have chosen not to love me, and that I have to do something with these infidels. I can't just un-create them. If I simply destroy all the unbelievers, I may as well have created only believers in the first place. Since I am omniscient, I would know in advance which of my creations would have a tendency to choose me. This would produce no conflict with free will since those who would not have chosen me would have been eliminated simply by not having been created in the first place. (I could call it Supernatural Selection.) This seems much more compassionate than hell.

You can't have a love relationship with someone who is not your equal. If you humans don't have a guaranteed eternal soul, like me, then you are worthless as companions. If I can't respect your right to exist independently, and your right to choose something other than me, then I couldn't love those of you who do choose me. I would have to find a place for all those billions of eternal souls who reject me, whatever their reasons might be. Let's call it "hell," a place that is not-God, not-me. I would have to create this inferno, otherwise neither the unbelievers nor I could escape each other. Let's ignore the technicalities of how I could manage to create hell and then separate it from myself, apart from whom nothing else exists. (It's not as though I could create something and then simply throw it away—there is no cosmic trash heap.) The point is that since I am supposedly perfect, this place of exile must be something that is the opposite. It must be ultimate evil, pain, darkness and torment.

If I created hell, then I don't like myself.

And if I did create a hell, then it certainly would not be smart to advertise that fact. How would I know if people were claiming to love me for my own sake, or simply to avoid punishment? How can I expect someone to love me who is afraid of me? The threat of eternal torment might scare some people into obedience, but it does nothing to inspire love. If you treated me with threats and intimidation, I would have to reconsider my admiration for your character.

How would you feel if you had brought some children into the world knowing that they were going to be tormented eternally in a place you built for them? Could you live with yourself? Wouldn't it have been better not to have brought them into the world in the first place?

I know that some of you feel that hell is just a metaphor. Do you feel the same way about heaven?

Anyway, this whole love argument is wrong. Since I am perfect, I don't lack anything. I can't be lonely. I don't need to be loved. I don't even want to be loved because to want is to lack. To submit to giving and receiving love is to admit that I can be hurt by those who choose not to love me. If you can hurt me, I am not perfect. If I can't be hurt, I can't love. If I ignore or erase those who do not love me, sending them off to hell or oblivion, then my love is not sincere. If all I am doing is throwing the dice of "free will" and simply reaping the harvest of those who choose to love me, then I am a selfish monster. If you played such games with people's lives, I would call you insensitive, conceited, insecure, selfish and manipulative.

I know you have tried to get me off the hook. You explain that Yours Truly is not responsible for the sufferings of unbelievers because rejection of God is their choice, not mine. They had a corrupt human nature, you explain. Well, who gave them their human nature? If certain humans decide to do wrong, where do they get the impulse? If you think it came from Satan, who created Satan? And why would some humans be susceptible to Satan in the first place? Who created that susceptibility? If Satan was created perfect and then fell, where did the flaw of perdition come from? If I am perfect, then how in God's name did I end up creating something that would not choose perfection? Someone once said that a good tree cannot bring forth evil fruit.

Here is the title for your next theological tome: Was Eve Perfect? If she was, she would not have taken the fruit. If she wasn't, I created imperfection.

Maybe you think all of this gives me a purpose—putting Humpty Dumpty back together—but it actually gives me a headache. (If you won't permit me a simple headache, then how can you allow me the pain of lost love?) I could not live with myself if I thought my actions were causing harm to others. Well, I shouldn't say that. Since I think you created me, I suppose I should let you tell me what I could live with. If you think it is consistent with my character to tolerate love and vengeance concurrently, then I have no choice. If you are my creator, then I could spout tenderness out of one side of my mouth and brutality out of the other. I could dance with my lover on the bones of my errant children and pretend to enjoy it. I would be very human indeed.

I have a thousand questions, but I will ask you just two more:

How do I decide what is right and wrong?
I don't know how I got here, but I'm here. Let's just say that my purpose is to make good people out of my creations. Let's say that I am here to help you learn how to be perfect like me, and that the best way to achieve that is for you to act just like me—or act like I want you to act. Your goal is to become a mirror of me. Won't that be splendid? I'll give you rules and principles and you try to follow them. This may or may not be meaningful, but it will keep us both busy. I suppose that from your point of view this would be terribly meaningful, since you think I have the power to reward and punish.

I know that some of you Protestant theologians think that I give rewards not for good deeds, but simply for believing in my son, Jesus, who paid the punishment for your bad deeds. Well, Jesus spent only about 36 hours of an eternal life sentence in hell and is now back up here in ultimate coziness with me. Talk about a wrist-slap! He was not paroled for good behavior—he was simply released. (He had connections.) If my righteous judgment demanded absolute satisfaction, then Jesus should have paid the price in full...don't you think?

Beyond that, it is entirely incomprehensible to me why you think I would accept the blood of one individual for the crime of another. Is that fair? Is that justice? If you commit a felony, does the law allow your brother to serve the jail sentence for you? If someone burglarized your home, would you think justice was served if a friend of the burglar bought you new furniture? Do you really think that I am such a bloodthirsty dictator that I will be content with the death of anyone for the crime of another? And are you so disrespectful of justice that you would happily accept a stand-in for your crimes? What about personal responsibility? Should I welcome believers into heaven who have avoided the rap for their own actions. Something is way out of kilter here.

But let's ignore these objections. Let's assume that Jesus and I worked it all out and that evil will be punished and good rewarded. How do I know the difference? You are insisting that I not consult any rulebook. You are asking me to be the Final Authority. I must simply decide, and you must trust my decision. Am I free to decide whatever I want?

Suppose I decide that I would like you to honor me with a day of my own. I like the number seven, I don't know why, maybe because it is the first useless number. (You never sing any hymns to me in 7/4 time.) Let's divide the calendar into groups of seven days and call them weeks. For harmony, I'll divide each lunar phase into roughly seven days. The last day of the week—or maybe the first day, I don't care— I'll set aside for myself. Let's call it the Sabbath. This all feels good, so I suppose it is the right thing to do. I'll make a law ordering you to observe the Sabbath, and if you do it then I will pronounce you good people. In fact, I'll make it one of my Ten Commandments and I'll order your execution if you disobey it. This all makes perfect sense, though I don't know why.

Help me out here. How am I supposed to choose what is moral? Since I can't consult any authority, the thing to do, it appears, is to pick randomly. Actions will become right or wrong simply because I declare them to be so. If I whimsically say that you should not make any graven or molten images of "anything that is in heaven above, or that is in the earth beneath, or that is in the water under the earth," then that is that. If I decide that murder is right and compassion is wrong, you will have to accept it.

Is that all there is to it? I just decide, willy-nilly, what is right and what is wrong? Or worse, I decide based on whatever makes me feel good? I have read in some of your literature that you denounce such self-centered attitudes.

Some of you say that since I am perfect, I can't make any mistakes. Whatever I choose to be right or wrong will be in accordance with my nature. And since I am perfect, then my choices will be perfect. In any event, my choices will certainly be better than your choices, you feel. But what does "perfect" mean? If my nature is perfect, then I am living up to a standard. If I am living up to a standard, then I am not God. If perfection means something all by itself, apart from me, then I am constrained to follow its path. If, on the other hand, perfection is defined simply as conformity to my nature, then it doesn't mean anything. My nature can be what it wants, and perfection will be defined accordingly. Do you see the problem here? If "perfection" equals "God," then it is just a synonym for me and we can do away with the word. Actually, we could do away with either word. Take your pick.

If I am perfect, then there are certain things that I cannot do. If I am not free to feel envy, lust or malice, for example, then I am not omnipotent. I cannot be more powerful than you if you can feel and do things that I cannot.

Additionally, if you feel that God is perfect by nature, what does "nature" mean? The word is used to describe the way things are or act in nature, and since you think I am above nature you must mean something else, something like "character" or "attributes." To have a nature or character means to be one way and not another. It means that there are limits. Why am I one way and not another? How did it get decided that my nature would be what it is? If my nature is clearly defined, then I am limited. I am not God. If my nature has no limits, as some of you suggest, then I have no nature at all and to say that God has "such-and-such a nature" is meaningless. In fact, if I have no limits, then I have no identity. And if I have no identity, then I do not exist.

Who am I?

This brings me back to the conundrum: if I don't know who I am then how can I decide what is right? Do I just poke around in myself until I come up with something?

There is one course I could pursue, and some of you have suggested this for yourselves. I could base my pronouncements on what is best for you humans. You people have physical bodies that bump around in a physical world. I could determine those actions that are healthy and beneficial for material beings in a material environment. I could make morality something material—something that is relative to human life, not to my whims. I could declare (by conclusion, not by edict) that harming human life is bad, and that helping or enhancing human life is good. This would be like providing an operation manual for something I designed and manufactured. It would require me to know all about human nature and the environment in which you humans live, and to communicate these ideas to you.

This makes a lot of sense, but it changes my task from one of determining morality to one of communicating morality. If morality is discovered in nature then you don't need me, except maybe to prod you along. I saw to it that you have capable minds with the ability to reason and do science. There is nothing mysterious about study-ing how humans interact with nature and with each other, and you should be able to come up with your own set of rules. Some of you tried this millennia before Moses. Even if your rules contradict mine, I couldn't claim any higher authority than you. At least you would be able to give reasons for your rules, which I can only do by submitting to science myself.

If morality is defined by how human beings exist in nature, then you don't need me at all. I am off the hook! From what I have read, most of you have your feet on the ground with no help from me. I could hand down some stone tablets containing what I think is right and wrong, but it would still be up to you to see if my rules work in the real world. I think we all agree that grounded reason is better than the whim of an ungrounded deity.

This is a wonderful approach, but what bothers me is that while this may help you know what is moral in your environment, it doesn't help me much. I don't have an environment. I'm out here flapping in the breeze. I envy you.

Nor does the humanistic approach help those of you who want morality to be rooted in something absolute, outside of yourselves. It must be frightening for those of you who need an anchor to real-ize that there is no bottom to the ocean. Well, it's frightening for me also. I don't have an anchor of my own. That's why I'm asking for your help.

Thank you for reading my letter and for letting me impose on your busy schedule. Please answer at your convenience. I have all the time in the world.

Sincerely,

Yours Truly

PART 3

What's Wrong
With Christianity

Chapter Ten
The Bible and Morality

Believers in God do not have a corner on the morality market. During all my years of preaching, I simply assumed that the bible was the rock-solid foundation of morality, and it never crossed my mind to examine that assumption. Yet as I morphed from faith to reason, I started looking at the "Word of God" in a different light. In the next chapter I lay out a natural basis for morality—how to be good without God—and show how we nonbelievers actually have a better grasp of ethics than those who take the bible seriously. But first I need to shine the light on why I no longer consider the bible to be a "Good Book."

The word "moral" appears nowhere in the bible. Neither does "morality," "ethics" or "ethical." To inquire if the bible is a good moral guide is to ask a question that originates outside the bible.

This does not mean that the bible has nothing to say about behavior. The phrase "to do right" appears throughout scripture, but this is usually followed by "in the sight of the Lord." To do right in one's "own eyes" is considered evil. There are a few passages that talk about doing that which is right or good without an explicit connection to deity, but taken in the general context of biblical theology all behavior that Christians and Jews consider to be good is measured against the "righteousness" of God, not against moral or ethical principles of humanity. Proverbs 16:25 says, "There is a way that seemeth right unto a man, but the end thereof are the ways of death."

Ironically, the first place the phrase "do right" is used in the bible is when Abraham questioned the morality of God. Abraham argued with God and succeeded in getting him to change his mind about slaughtering innocent victims in Sodom: "That be far from thee to do after this manner, to slay the righteous with the wicked; and that the righteous should be as the wicked, that be far from thee; Shall not the

Judge of all the earth do right?" (Genesis 18:25) *Shall not the judge of all the earth do right?*

God did change his mind about the minimum number of good people required to prevent the slaughter, but he went ahead and murdered all the inhabitants of Sodom anyway, including all of the "unrighteous" children, babies and fetuses. It appears that Abraham was more moral than his god, a matter to be examined later. And his question is quite valid: "Shall not the Judge of all the earth do right?" When a parent who smokes tells a child not to smoke, the child can be forgiven for asking, "What about you?" If the basis for morality rests with a single entity, then what makes that entity accountable? What makes God moral?

True Christians should not ask if the bible is moral, or if God is moral. If God is the source of morality, then asking if God is moral is like asking if goodness is good. To ask seriously if God or the bible is moral (with a possible negative answer) is to assume that "moral" means something apart from God, and that we already know what it means independently of the bible. If the word "moral" has meaning by itself, then right and wrong can be understood apart from God, and judging the morality of God puts him under the jurisdiction of a higher level of criticism. This is true even if the judgment is favorable. To the believer, questioning the morality of God is blasphemy. It implies that the "supreme judge" can be judged.

But, of course, "Is God moral?" is a perfectly legitimate question. Not only does it make sense to freethinkers, who are outside the religious circle and therefore not required to reduce it to a simple ontological tautology describing the perfection of deity, but it has to make some kind of sense to Christians, if they are honest, in order for them to be able to worship. Can you worship someone who has not earned respect? When Christians or Jews say that "God is good" aren't they judging God? Don't they think his character merits praise and adoration? Or, are they simply giving blind obedience to whatever happens to be omnipotent? (I might "respect" the strength of a hurricane, but I would not call it good nor would I worship it.) Most of us do not consider it an admirable moral quality to praise power alone. So, if believers deem God to be good, then it must be because they have judged God to be morally worthy of respect. You can't praise what you don't admire.

The question turns out to be something of a trap for believers. If pressed they will have to back off from judging God, and will have to admit that God is moral by definition alone. It doesn't really matter how God acts: God is good because God said he is good, and we should worship him not because he has earned our admiration but because he has demanded it. Morality is not a question with which mere human minds should wrestle, believers insist. It is something that should be determined by the perfect, omniscient, omnipotent mind of God.

Judaism, Christianity and Islam, the "revealed" religions that directly or indirectly share the Jewish Law, pretend to find their answer to morality in a holy book that originates from a mind that exists outside the material world. Their way to be moral is simply stated: obey Scripture.

Regardless of whether humanism or other naturalistic ethical systems are successful, or even possible, and regardless of whether we truly need an external moral code, the question can still be raised about the adequacy of any particular religious solution. Is the bible a good book? Is the bible an acceptable guide for moral behavior?

The bible is indeed filled with very specific commandments for living. Let's look at one of them. The Fourth Commandment says, "Remember the Sabbath day, to keep it holy." This is one of the Big Ten, so it can't be ignored. At face value it seems straightforward enough, but what exactly does it mean? How do you "remember" the Sabbath and what happens if you fail? In the book of Numbers the "Lord" gives a specific example of how the Sabbath law is applied, but he first explains that there is a difference between sinning deliberately and sinning accidentally, comparable to the modern idea of "intent." Although this provides for varying degrees of sentencing, it does not mitigate the crime itself. A sin is still a sin:

"And if any soul sin through ignorance, then he shall bring a she goat of the first year for a sin offering... But the soul that doeth ought [sin] presumptuously, whether he be born in the land, or a stranger, the same reproacheth the Lord; and that soul shall be cut off from among his people. Because he hath despised the word of the Lord, and hath broken his commandment, that soul shall utterly be cut off; his iniquity shall be upon him." (Numbers 15:27, 30-31)

Strong language. There is accidental sin and there is deliberate sin, though it seems that the former should hardly count as a "sin." In any event, the passage that immediately follows this clarification shows what happens to a person who *deliberately* breaks the Sabbath law:

"And while the children of Israel were in the wilderness, they found a man that gathered sticks upon the Sabbath day. And they that found him brought him unto Moses and Aaron, and unto all the congregation. And they put him in ward, because it was not declared what should be done to him. And the Lord said unto Moses, The man shall be surely put to death: all the congregation shall stone him with stones without the camp. And all the congregation brought him without the camp, and stoned him with stones, and he died; as the Lord commanded Moses." (Numbers 15:32-36)

This is clear: don't pick up sticks on Saturday. If you pick up sticks, God's followers will pick up stones. Is *this* a good guide for morality? When I was a child, each year my family would spend weeks camping in the mountains of California. My brothers and I had the job of picking up kindling wood for the fire. This often happened on the weekend. Didn't my born-again parents read the bible? (Perhaps my sin was one of "ignorance." Where am I going to find a she goat?) The man who was stoned to death was likely gathering firewood to cook food to feed his family. *He* was the one acting morally.

Some believers assert that these primitive Old Testament laws are no longer relevant and have been superseded by Jesus—but that proves the point! If they use such an argument, they are admitting that at least part of the bible is not acceptable for today's society. How many of us stop and think what day of the week it is before we pick up sticks? However you interpret it, the 15th chapter of Numbers is still in the bible, the Sabbath law is still in the Ten Commandments, and we see no condemnation of such barbarism, no moral outcry, no denunciation by Christians of these shameful acts committed by their "loving God" in the "Good Book." We see no pages being torn out of bibles with disgust. What if an ayatollah were to command the execution of a person who picked up sticks on an Islamic holy day because it offended Allah? What would we think of such bloodthirsty, immoral arrogance?

In dealing with such troublesome scriptural issues as capital punishment for picking up sticks on Saturday (the Jewish Sabbath) or Sunday (the Christian Sabbath), some liberal Christians will agree that portions of the bible are now outmoded. The text should not be taken literally, they claim. We should seek instead the "spiritual lesson" that underlies the specific example. (That would be like saying, "I am going to teach you a lesson about obedience by telling you that I killed someone. Don't worry about the violence or that person's life, because I love you and want you to learn how righteous I am.")

There is a subset of fundamentalists, called Dispensationalists, who claim that the Old Testament rules were in effect only for that period of history, and that we now have different rules because God's plan is unfolding in stages, or dispensations. (Though Jesus said he came to uphold "every jot and tittle" of the Old Testament law.) Other evangelical Christians will assert that tougher measures were required during the struggling infancy of the besieged Israelite nation. God's chosen people were at war so some "moral rationing" was justified—but that now that Christianity is on the scene such measures are no longer needed. (Though they still preach that the world is more corrupt than ever, and that the forces of evil continue to attack believers.) All of these liberal arguments, at minimum, admit that there are at least some parts of the current bible that are now no longer relevant to proper human behavior. All of us, believers and nonbelievers alike, whatever our reasoning, have to agree that the bible can be downright brutal.

Apologize, theologize, demythologize, liberalize and rationalize all you want—those barbaric scriptures are still being sold in bookstores. Many courts use the bible as the standard of truth telling and U.S. presidents place their hand upon it during inauguration—a practice, incidentally, not mandated by the Constitution. But any version of a "holy book" that contains barbaric decrees cannot be *entirely* palatable to the modern world. Perhaps it could be argued that some parts are still relevant, but the bible as a whole is undeniably flawed.

Believers often accuse skeptics of ignoring the good while picking out only the bad parts of the bible. Believers ask why we don't join them in emphasizing that which is good and beautiful in the bible? This might appear to be a fair question until it is turned around and we ask them why they don't join us in denouncing the ugly parts. Then, they don't see the questions as being quite so fair.

Suppose you invited me to your house to see your beautiful garden. "Here, look at this beautiful iris," you might say.

I might nod my head and smile. "Yes, that is beautiful." I've seen better, but that is not bad.

"And over here, look at this gorgeous rose."

"Wow, that is pretty," I might agree, but as I look around the garden I see that it is overrun with weeds and trash. Some of the plants show obvious signs of disease and decay, and bugs are chewing many of the leaves.

Noticing my distraction, you might say, "Oh, just ignore that. I want you to see the good parts."

"But you invited me here to see your 'beautiful garden,' and I have to say I am disappointed. You do have some nice flowers, which actually stand out against the unsightliness around them, but the general impression is chaotic and hideous."

"But you are not looking at it the right way. You have to ignore all that. Those things you are choosing to stare at do not bother me. Adjust your focus. Don't concentrate on the bad; look for the good. The disease is not my fault. Someone else threw the trash in there—the original garden was perfect. Who is to say what is a weed? I can't pull out the weeds because then there would be no contrast and we wouldn't appreciate how beautiful the flowers are."

"Yes, a few flowers are nice, but on balance this is an ugly sight. You are not a good gardener."

"I thought you were my friend!"

"Well, what are friends for?"

Those who can look at the bible objectively, who are not handicapped with the requirement that it be worshiped or respected, notice that there are problems with using it as a guide for behavior:

1. The bible argues from authority, not from reason, claiming that "might makes right."

2. The bible nowhere states that every human being possesses an inherent right to be treated with respect and fairness—humans don't matter as much as God does.

3. The biblical role models, especially Yahweh, Elohim and Jesus, are very poor moral examples, often ignoring their own good teachings (what few there are) and ruthlessly pursuing their own tyrannical teachings.

4. Many moral precepts of the bible are just plain bad, even dangerous.

5. On closer inspection, the few "positive" teachings are uninspired, unoriginal, inadequate and irrelevant. (See below.) On balance, this is an ugly garden.

Author Ruth Green calls the bible a "moral grab bag." Many pick and choose from its pages, most ignore it, and those few who do use it as a guide for behavior do so for religious rather than moral reasons. Those believers who are good people—and I think most of them are—and who credit the bible for their standards are giving credit where credit is not due. Christians, it turns out, don't have a corner on morality. On average they are no more moral than unbelievers. Some might argue that they are *less* moral. Those few shining examples from the Christian community shine no brighter than the caring unbelievers. But for all their talk about the need for moral guidance, they cannot substantiate the claim that the bible is a good guide for modern behavior.

MIGHT MAKES RIGHT

When someone tells you to do something it is natural to ask, "Why?" Why remember the Sabbath? The bible tells us that we should remember the Sabbath "to keep it holy." The word "holy" means "set apart," "sacred" or "clean" and has nothing to do with "good" or "right." In other words, this commandment does not deal with ethics; it deals with the superiority of God. When true believers say that something is "wrong," it is because it has been *decreed* wrong by a "holy" deity, not because there is a good ethical reason. The child asks, "Daddy, why can't I do this?" and Daddy responds, "Because I said so!" If the commandment is violated, it becomes a crime of disobedience—the authority figure should not be offended.

"Vengeance belongeth unto me, I will recompense, saith the Lord. And again, The Lord shall judge his people. It is a fearful thing to fall into the hands of the living God." (Hebrews 10:30-31)

"Be not afraid of them that kill the body, and after that have no more that they can do. But I will forewarn you whom ye shall fear: Fear him, which after he hath killed hath power to cast into hell; yea, I say unto you, Fear him." (Jesus, Luke 12:4-5)

"The fear of the Lord is the beginning of wisdom." (Solomon, Proverbs 1:7)

The humanist, on the other hand, looks for some reason or principle independent of authority. The child asks, "Why can't I do this?" Daddy or Mommy responds, "If you do it, you will get hurt. I love you and don't want you to get hurt." Or the parent says, "If you do this, someone else will get hurt." The crime is against humanity, not against Daddy. A deity might give reasons for its decrees, but they must be irrelevant. If God gives reasons, then he is appealing to a court outside himself—a court to which we could just as well appeal directly, circumventing his authority. If God needs reasons, then he is not God.

To the theist, punishment is administered by the offended Daddy. Whoever "reproacheth the Lord" shall be chastised. To the humanist, however, consequences, not punishment, happen as a natural effect of the behavior itself. This does not mean that a humanist parent will allow a child to run into a busy street; it means that the moral basis for restraint is found in the traffic, not in the "Word of Daddy." The humanist's child who disobeys and runs into the street is not committing a "sin" by offending the ego or "holiness" of the parents—the evil of the situation exists in the potential for getting run over by a moving vehicle. In other words, it exists in nature.

If there were something dangerous about picking up sticks on the weekend, then humanity should know it by now. Since we all agree that such an act in itself is harmless, then whoever executes a person for committing such a "crime" is an immoral person. Even if there were something wrong about picking up sticks—perhaps akin to threatening the morale of the troops—it is not so terribly wrong that it deserves capital punishment. We don't send jaywalkers to the gas chamber, or hang children for stealing cookies.

Unless… unless you argue from authority and the authority figure decrees, for no good reason, that such an action offends *Him*. People who believe they are living under the thumb of such a vain and petty lord are not guided by ethics; they are guided by fear. The bible turns out to be not a moral code, but a whip.

Rather than asking believers the silly (to them) question "Is God moral?" it might be more meaningful to ask: "What would the bible have to say in order to be immoral?" If the bible ordered killing, would that be immoral? Or, what if it mandated rape? What if it commanded stealing, lying or adultery? What if its main characters called names, issued threats and acted irrationally? Then would it be immoral? Exactly how bad would the bible have to get before it is discarded? Do Christians ever dare ask this question? (The bible does command or encourage all of these things, by the way.)

Such a question is contrary to the Christian agenda of faith in scripture and loyalty to Jesus. It is the nature of belief not to examine too closely the object of that belief. "Love is blind," or perhaps blind is love. It would be an insult to ask your lover to prove that he or she is not a bad person. Most believers have had it drummed into their heads, Sunday after Sunday, that the bible is a "Good Book." They are taught that thinking for yourself is at least woefully inadequate, if not completely evil. Proverbs 3:5 says, "Trust in the Lord with all thine heart; and lean not unto thine own understanding." II Corinthians 10:5 says, "[bring] into captivity every thought to the obedience of Christ." This is a circular argument, of course. Don't question the bible. Why? Because the bible says so.

Few Christians ask whether the bible is morally acceptable. (If they do, they are labeled "liberals.") Such questioning is heretical to most believers. Whether or not you assume or judge the bible to be morally acceptable, the important question to believers is whether or not you accept its authority. In the minds of Christians, authority equals morality. God is sovereign.

"Do this because I said so" is the kind of thing you say to a small child. A toddler may not be mature enough to follow a line of reasoning, so parents might have to exercise authority to prohibit something dangerous. But the "authority" in this case is not what determines whether something is right or wrong. It is simply an exercise of the minimum restraint necessary to enforce protective, rational guidelines until the child is old enough to reason independently. The parent who treats a toddler in such a manner, temporarily emphasizing authority over rationale, still should be able to explain to another adult why the child's action would be dangerous or undesirable. The child, in later years, should be able to obtain a reasonable explanation from the parent. If not, the parent is a petty tyrant.

Besides being childish, the morality-as-authority argument is dangerous. People who do not question authority become easy prey to dictators. Cult leaders can manipulate followers who give them blind obedience. Many of the 900 followers of the Rev. Jim Jones drank the poisonous punch, *aware* of what was happening, because they were convinced that he was next to God. The Catholic and Lutheran

Nazis wore "God is with us" on their belts, convinced that Hitler was doing the work of Jesus in exterminating the Jews, as he claimed in one of his speeches. Certain Christian fanatics, such as the Christian Scientists, Pentecostals and other fundamentalists, allow their children to die of treatable illnesses because their church tells them that circumventing God's natural plan is a sin, or that Jesus will heal "all manner of diseases."

Here's a good question for those who think God's authority is the basis for morality: If God told you to kill someone, would you do it? Some Christians will immediately answer "Yes," arguing that some killing is justified (death penalty, war, self-defense), or that the "giver of life" has the simple right to take life.

Then try this question on a male believer: If God told you to rape someone, would you do it? Some Christians, ignorant of biblical injunctions to rape, might answer, "God would never ask me to do that." But this simply avoids the question. If God is the source of all morality, and if God asked you to do something that *you* considered immoral, would it matter what you thought? According to the bible we should simply obey God, even when it is difficult. Abraham found it difficult to obey God's command to kill his son, Isaac, but he was prepared to do it and his obedience was considered praiseworthy! Jephthah found it hard to murder his daughter, but he was obligated by a vow to God to go through with it, and he did, without condemnation. Both of these men, if they were truly moral, would have defied God regardless of the divine consequences. They should have said to God, "You may have the might, but you don't have the right." (Or, as I might say, "God, you created hell—you can go to hell.")

Suppose a man were to say to his wife, "Prove how much you love me by helping me rob a bank. And if you don't help, I will beat you." We would call such a bully abusive and criminal. Yet this same bankrupt chain-of-command mentality is taught in the bible: God decides what is right and wrong and if you don't play along you are punished in hell.

Speaking for myself, if the biblical heaven and hell exist, I would choose hell. Having to spend eternity pretending to worship a petty tyrant who tortures those who insult his authority would be more hellish than baking in eternal flames. There is no way such a bully can earn my admiration.

HUMANS HAVE NO INTRINSIC RIGHT TO FAIRNESS OR RESPECT

The bible nowhere states that every human being possesses an inherent right to be treated with respect or fairness. Generally, everything flows from God to humans, not the other way around. A true moral guide should have some principles. If humans are supposed to treat other humans in certain ways, or to avoid treating humans in other ways, then there should be some examination of the general value of human life and of human *rights*. Yet this is not to be found anywhere in the bible.

There are a few places where God appeared to respect certain key players, such as when the angel asked the Virgin Mary for her permission to be impregnated by the Holy Ghost. But even then her response was submissive rather than egalitarian: "Behold the handmaid of the Lord." (Luke 1:38) It is all on God's side. If God can grant rights then he can take them away, meaning that there actually are no human rights in God's scheme.

The biblical view of human nature is negative. Humans don't deserve respect; they deserve damnation. We are all tainted with Original Sin. Romans 3:12 says, "There is none that doeth good, no, not one." Eleven verses later Romans says, "For all have sinned, and come short of the glory of God." Job (the sexist) said, "Man that is born of a woman is of few days, and full of trouble... Who can bring a clean thing out of an unclean? Not one." (Job 14:1-4)

The view that humans are intrinsically evil is hardly commensurate with an ethical system based on mutual respect. On the contrary, it tends to produce a negative self-image in those who were raised in bible-believing churches, and a cynicism toward other humans. It can become something of a self-fulfilling prophecy. Witness televangelist Jimmy Swaggart, who preached that we are all corrupt and then proved it himself! If he had been raised with a healthier view of human nature, he may not have blown sexual temptation into such a demon in his mind, becoming obsessed with what he railed against. (Or was it the other way around? In either case, the bible fueled the problem.)

It is also historically clear that the true bible believers have little respect for the human rights of anyone outside of their church. I know Christians who will do business only with other Christians, when possible. We all know about the way Christians and other religionists have treated outsiders: Native Americans, Jews, American blacks and South-African natives, and scores of pagan peoples around the world who had the misfortune of being born and raised outside of the "true" faith. We all know about the Crusades in the name of Jesus, the Spanish Inquisition, the Catholic-Protestant bloodshed in Northern Ireland and the militant Christian factions in the Middle East.

Modern warm and fuzzy American Protestants who try to distance themselves from such intolerance and brutality should ask themselves: would I prefer my son or daughter to marry a Catholic, Jew, Muslim or atheist? Paul advised Christians: "Be ye not unequally yoked together with unbelievers: for what fellowship hath righteousness with unrighteousness? And what communion hath light with darkness?" (II Corinthians 6:14) The intrinsic intolerance of Christianity cannot be candy-coated.

Matthew 7:18-20 says, "A good tree cannot bring forth evil fruit, neither can a corrupt tree bring good fruit... Wherefore by their fruits ye shall know them." Those of us outside the historically bloody religions have no restraints against denouncing the "fruit" that has been produced by such trees as Christianity. If the bible contains any seeds of respect or fairness toward other humans, it is sadly absent from a reading of the text or from the institutions produced by it.

Good deeds, in the bible, are almost always connected with heavenly reward, "God's will," avoiding punishment or with a missionary agenda. Most "Christian charity" is given to prove the superiority of Christianity or to win converts, not because human life is good, valuable and worthy of respect in its own right.

Truly good Christian individuals don't find their motivation in the bible. They do good because they are good people. Bertrand Russell said, "Men tend to have the beliefs that suit their passions. Cruel men believe in a cruel God and use their belief to excuse their cruelty. Only kindly men believe in a kindly God, and they would be kindly in any case."

BIBLE CHARACTERS ARE POOR ROLE MODELS

We hear a lot of "God is love" sermons from the pulpit, but even a cursory glance at the bible reveals that God kills a lot of people. He drowned the entire population of the planet, saving one family. He sent a plague to kill all the first-born children in Egypt, human and animal. He rained fire and brimstone on Sodom, killing everyone—boys, girls, babies, pregnant women, animals. He sent his Israelite warriors to destroy the neighboring pagan tribes—men, women and children.

In I Samuel 6, the ark of the Lord was being transported across country and five farmers of Bethshemesh "rejoiced to see it." They opened the box and made a burnt offering to the Lord, and for this terrible sin God "smote the men of Bethshemesh, because they had looked into the ark of the Lord, even he smote of the people fifty thousand and threescore and ten men: and the people lamented, because the Lord had smitten many of the people with a great slaughter." Is it moral to kill 50,000 people for a petty offense? And exactly what was the crime? These men were trying to worship this very god, in their own way. Wouldn't a God of mercy understand their innocent mistake? What if one of my children gave me a birthday card with the words "Daddy, I luv you" and I punished them for spelling the word wrong? (By the way, is it reasonable to think there was a settlement of more than 50,000 at that time in history?)

In I Samuel 25, an industrious man named Nabal refused to hand his produce over to David and his troops who were passing through the area. "Shall I then take my bread, and my water, and my flesh that I have killed for my shearers, and give it unto men, whom I know not whence they be?" That is not an unreasonable complaint. Nabal had a moral obligation to his workers. In punishment for protecting what he rightfully owned, "the Lord smote Nabal, that he died."

In Numbers 25:16-17, "The Lord spake unto Moses, saying, Vex the Midianites, and smite them." Here is what happened six chapters later: "And they warred against the Midianites, as the Lord commanded Moses; and they slew all the males... And the children of Israel took all the women of Midian captives, and their little ones, and took the spoil of all their cattle, and all their flocks, and all their goods. And they burnt all their cities wherein they dwelt, and all their goodly castles, with fire. And they took all the spoil, and all the prey, both of men and beasts." Well, this isn't so bad, is it? They slaughtered the men and burned the cities, but they did save the women and children. Read on:

"And Moses was wroth with the officers... And Moses said unto them, Have ye saved all the women alive? Now therefore kill every male among the little ones, and kill every woman that hath known man by lying with him. [How would they know this?] But all the women children, that have not known a man by lying with him, keep alive for yourselves."

It gets worse. As they were dividing up the "booty" they counted all the animals, gold, jewels "and thirty and two thousand persons in all, of women that had not known man by lying with him" and "the Lord's tribute was thirty and two persons." It does not say exactly what happened to these 32 lucky girls, but after watching their fathers, sisters, brothers and mothers butchered by the Israelite marauders, they may have preferred to honor their own families and become burnt offerings rather than serve as "booty" for the priests of Jehovah.

Who will dare claim that this is moral? This is God himself, acting like a god. Listen to these threats of the loving God from Leviticus 26:14-38:

- "If ye will not hearken unto me, and will not do all these commandments...I will appoint over you terror, consumption, and the burning ague, that shall consume the eyes, and cause sorrow of heart: and ye shall sow your seed in vain, for your enemies shall eat it...and ye shall be slain before your enemies.

- I will punish you seven times more...for your land shall not yield her increase, neither shall the trees of the land yield their fruits... I will also send wild beasts among you, which shall rob you of your children, and destroy your cattle...and I will bring a sword upon you,...

- I will send the pestilence among you...ten women shall bake your bread in one oven...and ye shall eat and not be satisfied... And ye shall eat the flesh of your sons, and the flesh of your daughters...and I will make your cities waste...and I will bring the land into desolation: And I will scatter you among the heathen, and will draw out a sword after you... Then shall the land enjoy her sabbaths, as long as it lieth desolate...even then shall the land rest, and enjoy her sabbaths...and ye shall perish among the heathen."

So, the Sabbath will be observed, even if God has to kill everyone to make it happen. Does this string of threats spew from a stable or loving mind?

Deuteronomy repeats many of these threats, including the appetizing, "And thou shalt eat the fruit of thine own body, the flesh of thy sons and of thy daughters, which the Lord thy God hath given thee, ...so that the man that is tender among you, and very delicate, his eye shall be evil toward his brother, and toward the wife of his bosom, and toward the remnant of his children which he shall leave." You bet. All you tender-meated people should look over your shoulders!

The biblical God punishes children and grandchildren for things they did not do, and calls this "mercy." Exodus 34:6-7: "And the Lord passed by before him, and proclaimed, The Lord, The Lord God, merciful and gracious, longsuffering, and abundant in goodness and truth, Keeping mercy for thousands, forgiving iniquity and transgression and sin, and that will by no means clear the guilty; visiting the iniquity of the fathers upon the children, and upon the children's children, unto the third and to the fourth generation." Who thinks *this* is moral?

If your great-grandfather was a horse thief, should you be thrown in jail? (And to those American believers of European descent who do think reparations are due to the descendants of victims, I would ask them to give me their houses and property, if they are serious. It was their ancestors, after all, who stole the land from my ancestors.)

A moral and wise adult knows that children are sometimes ornery—kids will be kids. But God seems not to understand this. In II Kings 2:23-24, he massacred 42 loud-mouthed children: "And he [Elisha] went up from thence unto Bethel: and as he was going up by the way, there came forth little children out of the city, and mocked him, and said unto him, Go up, thou bald head; go up, thou bald head. And he turned back, and looked on them, and cursed them in the name of the Lord. And there came forth two she bears out of the wood, and tare forty and two children of them." This sounds like an R-rated version of *Little Red Riding Hood* or the *Three Little Pigs*, but true bible believers are forced to pretend that this nonsense is historical as well as moral.

God's thirst for blood sacrifice is unparalleled, starting with Cain and Abel. Millions of animals were slaughtered to appease the anger and vanity of the Israelite deity. God even accepted a *human* sacrifice:

Jephthah's daughter (Judges 11:30-40). In II Samuel 21:1-14 the sacrifice of seven of Saul's sons, who were hanged, caused God to be appeased.

In Leviticus 27:28-29, God orders that "devoted" (sacrificed) humans must be put to death: "No devoted thing...both of man and beast...shall be sold or redeemed...but shall surely be put to death." This is human sacrifice, pure and simple. (I suppose believers better not have any devoted pets, either.)

God sold the Israelites to the king of Mesopotamia for eight years (Judges 3:8). It doesn't say what God did with the money. He also sold them to the Moabites for 18 years (3:14), to Canaan for 20 years (4:2-3), to the Midianites for seven years (6:1), to the Philistines for 40 years (13:1) and to the Babylonians for 70 years. That's more than a century and a half of slavery—more than twice as long as slavery existed in the United States. Is *this* moral?

In Exodus 21, right after the Ten Commandments, God gives us laws for dealing with slaves. "If thou buy an Hebrew servant, six years he shall serve...his master shall bore his ear through with an aul...and if a man sell his daughter to be a maidservant, she shall not go out as the manservants do..." and so on. Not only is this unabashed slavery, it is *sexist* slavery, treating women as less valuable property. God never denounces the institution of slavery. He encourages it.

God discriminated against the disabled: "For whatsoever man he be that hath a blemish, he shall not approach: a blind man, or a lame, or he that hath a flat nose, or any thing superfluous. Or a man that is brokenfooted, or brokenhanded, Or crookbacked, or a dwarf, or that hath a blemish in his eye, or be scurvy, or scabbed, or hath his stones [testicles] broken...that he profane not my sanctuaries." (Leviticus 21:18-23) Whose fault is it if you are born a dwarf? I've seen some priests with flat noses approaching the altar—why are they disobeying scripture? Don't they know God is prejudiced against the disabled?

God engages in deliberate deceit. Ezekiel 14:9 says, "And if the prophet be deceived when he hath spoken a thing, I the Lord have deceived that prophet." II Thessalonians 2:11 reports: "God shall send them strong delusion, that they should believe a lie."

God uses language that would never be allowed in church: "Behold, I will corrupt your seed, and spread dung upon your faces, even the dung of your solemn feasts." (Malachi 2:3) "The Lord commanded: And thou shalt eat it as barley cakes, and thou shalt bake it with dung that cometh out of man, in their sight." (Ezekiel 4:12) In other words, God said, "Eat shit." Is this proper language for a moral example? Also:

- "I will cut off from Jeroboam him that pisseth against the wall." (I Kings 14:10)

- "I will discover thy skirts upon thy face, and I will show the nations thy nakedness and thy kingdoms thy shame." (Nahum 3:5,6)

And the following misogynist verse celebrates sexual molestation: "Therefore the Lord will smite with a scab the crown of the head of the daughters of Zion, and the Lord will discover ("lay bare"—*NRSV*) their secret parts." (Isaiah 3:17) "Secret parts" is a euphemistic translation of the Hebrew word *poth,* which refers to the vagina, literally "hinged opening." Some pseudo-translations, such as the *NIV,* have tried to cover up this embarrassing image of a molesting deity by dishonestly translating *poth* as "scalp."

God created evil (Isaiah 45:7) and hell. God blames everyone for Adam's sin. God is partial to one race of people, which is racism. He gets jealous (Exodus 20:5) and, in fact, he says that his *name* is Jealousy: "For the Lord, whose name is Jealous, is a jealous God." (Exodus 34:14) The Israelites can perhaps be forgiven for referring to their deity by the generic name for "God" ("El" or "Elohim") or by the unpronounceable "YHWH" rather than by his real name. It just doesn't sound right to begin a prayer with "Dear Jealous."

There is not enough space to mention all of the places in the bible where God committed, commanded or condoned murder. In Ruth Green's *Born Again Skeptic's Guide to the Bible,* it takes 10 tightly typeset pages just to list briefly the killings of Jehovah. Is this the kind of character we would let our kids spend the day with? This sounds more like the stuff of a violent, X-rated movie than a guide for moral behavior.

Hearing these indictments, some Christians might ask, "Why are you attacking God?" I would respond, "Why are you looking the other way?" Christian apologists can dig up bible verses that say or demonstrate that "God is love," but how does this help? The most that can be proved with oppositional verses is that the bible is contradictory. Hitler's love for his wife, dog and close followers did not excuse the Holocaust.

WHAT ABOUT JESUS?

Some Christians will complain that we should not be concerned with the Old Testament deity because Jesus has superseded all of that. The words and actions of Jesus Christ are the perfect role model, they claim. Let's see if that is true.

In Luke 12:47,48, Jesus said: "And that servant [Greek *doulos* = slave] which knew his Lord's will, and prepared not himself, neither did according to his will, shall be beaten with many stripes. But he that knew not, and did commit things worthy of stripes, shall be beaten with few stripes." Jesus encouraged the beating of slaves! Is this an example of moral superiority? Some Christians will argue that this is just a parable based on the culture of the day, and that Jesus did not mean it to be taken literally. But an examination of the context proves otherwise. Jesus had just given a parable about servants a few verses earlier, and Peter had asked for an elaboration (12:41). The quote about beating slaves is in the explanation, not the parable. Besides, what an ugly thing to say! Even if it were a metaphor, it is a poor choice of words. It would be like a politician making an anti-Semitic or black joke and then saying, "I wasn't serious."

Why did Jesus, the unrivaled moral example, never once speak out against slavery? Why did the loving, wise Son of God forget to mention that human bondage is a brutal institution? Why did he incorporate it into his teachings, as if it were the most natural thing in the world? I'll tell you why: because he supported it. The Old Testament endorses and encourages slavery, and Jesus, being equal to God, supposedly wrote the old laws, so he *had* to support slavery. This is not to concede that a man named Jesus actually uttered these words in history. It merely demonstrates that the Gospels were written by human beings who were locked into their culture. Not only did they refuse to denounce slavery, they could not conceive that there was anything wrong with it.

Jesus never spoke out against poverty or did anything to eliminate it. In fact, like Mother Teresa, he taught that the poor should accept their lot in life. In Mark 14:3-9, some of Christ's disciples objected to the waste of a costly ointment used to anoint Jesus' head, "for it might have been sold for more than three hundred pence, and have been given to the poor." Jesus responded, "Ye have the poor with you always, and whensoever ye will ye may do them good: but me ye have not always."

This is selfish and callous. He offers no plan or hope for eliminating poverty and treats feeding the poor as an optional activity that is not as important as worshipping *him*—like many modern evangelists who squander contributions from the faithful on lavish lifestyles. Or like the pope, who lives in opulence. Where were the wise words of Jesus regarding waste and inequality? Where were the social programs that would lessen poverty?

Jesus indicated that he and his followers were a special class, above the rest, free to take liberally from the property and work of others. In Mark 2:23 he and his disciples roamed through cornfields, taking what they wanted, which was doubly unlawful since it was the Sabbath. In Matthew 21, Jesus instructed his disciples to take a horse without first asking the owner. This is the kind of attitude that a landlord or king might have adopted toward the peasants.

Jesus upheld the Old Testament view of women. Not a single woman was chosen to be among the 12 disciples or to sit at the Last Supper. This is cited as one of the reasons the pope does not approve of ordaining women. But does he forget that the disciples, besides being male, were also all Jews? How can there be an Italian, Polish or German pope, an Irish bishop or a Mexican priest?

Jesus was violent. He cast some devils into swine and "the whole herd of swine ran violently down a steep place into the sea, and perished in the waters." (Matthew 8:32) Why not show a little more respect for life? He also made a whip and threatened to harm the money changers, driving them out of the temple. (John 2:15) These were people who were practicing free enterprise, most likely using their profits to provide for their families. More than that, they were offering a service to worshippers who would otherwise be unable to donate to the temple devoted to Jesus' father, hence to Jesus himself! Was he totally nuts?

His violence was tempered with irrationality. "Now in the morning as he returned into the city, he hungered. And when he saw a fig tree in the way, he came to it, and found nothing thereon, but leaves only, and said unto it, Let no fruit grow on thee henceforward for ever. And presently the fig tree withered away." (Matthew 21:18-19, repeated in Mark 11:13-14, which adds that it was not even fig season.) Is it kind or rational to destroy a plant that happens to be out of season when you are hungry? Is such behavior indicative of mental health?

In Luke 19 Jesus told a parable which includes these ruthless words: "But those mine enemies, which would not that I should reign over them, bring them hither, and slay them before me." He is clearly comparing the "Lord" in the parable to himself. In Matthew 10:34 Jesus said, "I came not to send peace, but a sword." In Luke 22:36 he told his disciples that "he that hath no sword, let him sell his garment, and buy one."

He was callous. In Matthew 15:22-28, Jesus refused to heal a sick child until the mother pressured him. What if the mother had not been persistent? Would he have withheld his magical favors and let the child die? And why would God have to be asked in the first place? If my children are gravely ill and I don't take them to the hospital and they later ask me why, and I say "Because you didn't ask me" or "Because you didn't ask me humbly enough," can I be called a good parent?

In Matthew 19:12, showing his pro-life sensibilities, Jesus encourages castration: "There be eunuchs, which have made themselves eunuchs for the kingdom of heaven's sake. He that is able to receive it, let him receive it." Modern believers are eager to interpret this verse figuratively. The *New International Version* loosely (and hopefully) translates "made eunuch" as "renounced marriage." But the literal meaning is "castrate" and many devout Christian men in history have done it to themselves, including the early church father Origen and entire monastic orders. Jesus gives no indication that he is speaking in a parable, or that his words mean anything other than what he said. *He that is able to receive it, let him receive it.* This is no moral precept—this is sick. Castration keeps babies from being born just as effectively as abortion, so why aren't pro-lifers picketing churches that follow Jesus? After all, Jesus never once mentioned abortion, pro or con. He never gave advice to women about how to deal with an unwanted pregnancy. So, modern Christians who do give such advice are acting very un-Christlike.

We hear a lot of talk about the humble Jesus, but his words reveal something different. He looked at his disciples "with anger." (Mark 3:5) He said that he was "greater than the temple" (Matthew 12:6), "greater than Jonas [Jonah]" (Matthew 12:41) and "greater than Solomon." He also appeared to suffer from the paranoia that afflicts dictators: "He that is not with me is against me." (Matthew 12:30) Of course, that is not true. Jesus did not grasp the simple concept of neutrality. Would he also say, "He that is not against me is with me?"

But probably the worst of all of Jesus' ideas is the teaching of hell. He did not invent the concept of eternal punishment, but the promotion of the Christian doctrine of hell originated with Jesus. In the Old Testament, hell is just death or the grave. With Jesus, hell became a place of everlasting torment. In Mark 9:43, Jesus said that hell is "the fire that never shall be quenched." In Matthew 13:41-42, Jesus gives us a graphic (and almost gleeful) description of the place he created: "The Son of man shall send forth his angels, and they shall gather out of his kingdom all things that offend, and them which do iniquity; and shall cast them into a furnace of fire: there shall be wailing and gnashing of teeth." Hitler's gas ovens were horrendous and the suffering was unspeakable, but they did not burn forever. The murdered victims of the Holocaust suffer no more, but the victims of God's anger will scream forever and ever.

I don't believe in Jesus or in God, so I qualify as one of those "things that offend" in the above verse. Anyone who thinks it is moral for someone like me—a person who has used reason and kindness to come to conclusions—to be eternally punished for my views hasn't the faintest concept of morality. Any system of thought or any religion that contains such a threat of physical violence is morally bankrupt. For this reason alone, Jesus deserves to be denounced as a tyrant.

And who could possibly think he was wise? The moral teachings of Jesus include these pearls of wisdom:

- don't make any plans for the future (Matthew 6:34)

- don't save any money (Matthew 6:19-20)

- don't become wealthy (Mark 10:21, 25)

- sell everything you have and give it to the poor (Luke 12:33)

- don't work to obtain food, such as meat, because it doesn't last forever (John 6:27)

- don't have sexual urges (Matthew 5:28)

- marrying a divorced woman is committing adultery (Matthew 5:32)

- act in such a way that people will want to persecute you (Matthew 5:11)

- let everyone know that you are special and better than the rest (Matthew 5:13-14)

- hate your family (Luke 14:26)

- take money from those who have no savings and give it to the rich investors (Luke 19:23-26)

- if someone steals from you, don't try to get it back (Luke 6:30)

- if someone hits you, invite them to do it again (Matthew 5:39)

- if you lose a lawsuit, give more than the judgment (Matthew 5:40)

- if someone forces you to walk a mile, walk two miles (Matthew 5:41)

- if anyone asks you for anything, give it to them without question (Matthew 5:42)

- if you do something wrong with your hand, cut it off, and if you do something wrong with your eye, pluck it out (Matthew 5:29, 30—said in a sexual context)

- if you are a man, then a good way to make points with "the kingdom" is to avoid women (Matthew 19:12)

Much could be said about the moral character of other biblical personages, such as Noah (drunkard), Abraham (who lied about his wife), Lot (incestuous father), Moses (a murderer), David (adulterer and murderer), Solomon (polygamist), Peter (who swung swords and lied like a coward), Paul (who told women to keep silent) and many others. Believers could argue that these are mere mortals, that we should expect them sometimes to act according to their corrupt human nature, and that this actually proves the need for a Savior who can love evil creatures in spite of our humanity. Only in a theological context might this be a plausible, if unsatisfactory, response. The fact remains that it is difficult to find consistent examples of moral behavior in the bible. We might grant the benefit of the doubt to the human characters in the bible, but why should we expect any better when the deities themselves—God and Jesus—act like thugs or lunatics who ought to be locked up?

MANY MORAL PRECEPTS OF THE BIBLE ARE UNACCEPTABLE

We have already noted that the bible encourages slavery. It took the Civil War to rid ourselves of the fruits of such inhumanity in the United States, a task that was made more difficult due to the preachers (mainly standing in southern pulpits) who used the bible to defend their position. Not all churches were actively pro-slavery, but those that were found little difficulty supporting slavery with scripture. Why would a moral deity not have known this would happen? A single word from Jesus, if he were truly God, would have shaved 2,000 years off the time it took us to progress out of human bondage in most parts of the world. Unfortunately, it does still exist in some countries and regions.

Even though the phrase "original sin" does not appear in the bible, the scriptural concept that human nature is intrinsically evil has been an insidious doctrine. Jesus admits that mere humans can do good things, but we are nevertheless evil by nature: "If ye then, being evil, know how to give good gifts unto your children..." (Matthew 7:11, Luke 11:3) What worse psychological damage could be done to children than to tell them that they basically are no good? What does this do to self-image? How many children go to sleep at night afraid of hell?

Jesus said, "If a man abide not in me, he is cast forth as a branch, and is withered; and men gather them, and cast them into the fire, and they are burned." (John 15:6) All through history, the church has interpreted this verse literally, using it to execute heretics with fire and other forms of capital punishment. Somebody tell Bruno, Servetus and other victims of the Catholic Inquisition and Protestant Reformation that the bible is a morally superior book.

Exodus 22:18 says, "Thou shalt not suffer a witch to live." This one verse was responsible for the murder of thousands, perhaps millions, of women who were believed to be witches. Anyone who thinks this is a good moral teaching should become a fascist. It is manifestly *immoral* to deal with enemies, real or perceived, by genocide.

One of the most damaging ideas in the bible is the concept of a Lord and Master. The loftiest biblical principles are obedience, submission and faith, rather than reason, intelligence and human values. Worshippers become humble servants of a dictator, expected to kneel before this king, lord, master, god—giving adoring praise and taking orders. According to the bible, we all eventually will be *forced* to bow before Jesus: "every knee shall bow to me, and every tongue shall confess to God." (Romans 14:11) The master/slave relationship has become so ingrained in the Jewish/Christian/Muslim world that independent thinkers are considered heretical, evil rebels. Prophets, popes and ayatollahs have capitalized on this dichotomy of abasement in order to manipulate gullible followers. And even if they hadn't—even if the church had had a blameless history—why is there merit in submission?

The United States of America is a proudly rebellious nation. We fought a revolution to kick the lord and master out of our affairs. It was a good and moral act to rebel against the tyranny of the king. It seems incongruous that so many Americans, who would never tolerate a dictator in government, are so eager to pay tribute to a universal Lord. Jesus said, "Render therefore unto Caesar the things which are Caesar's; and unto God the things that are God's." But what about the individual? What about democracy? Jesus considered that human beings are cogs in someone else's machine, be it God's or Caesar's. This goes against the grain of a modern representative society. It is not moral to be told to submit to a Caesar or to a god.

WHAT ABOUT THE GOOD TEACHINGS OF THE BIBLE?

Most Christians talk a lot about the bible, but don't know what it says. They *think* it is filled with wonderful advice. Many of them act shocked, incredulous or offended when skeptics quote horrible scriptures. During many debates and TV and radio shows on which I have quoted unsavory bible verses, biblically illiterate callers or audience members have asked me, "What bible are you reading?" And I might reply, "What bible are you *not* reading?" Most "positive" teachings in the bible are uninspired, inadequate or dangerous.

I participated in a debate in Atlanta in 1988 on the subject "Is the bible an acceptable guide for moral behavior?" My opponent was Dr. Walter Lowe, professor of systematic theology at Candler School of Theology at Emory University. During his entire prepared statement he never once used the bible to support his position! He spent his time debunking the critical mindset of skeptics and presenting a "framework" for certain liberal understandings of Christianity, as if the mere discounting of skepticism could stand in place of evidence that the bible is a good book. My presentation was filled with specific quotes demonstrating that there is much immorality in the bible. His rebuttal was simply to label my interpretation of scripture as "fundamentalist." I was unwilling to give the bible the benefit of the doubt, he claimed, or to understand that the moral principles are contained over and above what the text actually says.

I hear this criticism a lot. If we freethinkers were mature and sophisticated enough to study the scriptures as they *should* be studied (higher criticism, context, metaphor, cultural elements, and so on), then we would have fewer problems understanding them. But this is nothing more than saying, "If you held my point of view, then you would hold my point of view." *Everyone* thinks his or her interpretation of the bible is the correct one. I agree that taking the bible at face value is simplistic; however, liberal scholars should admit that skepticism regarding scriptural integrity is greater among liberal experts. They cannot deny that there is a storm of disagreement among scholars, theologians and ordinary believers about the "true" meaning of the text.

If a god is trying to get his message across to the masses of humanity, why did he do it in such a way that the only people qualified to grasp its true significance are those with doctorates in biblical studies? And then, how do we know which authorities to believe? What the bible means *in plain English* is what most people read. If it embarrasses itself in plain English, then it fails to make its point. In any event, Dr. Lowe did not explain how his sophisticated liberal understanding makes the brutal scriptures less brutal. No matter how you interpret it, administering the death penalty for picking up sticks is cruel and barbaric.

We freethinkers actually do know what the bible says. Mark Twain said: "It's not the parts of the bible I don't understand that bother me; it's the parts I do understand."

Toward the end of the debate I asked Dr. Lowe to give an example of a good moral teaching in the bible. He was unable to cite a single verse. Curiously, he did not mention the Ten Commandments, the Beatitudes, "turn the other cheek," "love thy neighbor as thyself" or the Golden Rule, passages that historically have stood as shining examples in the "Good Book." Yet a closer look at even these "good" teachings shows that the shine is rather dull.

THE TEN COMMANDMENTS

After a speech in which I mentioned a lawsuit by the Freedom From Religion Foundation seeking to move the Ten Commandments from the Colorado capitol grounds to an appropriate private location, such as a church, a woman asked me, "How can you object to the Ten Commandments? They are the most perfect set of laws ever given to humans! Our country is based on those laws." People who make such statements apparently have never studied the Ten Commandments (or American history).

Only three of the Ten Commandments have any relevance to American law: homicide, theft and perjury. (Adultery and Sabbath laws are still on the books in some states, but they are artifacts of theocracy.)

The first four commandments have nothing at all to do with ethics or moral behavior:

First Commandment: "Thou shalt have no other gods before me." This was spoken by *Elohim* (ironically, a plural name for the god *El*), who is the "Lord" of the Israelites. This is the equivalent of establishing the nation of Israel, not the United States of America. It can be taken as either monotheistic (only one god) or henotheistic (only one supreme god), and in any case is contrary to the American constitutional guarantees of freedom of conscience and against an establishment of religion. In the United States, we are free to worship many gods, one god or no gods at all. Elohim does not appear in any of the governing documents on which our country was founded.

Second Commandment: "Thou shall not make for yourself a graven image, or any likeness of anything that is in heaven above, or that is in the earth beneath, or that is in the water under the earth." This statement, ironically, appears on a graven image monolith of the Ten Commandments in many locations. As law, it would violate free speech. At face value, it rules out all art! (Later versions of this commandment prohibit "molten" images.) And how do Catholics get around this? Their churches and homes are filled with images of saints and virgins. Actually, the Catholic Church tried to get around this injunction by deleting the second commandment altogether! Some of the granite markers of the Ten Commandments that have been put on public property actually (humorously) omit this one and cut the last commandment into two prohibitions against coveting in order to round it out to ten.

Third Commandment: "Thou shalt not take the name of the Lord thy God in vain." This would be like prohibiting criticism of the president or other public officials. It is undemocratic and contrary to free speech.

Fourth Commandment: "Remember the sabbath day." According to the biblical application of this law (as we already saw in Numbers 15), millions of Americans deserve capital punishment.

The first four commandments are religious edicts, not moral guidelines. They have nothing to do with ethics or how we should treat each other. They certainly have no official place in a country that "shall make no law respecting an establishment of religion."

Fifth Commandment: "Honor thy father and thy mother: that thy days may be long upon the land" is the first statement in the Decalogue that approaches morality, although there are no details here explaining exactly how to honor parents. Do we obey them in everything? How long do we obey them? Until they die? There is obviously some merit in the idea expressed by this commandment, but there is precious little guidance here beyond a general principle that parents should be respected. Isn't this just another variation of the bible's "respect authority" message? Wouldn't a moral principle suggest that you should not do anything to hurt your parents, that you should not take advantage of them, and that you should treat them with the basic respect deserved by all human beings? What if your parents are uneducated and poor advisors? What if they belong to a kooky or abusive religious cult? What if they are evil? We all know that some parents do not deserve to be honored or obeyed. How do you "honor" a father who commits incest? Notice also that the rationale "that thy days may be long" is an appeal to self-interest, not to the value of parents as human beings.

Sixth Commandment: "Thou shalt not kill" is the first genuine moral statement in the Decalogue because it deals with the issue of real harm in the real world, although it is unqualified. Does this mean that capital punishment is wrong? What about self defense? What about war? What about euthanasia requested by the terminally ill? The drawback of this law is its absoluteness—good laws make distinctions. Since the actions and commands of God burst with bloodthirstiness, this commandment seems to lose its import. Besides, prohibitions of murder existed long before the Ten Commandments or the Israelites appeared on the scene. It is not as if the human race never would have figured out that it is wrong to kill without some tablets coming down from a mountain. Laws against murder and manslaughter based on self-preservation and social stability have found their way into almost every culture before and after Moses, and it would be odd if the Israelites did not have a similar principle. (See Chapter 11 for more on this commandment.)

Seventh Commandment: "Thou shalt not commit adultery" is also a good idea, though it is not against the law. And if it were, it hardly merits the death penalty: "And the man that committeth adultery with another man's wife, even he that committeth adultery with his neighbor's wife, the adulterer and the adulteress shall surely be put to death." (Leviticus 20:10) Adultery involves a broken promise between consenting adults and has nothing to do with a government. In many, if not most, cases it is destructive to a relationship and affects children if the marriage falls apart as a result. (Other things, such as fundamentalism, can cause the same problem.) But adultery by consenting adults does not fall into the category of a malicious or harmful felony. It is a legitimate concern of ethics; however, it is no crime. Why don't the Ten Commandments mention rape? What about incest? How about the more useful "Thou shalt not beat thy wife?" Why don't the Ten Commandments tell husbands that it is immoral to force an unwilling wife to have intercourse? Why doesn't the bible say that it is wrong for you to have sex, even with your spouse, if you knowingly have a sexually transmitted disease (which the bible would do if it were relevant to today). Although adultery is important, does it rate the Big Ten? In the bible, women were considered the property of men (see Tenth Commandment), so adultery was really a crime of theft.

Eighth Commandment: "Thou shalt not steal" is generally good advice and makes good law. Except in wartime most cultures, before and after the bible, have observed statutes that respect the property of others. But what about exceptions? The Ten Commandments, couched in absolute terms, allow no situational dilemmas. Would it be immoral to steal bread from a wealthy person to feed your starving child? Isn't Robin Hood considered a folk hero? Nevertheless, most cultures recognize that taking someone's rightful property without permission, in principle, is generally wrong. Do Christians claim that without the Tablets from Mount Sinai it never would have dawned on the human race that stealing is wrong?

Ninth Commandment: "Thou shalt not bear false witness" is also a generally good principle, but there is no universal law in America against telling lies. We have adequate laws against perjury and false advertising. But we all know that it is sometimes necessary to tell a lie in order to protect someone from harm. Lies in wartime are considered virtuous. The biblical prostitute Rahab was considered virtuous because she lied to protect Israelite spies (Hebrews 11:31). If I knew the whereabouts of a woman who was being hunted by her abusive husband, I would consider it a moral act to lie to the man. True morality is being able to weigh and compare the relative merits of the consequences of one action against another. It is flexible. The bible, on the other hand, makes absolute statements without admitting the possibility of ethical dilemmas. As with killing and stealing, most cultures through history have made honesty a high ideal, with or without the Ten Commandments.

Tenth Commandment: "Thou shalt not covet thy neighbor's house... wife... manservant... maidservant... ox... ass... nor any thing that is thy neighbor's." If there were a law based on this commandment, our entire system of free enterprise would collapse! Notice that this treats a wife like property. It does not say "Thou shalt not covet thy neighbor's husband" because it is assumed that everything, including law, is directed at males. This is a plainly silly commandment. How can you command someone not to covet? And why would you? If stealing is wrong, then there is no need for this commandment. If I tell you that you have a beautiful house and that I wish I had it for myself, is that immoral? (Some claim that "covet" in this verse more properly means "to cast an evil eye" or spell upon something, and this should be viewed as a prohibition of sorcery. But the Hebrew word *châmad*, according to *Strong's Concordance*, means "to delight in: beauty, greatly beloved, covet, delectable thing, delight, desire, goodly, lust, pleasant, precious thing.")

So the Ten Commandments are composed of four religious edicts that have nothing to do with ethics, three one-dimensional prohibitions that are irrelevant to modern law, and three shallow absolutes that are useful but certainly not unique to the Judeo-Christian system. Any one of us could easily come up with a more sensible, thorough and ethical code for human behavior.

From the perspective of biblical criticism, there is a more serious problem with the traditional Ten Commandments. It is the wrong batch of laws! The common listing (such as inscribed on the tombstone-like granite monuments at the Denver and Austin capitols) is from Exodus 20, but most people don't realize that these laws are not called the Ten Commandments in that chapter.

When Moses took his first trip up the mountain, he came back down with no stone tablets at all. He simply spoke what he said God told him and that list of edicts in Exodus 20 is what made it into Jewish and Christian tradition (as well as the humorously tacky movie by that name) as the "Ten Commandments."

Moses went back up the mountain a second time, and this time he did come back with laws engraved by the finger of God with ten commandments, though not formally called the Ten Commandments. Moses smashed those tablets to pieces when he saw the children of Israel worshipping the golden calf. (Wow. If I were carrying an original hand-written document from God, I would take better care of it than that.)

So, Moses went back up the mountain a third time to get a replacement, and what God told him would be identical to the previous list. (This clearly means they were more important than what was merely spoken in Exodus 20.) The set of laws inscribed on the second set of tablets that Moses brought back from his third trip up the mountain, listed in Exodus 34:28 and Deuteronomy 4:13 (a retelling of Exodus 34), is the only set called the Ten Commandments. It is quite revealing to read Exodus 34: "And the Lord said unto Moses, Hew thee two tables of stone like unto the first: and I will write upon these tables the words that were in the first tables, which thou brakest. And be ready in the morning, and come up in the morning unto mount Sinai..." Moses obeyed, "And he was there with the Lord forty days and forty nights; he did neither eat bread, nor drink water. And he wrote upon the tables the words of the covenant, the Ten Commandments." Here is the list Moses got the third time around, the final authorized, edited and proofed version of the Ten Commandments:

1. Thou shalt worship no other god. (The same as Exodus 20; so far so good.)

2. Thou shalt make thee no molten gods. (So, graven images are okay now?)

3. The feast of unleavened bread shalt thou keep. (My family never did this!)

4. Six days thou shalt work, but on the seventh day thou shalt rest. (Another match.)

5. Thou shalt observe the feast of weeks. (What is this? When is this?)

6. Thrice in the year shall all your menchildren appear before the Lord God. (Boys only? And how, exactly, do they get up there every four months?)

7. Thou shalt not offer the blood of my sacrifice with leaven. (What?)

8. Neither shall the sacrifice of the feast of the passover be left until the morning. (Because the meat will spoil overnight?)

9. The first of the firstfruits of thy land thou shalt bring unto the house of the Lord thy God. (This applies to farmers, so most of us are off the hook.)

10. Thou shalt not seethe a kid in his mother's milk. (No problem. That one's easy to keep.)

What is this? These are the real Ten Commandments? They only have a 20 percent match with Exodus 20. Did the rules change between visits? Did God lose his memory? What happened to homicide, theft and perjury? Is adultery okay now? What might have happened with a fourth visit, or a fifth? Notice that these are not additional commandments: they are "the words that were in the first tables, which thou brakest." If you have ever been tempted to boil a goat in the milk of its mother, now you know better. If I were still a Christian, I would be embarrassed that the God I thought I admired could be so forgetful and so petty. And so downright weird.

Other religions have lists of laws. The Ten Precepts of Buddhism (at least 500 B.C.E.) include 1) abstinence from destroying life, 2) abstinence from stealing, 3) abstinence from impurity, 4) abstinence from lying, 5) abstinence from strong drinks and intoxicating liquor, and five more rules for monks only. Notice that these are "precepts," not commandments, and though they also devote wasted space to religious rules, they were probably easier to carry. They show that we humans are not so stupid that we couldn't figure out on our own that there is something wrong with killing, stealing and lying, and we did this long before the Israelites claimed the copyright. The human race has a tendency to make behavior lists and the biblical Ten Commandments are not unique.

Did things get any better with Jesus? The Old Testament is, after all old. As Julia Sweeney says in her hilarious play and movie *Letting Go of God*: "The world 'Old' is right there in the title!" Perhaps the "New" Testament will be an improvement.

THE GOLDEN RULE

The phrase "Golden Rule" does not appear in the bible. Neither does the famous "do unto others" wording. What Jesus was actually reported to have said is this: "Therefore all things whatsoever ye would that men should do to you, do ye even so to them: for this is the law and the prophets." (Matthew 7:12) The author of Luke relates it this way: "And as ye would that men should do to you, do ye also to them likewise." (Luke 6:31)

Matthew's version is interesting. It appears to parallel an earlier wording of the same idea by Rabbi Hillel in 10 C.E.: "What is hateful to you, do not to your fellowmen. That is the entire Law; all the rest is commentary." (Talmud, Shabbat, 31a) The Golden Rule is not unique to Jesus, nor did it start with Christianity.

In Hinduism (Brahmanism), around 300 B.C.E.: "This is the sum of duty: Do naught unto others which would cause you pain if done to you." (Mahabharata, 5, 1517. The Vedic period of Hinduism goes back to 1500 B.C.E.)

In Buddhism we read: "Hurt not others in ways that you yourself would find hurtful." (Udana-Varga, 5, 18)

In Confucianism, which started around 500 B.C.E.: "Surely it is the maxim of loving-kindness: Do not unto others that you would not have them do unto you." (Analects, 15, 23)

In Taoism we have, "Regard your neighbor's gain as your own gain, and your neighbor's loss as your own loss." (T'ai Shang Kan Ying P'ien. The date of this writing is uncertain, but it was probably between 900-1200 C.E. Taoism came into its own around the fourth century B.C.E.)

Zoroastrianism: "That nature alone is good which refrains from doing unto another whatsoever is not good for itself." (Dadistan-i-dinik, 94, 5. This particular quote came after Christianity, but the religion goes back to about 1500 B.C.E.)

Some theologians claim that the Christian version of the Golden Rule is superior because it is phrased as the positive "Do" rather than the negative "Do not." (So, what does that say about the thou-shalt-nots of the Ten Commandments?)

I personally think that the negative version is more useful. The problem with "Do unto others" is, what if you have bad taste? What if you are a masochist? Should you "do unto others" what you would like to have done unto yourself? What if you enjoy being preached at? Should you pester those who might not enjoy it? Should you prepare meals or buy gifts for others based on what *you* like? What if you are an ascetic? Would you withhold a comfortable life from others? What if you have bizarre sexual preferences? Should you do unto others as you would have them do unto you?

This rule does not deserve a gold medal. It would be better titled the "Bronze Guideline."

While the positive version tells you to "do unto others," there are many people who don't want anything done to them at all. Although phrased positively, the Golden Rule does not give any positive guidance. It does not say, "Do kind things, peaceful things, compassionate things to others." The negative version, on the other hand, allows people to be left alone. It rightly recognizes the essence of morality: try to minimize harm. I like the Hindu and Buddhist versions because they identify harm as the real culprit in moral decisions.

Whether phrased positively or negatively, what do you do with a wife who hates back rubs and a husband who loves them? The positive expression of the rule would tell the husband to give his wife a back rub, which she doesn't want. The negative version would tell the wife not to give her husband a back rub, which he would love to have! Either way they lose.

Jesus' Bronze Guideline has sometimes been called the Law of Reciprocity. The general concept is to reflect on how your actions affect others, which is essential to ethical reasoning. But since it is not unique to Jesus, and since the Christian version is poorly phrased, it hardly supports the claim that the bible is a superior guide for moral behavior.

LOVE THY NEIGHBOR

Closely related to the Golden Rule is "love thy neighbor." In Leviticus 19:18 we find the commandment: "Thou shalt not avenge, nor bear any grudge against the children of thy people, but thou shalt love thy neighbor as thyself." Although this is not found in any version of the Ten Commandments, Jesus and Paul treat it as if it were on the main list.

In Matthew 19:16 a man asked Jesus how to achieve eternal life and Jesus replied, "Keep the commandments." The man asked, "Which? Jesus said, "Thou shalt do no murder, Thou shalt not commit adultery, Thou shalt not steal, Thou shalt not bear false witness, honour thy father and thy mother: and, Thou shalt love thy neighbor as thyself." If God had known that "love thy neighbor" was to be one of the biggies, why did he not include it in his Big Ten? Couldn't the rule about boiling a goat in its mother's milk be moved somewhere else to make space for it? (Of course, this was before word processors, and once something is engraved in stone...) On the other hand, perhaps this rearranging of rules in midstream is evidence of moral development. Maybe God, once he became a human being, actually became a better person. Maybe gods have to grow up, too. At face value, loving your neighbor does seem superior to worrying about mixing blood and leaven.

This passage does present a problem for most Protestants, who are taught that salvation comes by faith alone, not by keeping the commandments. When the man asked Jesus how to achieve eternal life, why didn't Jesus say "Believe on me" as Martin Luther preached instead of "Keep the commandments" as the popes preached? The bible is contradictory.

In Romans 13:8-9 Paul lists some important commandments and also includes "love thy neighbor": "for he that loveth another hath fulfilled the law. For this, Thou shalt not commit adultery, Thou shalt not kill, Thou shalt not steal, Thou shalt not bear false witness, Thou shalt not covet; and if there be any other commandment, it is briefly comprehended in this saying, namely, Thou shalt love thy neighbour as thyself." In Galatians 5 Paul wrote: "For all the law is fulfilled in one word, even in this; Thou shalt love thy neighbour as thyself." James 2:8 said it also. So, according to Jesus, we should remove those Ten Commandments from government property. All we need is love. Love is all we need.

While we all agree that love is good, this rule is not specific. It does not give any advice about how to treat others. What about people who do not love themselves—how can they love others "as themselves?" What if you were raised in a dysfunctional and abusive family and have a very low self-image? What if you are suicidal?

It is important to understand that "love thy neighbor" in the Old Testament meant something less than in the New Testament. In the Leviticus wording it deals with "the children of thy people," not with the entire earth. The word "neighbor" simply meant fellow Israelite. This is obvious when we observe how God's people treated other nations. In the context of the Old Testament, "love thy neighbor" is actually discriminatory. It would be like Ku Klux Klan leaders advising their followers to "love your white neighbors." It was perfectly allowable for God's people to hate the heathen. King David said that he hated them "with perfect hatred." (Psalm 139:22)

Jesus enhanced the concept by making it universal: "Ye have heard that it hath been said, Thou shalt love thy neighbour, and hate thine enemy. But I say unto you, Love your enemies, bless them that curse you, do good to them that hate you, and pray for them which despitefully use you, and persecute you." This is an improvement over Israelite imperialism, but the fact that it is less discriminatory does not necessarily make it an exceptional moral guide. We certainly can't base any laws on this—no one will go to prison for not loving. Some Christians feel that "love your enemy" is so unnatural, so nonintuitive, so shockingly different, that it elevates Jesus to a whole new level of compassion. But I think it is actually less moral than our natural human instincts. There are some enemies who ought not to be loved. Some enemies should be hated. If love is just a blanket imperative that ignores the qualities of its object, then it becomes meaningless. Sure, we humanists can "love" the human race, treating all people fairly—innocent until proven guilty, if you will—but as moral agents we have an obligation *not* to love at times.

Love can't be commanded. No one has the right to tell me to love someone else. I can treat people with fairness. I can give respect where respect is due. But I can't just turn on love. Love, if it has any special meaning at all, is reserved for those who are dear to me, for those who have earned my admiration, for those whom I find attractive or lovable. It is contrary to human nature to expect that I can have equal feelings for all people, and it cheapens love to bring everyone to the same level. When you say "I love you" to your spouse or lover, try adding "but it could have been anyone else because I love all my neighbors and enemies, too."

What if my neighbor is a jerk? What if after all my sincere attempts to be friendly and fair, my neighbor continues to act destructively? Is it healthy for me to pretend to love this person? I might be concerned for this person's lifestyle (or I might not) and wish to see an improvement for his or her sake as well as mine, but I certainly am not going to feign love. The biblical Jesus should have known better than to command believers to fake an emotion that is often inappropriate, unnatural and insincere.

(At the Freethought Advance in Lake Hypatia, Alabama, a few years ago, a contest was held to see who would come up with the best response when someone says, "Jesus loves you." The winner was: "Yes, I know. Everybody loves me.")

As with most other biblical rules, Jesus makes "love thy neighbor" a condition for reward: "For if ye love them which love you, what reward have ye? Do not even the publicans do the same? Be ye therefore perfect, even as your Father which is in heaven is perfect." (Matthew 5:46-48. The biblical god didn't love everyone, so he isn't perfect either.) Try saying to someone you love: "The reason I love you is because I am trying to attain perfection and hope to be rewarded someday." These sayings are based on self-interest and a "spiritual" goal that is out of touch with the real world where morality matters. A better guide for human behavior would take into account the physical conditions, the individual cases, the nature of human feelings and the results of certain actions before making a blanket commandment. "Love thy neighbor" might make a lofty sentiment, but it is an impractical moral guideline.

THE BEATITUDES

The word "Beatitude" does not appear in the bible. The Beatitudes describe the first eight sayings of the "Sermon on the Mount" (also a phrase absent from the bible) spoken by Jesus in the fifth chapter of Matthew, all beginning with "Blessed are..."

Five of the eight Beatitudes have nothing to do with morality. At face value the entire group is more of a religious pep talk than a code of ethical behavior. They are all in the passive voice. None of them are truly ethical in themselves since they are all conditions for a future reward. A true ethical code might mention the benefits ("Blessed are") of certain actions, but should stress the inherent value of the behavior on its own merits before detailing the gain or loss for the individual. The eight Beatitudes are:

(1) "Blessed are the poor in spirit: for theirs is the kingdom of heaven." This praises a condition that is not admirable. Are we all supposed to become "poor-spirited?" What does "poor in spirit" mean? This verse does not advocate any specific, positive ethical action. It only says that if you happen to be "poor in spirit" then be happy because you are going to heaven. Verses such as these have been cited to keep slaves and women in their place with promises of "pie in the sky."

(2) "Blessed are they that mourn: for they shall be comforted." As with the first one, this does not advocate any behavior, unless it is interpreted as a command to go into mourning. Instead, why not encourage people to comfort those who are in mourning?

(3) "Blessed are the meek: for they shall inherit the earth." This is not advocating meekness, it is merely stating that if you happen to be a meek person then don't feel bad about it because you won't be left out. This might have some worth if meekness is equated with gentleness and pacifism, but even then it is valued only as a condition for a major

payoff in the future. This is like saying, "Be nice to Grandma because she might put you in her will." Incidentally, meekness is one attribute that is rarely seen in Christian history, current or past. How meek is the popular hymn "Onward, Christian Soldiers"? How much meekness is found in televangelists? How meek is the pope? Are the faces of the anti-abortionists filled with gentleness as they scream threats and physically block access to clinics, all in the name of God? How meek was Jesus when he cursed the fig tree, drove out the money changers, murdered a herd of swine or looked at his disciples with anger? How meek are the Christians who shout insulting and threatening messages on the answering machine at the Freedom From Religion Foundation? Meekness might be a useful survival tactic of those who are supposed to be in submission to a powerful master, such as slaves or Christian wives, but since much of life calls for firm, decisive and sometimes forceful action in order to correct inequalities and abuses, "meekness" seems like a rather weak and useless order.

(4) "Blessed are they which do hunger and thirst after righteousness: for they shall be filled." This merely encourages religious rituals, such as prayer. It offers no advice about how to treat other human beings. If "righteousness" is interpreted politically, then this is a dangerous verse. Righteousness breeds censorship, segregation, persecution, civil inequality and intolerance. Millions of people have been killed and persecuted by the righteousness of others. If "righteousness" can be interpreted to mean "morality," then why hunger and thirst after it? Why not just be moral? If you have to hunger and thirst for goodness, then you are admitting you are not such a good person in the first place. Forget about original sin and just start acting ethically.

(5) "Blessed are the merciful: for they shall obtain mercy." This might be admirable, but how many of us (besides parents) are ever in a position to bestow mercy? The ability to grant mercy implies an authoritative control over others: slavemaster, king, military leader, judge. Christian parents ought to observe this mandate when they are about to follow the biblical command to spank their children. The motivation for this Beatitude is wrong: "for they shall obtain mercy." This beatitude is actually a threat, implying that God will not be merciful to those who are not merciful. Why would God not want to be merciful? Wouldn't the "crime" of a lack of mercy be one of the situations producing a need for God's mercy? A better moral principle might say, "Blessed are

the cautious, because no human being has the right to go overboard in defending against the harm of another."

There is a potential dark side to this verse. Many believers are eager to forgive the sins of their pastors, priests and other church leaders, unwilling to denounce them or to seek criminal or civil justice when they commit crimes. This is painfully evident in the many cases of pedophilia and child abuse by priests and ministers. Many church members rally to the support of the minister, consoling him with "mercy" in his time of need—while blaming or ignoring the victims. If this beatitude produces such a lack of accountability, then it is truly an evil verse.

(6) "Blessed are the pure in heart: for they shall see God." What does "pure" mean, in real terms? If it means "the lack of desire to hurt others" then it is not bad. If it means "being spiritual, separate from worldly concerns" then it is bigoted and potentially dangerous. No ethical benefits arise from anti-social or self-denying attitudes. The Apostle Paul talked about having a "pure conscience" and this might be considered an admirable attitude in certain groups, but if there is no elaboration about how this affects conduct, then it is useless as a moral guide. Besides all that, how in the world can a person be "pure in heart" if we are all born sinners?

(7) "Blessed are the peacemakers: for they shall be called the children of God." This is the best of the bunch. We all want peace, but how do we get it? Was the bomb at Hiroshima peaceful because it ended the war? Are nuclear warheads "blessed?" The United States is currently "at peace" with the Native Americans; however, was United States policy therefore peaceful and blessed toward the Indians? Besides, Jesus contradicted his own advice by warning, "Think not that I am come to send peace on earth: I came not to send peace, but a sword." Bible scholar Hector Avalos, in his book *Fighting Words: The Origins of Religious Violence,* points out that the word "peace" in scripture doesn't have the same meaning as the modern-day, warm and fuzzy, "let's all get along" version. Peace was a military concept, not an ideal of tolerance. "Shalom" should more accurately be translated as "pacification." In Deuteronomy 20:10-11 God told his chosen people: "When you draw near to a town to fight against it, offer it terms of peace. If it accepts your terms of peace and surrenders to you, then all the people in it shall serve you at forced labor." In other words, there will be "peace on

earth" when non-Jews are either killed or turned into slaves. According to Jesus, these holy marauding peacemakers are "blessed."

(8) "Blessed are they which are persecuted for righteousness' sake: for theirs is the kingdom of heaven. Blessed are ye when men shall revile you, and persecute you, and shall say all manner of evil against you falsely, for my sake. Rejoice, and be exceeding glad: for great is your reward in heaven: for so persecuted they the prophets which were before you." This Beatitude is dangerous. Besides being in the passive voice and not advocating any specific moral behavior, "Blessed are they which are persecuted" appears to invite, encourage and praise confrontation and dispute among human beings. Some have even interpreted this verse as a command to go out and "get persecuted." This persecution complex, admittedly not shared by all Christians, contradicts the seventh Beatitude! If you stir up trouble for Jesus, you are blessed and will receive a great "reward in heaven." You are supposed to "rejoice, and be exceeding glad" when your actions incite others to treat you badly.

Persecution is something that could happen to anyone, whether that person has integrity or not, in the course of supporting a cause. Freethinkers have garnered their share of hostility while working for the separation of church and state (are we therefore "blessed"?). But to seek persecution and to "rejoice" in it is perverse. Are we supposed to say, "Yay! Someone called me an idiot! Hooray! I got another death threat!"?

The Beatitudes are immature: "If you kids will stop fighting and pay attention to me, I'll take you to the movies." Since they give little behavioral advice, stressing inner attitudes of being, they sometimes are called the "be-attitudes" by preachers. (Not the "do-attitudes.") They are fluff. Offering skimpy moral guidance, they turn out to be mere platitudes to keep the poor and disenfranchised content to stay in their place. They are not good guides for behavior.

TURN THE OTHER CHEEK

I have heard Christians say that "turning the other cheek" is what makes Christianity unique, comparing it to Martin Luther King's nonviolent resistance. Here is how Jesus phrased it in the Sermon on the Mount: "Ye have heard that it hath been said, An eye for an eye, and a tooth for a tooth: but I say unto you, That ye resist not evil: but whosoever shall smite thee on thy right cheek, turn to him the other also." (Matthew 5:38-39)

At face value (no pun intended) this appears to be a plea for pacifism, and if it is interpreted as such then it is acceptable. Most of us agree that it is usually more moral to avoid violence. We tell children not to hit other kids in the schoolyard even if they hit first, and to try to resolve differences in other ways. But the way Jesus put it, this is not nonviolent resistance—it is violent nonresistance! To invite an abusive person to engage in further abuse is not pacifism. It is reckless. If someone breaks into my house and threatens our family, should I stand idle and let it happen? If a woman is raped, should she love her enemy and invite him back to her home? Do Christian members of the National Rifle Association think they should let go of their guns?

Some might argue that the phrase "turn the other cheek" is just a figure of speech and that Jesus did not actually mean we should encourage maltreatment. But reading the context in Matthew 5:40-42 reveals that this is indeed what he meant, ordering believers to reward doubly those who steal or kidnap.

A more sensible rule would say, "If someone smites thee on thy right cheek, then get away from that person! Defend yourself to avoid further harm. Ask for help, file charges, or try to stop the abuse from happening to someone else. Let the person know that this kind of behavior is unacceptable. Never invite abuse."

HUMANISM OFFERS MORALITY

The bible does contain a smattering of potentially useful advice, such as the admonition against laziness in Proverbs 6:6-11, but even this admirable attempt to improve character fails to point out that there is nothing immoral about laziness itself. Ethical considerations are situational and laziness would be wrong only if it caused unnecessary harm to someone. On the whole, the bible does not have a grasp of ethics.

Even if we all agreed that an absolute moral code were necessary, we would have a serious practical problem. How do we know what that code is? Who decides how the bible is interpreted? Millions of devout, bible-believing Christians and Jews who study scripture carefully cannot agree on many important moral issues. They come down on different sides of the debate about capital punishment, abortion, physician-assisted suicide, death with dignity, ordination of women, women's rights, gay rights, birth control, war and many other issues. What good does it do to have a divine code of ethics if no one knows what it is?

If morality means anything, it means that we are accountable to others. Christians believe that we are accountable not to people, but to God. Since God is nonexistent, then they are accountable to no one. Even if a god does exist, they are in practice not directly accountable to anyone in the real world, which amounts to the same thing. Since bible believers are accountable to God and not to humanity, they can ask for forgiveness from God for any crimes they commit against humanity. In other words, they can act with impunity. And they often do.

It does no good to say that Jesus died on the cross to pay for our sins. I don't have any sins, but if I did I wouldn't want Jesus to die for my sins. I would say, "No, thanks. I will take responsibility for my own actions." What self-respecting person would want otherwise? If I commit a crime, Jesus can die a million deaths and still not change the fact that the guilt lies with me. If I am convicted of a felony, does the law allow someone else to go to prison in my place? What good would that do? It would make a mockery of law and justice and would turn me into an even more reprehensible character, fobbing responsibility off on another. To sing "Jesus died for my sin" is to admit that wrongful actions have nothing at all to do with consequences against flesh-and-blood sentient creatures who hurt.

Humanists are accountable to real, natural, breathing human beings (and other sentient animals), and to enforceable human laws, not to an unprovable, pie-in-the-sky deity. This makes humanism superior as a guide for moral behavior. Humanism is not just better than the bible—the Bad Book—it is the only way we can be moral.

Chapter Eleven
Murder, He Wrote

The Freedom From Religion Foundation has a series of inexpensive "nontracts" that are very popular with members. They have been used to counter proselytizers and to introduce inquiring friends to the reasonableness of freethought. They are called "nontracts"—tracts for nonbelievers—because "tract" can connote propaganda. Most freethinkers are happy to live and let live and only respond when confronted by believers, although one unbeliever became so exasperated over a local church that he sneaked into the sanctuary and inserted *Dear Believer* into every hymnbook. (I don't recommend doing this, but I suppose it is not unfair.)

The nontracts have been passed out all over the continent, and guess who gets the fallout. The Foundation office regularly receives letters from the recipients and has even picked up a few members among supportive readers. One fellow read *Ten Common Myths About Atheists* on a laundromat bulletin board and promptly joined. Usually, however, we hear from believers who want to correct our heresy.

The *Bible Contradictions* nontract provokes the longest letters. We get these tortured point-by-point defenses of the "inerrant word of God" from fundamentalist preachers and other Christians who think the discrepancies can be explained. What they lack in logic they make up for in length.

The first contradiction in the nontract deals with the Ten Commandments, contrasting Exodus 20:13, "Thou shalt not kill," with Exodus 32:27, "Slay every man his brother." The bible is filled with killings and mass murders that are committed, commanded or condoned by deity. If this is not a contradiction, then all squares are round.

Yet most believers think they can square up this discrepancy with circular reasoning, or with creative *ad hoc* arguments. The most common claim offered in defense of this contradiction is that Exodus 20:13

really says, "Thou shalt not *murder*." To murder is to kill unlawfully, maliciously or premeditatedly. If the Commandments forbid only "murder," then it can be argued that other forms of killing are allowed, or even encouraged. God can ordain capital punishment, or command a holocaust of heathens without breaking his own law.

Of course, it is a useless tautology to define murder as an "unlawful" killing in this context. Since the Ten Commandments supposedly *are* the law, they would be merely saying, "It is unlawful to kill unlawfully." This type of circular thinking excuses anyone who kills "in the name of the Lord, the source of law." It is not only illogical, but also immoral, to claim that there is a law above the law that can justify unnecessary bloodshed. Many Christians claim that the genocide of idolaters is permitted because "God knows best." But every murderer feels some kind of justification for the crime. Why is God special? Why should a deity get away with atrocities that would send you or me straight to prison?

Malice is a desire to cause harm, so if murder means anything it means a deliberately cruel taking of life. Except for euthanasia—a nonmalicious and (usually) requested termination of waning life—and perhaps self defense—where killing might regrettably be the minimal amount of violence necessary to prevent a greater harm—few would doubt that killing a person is harmful, no matter who does the killing.

Do the Ten Commandments really say that "Thou shalt not murder"? The Hebrew word for "kill" in Exodus 20:13 is *ratsach*. (The word for "slay" in the contradictory command in Exodus 32:27 is *haraq*.) Depending on which version you use, there are about 10 Hebrew words which are translated to mean "kill." The five most common in Hebrew order (with translation in order of *King James* frequency) are:

muth:	(825) die, slay, put to death, kill
nakah:	(502) smite, kill, slay, beat, wound, murder
haraq:	(172) slay, kill, murder, destroy
zabach:	(140) sacrifice, kill
ratsach:	(47) slay [23], murder [17], kill [6], be put to death [1]

I am using the King James Version for convenience. Other translations will be a bit different, but this gives the general idea. Modern preachers must be smarter than Hebrew translators if they claim that *ratsach* means "murder" exclusively. *Muth, nakah, haraq, zabach* and *ratsach* appear to be spilled all over the bible in an imprecise and overlapping jumble of contexts, in much the same way modern writers will swap synonyms.

The word often means something that we would call "manslaughter" in our modern society. Referring to the "cities of refuge" set up by Moses to shelter killers, Deuteronomy 4:42 says "that the slayer [*ratsach*] might flee thither, which should kill [*ratsach*] his neighbor unawares, and hated him not in times past." This accidental killing is hardly murder—it is neither premeditated nor malicious.

Numbers 35:6-34 gives perhaps the best glimpse of how the words were used interchangeably. "Then ye shall appoint you cities for refuge from the avenger; that the slayer [*ratsach*] may flee thither, which killeth [*nakah*] any person at unawares." (35:11) "He that smote [*nakah*] him shall surely be put to death [*muth*]; for he is a murderer [*ratsach*]." (35:21)

Again showing that *ratsach* can be accidental: "But if he thrust him suddenly without enmity, or have cast upon him any thing without laying of wait, or with any stone...seeing him not...and was not his enemy, neither sought his harm: Then the congregation shall judge between the slayer [*ratsach*] and the revenger of blood according to these judgments." (35:22-24)

Verse 27 shows that *ratsach* can be considered a justified killing: "[if] the revenger of blood kill [*ratsach*] the slayer [*ratsach*]; he shall not be guilty of blood." Verses 30 and 31 show how the words are interchanged, and also indicate that *ratsach* was used for capital punishment: "Whoso killeth [*nakah*] any person, the murderer [*ratsach*] shall be put to death [*ratsach*] by the mouth of witnesses... Moreover ye shall take no satisfaction for the life of a murderer [*ratsach*], which is guilty of death: but he shall surely be put to death [*muth*]."

If this doesn't remove all doubt then consider Proverbs 22:13: "The slothful man saith, There is a lion without, I shall be slain [*ratsach*] in the streets." Can animals be guilty of murder?

As a desperate final straw, naive apologists might point to Matthew 19:18 where Jesus recites the Commandment, "Thou shalt do no murder [*phoneuo*]." But of the 12 times *phoneuo* appears in the bible, this is the only place where it is translated as "murder." It is translated as "kill" everywhere else, and the Revised Version, The Amplified Bible, the New Catholic Bible and the New American Bible use "kill" in

Matthew 19:18. The writer of Matthew was quoting the Septuagint, a Greek translation of the Hebrew scriptures, and this is an example of the difficulty of handling three slippery languages at once. It is hardly a persuasive argument in favor of "Thou shalt not murder," and most likely reflects a translator bias.

Considering the biblical evidence, "Thou shalt not kill" is a better translation of the sixth commandment than "Thou shalt not murder." There is a very slight argument in favor of inerrantists, however. Even though the biblical deity overindulged in *nakah, haraq* and *muth*, there is no instance where God did any *ratsach* himself. It was ordered and approved by God, but never directly committed by God, not by that verb. But since the use of *ratsach* is relatively sparse, it may just be that the writers of the bible never got around to assigning this particular word to godly massacres.

But all of this is irrelevant when we find verses repeating "Thou shalt not kill" in other Hebrew words. Leviticus 24:17 says, "And he that killeth [*nakah*] any man shall surely be put to death [*muth*]." Exodus 21:12, just 21 verses after the Ten Commandments, says, "He that smiteth [*nakah*] a man, so that he die, shall be surely put to death." According to Scripture it doesn't matter what word you use: killing is against the law.

Joshua *nakah*'ed the people of Ai (Joshua 8:21), and David *nakah*'ed Goliath (I Samuel 19:5). This was considered justifiable killing in spite of the fact that *nakah* was expressly forbidden. What does this do to the "*ratsach* = murder" defense? If Joshua and David are not criminals, then the bible is again proved contradictory.

Some might argue that no matter how the Ten Commandments are translated, we still need them as a basis for law and order. But do we really? If Moses had not existed would it have never occurred to us that murder is immoral? Without "The Law" would we all be wandering around like little gods, stealing, raping and spilling blood whenever our vanity was offended? The first four Commandments have nothing to do with ethics (see Chapter 10), and any value in the remainder is based on rational humanistic principles that long predated the Jewish religion. It is wrong to kill, *even* according to the bible. And since the biblical god and his followers were murderers, the bible is contradictory.

When the Israelite warriors marched through a village, slaughtering and plundering in the name of the Lord, ripping up animals, children, men and women and saving the virgins alive for themselves (Numbers 31:15-18), they didn't say to the pregnant woman with a sword in her belly, "By the way, I want you to know that I am not *murdering* you. I am lawfully killing you in God's name." And regardless, would such a fine semantic distinction make much difference to the victims of righteousness?

Chapter Twelve
For Goodness Sake

If we did a good act merely from the love of God and a belief that it is pleasing to Him, whence arises the morality of the Atheist?... Their virtue, then, must have had some other foundation than the love of God.
—**Thomas Jefferson**

You notice a person drowning in a river. What should you do? If you agree with Jefferson, you will consider yourself a "social animal" with an "instinct" to compassion, whether you believe in a god or not. If you are a humanist, you will empathize with the sufferings of another human being. If you are a Christian, you will believe that the person's life has value because he or she was "created in the image of God." But whatever your basis for value, you still have to decide: "Should I jump in?" You can't pull a list from your back pocket to look up "Rule 127: What to do when someone is drowning." You can't consult engraved stone tablets for a commandment that says that "Thou shalt jump into rivers to save drowning people."

Behavioral dilemmas involve a conflict of values, and in real life this means they are always situational. You can't simply follow a blind code. You have to compare the relative merits of the consequences of different actions, and the only way to do that is to exercise reason. How far out in the river is the person? How strong is the current? How good a swimmer are you? Are you likely to cause two deaths instead of one? How many children are you responsible for supporting?

It would be pointless to ask, "Is it moral to dive in?" The only purpose of this irrelevant question might be to make you feel virtuous, or guilty.

Perhaps you bravely take the risk and dive in. Or, regrettably, you might reason that the most moral action would be not to jump in the river, but to run for help. Your basis for value is not important—the facts of the situation are.

Quoting Dostoyevsky ("If God does not exist, everything is permissible"), many believers suggest that it is only theists who can have values. Like Jefferson, though, they certainly know this is not true. We atheists are just as likely as Christians to jump in that river—perhaps more likely.

During my struggle to break free from the cocoon of Christianity, the most difficult issue with which I grappled was the idea of relativism. I used to preach that relativism leads to chaos, that without absolutes "anything goes." I'd say that like ships without rudders or machines without operating instructions, human beings without absolutes simply wander through life, hit-or-miss, trying this or that, never knowing what is right or wrong. It made a good sermon.

Most Christians feel that the basis for morality must be something absolute. This rock-solid foundation must be rooted outside humanity, they claim, providing an external and objective reference by which human behavior can be measured. Without this "cosmic code" for living, we would all choose or manufacture our own individual ethics relative to personal wants, whims and needs. An "inner directed" morality, most Christians insist, leads to relativism—and relativism, to them, is sin.

Additionally, believers claim that without an external code that is absolute, there is no ethical imperative. Why be good if there is no punishment, no reward, no all-knowing police officer to enforce the rules? They believe that if there is no god, then there is no accountability. Since human nature, they insist, is intrinsically corrupt (look at history or current headlines), the tendency will be toward destruction and evil unless there are strict laws and absolute enforcement. We are rambunctious children who need to be broken like wild horses, or reined in and controlled by our wise parents. The fear of punishment and the loss of parental approval provide the necessary moral imperative.

I used to find this argument persuasive. For about a year after rejecting religion I felt uncomfortable flapping my own wings. It took some getting used to the idea that I could chart my own moral course through life—that I *must* chart my own moral course through life. Although there is no ultimate universal guide, I do have a mind, which I realized is the only rudder I will ever have or need. To use yet another metaphor, I felt as though I were on trial and that right in the middle of the proceedings my lawyer died and I was left to represent myself before the bench, which was scary enough until I looked up and saw that the bench was vacant! I was the plaintiff, the defendant, the attorney and the judge! The responsibility was almost enough to drive me back to my cell, back to the cocoon of absolutes.

On the other hand, it did not take long to discover that there is no great mystery to morality. Although a few extreme ethical dilemmas might arise in one's lifetime, basic day-to-day morality is a simple matter of kindness, respect and reason.

Once I shed the religio-psychological frame of mind, I learned that the Christian "struggle" with morality is overblown. I learned that relativism is all we've got. Human values are not absolutes—they are relative to human needs. The humanistic answer to morality, if the question is properly understood, is that the basis for values lies in nature. Since we are a part of nature, and since there is nothing "beyond" nature, it is necessary to assign value to actions in the context of nature itself. Most of us do this daily since we are born and raised in nature; as a matter of fact, we do it without much thought or distress.

One simplified example of how nature provides the basis for value: the human body requires water for survival. Since most humans want to survive, withholding water can be considered immoral. There is nothing cosmically "good" about water or cosmically "evil" about the lack of it. It is all relative to natural human needs. If we had evolved to require arsenic, then offering arsenic would be appreciated while serving water might be a crime. It would miss the point to complain that "water versus arsenic" is irrelevant because it addresses nouns rather than verbs—that instead we should be discussing the relative merits of "withholding versus not withholding."

Morality implies avoiding or minimizing harm. This is by definition. No matter how elaborate the philosophical arguments become, moral decisions in the daily world still boil down to assessing the value of things like water and arsenic—natural things—and their effects on other natural things, such as our bodies.

"Value" is a concept of relative worth. And since concepts, as far as we know, exist only in brains, which are material things, it is meaningless, even dangerous, to talk of cosmic moral absolutes. The assessment of value requires the use of reason. In other words, morality comes from *within* humanity. If intelligent life had not appeared on this planet, morality would not exist.

Morality is in the mind—and reason is in the mind. No matter where you look for morality, it all comes down to the mind. Those believers who distrust the human mind are still required to look to some kind of mind for guidance, whether the mind of a god, prophet, preacher or pope. If there were a god, then its moral decrees would originate from *its* mind. (I am using the word "mind" as a function of the brain, just as digestion is a function of the stomach or circulation is a function of the heart. I do not mean to concede that the natural brain/mind of a human is any way comparable to the intangible, "spiritual" mind of a deity—whatever that might mean—that believers imagine existing somewhere outside of nature.)

Why should the mind of a deity—an outsider—be better able to judge human actions than the minds of humans themselves? Has God ever been thirsty? The human mind and human actions are part of the natural world; the mind of a god is not. Human minds interact with each other in the real world. A human mind feels physical pain. The human mind can know sorrow, grief, regret and embarrassment, while the mind of a perfect deity cannot. Can a god shed a tear, smell a flower or hug a child? Does a god perspire after a day of hard work under a burning sun, or shiver while trudging through a blizzard? Which mind is in a better position to make judgments about human actions and feelings? Which mind has more credibility? Which has more experience in the real world? Which mind has more of a right?

Christians who argue that Jesus became human, that the "Word became flesh," to give the supernatural deity an opportunity to relate to natural human suffering forget that the Ten Commandments were written long before the first century. The Man from Galilee said, "Think not that I am come to destroy the law, or the prophets: I am not come to destroy, but to fulfill. For verily I say unto you, Till heaven and earth pass, one jot or one tittle shall in no wise pass from the law, till all be fulfilled." (Matthew 5:17-18) The Law, according to the bible, originated in the mind of God long before he stuck his toe into our world.

In any event, how can the temporal sufferings of Jesus compare to the sufferings of the entire human race? Did Jesus ever experience the pain of childbirth? The billions of women going through labor are much more life giving, much more nurturing of value than a few hours of self-imposed bleeding on a cross. The short life of Jesus can hardly compare with the suffering of brave heretics who have been persecuted for criticizing Christianity, or with the agony of the "witches" who were burned, drowned and hanged by bible believers (quoting Exodus 22:18: "Thou shalt not suffer a witch to live"). Nor can the one day of suffering Jesus supposedly endured compare with the Holocaust, the genocide of Native Americans or the pain of those who were tortured during the Inquisition. His supposed contribution to the world hardly compares with the hard work, sacrifice and discipline of intelligent individuals who have dedicated their lives to science and medicine. Just because Jesus was considered a Higher Power does not make his alleged suffering any higher than yours or mine.

Why do believers assume that a *higher* power is necessarily a more moral power? How do they know it is not the other way around? If you look at nature, you discover that there is very little crime in the plant kingdom. (Ignoring dandelions.) Is it a felony when an eagle kills a field mouse? Immorality, crime, malice and cruelty belong to the "higher" forms of life. Chimpanzees and other primates sometimes show behavior that appears malicious, but they are "higher" animals. "Higher" does not mean "better"—it means perhaps more complex, or more conscious, or more cultural, or "more like us humans." If there is a Higher Power, shouldn't we be all the more suspicious of its motives and actions? A Higher Power can create a Higher Crime. Perhaps we would all benefit from revering the Lower Powers of the universe, and would improve morality if we were to get back in touch with the fact that we are animals living in a natural environment, and that we are truly part of nature, not something separate and above.

For simplicity, I am using "morality" and "ethics" synonymously in this book, though they are technically not the same. My understanding is that ethics is the study of behavioral values, while morality is a set of values a particular culture chooses. Ethics deals with principles while morality deals with rules. Simplistically stated, ethics *asks* what is actually good or bad, while morality *states* what is good or bad. The two words often overlap. For example, if you walk down the middle of the street naked by a schoolyard many cultures will call you immoral, though there is nothing inherently unethical about such an act. Killing a person for no reason other than pleasure is both unethical and immoral. Insulting a prophet may be immoral to a particular group of religious people, but it is not unethical outside of that framework.

For me, the phrase "moral relativism" refers to the differences between cultural mores, while "ethical relativism" refers to the same act being right or wrong depending on the situation. I know that some thinkers use ethical relativism to mean moral relativism, and I want to make the distinction clear. I do not embrace moral relativism, but I do embrace ethical relativism. Moral relativism means that the same action in the same context can be right in one culture and wrong in another. Ethical relativism (to me) means that the same action can be right in one context and wrong in another. For me, ethical relativism means situational ethics. In this book, my own informal usage treats the word "moral" as a synonym for "ethical," not the other way around. It may not be "nice" to criticize Jesus or God, resulting in some hurt feelings, but it is not unethical—and since I treat ethics and morality roughly synonymously, I would say it is not immoral to criticize religion. In fact, if we consider ourselves to be moral (or ethical), we ought not to refrain from denouncing religious teachings and practices that cause harm.

"How does an atheist account for the existence of objective moral values?" is a question I often hear. "If you don't believe in God, then what is your basis for morality?" To me, the answer is obvious: we atheists find our basis for morality in nature. Where else would we look?

Most atheists think moral values are real, but that does not mean they are "objective." They can't be. A value is not a "thing"—it is a function of a mind (which is itself a function). To be objective is to exist independently of a mind. So, an "objective value" is an oxymoron: the existence in the mind of something that is independent of the mind.

Most atheists think that values, though not objective things in themselves, can be objectively justified by reference to the real world. Our actions have consequences, and those consequences can be objectively measured.

Although most atheists accept the importance of morality, this is not conceding that morality exists in the universe—that it is a cosmic object waiting to be discovered. The word "morality" is just a label for a concept, and concepts exist only in minds. If no minds existed, no morality would exist.

There is no big mystery to morality. Morality is simply acting with the intention to minimize harm. Since harm is natural, its avoidance is a material exercise. Organisms suffer as they bump into their environment and each other, and as rational animals with some ability to anticipate the future, we humans have some choice about how this happens. If we try to minimize harm and enhance the quality of life, we are moral. If we don't, we are immoral or amoral, depending on our intentions. Even if we make a mistake, we can still be called moral or ethical if it is truly our intention to minimize harm. And the way to avoid making a mistake is to try to be as informed as possible about the likely consequences of the actions being considered. To be moral, atheists have access to the simple tools of reason and kindness. There is no cosmic code book directing our actions.

Of course, relative to humanity, certain general actions can be deemed almost uniformly right or wrong. Without the Ten Commandments, would it never have dawned on the human race that there is a problem with killing? Prohibitions against homicide and theft existed millennia before the Israelite story of Moses coming down from Sinai.

The way to be moral is to first learn what causes harm and how to avoid it. This means investigating nature—especially human nature: who we are, what we need, where we live, how we function and why we behave the way we do.

Why should I treat my neighbor nicely? Because we are all connected. We are part of the same species, genetically linked. Since I value myself and my species, and the other species to which we are related, I recognize that when someone is hurting, my natural family is suffering. By nature, those of us who are mentally healthy recoil from pain and wish to see it ended.

Of course, we often act in positive ways to stop the pain of others. This is compassion. Although I don't think there is a "moral imperative" nor a "compassion imperative"—you can be considered moral if you are passively not causing unnecessary harm—I do think most human beings who are mentally healthy will empathize with the sufferings of others and will naturally want to reach out. Atheists can perhaps express compassion more easily than believers can because we are not confused by:

- Fatalism: "Whatever happens is God's will."

- Pessimism: "We deserve to suffer."

- Salvation: "Death is not the end."

- Retribution: "Justice will prevail in the afterlife."

- Magic: "Pray for help."

- Holy war: "Kill for God."

- Forgiveness: "I won't be held responsible for my mistakes."

- Glory: "Suffering with Christ is an honor."

Since this is the only life we atheists have, each decision is crucial and we are accountable for our actions right now.

Yet notice how leading theists deal with the real world: "Ye have the poor with you always," said the "loving" Jesus, who never lifted a finger to eradicate poverty, wasting precious ointment on his own luxury rather than selling it to feed the hungry (Matthew 26:6-11). "I think it is very beautiful for the poor to accept their lot, to share it with the passion of Christ," Mother Teresa added. "I think the world is much helped by the suffering of the poor people." So much for theistic compassion!

Jefferson may have been wrong to call compassion an "instinct" because many appear not to have it—it seems optional. Or perhaps he was right and the "compassion gene" (to oversimplify) varies across the population like any other human feature (height, intelligence, musical ability, etc.), and some of us have more of the instinct than others have. But it is fortunate that there are enough of us who love life to protect ourselves from those who don't. We have systems of law, enforcement, justice and defense. We encourage kind, ethical actions through moral education and critical thinking. And though there is no cosmic moral imperative, all of us who value life and consider ourselves moral—atheists and believers alike—can choose to actively exhort others to join us in expressing our innate feelings of altruism and compassion.

Compassion is, after all, a characteristic of being human. When someone commits a horrible act, what do we say? "That was an inhuman thing to do!" We assume that the natural "human" attitude is nonviolent and peaceful. We are not corrupt, evil creatures. A few of us are off to the side of "saintliness" (to borrow a word), and a few of us are off to the other side, the side of mental disease, with sociopaths and criminals. On the bell curve of morality and compassion, however, most of us fall somewhere in the large middle area.

Many believers, including Christians who are ordered to "bring into captivity every thought unto the obedience of Christ," have an underlying distrust of human reasoning. Yearning for absolutes, they perceive relativism—the recognition that actions must be judged in context—as something dangerous when it is the only way we can be truly moral.

Theists are afraid people will think for themselves; atheists are afraid they won't.

When theists make a case for "natural rights," they often point to Locke, Jefferson, Paine and other enlightened thinkers of the Age of Reason. It is enlightening to notice that they rarely quote from the bible. Nowhere in Scripture will you find an acknowledgment that each individual has an "inalienable right" to be treated with fairness and respect, or that "We, the People" are capable of governing ourselves. There is no democracy in the "word of God." In the bible, humans are "worms" and "sinners" deserving damnation and "slaves" who should humbly submit to all kings, heavenly and earthly.

Championing the "consent of the governed" over the authority of a sovereign, the Declaration of Independence is unabashedly anti-biblical. We Americans are a proudly rebellious people who fought a Revolutionary War to kick the King of England out of our affairs. Then, we produced a godless Constitution, the first to separate church and state.

But many American Christians see it differently: "Had Jefferson been influenced by Darwin instead of Locke," writes Clifford Goldstein, editor of the Seventh Day Adventist *Liberty Magazine,* "Joseph Stalin's views on religious liberty would have been deemed progressive." In a

"Darwinian universe," Goldstein contends, truth rests "on a foundation as whimsical as the electorate or whichever despot happens to be
in control."

Oh? How does truth fare in the "theistic universe" where the despot
is named Jehovah? We saw in the previous chapter how horribly immoral
the God of the bible and his son, Jesus, acted. The God of Scripture
slaughtered entire groups of people that offended his vanity. "Happy
shall be he that taketh and dasheth thy little ones against the stones,"
he advised (Psalm 137:9), threatening those with the wrong religion
that "their women with child shall be ripped up." (Hosea 13:16) He
also sent bears to attack 42 children who teased a prophet (II Kings
2:23-24), punished innocent offspring to the fourth generation (Exodus
20:5), discriminated against the handicapped (Leviticus 21:18-23) and
promised that fathers and sons would eat each other (Ezekiel 5:10),
among other actions that we would find repugnant in a human being.
In this theistic universe, morality is severed from reality and reduced
to flattering the Sovereign.

If on a Saturday, for example, you notice a man gathering wood
to warm his family, what should you do as a Christian commanded to
"remember the Sabbath?" According to Numbers 15:32-36, you should
stone him to death! Is this not whimsical?

Jesus incorporated slavery into his parables as if it were the most
natural order, only cautioning masters to beat some slaves less severely
than others (Luke 12:46-47). The Heaven's Gate cult, like Origen,
accepted Jesus' advice: "There be eunuchs which have made themselves
eunuchs for the kingdom of heaven's sake. He that is able to receive it,
let him receive it." (Matthew 19:12) Is this good advice?

There are some good teachings in the bible, of course, but is a garden overrun with weeds still beautiful? Jefferson thought that most of
Jesus' words were insulting, although he spotted a few good teachings
that were as "easily distinguishable as diamonds in a dunghill." (To
John Adams, October 1813)

Goldstein has it backwards. Had Jefferson been influenced by
Jehovah instead of Locke, Adolph Hitler's views on religious liberty
would have been deemed progressive! Hitler allowed Darwinism to be
twisted for a political purpose, framing evolution in a "social" way not
intended by Darwin himself. But it wasn't Darwinism that gave the
theistic Hitler his basis for morality: "I am convinced that I am acting

as the agent of our Creator. By fighting off the Jews, I am doing the Lord's work." (*Mein Kampf*) Hitler credited *Jesus* as his inspiration. In a 1926 Nazi Christmas celebration, he boasted, "Christ was the greatest early fighter in the battle against the world enemy, the Jews... The work that Christ started but could not finish, I—Adolf Hitler—will conclude." The creationist Hitler shared a thirst for blood with the bombastic biblical God in whose "image" he thought he was created.

There is no practical value in claiming that "natural rights" are rooted outside of nature. People who find "moral absolutes" in the revelation of a deity have never agreed what those absolutes are. Take any of society's moral issues of the day—capital punishment, abortion, stem-cell research, physician-assisted suicide, women's rights, divorce, gay rights, corporal punishment, animal rights, slavery, pacifism, environmental protection, birth control, overpopulation, state/church separation—and you will notice that praying, bible-believing Christians have come down on opposite sides.

If the bible gives us absolute moral guidance, then where is it? Why don't sincere believers agree on these important questions? It's clear that the bible is an inadequate behavioral guide, and that the tyrannical god of Scriptural mythology leads us to a lack of values.

When Jefferson wrote about the "Creator" in the Declaration of Independence, he was not talking about the Christian god. As a Deist, he viewed the "Creator" as a much less personal being than the biblical deity. The god of Deism was more like "nature" than "Jehovah."

When Jefferson claimed that all people are "endowed by their Creator with certain inalienable rights," he could not have meant "endowed" in the sense of a sovereign granting a privilege that might be denied. If something can be endowed, then it can be un-endowed. If a right is inalienable, it can't be withheld or withdrawn, not even in principle. An "inalienable right," if rights are endowed, is an oxymoron.

Human rights, if they are inalienable, could not have been granted—not by a government, society or god. A "natural right" is a claim to a freedom, privilege or power that you possess inherently, by nature (though you still might have to convince others to recognize and grant that right). Natural rights, if they exist, are indeed inalienable—but then they could not have been "endowed." We simply own them.

Jefferson meant, figuratively, that since we are "endowed by nature" with common human needs, we are justified in expecting society to honor our right to life, liberty and the pursuit of happiness.

Christians think we should treat others nicely because we were all created in the "image of God." This gives us value, they suppose.

But they don't explain why. Why does the image of a god provide greater value than some other image? Why does it give any value at all? What does "image of God" mean?

"God is a Spirit," Jesus supposedly said, but what is that? The word "spirit" has never been defined, except in terms that tell us what it is not: immaterial, intangible, noncorporeal, supernatural. No one has ever described what a spirit *is*. "To talk of immaterial existences," Jefferson wrote, "is to talk of nothings. To say that the human soul, angels, God, are immaterial, is to say, they are nothings, or that there is no God, no angels, no soul. I cannot reason otherwise." (To John Adams, August 1820.) This does not mean Jefferson was an atheist. He conceived of God as a material being, or as nature itself, which is consistent with Deism.

Since "god" has never been defined, much less proved, its "image" can't be used as a basis for anything. "Nature," on the other hand, means something. Darwinism shows us that all living organisms are the result of a natural evolutionary process. We have been fashioned by the laws of nature.

This revelation can only fail to impress you if you have been taught that there is something wrong with nature, something shameful about being a mere animal in a debased realm beneath the supernatural, whatever that is. Many theists seem eager to play this game of nature bashing. The "blind chance" of evolution, they say, is a brute force incapable of producing something as "lofty" as us humans.

But evolution is not blind chance. It is design that incorporates randomness—not intelligent design, but design by the laws of nature, by the limited number of ways atoms interact mathematically and molecules combine geometrically. It is design by extinction, by the way a changing environment automatically disallows organisms that happen not to be adapted, leaving the "fittest" behind, if any. The randomness of genetic variation is a strength of evolution, providing a greater chance that something will survive.

This is amazing. Instead of speculating about an unknown "creator," we can actually look at our origins. Evolution shows how complexity arises from simplicity. Creationism can't do that. Creationism tries to explain complexity with more complexity, which only replaces one mystery with another mystery. If functional complexity requires a designer, then how do you account for the functional complexity of the mind of the designer?

Darwin's enlightening concept is empirical, testable, provable and relevant to creatures that inhabit a physical planet. It shows us who we really are. We are not above nature. We are not just a part of nature. We *are* nature. We are natural creatures in a natural environment. Through the startlingly sloppy, painfully unpredictable, part-random, part-determined process of natural selection, life has become what it is: imperfect yet doggedly hanging on.

And that's what makes life valuable: it didn't have to be. It is dear. It is fleeting. It is vibrant and vulnerable. It is heart breaking. It can be lost.

It will be lost.

But we exist now. We are caring, intelligent animals and can treasure our brief lives. Why is eternal better than temporal, or supernatural "higher" than natural? Doesn't rarity increase value? God is an idea, not a natural creature. Why should his "image" be more valuable than our own "nature?" What right does an immaterial existence—a ghost in the sky—have to tell us natural creatures what is valuable?

If we were created in his unknowable image, then we have no idea who we are. But being fashioned in the "image of nature," we do know who we are and we can find out more. Right in our backyard, here on earth, we can investigate, study and continue to improve conditions on this planet. It wasn't faith that eradicated smallpox. Contemplating the "image of god" will not cure cancer or AIDS.

Science has given us much. What has theology ever provided?

Theology has given us hell.

The threat of damnation is designed to be an incentive to right action, but this is a phony morality. Humanists think we should do good for goodness' sake, not for the selfish prospect of reaping individual rewards or avoiding punishment. Any ideology that makes its point by threatening violence is morally bankrupt. (Hitler's horrible ovens, at least, were relatively quick. The torment Jesus promised is a "fire that shall never be quenched.") Anyone who believes in hell is at heart not moral at all.

If the only way you can be forced to be kind to others is by the threat of hell, that shows how little you think of yourself. If the only way you can be motivated to be kind to others is by the promise of heaven, that shows how little you think of others.

Most atheists will say, "Be good, for goodness' sake!"

Chapter Thirteen
Bible Contradictions

"It ain't those parts of the bible that I can't understand that bother me, it is the parts that I do understand."
—**Mark Twain**

Paul said that "God is not the author of confusion" (I Corinthians 14:33), yet never has a book produced more confusion than the bible. There are hundreds of denominations and sects, all using the "inspired Scriptures" to prove their conflicting doctrines. Why is this? Why do translations differ? Why do educated theologians disagree over Greek and Hebrew meanings? Why such muddle? "If the trumpet give an uncertain sound," Paul wrote in I Corinthians 14:8, "who shall prepare himself to the battle? So likewise ye, except ye utter by the tongue words easy to be understood, how shall it be known what is spoken? For ye shall speak into the air." Exactly! Paul should have practiced what he preached. For almost two millennia, the bible has been producing a most "uncertain sound."

The problem is not with human limitations. The problem is the bible itself. People who are free of theological bias notice that the bible contains hundreds of discrepancies. Should it surprise us when such a literary and moral mishmash, taken seriously, causes so much discord? Here is a brief sampling of biblical contradictions.

SHOULD WE KILL?

Exodus 20:13 "Thou shalt not kill."

Leviticus 24:17 "And he that killeth any man shall surely be put to death."

Exodus 32:27 "Thus sayeth the Lord God of Israel, Put every man his sword by his side, ...and slay every man his brother, ...companion, ...neighbor."

I Samuel 6:19 "...and the people lamented because the Lord had smitten many of the people with a great slaughter."

I Samuel 15:2, 3, 7, 8 "Thus saith the Lord... Now go and smite Amalek, and utterly destroy all that they have, and spare them not; but slay both man and woman, infant and suckling, ox and sheep, camel and ass... And Saul smote the Amalekites... and utterly destroyed all the people with the edge of the sword."

Numbers 15:36 "And all the congregation brought him without the camp, and stoned him with stones, and he died; as the Lord commanded Moses." (This was a believing Israelite, not an infidel.)

Hosea 13:16 "...they shall fall by the sword: their infants shall be dashed in pieces, and their women with children shall be ripped up."

Psalm 137:9 "Happy shall he be that taketh and dasheth thy little ones upon the stones."

For a discussion of the defense that the Commandments prohibit only murder, see Chapter 11.

SHOULD WE TELL LIES?

Exodus 20:16 "Thou shalt not bear false witness."

Proverbs 12:22 "Lying lips are an abomination to the Lord."

versus

I Kings 22:23 "The Lord hath put a lying spirit in the mouth of all these thy prophets, and the Lord hath spoken evil concerning thee."

II Thessalonians 2:11 "And for this cause God shall send them strong delusion, that they should believe a lie."

Also, compare Joshua 2:4-6 with James 2:25 to see how a lying prostitute was praised for her dishonesty. (I don't think telling a lie is always wrong, and neither does the bible.)

SHOULD WE STEAL?

Exodus 20:15 "Thou shalt not steal."

Leviticus 19:13 "Thou shalt not defraud thy neighbor, neither rob him."

versus

Exodus 3:22 "And ye shall spoil the Egyptians."

Exodus 12:35-36 "And they spoiled [plundered, NRSV] the Egyptians."

Luke 19:29-34 "[Jesus] sent two of his disciples, Saying, Go ye into the village…ye shall find a colt tied, whereon yet never man sat: loose him, and bring him hither. And if any man ask you, Why do ye loose him? thus shall ye say unto him, Because the Lord hath need of him… And as they were loosing the colt, the owners thereof said unto them, Why loose ye the colt? And they said, The Lord hath need of him."

I was taught as a child that when you take something without asking for it, that is stealing.

SHALL WE KEEP THE SABBATH?

Exodus 20:8 "Remember the sabbath day to keep it holy."

Exodus 31:15 "Whosoever doeth any work in the sabbath day, he shall surely be put to death."

Numbers 15:32, 36 "And while the children of Israel were in the wilderness, they found a man that gathered sticks upon the sabbath day… And all the congregation brought him without the camp, and stoned him with stones, and he died; as the Lord commanded Moses."

versus

Isaiah 1:13 "The new moons and sabbaths, the calling of assemblies, I cannot away with; it is iniquity."

John 5:16 "And therefore did the Jews persecute Jesus and sought to slay him, because he had done these things on the sabbath day."

Colossians 2:16 "Let no man therefore judge you in meat, or in drink, or in respect of an holy-day, or of the new moon, or of the sabbath days."

SHALL WE MAKE GRAVEN IMAGES?

Exodus 20:4 "Thou shalt not make unto thee any graven image, or any likeness of anything that is in heaven…earth…water."

Leviticus 26:1 "Ye shall make ye no idols nor graven image, neither rear you up a standing image, neither shall ye set up any image of stone."

Deuteronomy 27:15 "Cursed be the man that maketh any graven or molten image."

versus

Exodus 25:18 "And thou shalt make two cherubims of gold, of beaten work shalt thou make them."

I Kings 7:15, 16, 23, 25 "For he [Solomon] cast two pillars of brass… and two chapiters of molten brass… And he made a molten sea…it stood upon twelve oxen…[and so on]"

ARE WE SAVED THROUGH WORKS?

Ephesians 2:8, 9 "For by grace are ye saved through faith… not of works."

Romans 3:20, 28 "Therefore by the deeds of the law there shall no flesh be justified in his sight."

Galatians 2:16 "Knowing that a man is not justified by the works of the law, but by the faith of Jesus Christ."

versus

James 2:24 "Ye see then how that by works a man is justified, and not by faith only."

Matthew 19:16-21 "And, behold, one came and said unto him, Good Master, what good thing shall I do, that I may have eternal life? And he [Jesus] said unto him...keep the commandments... The young man saith unto him, All these things have I kept from my youth up: what lack I yet? Jesus said unto him, If thou wilt be perfect, go and sell that thou hast, and give to the poor, and thou shalt have treasure in heaven."

The common defense here is that "we are saved by faith *and* works." But Paul said "not of works."

SHOULD GOOD WORKS BE SEEN?

Matthew 5:16 "Let your light so shine before men that they may see your good works."

I Peter 2:12 "Having your conversation honest among the Gentiles: that...they may by your good works, which they shall behold, glorify God in the day of visitation."

versus

Matthew 6:1-4 "Take heed that ye do not your alms before men, to be seen of them . . . that thine alms may be in secret."

Matthew 23:3, 5 "Do not ye after their [Pharisees'] works... all their works they do for to be seen of men."

SHOULD WE OWN SLAVES?

Leviticus 25:45-46 "Moreover of the children of the strangers that do sojourn among you, of them shall ye buy, ...and they shall be your possession... they shall be your bondmen forever."

Genesis 9:25 "And he [Noah] said, Cursed be Canaan; a servant of servants shall he be unto his brethren."

Exodus 21:2, 7 "If thou buy an Hebrew servant, six years he shall serve: and in the seventh he shall go out free for nothing... And if a man sell his daughter to be a maidservant, she shall not go out as the manservants do."

Joel 3:8 "And I will sell your sons and your daughters into the hand of the children of Judah, and they shall sell them to the Sabeans, to a people far off: for the Lord hath spoken it."

Luke 12:47, 48 [Jesus speaking] "And that servant, which knew his lord's will, and prepared not himself, neither did according to his will, shall be beaten with many stripes. But he that knew not, and did commit things worthy of stripes, shall be beaten with few stripes."

Colossians 3:22 "Servants, obey in all things your masters."

versus

Isaiah 58:6 "Undo the heavy burdens... let the oppressed go free, ... break every yoke."

Matthew 23:10 "Neither be ye called Masters: for one is your Master, even Christ."

Pro-slavery bible verses were cited by many churches in the South during the Civil War, and were used by some theologians in the Dutch Reformed Church to justify apartheid in South Africa. There are more pro-slavery verses than cited here.

DOES GOD CHANGE HIS MIND?

Malachi 3:6 "For I am the Lord; I change not."

Numbers 23:19 "God is not a man, that he should lie; neither the son of man, that he should repent."

Ezekiel 24:14 "I the Lord have spoken it: it shall come to pass, and I will do it; I will not go back, neither will I spare, neither will I repent."

James 1:17 "...the Father of lights, with whom is no variableness, neither shadow of turning."

versus

Exodus 32:14 "And the Lord repented of the evil which he thought to do unto his people."

Genesis 6:6, 7 "And it repented the Lord that he had made man on the earth... And the Lord said, I will destroy man whom I have created from the face of the earth... for it repenteth me that I have made him."

Jonah 3:10 "...and God repented of the evil, that he had said that he would do unto them; and he did it not."

See also II Kings 20:1-7, Numbers 16:20-35, Numbers 16:44-50.

See Genesis 18:23-33, where Abraham gets God to change his mind about the minimum number of righteous people in Sodom required to avoid destruction, bargaining down from 50 to 10. (An omniscient God must have known that he was playing with Abraham's hopes for mercy—he destroyed the city anyway.)

DOES GOD KNOW THE FUTURE?

Isaiah 46:10 [God talking] "I make known the end from the beginning, from ancient times, what is still to come."

versus

Genesis 22:12 [God talking to Abraham when he was about to sacrifice his son Isaac] "Lay not thine hand upon the lad, neither do thou any thing unto him: for now I know that thou fearest God, seeing thou hast not withheld thy son, thine only [son] from me."

When God said that "now I know" this means he did not know before. This also contradicts I Chronicles 28:9, which says "for the LORD searcheth all hearts, and understandeth all the imaginations of the thoughts."

ARE WE PUNISHED FOR OUR PARENTS' SINS?

Exodus 20:5 "For I the Lord thy God am a jealous God, visiting the iniquity of the fathers upon the children unto the third and fourth generation." (Repeated in Deuteronomy 5:9.)

Exodus 34:6-7 "...The Lord God, merciful and gracious...that will by no means clear the guilty; visiting the iniquity of the fathers upon the children, and upon the children's children, unto the third and to the fourth generation."

I Corinthians 15:22 "For as in Adam all die..."

versus

Ezekiel 18:20 "The son shall not bear the iniquity of the father."

Deuteronomy 24:16 "The fathers shall not be put to death for the children, neither shall the children be put to death for the fathers: every man shall be put to death for his own sin."

WHOSE FAULT WAS IT THAT MOSES COULD NOT ENTER THE PROMISED LAND?

Deuteronomy 32:48-52 [God telling Moses that it was his and Aaron's fault] "This is because both of you broke faith with me in the presence of the Israelites at the waters of Meribah...and because you did not uphold my holiness among the Israelites."

Numbers 27:12-13 [God to Moses] "Ye rebelled against my commandment."

versus

Deuteronomy 1:37 [Moses talking to the people, shifting the blame] "Because of you, the Lord became angry with me." (See also Deuteronomy 3:26 and 4:20-22.)

IS GOD GOOD OR EVIL?

Psalm 145:9 "The Lord is good to all."

Deuteronomy 32:4 "A God of truth and without iniquity, just and right is he."

versus

Isaiah 45:7 "I make peace and create evil. I the Lord do all these things."

Lamentations 3:38 "Out of the mouth of the most High proceedeth not evil and good?"

Jeremiah 18:11 "Thus saith the Lord; Behold, I frame evil against you, and devise a device against you."

Ezekiel 20:25, 26 "I gave them also statutes that were not good, and judgments whereby they should not live. And I polluted them in their own gifts, in that they caused to pass through the fire all that openeth the womb, that I might make them desolate, to the end that they might know that I am the Lord."

Regarding Isaiah 45:7, where God says "I make peace and create evil," we notice that some versions dishonestly translate "evil," or *ra*, as "calamity" or another softer word—although even this paints God as a troublemaker. However, that Hebrew word *ra* clearly means "moral evil," as it is used in Genesis 3, the most important moral tale in the entire bible, the story of the fall of the human race: "For God doth know that in the day ye eat thereof, then your eyes shall be opened, and ye shall be as gods, knowing good and evil... And the LORD God said, Behold, the man is become as one of us, to know good and evil." (Genesis 3:5, 22) That word "create," by the way, is *bara*, used in the first verse of the bible.

DOES GOD TEMPT PEOPLE?

James 1:13 "Let no man say...I am tempted of God: for God cannot be tempted with evil, neither tempteth he any man."

versus

Genesis 22:1 "And it came to pass after these things, that God did tempt Abraham."

IS GOD PEACEABLE?

Romans 15:33 "The God of peace."

Isaiah 2:4 "...and they shall beat their swords into plowshares, and their spears into pruninghooks: nation shall not lift up sword against nation, neither shall they learn war any more."

versus

Exodus 15:3 "The Lord is a man of war."

Joel 3:9-10 "Prepare war, wake up the mighty men, let all the men of war draw near; let them come up: Beat your plowshares into swords, and your pruninghooks into spears: let the weak say, I am strong."

WHO WAS THE PRIEST IN THE STORY OF DAVID AND THE SHEWBREAD?

I Samuel 21:1-6 " Then came David to Nob to Ahimelech the priest... So the priest gave him hallowed bread: for there was no bread there but the shewbread."

versus

Mark 2:26 "How he [David] went into the house of God in the days of Abiathar the high priest, and did eat the shewbread, which is not lawful to eat but for the priests, and gave also to them which were with him?

Some apologists claim that "days of Abiathar" (a priest after the time of David) is metaphorical. If this defense is allowed, then there could be no possible contradiction anywhere, inside or outside of the bible. We can simply claim metaphor where we don't like what the actual text says.

WHEN WAS JESUS BORN?

Before 4 B.C.E.: Matthew 2:1 "Now when Jesus was born in Bethlehem of Judaea in the days of Herod the king..." (King Herod died in 4 B.C.E.)

versus

After 6 C.E.: Luke 2:1-4 "And it came to pass in those days, that there went out a decree from Caesar Augustus that all the world should be taxed. (And this taxing was first made when Cyrenius was governor of Syria.)... And Joseph also went up from Galilee, out of the city of Nazareth, unto the city of David, which is called Bethlehem..." (Cyrenius became governor of Syria in 6 C.E.)

Cyrenius is also spelled "Quirinius." For an in-depth analysis, see *The Date of the Nativity in Luke*, by Richard Carrier (www.infidels.org/library/modern/richard_carrier/quirinius.html).

WAS JESUS PEACEABLE?

John 14:27 "Peace I leave with you, my peace I give unto you."

Acts 10:36 "The word which God sent unto the children of Israel, preaching peace by Jesus Christ."

Luke 2:14 "...on earth peace, good will toward men."

versus

Matthew 10:34 "Think not that I am come to send peace on earth: I came not to send peace, but a sword. For I am come to set a man at variance against his father, and the daughter against her mother, and the daughter in law against her mother in law. And a man's foes shall be they of his own household."

Luke 22:36 "Then said he unto them...he that hath no sword, let him sell his garment, and buy one."

WAS JESUS TRUSTWORTHY?

John 8:14 "Though I bear record of myself, yet my record is true."

versus

John 5:31 "If I bear witness of myself, my witness is not true."

"Record" and "witness" in the above verses are the same Greek word (*martyria*).

SHALL WE CALL PEOPLE NAMES?

Matthew 5:22 "Whosoever shall say Thou fool, shall be in danger of hellfire." [Jesus speaking]

versus

Matthew 23:17 "Ye fools and blind." [Jesus speaking]

Psalm 14:1 "The fool hath said in his heart, There is no God."

HAS ANYONE SEEN GOD?

John 1:18 "No man hath seen God at any time."

Exodus 33:20 "Thou canst not see my face: for there shall no man see me, and live."

John 6:46 "Not that any man hath seen the Father, save he which is of God [Jesus], he hath seen the Father."

I John 4:12 "No man hath seen God at any time."

versus

Genesis 32:30 "For I have seen God face to face."

Exodus 33:11 "And the Lord spake unto Moses face to face, as a man speaketh unto his friend."

Isaiah 6:1 "In the year that king Uzziah died I saw also the Lord sitting upon a throne, high and lifted up, and his train filled the temple."

Job 42:5 "I have heard of thee by the hearing of the ear: but now mine eye seeth thee."

HOW MANY GODS ARE THERE?

Deuteronomy 6:4 "The Lord our God is one Lord."

versus

Genesis 1:26 "And God said, Let us make man in our image."

Genesis 3:22 "And the Lord God said, Behold, the man has become as one of us, to know good and evil."

I John 5:7 "And there are three that bear witness in heaven, the Father, the Word, and the Holy Ghost: and these three are one."

It does no good to claim that "Let us" is the magisterial "we." Such usage implies inclusivity of all authorities under a king's leadership. Invoking the Trinity solves nothing because such an idea is more contradictory than the problem it attempts to solve. (By the way, the text of I John 5:7 does not appear in any ancient Greek manuscript. It was added much later by the Catholic Church into the Latin Vulgate. See *Misquoting Jesus* by Bart Ehrman for documentation of this fraudulent tampering with the bible.)

ARE WE ALL SINNERS?

Romans 3:23 "For all have sinned, and come short of the glory of God."

Romans 3:10 "As it is written, There is none righteous, no, not one."

Psalm 14:3 "There is none that doeth good, no, not one."

versus

Job 1:1 "There was a man... whose name was Job; and that man was perfect and upright."

Genesis 7:1 "And the Lord said unto Noah, Come thou and all thy house into the ark; for thee have I seen righteous before me in this generation."

Luke 1:6 "And they were both righteous before God, walking in all the commandments and ordinances of the Lord blameless."

HOW OLD WAS JEHOIACHIM WHEN HE BECAME KING?

II Kings 24: 8 "Jehoiachim was 18 years old when he became king, and he reigned in Jerusalem three months."

II Chronicles 36:9 "Jehoiachim was 8 years old when he became king, and he reigned in Jerusalem 3 months and 10 days."

HOW OLD WAS AHAZIAH WHEN HE BEGAN TO REIGN?

II Kings 8:26 "Two and twenty years old was Ahaziah when he began to reign."

II Chronicles 22:2 "Forty and two years old was Ahaziah when he began to reign."

All scholars, including inerrantists, admit that the previous two numerical examples are indeed discrepant in the oldest documents we possess, but some claim this is merely due to a copyist error, not a contradiction in the original text. (A piece of papyrus flaked off or a scribe's vision was weak.) Of course, we don't have the "originals" (if indeed they were written rather than oral), so there is no way to confirm this convenient assumption. Also, it should be pointed out that an omnipotent, omniscient, all-caring deity might have guaranteed that his all-important message be conveyed in a less sloppy manner. Although the New International Version, for example, changes the text of II Chronicles 22:2 from "forty-two" to "twenty-two," presumably to avoid the appearance of a contradiction, they are honest enough to include a footnote saying: "Hebrew forty-two."

SHOULD WE SWEAR AN OATH?

Numbers 30:2 "If a man vow a vow unto the Lord, or swear an oath... he shall do according to all that proceedeth out of his mouth."

Genesis 21:22-24, 31 "...swear unto me here by God that thou wilt not deal falsely with me... And Abraham said, I will swear... Wherefore he called that place Beersheba ["well of the oath"]; because there they sware both of them."

Hebrews 6:13-17 "For when God made promise to Abraham, because he could swear by no greater, he sware by himself...for men verily swear by the greater: and an oath for confirmation is to them an end of all strife. Wherein God, willing more abundantly to shew unto the heirs of promise the immutability of his counsel, confirmed it by an oath."

See also Genesis 22:15-19, Genesis 31:53, and Judges 11:30-39.

versus

Matthew 5:34-37 "But I say unto you, swear not at all; neither by heaven... nor by the earth... Neither shalt thou swear by thy head... But let your communication be, Yea, yea; Nay, nay: for whatsoever is more than these cometh of evil."

James 5:12 "...swear not, neither by heaven, neither by the earth, neither by any other oath: but let your yea be yea; and your nay, nay; lest ye fall into condemnation."

WHEN WAS JESUS CRUCIFIED?

Mark 15:25 "And it was the third hour, and they crucified him."

versus

John 19:14-15 "And about the sixth hour: and he saith unto the Jews, Behold your King! But they cried out... crucify him."

It is an *ad hoc* defense to claim that there are two methods of reckoning time here. It has never been shown that this is the case.

SHALL WE OBEY THE LAW?

I Peter 2:13 "Submit yourself to every ordinance of man...to the king, as supreme; Or unto governors."

Matthew 22:21 "Render therefore unto Caesar the things which are Caesar's."

See also Romans 13:1, 7 and Titus 3:1.

versus

Acts 5:29 "We ought to obey God rather then men."

HOW MANY ANIMALS ON THE ARK?

Genesis 6:19 "And of every living thing of all flesh, two of every sort shalt thou bring into the ark."

Genesis 7:8-9 "Of clean beasts, and of beasts that are not clean, and of fowls, and of every thing that creepeth upon the earth. There went in two and two unto Noah into the ark, the male and the female, as God had commanded Noah."

Genesis 7:15 "And they went in unto Noah into the ark, two and two of all flesh, wherein is the breath of life."

versus

Genesis 7:2 "Of every clean beast thou shalt take to thee by sevens, the male and his female: and of beasts that are not clean by two, the male and his female."

WERE WOMEN AND MEN CREATED EQUAL?

Genesis 1:27 "So God created man in his own image, in the image of God created he him; male and female created he them."

versus

Genesis 2:18, 23 "And the Lord God said, It is not good that the man should be alone; I will make him an help meet for him... And Adam said, This is now bone of my bones, and flesh of my flesh: she shall be called Woman, because she was taken out of Man."

WERE TREES CREATED BEFORE HUMANS?

Genesis 1:12-31 "And the earth brought forth grass, and herb yielding seed after his kind, and the tree yielding fruit, whose seed was in itself, after his kind:... And the evening and the morning were the third day... And God said, Let us make man in our image... And the evening and the morning were the sixth day."

Genesis 2:5-9 "And every plant of the field before it was in the earth, and every herb of the field before it grew: for the Lord God had not caused it to rain upon the earth, and there was not a man to till the ground... And the Lord God formed man of the dust of the ground... And the Lord God planted a garden eastward in Eden; and there he put the man whom he had formed. And out of the ground made the Lord God to grow every tree that is pleasant to the sight, and good for food."

DID MICHAL HAVE CHILDREN?

II Samuel 6:23 "Therefore Michal the daughter of Saul had no child unto the day of her death."

versus

II Samuel 21:8 "But the king took the two sons of Rizpah...and the five sons of Michal the daughter of Saul."

HOW MANY STALLS DID SOLOMON HAVE?

I Kings 4:26 "And Solomon had forty thousand stalls of horses for his chariots, and twelve thousand horsemen."

versus

II Chronicles 9:25 "And Solomon had four thousand stalls for horses and chariots, and twelve thousand horsemen."

DID PAUL'S MEN HEAR A VOICE?

Acts 9:7 "And the men which journeyed with him stood speechless, hearing a voice, but seeing no man."

versus

Acts 22:9 "And they that were with me saw indeed the light, and were afraid; but they heard not the voice of him that spake to me."

See Chapter 14 for a deeper analysis of this contradiction.

IS GOD OMNIPOTENT?

Jeremiah 32:27 "Behold, I am the Lord, the God of all flesh: is there anything too hard for me?"

Matthew 19:26 "But Jesus beheld them, and said unto them, With men this is impossible; but with God all things are possible."

versus

Judges 1:19 "And the Lord was with Judah; and he drave out the inhabitants of the mountain; but could not drive out the inhabitants of the valley, because they had chariots of iron."

DOES GOD LIVE IN LIGHT?

I Timothy 6:15-16 "...the King of kings, and Lord of lords; Who only hath immortality, dwelling in the light which no man can approach..."

James 1:17 "...the Father of lights, with whom is no variableness, neither shadow of turning."

John 12:35 "Then Jesus saith unto them,... he that walketh in darkness knoweth not wither he goeth."

Job 18:18 "He [the wicked] shall be driven from light into darkness, and chased out of the world."

Daniel 2:22 "He [God] knoweth what is in the darkness, and the light dwelleth with him."

See also Psalm 143:3, II Corinthians 6:14 and Hebrews 12:18-22.

versus

I Kings 8:12 "Then spake Solomon, The Lord said that he would dwell in the thick darkness." (Repeated in II Chronicles 6:1)

II Samuel 22:12 "And he made darkness pavilions round about him, dark waters, and thick clouds of the skies."

Psalm 18:11 "He made darkness his secret place; his pavilion round about him were dark waters and thick clouds of the skies."

Psalm 97:1-2 "The Lord reigneth; let the earth rejoice...clouds and darkness are round about him."

DOES GOD ACCEPT HUMAN SACRIFICE?

Deuteronomy 12:31 "Thou shalt not do so unto the Lord thy God: for every abomination to the Lord, which he hateth, have they done unto their gods; for even their sons and their daughters they have burnt in the fire to their gods."

versus

Genesis 22:2 "And he said, Take now thy son, thine only son Isaac, whom thou lovest, and get thee into the land of Moriah; and offer him there for a burnt offering upon one of the mountains which I will tell thee of."

Exodus 22:29 "For thou shalt not delay to offer the first of thy ripe fruits, and of thy liquors; the firstborn of thy sons shalt thou give unto me."

Judges 11:30-39 "And Jephthah vowed a vow unto the Lord, and said, If thou shalt without fail deliver the children of Ammon into mine hand, Then it shall be, that whatsoever cometh forth of the doors of my house to meet me, when I return in peace from the children of Ammon, shall surely be the Lord's, and I will offer it up for a burnt offering. So Jephthah passed over unto the children of Ammon... and the Lord delivered them into his hands... And Jephthah came to Mizpeh unto his house, and, behold, his daughter came out to meet him with timbrels and with dances: And it came to pass at the end of two months, that she returned unto her father, who did with her according to his vow which he had vowed."

II Samuel 21:8-14 "But the king [David] took the two sons of Rizpah... and the five sons of Michal...and he delivered them into the hands of the Gibeonites, and they hanged them in the hill before the Lord:

and they fell all seven together, and were put to death in the days of harvest... And after that God was intreated for the land."

Hebrews 10:10-12 "...we are sanctified through the offering of the body of Jesus Christ... But this man, after he had offered one sacrifice for sins forever, sat down on the right hand of God."

I Corinthians 5:7 "...For even Christ our passover is sacrificed for us."

WHO WAS JOSEPH'S FATHER?

Matthew 1:16 "And Jacob begat Joseph the husband of Mary, of whom was born Jesus."

versus

Luke 3:23 "And Jesus himself began to be about thirty years of age, being (as was supposed) the son of Joseph, which was the son of Heli."

The above list is a very small portion of the thousands of biblical discrepancies that have been catalogued by scholars. See Chapter 15 and Chapter 16 for additional discrepancies specific to the birth narratives and resurrection of Jesus. All of these contradictions have been carefully studied, and when necessary the original languages have been consulted. Although it is always important to consider the original languages, why should that be necessary with the "word of God?" A respectable deity should have made his crucial message unmistakably clear to everyone, everywhere, at all times, in all languages. No one should have to learn a dead tongue to understand God's message, especially an ancient language about which there is scholarly disagreement. If the English translation is flawed or imprecise, then God failed to get his point across to English speakers. A true fundamentalist should consider the English version of the bible to be just as inerrant as the original because if we admit that human error was possible in the translation, then it was equally possible in the original writing. (Some fundamentalists do assert that the King James Version is perfect. One preacher reportedly said, "If the King James Version was good enough for the Apostle Paul, then it's good enough for me.")

While examining these contradictions, be aware of the fact that some modern translations have dishonestly changed the meaning of words to make the discrepancies disappear. (See Chapter 14 for a specific example.) I am using the King James Version not because I think it is the best English translation, but because it tends to be honest in portraying these discrepancies at face value—more honest than some of the later translations that try to paper them over. It is a good idea to consult a number of versions for comparison, especially if you don't read the Hebrew or Greek.

Why should it surprise us that the bible is contradictory? Pick up any newspaper and you will find contradictions. You can probably find one in this book, and the same person wrote all the chapters. (Of course, I am not claiming divine inspiration.) The bible was written by dozens of authors with diverse agendas, most of whom did not know each other, over hundreds of years. They were human beings. Human beings make mistakes. The bible does contain some truth, but no honest person can pretend it is a perfect book. Combined with the exaggerations, scientific inaccuracies, borrowings from pagan sources, evidence of tampering and clearly irrelevant passages aimed at bygone, primitive, superstitious people, the contradictions underscore the fact that, on balance, the bible is not a reliable source of truth.

Chapter Fourteen
Understanding Discrepancy

In the 9th chapter of Acts, Luke tells the story of the conversion of Saul, saying that "the men which journeyed with him stood speechless, *hearing a voice,* but seeing no man." (Acts 9:7, emphasis mine.) In the 22nd chapter of the same book, Luke quotes Paul's own words regarding the same experience: "And they that were with me saw indeed the light, and were afraid; but they *heard not the voice* of him that spake to me." (Acts 22:9, emphasis mine.) There is an apparent contradiction here: Luke says "hearing a voice" but Paul says "they heard not the voice." If the translation is correct, then Luke has made a mistake.

There are two approaches that defenders of the bible have used to try to clear up this discrepancy. The first claims that "hear" should be translated as "understand" in Acts 22:9, meaning that although the men heard the voice, they did not *hear* (understand) the voice. The second defense claims that the word "voice" should really be translated as "sound" in Acts 9:7, meaning that the men heard *something*, but did not know it was a voice.

"HEAR" OR "UNDERSTAND"?

I play professional piano. Although I sometimes use electronic keyboards in jazz bands, I much prefer the acoustic piano, especially for solo work. Nothing matches the beauty of physically produced tones resonating in a real piano of quality wood. The overtones mix in the air like no computer can duplicate.

The word acoustic comes from the Greek word *akouo,* meaning "to hear." Pronounced "ah-KOO-oh" by modern Greeks, it means to hear physically, acoustically. Both Acts 9:7 and Acts 22:9 use that word. *Akouo* does not mean "understand." New Testament Greek possesses other words for "understand." The main one is *suniemi,* which is "to understand in the sense of putting things together." (The word means "to send together.") There are also *noeo*, from the word for "mind"; *ginosko*, which means "to know"; and others. These verbs have noun counterparts: for example, *sunesis* ("understanding"), related to *suniemi*. The word *akouo* has no noun counterpart that works as a synonym for "understanding."

This does not mean, however, that "hear" cannot be rendered loosely as "understand" in some special cases. We do it in English in the informal phrase, "I hear you." We also use "see" sometimes in this manner: "Do you see what I mean?" A word for a physical sense can sometimes be used poetically to refer to a mental process, but the only way to know this is by context. It can't be done with grammar alone. *Akouo* always means "hear" at the literal level, but it might sometimes figuratively be perceived as "understand," depending on its usage in a particular passage.

There is only one instance where the King James Version (KJV) translates *akouo* as "understand." First Corinthians 14:2: "For he that speaketh in an unknown tongue speaketh not unto men, but unto God: for no man understandeth (*akouo*) him; howbeit in the spirit he speaketh mysteries." The New International Version (NIV) puts it this way: "Indeed, no one understands him; he utters mysteries with his spirit." It seems, in context, that "understand" can be used here because, although there is obviously some physical hearing involved, there is an ambiguity about how a "mystery" spoken by a "spirit" could be physically perceived.

The Greek in Acts 22:9 is: *ten de phonen ouk ekousan.* ("The voice they did not hear." *Ekousan* is aorist [past tense] of *akouo*, 3rd person plural). The KJV and the New Revised Standard Version (NRSV) say that the men did not "hear" the voice, but the NIV and Living Bible (LB, a paraphrase, not a translation), both produced by evangelicals, say that the men did not "understand" the voice, removing the appearance of a contradiction. On what grounds do the NIV and LB use such a translation? The narrative passage is not poetic. In fact, in the parallel Acts 9:7, telling the same story, the NIV and LB do use "hear," from the verb *akouo* with the same object. There is nothing in the context of either Acts 9:7 or Acts 22:9 to warrant an informal or poetic translation of *akouo*.

There are a few places in the New Testament where *akouo* (hear) and *suniemi* (understand) are paired and contrasted as synonyms, but the connection is explicit. In Matthew 13:13, Jesus reportedly said: "Therefore speak I to them in parables: because they seeing see not; and hearing (*akouo*) they hear (*akouo*) not, neither do they understand (*suniemi*)." If the second occurrence of *akouo* means "understand," all by itself, then it would not have been necessary for Luke to add, "neither do they understand." This underscores the fact that grammar is not enough to determine when *akouo* might be translated loosely.

The NIV and the LB wish us to think that Paul's men "heard (Acts 9:7) but did not understand (Acts 22:9)" the voice. But "hear" and "understand" are coupled together all through the New Testament as a contrast of two different words. Matthew 13:23 says, "But he that received good seed into the good ground is he that heareth (*akouo*) the word, and understandeth (*suniemi*) it." Matthew 15:10: "Hear (*akouo*) and understand (*suniemi*)." Mark 4:12: "and hearing they may hear (*akouo*), and not understand (*suniemi*)." Notice that Mark did not use *ouk akouo* (not hear) when he wanted to say "not understand." For similar constructions see also Matthew 13:15, Matthew 13:19, Mark 7:14, Luke 8:10, Acts 28:26,27 and Romans 15:21. Since such pairing and contrasting of the two different words "hear" and "understand" is so common in New Testament Greek, why didn't Luke take advantage of it in order to make his meaning clear in this instance?

There is nothing in Acts 22:9—nothing grammatical, contextual or explicit—to indicated that *akouo* should be translated anything other than "hear." In fact, the same words (often the very same phrase: *ouk ekousan*) occur throughout the New Testament, but neither the NIV nor the LB use "not understand" in those places. Look at Matthew 13:17 (NIV): "Many prophets and righteous people longed to see what you see, but did not see it, and to hear what you hear, but did not hear (*ouk ekousan*) it." If Acts 22:9 should be translated as "not understand," why not here? In fact, Matthew 13:17 is one instance where *akouo* might justifiably be loosely translated "understand" (though this would spoil the poetry), but the opportunity is not taken, maybe because there is no discrepancy to disguise. We should not take this as permission, however, to consider that Luke was using a similar literary device because 13 chapters separate Acts 9:7 and 22:9. It would only work if the words were closely paired poetically, in the same passage or sentence.

Look at Mark 8:18 (NIV): "Do you have eyes but fail to see, and ears but fail to hear?" The phrase "fail to hear" is *ouk akouete:* "You do not hear." Again, if Acts 22:9 should be "not understand," then why not here? Other examples are John 5:37: "You have neither heard his voice nor seen his form"; and Romans 10:18: "Did they not hear (*ouk ekousan,* identical with Acts 22:9)?" (See also Mark 6:11, Luke 10:24, Luke 16:31, John 10:8, Acts 9:12 and Romans 15:21.) Why is the NIV not consistent? Why does it use "understand" *only* in Acts 22:9?

If Luke had wanted Acts 22:9 to mean "not understand," he should have said so, either explicitly (with *suniemi* or some other verb for understand) or contextually. If he had wanted to contrast the two meanings, why didn't he follow the New Testament practice of pairing *akouo* and *suniemi*?

"VOICE" OR "SOUND"?

I once brought up this contradiction on an Arizona radio show where I was debating James White, a self-styled Christian apologist. White immediately retorted that since *phone* ("voice," pronounced "Pho-NEE" by modern Greeks) is in two different cases in these verses, it was meant to be understood differently: "voice" in one instance but "sound" in the other. He is right about the two different cases, but he is wrong about what this means. Greek scholars who have more than a superficial knowledge of the language would never use this argument.

Acts 9:7 has *tes phones* and Acts 22:9 has *ten phonen* for "the voice." The first is in the genitive case, and the second is in the accusative. Although the KJV and the NRSV use "voice" in both verses, the evangelical NIV and LB translate *phones* as "sound" in Acts 9:7 and *phonen* as "voice" in Acts 22:9. They appear to be suggesting that the genitive case should change the meaning of "voice." A number of Christian apologists, such as Gleason Archer, have used this argument. But they are wrong. In this instance, the genitive case does not change the meaning of the word in any way.

In many inflected languages, such as Greek, there is a flexibility of case usage (declension of nouns) with some verbs. Some verbs take their direct objects in more than just the accusative case. This is explicitly true of *akouo,* which can take either the accusative or the genitive with no change in meaning. If the apologists are right and the genitive cases does change the meaning here, then this would create dozens of contradictions elsewhere in the New Testament where such flexibility of case is common.

For example, the writers of Matthew and Luke both relate Jesus' parable of the wise man who built his house upon a rock. Matthew 7:24 quotes Jesus: "[W]hosoever heareth these sayings (*tous logous*) of mine, and doeth them, I will liken him unto a wise man." Luke 6:47, telling the *same* story, quotes Jesus: "Whosoever cometh to me, and heareth my sayings (*ton logon*), and doeth them, I will shew you to whom he is like." Both writers related the same speech, so it could not have meant two different things, but they used different cases for the object of *akouo*. Matthew used the accusative and Luke used the genitive. This is not a contradiction. There is a tiny inexactness about what declension Jesus might actually have used when he spoke these words in history (if he indeed spoke them in Greek, or spoke them at all), but there is no discrepancy. Matthew and Luke, each reconstructing the scene from memory (or perhaps from notes, from someone else's memory or translating from Aramaic), can be allowed some personal leeway in their choice of declensions. The New Testament Greek allows for such looseness. It is clear that the accusative and genitive case render exactly the same meaning following the word *akouo*.

Another example is when Matthew and Mark each report the appearance of Jesus before the high priest. Matthew 26:65 quotes the high priest: "Behold, now ye have heard his blasphemy (*blasphemian*)." Mark 14:64 tells the same story, quoting the high priest: "Ye have heard the blasphemy (*blasphemias*)." The writer of Matthew used the accusative for the object of *akouo* and the writer of Mark used the genitive. Again, there is no contradiction—just impreciseness about what actual word was spoken by the high priest. I suppose it is possible that one of the writers made a mistake, but since the case usage is flexible, translators don't even need to be charitable. They can simply assume there is no discrepancy.

Closer to home is Acts 9:4, Acts 22:7 and Acts 26:14, the story of Saul's conversion itself. (It is told three different times.) Acts 9:4: "And he fell to the earth and heard a voice (*phonen*) saying unto him, Saul, Saul, why persecutest thou me?" Acts 22:7: "And I fell unto the ground, and heard a voice (*phones*) saying unto me." Acts 26:14: "And when we were all fallen to the earth, I heard a voice (*phonen*) speaking unto me." Notice the different cases. Paul himself, telling the *same* story in the same context, uses two different cases. They cannot have meant two different things. In fact, the NIV and the LB agree, translating both the accusative and the genitive as "voice" in all three instances. If the apologists are correct when they say that the difference in case produces different words in Acts 9:7 and Acts 22:9, then the above example shows Paul contradicting himself. The apologists have shot themselves in the foot.

To be fair, there are places where *phone* can allowably be translated as "sound," but context rather than case determines this. *Phone* is used 140 times in the New Testament. It is translated as "voice" 131 times in the KJV. The other nine times it is translated as "sound" or "noise," but each of these is clearly figurative, referring to something that is not a person: "the noise (*phone*) of thunder," "sound (*phone*) of wind," "wings," etc. Notice that although the KJV translates Revelation 6:1 as "sound of thunder" (*phone*, dative case), the NRSV, NIV and LB stick with "voice." Here, where there actually *is* a poetic justification for using "sound," and a different case from the accusative, it is not taken. I think the literal "voice of thunder," a more interesting way of speaking, is more respectful of the poetic intention of the writer than "sound of thunder." Neither thunder nor wind actually have a "voice." But in Acts 9:7 there is no such poetic context. In fact, Luke goes out of his way to insist that it was a person: "hearing a voice, but seeing *no man*." (My emphasis.) If Paul's men thought they had heard an impersonal noise like thunder or wind, then it would not have been necessary to add the phrase "but seeing no man."

Why would the NIV and the LB use "sound" in Acts 9:7 instead of "voice"? There is no linguistic or contextual reason. It appears these evangelical translators are simply trying to paper over a discrepancy. The NIV and LB translators cannot claim a new, more advanced understanding of Greek. The NRSV was published *after* the NIV and LB, and it uses the literal "voice" in Acts 9:7. (From what I can tell, the NRSV seems to be the most popular translation among scholars.)

The motives of the NIV and LB translators are made clear in the preface to each book. The NIV, translated by a team of evangelical scholars (instigated by the National Association of Evangelicals), is introduced with these words: "We offer this version of the bible to him in whose name and for whose glory it has been made. We pray that it will lead many into a better understanding of the Holy Scriptures and a fuller knowledge of Jesus Christ the incarnate Word, of whom the Scriptures so faithfully testify." If there is a contradiction in the New Testament, then it could not "faithfully testify" anything. The NIV team was extremely selective in choosing its scholars: "[T]he translators were united in their commitment to the authority and infallibility of the bible as God's Word in written form. They believe that it contains the divine answer to the deepest needs of humanity, that it sheds light on our path in a dark world, and that it sets forth the way to our eternal well-being." This is not the agenda of a team of objective scholars. This is evangelism. If there is a contradiction in the bible, the NIV translators, who were confessedly committed *a priori* to infallibility, could never see it! (Some skeptics might be tempted to use the phrase, "There is none so blind as he who will not see." I would never stoop to such *ad hominem* tactics.)

The Living Bible does not claim to be a strict translation. It is a paraphrase by Dr. Kenneth Taylor, who admits in his preface: "[W]hen the Greek or Hebrew is not clear, then the theology of the translator is his guide, along with his sense of logic... The theological lodestar in this book has been a rigid evangelical position." *The theology of the translator is his guide.* In Acts 9:7 there is no lack of clarity: *phones* is "voice." But if your "theology" dictates that the bible must contain no errors, then a perfectly simple translation that results in a contradiction becomes "unclear," and you have to resort to sleight of hand to repair the damage to your theology.

What if an atheistic or skeptical organization were to translate the bible, putting together a team of staunch materialists, systematically excluding conservative or evangelical scholars, announcing a "rigid skeptical position," claiming to be "united in our commitment to the fallibility of the bible," and advertising the "hope that this translation will lead many astray from faith into a solid doubt of the reliability of Scriptures?" The evangelicals would scream! So would real scholars. Such prejudice clearly would taint the objectivity of the process.

One of the most popular evangelical verses is Revelation 3:20 (I used this often in my own evangelism), where Jesus is quoted as saying: "Behold, I stand at the door and knock: if any man hear my voice (*phones*), and open the door, I will come into him." The genitive case is used here, as it is in Act 9:7, yet the NIV uses "voice" and the LB says "hears me calling." Neither uses "knocking" or "sound."

These evangelical translators are not consistent. They only invoke the *ad hoc* (and faulty) genitive-case argument where it suits their inerrancy agenda.

Let's face it. Acts 9:7 and Acts 22:9 are contradictory. Writers make mistakes. In their confessed missionary zeal, the translators of the NIV and the Living Bible and other evangelical apologists have dishonestly tampered with the meaning of scripture, using a phony argument (a *phone* argument!) in order to deceive the readers and disguise an embarrassing discrepancy in their so-called "holy book."

Chapter Fifteen
Did Jesus Exist?

In all the years I was a Christian minister, I never preached a sermon about the evidence for a historic Jesus. There was no need for such a sermon. I stood before many congregations and associated with many ministers, evangelists and pastors, and not one of us ever spoke about the possibility that Jesus was a legend or that his story is more myth than history. We had heard, of course, that there were academic skeptics, but we dismissed them as a tiny fringe of quacks and atheists.

In my four years of religious study at Azusa Pacific College, I took many bible classes—an entire course about the book of Romans, another very useful class about Hebrew wisdom literature, and so on—but I was offered only one course in Christian apologetics. It was called "Christian Evidences" and I found it to be the least useful of all my studies. Not that it was a bad class, but it seemed so unnecessary. It provided an answer to a question nobody was asking. Since I preferred evangelism to academics, I found the information mildly interesting and somewhat confirming (though my faith did not need such confirmation), and mainly irrelevant. The class did not delve deeply into the ancient documents. We recited the roster of early historians and read some of the church fathers, and then promptly forgot them all. I figured that Christian scholars had already done the homework and that our faith rested on a firm historical foundation, and that if I ever needed to look it up I could turn to some book somewhere for the facts. I just never needed to look it up.

But when I became a freethinker, I did decide to look it up and was very surprised at what I found—or more precisely, at what I didn't find. I am now convinced that the Jesus story is a combination of myth and legend, mixed with a little bit of real history unrelated to Jesus. Here's what I found out:

1) There is no external historical confirmation for the New Testament stories.

2) The New Testament stories are internally contradictory.

3) There are natural explanations for the origin of the Jesus legend.

4) The miracle reports make the story unhistorical.

The Jesus of history is not the Jesus of the New Testament. A number of scholars[1] and writers, known informally as "mythicists," insist that Jesus did not exist at all. Others think there might have existed a self-proclaimed messiah figure named Yeshua (there were many others) on whom the New Testament story was loosely based. But even so, the latter group considers the exaggerated, miracle-working, resurrecting Jesus caricature in the Gospels to be a legend, a literary character produced by a later generation of believers. The legend position amounts to the same thing as myth to most believers, who worship only the Jesus of the Gospels. The Gospels, written many decades after the fact, are a blend of fact and fantasy—historical fiction—and although the proportions of the blend may differ from scholar to scholar, no credible historians take them at 100 percent face value.

Whether myth or legend, the life of Jesus is not corroborated. Not a single word about Jesus appears outside of the New Testament in the entire first century, even though many writers documented firsthand the early Roman Empire in great detail, including careful accounts of the time and place where Jesus supposedly taught.

Many Christian writers do claim, however, that there is overwhelming historical testimony for Jesus. At face value, the number of evidences does appear to be ample. Looking outside of the New Testament, many texts in apologetics will include a long list of names and documents that claim to confirm the story of Jesus: Josephus, Suetonius, Pliny, Tacitus, Thallus, Mara Bar-Serapion, Lucian, Phlegon, Tertullian, Justin Martyr, Clement of Rome, Ignatius, Polycarp, Clement of Alexandria,

---

1   Including John Allegro, G. A. Wells, Michael Martin (who leans towards Wells's view), Timothy Freke & Peter Gandy (*The Jesus Mysteries*), Robert Price (*Deconstructing Jesus*), Frank Zindler (*The Jesus The Jews Never Knew*), Earl Doherty (*The Jesus Puzzle*), and others.

Hippolytus, Origen, Cyprian and others. If you simply rattle off this list, you might be forgiven for saying, "Wow, that settles it!"

But then, if you ask a few questions you quickly realize that most of these names can be taken off the list. And if you scratch beneath the surface, they all have to be discarded. Some of these names are church fathers writing in the second to fourth centuries and are therefore too late to be considered reliable for first-century confirmation. Being church leaders, their objectivity is also questionable. These facts were not important to me as an evangelist nor would they raise any red flags in the minds of the average believer reading the average book of Christian "proofs."

The list does, however, include some nonbelievers—Jewish and Roman writers who were likely not biased towards Christianity—so it would appear that there can be little question about the historical confirmation of Jesus. Still, it is rarely if ever pointed out that none of these reports dates from the time of Jesus or even the following generation. Jesus supposedly lived sometime between 4 B.C.E. and 30 C.E., but there is not a single contemporary historical mention of Jesus, not by Romans or by Jews, not by believers or by unbelievers, not during his entire lifetime. The earliest candidate for extrabiblical confirmation, one small paragraph in Josephus, dates to the mid 90s C.E., which is more than 60 years after Jesus supposedly died. Even this turns out to be bogus. The lack of contemporary corroboration does not disprove his existence, of course, but it certainly casts great doubt on the historicity of a man who supposedly had a great impact on the world. Someone should have noticed.

The early years of the Roman Republic is one of most historically documented times in history. One of the writers alive during the time of Jesus was Philo-Judaeus (sometimes known as Philo of Alexandria). John E. Remsburg, in *The Christ*, writes:

"Philo was born before the beginning of the Christian era, and lived until long after the reputed death of Christ. He wrote an account of the Jews covering the entire time that Christ is said to have existed on earth. He was living in or near Jerusalem when Christ's miraculous birth and the Herodian massacre occurred. He was there when Christ made his triumphal entry into Jerusalem. He was there when the crucifixion with its attendant earthquake, supernatural darkness and resurrection of the dead took place—when Christ himself rose from the dead and in the presence of many witnesses ascended into heaven. These marvelous events which must have filled the world with amazement, had they really occurred, were unknown to him. It was Philo who developed the doctrine of the Logos, or Word, and although this Word incarnate dwelt in that very land and in the presence of multitudes revealed himself and demonstrated his divine powers, Philo saw it not."

Philo might be considered the investigative reporter of his day. He was there on location during the early first century, talking with people who should have remembered or at least heard the stories, observing, taking notes, documenting. He reported nothing about Jesus.

There was also a historian named Justus of Tiberius who was a native of Galilee, the homeland of Jesus. He wrote a history covering the time when Christ supposedly lived. This history is now lost, but a ninth-century Christian scholar named Photius had read it and wrote: "He [Justus] makes not the least mention of the appearance of Christ, of what things happened to him, or of the wonderful works that he did."[2] Notice that Photius made the assumption that Justus overlooked Jesus when it is also possible that there was nothing there to overlook in the first place.

FLAVIUS JOSEPHUS

My Dad's birthday present to me when I turned 19 was a copy of the complete works of Flavius Josephus. When it comes to hard evidence from outside the bible, this is the most common piece of historical documentation offered by Christian apologists. Outside of the New Testament, Josephus presents the only possible confirmation of the Jesus story from the first century.

At first glance, Josephus appears to be the answer to the Christian apologist's dreams. He was a messianic Jew, not a Christian, so he could not be accused of bias. He did not spend a lot of time or space on his report of Jesus, showing that he was merely reporting facts, not spouting propaganda like the Gospel writers. Although he was born in 37 C.E. and could not have been a contemporary of Jesus, he lived close enough to the time to be considered a valuable second-hand source. Josephus was a highly respected and much-quoted Roman historian. He died sometime after the year 100. His two major tomes were *The Antiquities of the Jews* and *The Wars of the Jews*.

2   Photius' *Bibliotheca*, code 33.

Antiquities was written sometime after the year 90 C.E. It begins, "In the beginning God created the heaven and the earth," and arduously parallels the Old Testament up to the time when Josephus is able to add equally tedious historical details of Jewish life during the early Roman period. In Book 18, Chapter 3, this paragraph is encountered (Whiston's translation):

"Now, there was about this time, Jesus, a wise man, if it be lawful to call him a man, for he was a doer of wonderful works—a teacher of such men as receive the truth with pleasure. He drew over to him both many of the Jews, and many of the Gentiles. He was [the] Christ; and when Pilate, at the suggestion of the principal men amongst us, had condemned him to the cross, those that loved him at the first did not forsake him, for he appeared to them alive again the third day, as the divine prophets had foretold these and ten thousand other wonderful things concerning him; and the tribe of Christians, so named from him, are not extinct at this day."

This truly appears to give historical confirmation for the existence of Jesus. But is it authentic? Most scholars, including most fundamentalist scholars, admit that at least some parts of this paragraph cannot be authentic. Many are convinced that the entire paragraph is a forgery, an interpolation inserted by Christians at a later time. There are at least seven reasons for this:

1) The paragraph is absent from early copies of the works of Josephus. For example, it does not appear in Origen's second-century version of Josephus, in *Origen Contra Celsum*, where Origen fiercely defended Christianity against the heretical views of Celsus. Origen quoted freely from Josephus to prove his points, but never once used this paragraph, which would have been the ultimate ace up his sleeve.

In fact, the Josephus paragraph about Jesus does not appear at all until the beginning of the fourth century, at the time of Constantine. Bishop Eusebius, a close ally of the emperor, was instrumental in crystallizing and defining the version of Christianity that was to become orthodox, and he is the first person known to have quoted this paragraph of Josephus. Eusebius once wrote that it was a permissible "medicine" for historians to create fictions—prompting historian Jacob Burckhardt to call Eusebius "the first thoroughly dishonest historian of antiquity."

The fact that the Josephus-Jesus paragraph shows up at this point in history—at a time when interpolations and revisions were quite common and when the emperor was eager to demolish gnostic Christianity and replace it with literalistic Christianity—makes the passage quite dubious. Many scholars believe that Eusebius was the forger and interpolater of the paragraph on Jesus that magically appears in the works of Josephus after more than two centuries.

2) Josephus would not have called Jesus "the Christ" or "the truth." Whoever wrote these phrases was a believing Christian. Josephus was a messianic Jew, and if he truly believed Jesus was the long-awaited messiah (Christ), he certainly would have given more than a passing reference to him. Josephus never converted to Christianity. Origen reported that Josephus was "not believing in Jesus as the Christ."

3) The passage is out of context. Book 18 ("Containing the interval of 32 years from the banishment of Archelus to the departure from Babylon") starts with the Roman taxation under Cyrenius in 6 C.E. and talks about various Jewish sects at the time, including the Essenes and a sect of Judas the Galilean, to which he devotes three times more space than to Jesus. He discusses Herod's building of various cities, the succession of priests and procurators, and so on. Chapter 3 starts with sedition against Pilate, who planned to slaughter all the Jews but changed his mind. Pilate then used sacred money to supply water to Jerusalem. The Jews protested. Pilate sent spies into the Jewish ranks with concealed weapons, and there was a great massacre. Then in the middle of all these troubles comes the curiously quiet paragraph about Jesus, followed immediately by: "And about the same time another terrible misfortune confounded the Jews…" Josephus, an orthodox Jew, would not have thought the Christian story to be "another terrible misfortune." If he truly thought Jesus was "the Christ," this would have been a glorious story of victory. It is only a Christian (someone like Eusebius) who might have considered Jesus to be a Jewish tragedy. Paragraph three can be lifted out of the text with no damage to the chapter. In fact, it flows better without it.

4) The phrase "to this day" shows that this is a later interpolation. There was no "tribe of Christians" during Josephus' time. Christianity did not get off the ground until the second century.

5) Josephus appears not to know anything else about Jesus outside of this tiny paragraph and an indirect reference concerning James, the

"brother of Jesus" (see below). He does not refer to the gospels now known as Matthew, Mark, Luke and John, or to the writings or activities of Paul, though if these stories were in circulation at that time he ought to have known about them and used them as sources. Like the writings of Paul, Josephus' account is silent about the teachings or miracles of Jesus, although he reports the antics of other prophets in great detail. He makes no mention of the earthquake or eclipse at the crucifixion, which would have been universally known in that area if they had truly happened. He adds nothing to the Gospel narratives, and says nothing that would not have been believed by Christians already, whether in the first or fourth century. In all of Josephus' voluminous works, there is not a single reference to Christianity anywhere outside of this tiny paragraph. He relates much more about John the Baptist than about Jesus. He lists the activities of many other self-proclaimed messiahs, including Judas of Galilee, Theudas the magician and the Egyptian Jew Messiah, but is mute about the life of one whom he claims (if he wrote it) is the answer to his messianic hopes.

6) The paragraph mentions that the "divine prophets" foretold the life of Jesus, but Josephus neglects to mention who these prophets were or what they said. In no other place does Josephus connect any Hebrew prediction with the life of Jesus. If Jesus truly had been the fulfillment of divine prophecy, as Christians believe (and Josephus was made to say), he would have been the one learned enough to document it.

7) The hyperbolic language of the paragraph is uncharacteristic of a careful historian: "...as the divine prophets had foretold these and ten thousand other wonderful things concerning him..." This sounds more like sectarian propaganda—in other words, more like the New Testament—than objective reporting. It is very unlike Josephus.

Christians should be careful when they refer to Josephus as historical confirmation for Jesus. If we remove the forged paragraph, as we should, the works of Josephus become evidence *against* historicity. Some Christian scholars are honest enough, however, to acknowledge these problems—how could they not?—agreeing that tampering has occurred, yet insisting that the passage can be un-doctored to uncover an original, plainer report by Josephus that was later modified by someone like Eusebius. This is not the bible, after all. If we remove the fraudulent "he was the Christ" and "to this day" and "ten thousand other wonderful things" and so on, we can still spot an unvarnished second-hand recognition of the existence of Jesus, these scholars insist. But then you have to wonder where to draw the line.

How do Christians prove it was only part of the paragraph, and not the entire thing, that was dishonestly added to the *Antiquities?* And even if they can do that, doesn't this prove too much? Instead of raising our confidence in the reliability of ancient writings, doesn't this actually demonstrate that at least some early Christians were eager to falsify documents? If you admit there was a propensity for believers to tamper with evidence, how do you know they kept their grubby hands off the New Testament? Those who would try to rescue Josephus with this tactic are shooting themselves in the foot. The bible *has* been tampered with, and the argument that saves one damns the other.

There is one other passage in the *Antiquities* that mentions Jesus as an aside. It is in Book 20, Chapter 9:

"Festus was now dead, and Albinus was put upon the road; so he assembled the sanhedrin of judges, and brought before them the brother of Jesus, who was called Christ, whose name was James, and some others, (or some of his companions). And when he had formed an accusation against them as breakers of the law, he delivered them to be stoned..."

This is flimsy, and even Christian scholars widely consider this to be a doctored text. The stoning of James is not mentioned in Acts. Hegesippus, a Jewish Christian, in 170 C.E. wrote a history of the church saying that James the brother of Jesus was killed in a riot, not by sentence of a court. Clement confirms this (quoted by Eusebius). Most scholars agree that Josephus is referring to another James here, possibly the same one that Paul mentions in Acts, who led a sect in Jerusalem. Instead of strengthening Christianity, this "brother of Jesus" interpolation contradicts history. Again, if Josephus truly thought Jesus was "the Christ," he would have added more about him than a casual aside in someone else's story.

Josephus was a native of Judea and a contemporary of the Apostles. He was governor of Galilee for a time, the province in which Jesus allegedly lived and taught. "He traversed every part of this province," writes Remsburg, "and visited the places where but a generation before Christ had performed his prodigies. He resided in Cana, the very city in which Christ is said to have wrought his first miracle. He mentions every noted personage of Palestine and describes every important event that occurred there during the first seventy years of the Christian era. But Christ was of too little consequence and his deeds too trivial to merit a line from this historian's pen."

THE SECOND CENTURY AND LATER

After Josephus there are other writers who mention Christianity, but even if we are confident that their writings are authentic, they are too late to claim the confirming impact of a first-century witness. Suetonius wrote a biography called *Twelve Caesars* around the year 112 C.E., mentioning that Claudius "banished the Jews from Rome, since they had made a commotion because of Chrestus," and that during the time of Nero "punishments were also inflicted on the Christians, a sect professing a new and mischievous religious belief..." Notice that there is no mention of Jesus by name. It is unlikely that Christianity had spread as far as Rome during the reign of Claudius, or that it was large enough to have caused a revolt. Chrestus does not mean Christ. It was a common name meaning "good," used by both slaves and free people and occurring more than 80 times in Latin inscriptions.

Even if Suetonius made a typo and truly meant Christus (Christ), he may have been referring only to the Jews in Rome who were expecting a messiah, not to Jesus of Nazareth. It could have been someone else, maybe a Roman Jew, who stepped forward. It is only eager believers who jump to the conclusion that this provides evidence for Jesus. Nowhere in any of Suetonius' writings did he mention Jesus of Nazareth. Even if he had, his history would not necessarily have been reliable. He also reported, for example, that Caesar Augustus bodily rose to heaven when he died, an event that few modern scholars consider historical.

In 112 C.E., Pliny (the younger) said that "Christians were singing a hymn to Christ as to a god..." That's it. In all of Pliny's writings, we find one small tangential reference, and not even to Christ, but to Christians. Again, notice the absence of the name Jesus. This could have referred to any of the other "Christs" who were being followed by Jews who thought they had found a messiah. Pliny's report hardly counts as history since he is only relaying what other people believed. Even if this sentence referred to a group of followers of Jesus, no one denies that Christianity was in existence at that time. Pliny, at the very most, might be useful in documenting the religion, but not the historic Jesus.

Sometime after 117 C.E., the Roman historian Tacitus wrote in his *Annals* (Book 15, chapter 44): "Nero looked around for a scape-goat, and inflicted the most fiendish tortures on a group of persons already hated for their crimes. This was the sect known as Christians. Their founder, one Christus, had been put to death by the procurator, Pontius Pilate in the reign of Tiberius. This checked the abominable superstition for a while, but it broke out again and spread, not merely through Judea, where it originated, but even to Rome itself, the great reservoir and collecting ground for every kind of depravity and filth. Those who confessed to being Christians were at once arrested, but on their testimony a great crowd of people were convicted, not so much on the charge of arson, but of hatred of the entire human race."

In this passage, Tacitus depicts early Christians as "hated for their crimes" and associated with "depravity and filth." This is not a flattering picture. But even if it is valid, it tells us nothing about Jesus of Nazareth. Tacitus claims no first-hand knowledge of Christianity. He is merely repeating the then common ideas about Christians. (A modern parallel would be a 20th century historian reporting that Mormons believe that Joseph Smith was visited by the angel Moroni, which would hardly make it historical proof, even though it is as close as a century away.) There is no other historical confirmation that Nero persecuted Christians. Nero did persecute Jews, and perhaps Tacitus was confused about this. There certainly was not a "great crowd" of Christians in Rome around 60 C.E., and the term "Christian" was not in use in the first century. Tacitus is either doctoring history from a distance or repeating a myth without checking his facts. Historians generally agree that Nero did not burn Rome, so Tacitus is in error to suggest that he would have needed a scapegoat in the first place. No one in the second century ever quoted this passage of Tacitus, and in fact it appears almost word-for-word in the writings of someone else, Sulpicius Severus, in the fourth century, where it is mixed in with other myths. The passage is therefore highly suspect and adds virtually no evidence for a historic Jesus.

In the ninth century a Byzantine writer named George Syncellus quoted a third-century Christian historian named Julius Africanus, who quoted an unknown writer named Thallus on the darkness at the crucifixion: "Thallus in the third book of his history calls this darkness an eclipse of the sun, but in my opinion he is wrong." All of the works of Africanus are lost, so there is no way to confirm the quote or to examine its context. We have no idea who Thallus was, or when he wrote. Eusebius (fourth century) mentions a history of Thallus in three books ending about 112 C.E. so the suggestion is that Thallus might have been a near contemporary of Jesus. (Actually, the manuscript is damaged, and "Thallus" is merely a guess from "_allos Samaritanos." That word "allos" actually means "other" in Greek, so it may have been simply saying "the other Samaritan.") There is no historical evidence of an eclipse during the time Jesus was supposedly crucified. The reason Africanus doubted the eclipse is because Easter happens near the full moon, and a solar eclipse would have been impossible at that time. (Even ancient skeptics knew that the full moon occurs when it is on the opposite side of the earth from the sun, where it is unable to move between the sun and the earth to produce an eclipse.)

There is a fragment of a personal letter from a Syrian named Mara Bar-Serapion to his son in prison, of uncertain date, probably second or third century, that mentions that the Jews of that time had killed their "wise king." However, the New Testament reports that the Romans, not the Jews, killed Jesus. The Jews had killed other leaders; for example, the Essene Teacher of Righteousness. If this truly is a report of a historical event rather than the passing on of folklore, it could have been a reference to someone else. It is worthless as evidence for Jesus of Nazareth, yet it can be found on the lists of some Christian scholars as proof that Jesus existed.

A second-century satirist named Lucian wrote that the basis for the Christian sect was a "man who was crucified in Palestine," but this is equally worthless as historical evidence. He is merely repeating what Christians believed in the second century. Lucian does not mention Jesus by name. This reference is too late to be considered historical evidence, and since Lucian did not consider himself a historian, neither should we.

All of these "confirmations" of Jesus are at best second-hand hearsay of what others were thought to have believed. They would be worthless in a court of law. It would be like a witness to a murder saying, "I did not see the act itself, but I read in a letter from someone who is now dead that they heard from a probably reliable source that someone actually believed that a person with the same or similar name committed the crime."

BOTTOM OF THE BARREL

In addition to Josephus, Suetonius, Tacitus and the others, there are a handful of highly questionable, so-called evidences that some Christians have put forward. These include Tertullian (197 C.E.), Phlegon (unknown date), Justin Martyr (about 150 C.E.) and portions of the Jewish Talmud (second through fifth centuries) that mention Jesus in an attempt to discredit Christianity, supposedly showing that even the enemies of Jesus did not doubt his existence. Though all of these late opinions are flimsy, some Christians make a showy point of listing them with little elaboration in their books of apologetics. Ministers can rattle off these "historical confirmations" with little fear that their congregations will take the time to investigate their authenticity.

I include one other very silly attempt here—the *Archko Volume*—not because it has ever come up in any of my debates or has been used by serious Christian apologists, but because it shows the lengths to which some believers will go to "prove" Christianity and how eagerly some gullible believers swallow such nonsense. And these are modern believers, supposedly more informed and sophisticated than the ancient writers.

A Christian actually mailed me a copy of the *Archko Volume*. This "eyewitness testimony" supposedly reports authentic, first-hand accounts of Jesus from the early first century. It includes letters from Pilate to Rome, glowing interviews of the shepherds outside Bethlehem who visited the baby Jesus at the manger after being awakened by angels, and so on. Its flowery King James prose makes entertaining reading, but it is not considered authentic by any scholar. It was written in the 19th century by a traveling salesman who said he translated it from original documents found in the basement of the Vatican. The "translations" were mailed overseas in installments, after payment for each one was received. No one has ever seen the original documents.

In *Evidence That Demands a Verdict,* Josh McDowell makes an argument that is common among apologists: "There are now more than 5,300 known Greek manuscripts of the New Testament. Add over 10,000 Latin Vulgate and at least 9,300 other early versions (MSS) and we have more than 24,000 manuscript copies of portions of the New Testament in existence today. No other document of antiquity even begins to approach such numbers and attestation. In comparison, the *Iliad* by Homer is second with only 643 manuscripts that still survive." Do you see how he is piling on numbers? What do the 10,000 Latin Vulgate copies have to do with original Greek manuscripts? This information might cause believers to applaud with smugness, but it misses the point. What does the number of copies have to do with authenticity?

If a million copies of this book are printed, does it make it any more truthful? Are the "historical" facts reported in the *Iliad* considered reliable? There are currently hundreds of millions of copies of the Koran in existence, in many forms and scores of translations. Does the sheer number of copies make it more reliable than, say, a single inscription on an Egyptian sarcophagus? This argument is a smokescreen. There are no original manuscripts (autographs) of the bible in existence, so we all agree that we are working from copies of copies. Critics might agree that some current translations of the New Testament are based on a reasonably accurate transcription of variations from early forms of some of the Greek documents, but what does this have to do with authenticity, reliability or truthfulness? And why are there variations at all? Yes, scribes sometimes made minor copying errors, but few believers realize how many discrepancies there are among the manuscripts. Bart Ehrman, in *Misquoting Jesus*, reminds us that there are more variants among the ancient documents than there are words in the New Testament.

Another argument made by Josh McDowell and others is the close interval of time between the events or original writing and the earliest copies in our possession. Homer wrote the *Iliad* in 900 B.C.E., but our earliest copy is from 400 B.C.E.—a span of 500 years. Aristotle wrote in 384-322 B.C.E. and the earliest copy of his work dates from 1100 C.E.—a gap of 1,400 years. In contrast, the New Testament was written (McDowell says) between 40 and 100 C.E., and the earliest copy dates from 125 C.E., a time span of 25 years. Actually, the earliest copy does not date from 125 C.E.—it is the earliest fragment, a few verses from the Gospel of John, that dates from then. There is no way to verify, from those few verses, whether the rest of John or any of the remainder of the New Testament is reliable. Most of the copies of the manuscripts that we have on hand date from a millennium later, so McDowell's implication is misleading.

All of this is important when considering the reliability of the *text* itself. A shorter interval of time allows for fewer corruptions and variants. (So, why are there so many variants, if the time was so short?) But even if the time interval were extremely brief, it has no relevance to the reliability of the *content*. If the New Testament should be considered reliable on this basis, then so should the *Book of Mormon*, which was supposedly written (copied by Joseph Smith) in 1823 and first published in 1830, a gap of only seven years. In addition to Joseph Smith, there are signed testimonies of 11 witnesses who claimed to have seen the gold tablets on which the angel Moroni wrote the *Book of Mormon*. We are much closer in history to the origin of Mormonism than to the origin of Christianity. There are millions of copies of the *Book of Mormon* and a thriving Church of Jesus Christ of Latter Day Saints (with millions of members and billions of dollars in assets) to prove its veracity. Though most scholars (pro and con) agree that the current edition of the *Book of Mormon* is a trustworthy copy of the 1830 version, few Christian scholars consider it to be reliable history.

NOT THE GOSPEL TRUTH

If we stick to the New Testament (we have no choice), how much can we know about the Jesus of history? Although the four Gospels—Matthew, Mark, Luke and John—have been placed first in the current ordering, they were not the first books written, nor were they written in that order. The earliest writings about Jesus are those of Paul, who produced his epistles no earlier than the mid 50s C.E. Strangely, Paul, who never met Jesus, mentions very little about the life of the historical Jesus. If Jesus had been a real person, certainly Paul, his main cheerleader, would have talked about him as a man. The Jesus of whom Paul writes is a disembodied, spiritual Christ, speaking from the sky, not a flesh and blood man of history. Paul never talks about Jesus' parents or the virgin birth or Bethlehem. He never mentions Nazareth, never refers to Jesus as the "Son of man" (as commonly used in the Gospels), avoids recounting a single miracle or deed committed by Jesus (except for reciting the Last Supper ritual), does not fix any historical activities of Jesus in any time or place, makes no reference to any of the 12 apostles by name, omits the trial and fails to place the crucifixion in a geographical location. Paul rarely quotes Jesus, and this is odd since he used many other devices of persuasion to make his points. There are numerous places in the teachings of Paul where he could have and should have invoked the teachings of Jesus, but he ignores them. He contradicts Jesus' teachings on divorce (I Corinthians 7:10), allowing for none while Jesus permitted exceptions. Jesus taught a trinitarian baptism ("in the name of the Father, Son and Holy Ghost"), but Paul and his disciples baptized in Jesus' name only—which makes perfect sense if the concept of the trinity was developed later. Paul never claims to have met the pre-resurrected Jesus. In fact, one of the most glaring contradictions of the bible appears in two different accounts of how Paul supposedly met the disembodied Christ for the first time (see Chapter 14).

The "silence of Paul" is one of the thorny problems confronting defenders of a historical Jesus. The Christ in Paul's writings is a different character from the Jesus of the Gospels. Paul adds not a speck of historical documentation for the story. Even Paul's supposed confirmation of the resurrection in I Corinthians 15:3-8 contradicts the Gospels when it says that Jesus first was seen of "Cephas [Peter], then of the twelve" (see Chapter 16).

The Gospels were written no earlier than 70 C.E., and most likely were written during the 90s C.E. and later. They all pretend to be biographies of Jesus. No one knows who wrote these books, the names having been added later as a matter of convenience. The writer of Matthew, for example, refers to "Matthew" in the third person. Neither Mark nor Luke appears in any list of the disciples of Jesus, and we have no way of knowing where they got their information. The general scholarly consensus is that Mark was written first (based on an earlier "proto-Mark" now lost, which shows that even the earliest Gospel contains second-hand data) and that the writers of Matthew and Luke borrowed from Mark, adapting and adding to it. Matthew, Mark and Luke are commonly known as the "synoptic Gospels" since they share much common material. The writer of John appears to have written in isolation, and the Jesus portrayed in his story is a different character. John contains little in common with the other three, and where it does overlap it is often contradictory.

There is very little that can be ascertained from the four Gospels about the historic Jesus. His birthday is unknown. In fact, the year of Jesus' birth *cannot* be known. The writer of Matthew says Jesus was born "in the days of Herod the king." Herod died in 4 B.C.E. Luke reports that Jesus was born "when Cyrenius [Quirinius] was governor of Syria." Cyrenius became governor of Syria in 6 C.E. That is a discrepancy of at least nine years. (There was no year zero.) Luke says Jesus was born during a Roman census, and it is true that there was a census in 6 C.E. This would have been when Jesus was at least nine years old, according to Matthew. There is no evidence of any earlier census during the reign of Augustus; Palestine was not part of the Roman Empire until 6 C.E. Perhaps Matthew was right, or perhaps Luke was right, but both could not have been right. (See Chapter 13 for the exact citations.)

Matthew reports that Herod slaughtered all the first-born in the land in order to execute Jesus. No historian, contemporary or later, mentions this supposed genocide, an event that should have caught someone's attention. None of the other biblical writers mention it.

The genealogies of Jesus present a particularly embarrassing (to believers) example of why the Gospel writers are not reliable historians. Matthew gives a genealogy of Jesus consisting of 28 names from David down to Joseph. Luke gives a reverse genealogy of Jesus consisting of 43 names from Joseph back to David. They each purport to prove that Jesus is of royal blood, though neither of them explains why Joseph's genealogy is relevant if he was not Jesus' father: Jesus was born of the Virgin Mary and the Holy Ghost. (I'd like to see the genome of the Holy Ghost's DNA.) Matthew's line goes from David's son Solomon, while Luke's goes from David's son Nathan. The two genealogies could not have been for the same person.

Matthew's line is like this: David, Solomon, 11 other names, Josiah, Jechoniah, Shealtiel, Zerubbabel, Abiud, six other names, Matthan, Jacob and Joseph. Luke's line is like this: David, Nathan, 17 other names (none identical to Matthew's list), Melchi, Neri, Shealtiel, Zerubbabel, Rhesa, 15 other names (none identical to Matthew's list), Matthat, Heli and Joseph.

Some defenders of Christianity assert that this is not contradictory at all because Matthew's line is through Joseph and Luke's line is through Mary, even though a simple glance at the text shows that they both name Joseph. No problem, say the apologists: Luke named Joseph, but he really meant Mary. Since Joseph was the legal parent of Jesus, and since Jewish genealogies are patrilineal, it makes perfect sense to say that Heli (their choice for Mary's father) had a son named

Joseph who had a son named Jesus. Believe it or not, many Christians can make these statements with a straight face. In any event, they will not find a shred of evidence to support such a notion.

There is an insurmountable problem to this argument: the two genealogies intersect. Notice that besides starting with David and ending with Joseph, the lines share two names: Shealtiel and Zerubbabel, both commonly known from the period of the Babylonian captivity. If Matthew and Luke present two distinct parental genealogies, as the apologists assert, there should be no intersection. In a last-ditch defense, some very creative apologists have hypothesized that Shealtiel's grandmother could have had two husbands and that her sons Jechoniah and Neri represent two distinct paternal lines, but this is painfully speculative.

The two genealogies are widely different in length. One would have to suppose that something in Nathan's genes caused every one of the men in his line to sire sons when they were 50 percent younger (on average) than the men in Solomon's line.

Matthew's line omits four names from the genealogy given in the Old Testament (between Joram and Jotham), and this makes sense when you notice that Matthew is trying to force his list into three neat groups of 14 names each. (Seven is the Hebrew's most sacred number.) He leaves out exactly the right number of names to make it fit. Some have argued that it was common to skip generations and that this does not make it incorrect. A great-great grandfather is just as much an ancestor as a grandfather. This might be true, except that Matthew explicitly reports that it was exactly *14* generations: "So all the generations from Abraham to David are fourteen generations; and from David until the carrying away into Babylon are fourteen generations; and from the carrying away into Babylon unto Christ are fourteen generations." (Matthew 1:17) Matthew is caught tinkering with the facts. His reliability as a historian is severely crippled.

Another problem is that Luke's genealogy of Jesus goes through Nathan, which was not the royal line. Nor could Matthew's line be royal after Jeconiah because the divine prophecy says of Jeconiah that "no man of his seed shall prosper sitting upon the throne of David, and ruling any more in Judah." (Jeremiah 22:30) Even if Luke's line is truly through Mary, Luke reports that Mary was a cousin to Elizabeth, who was of the tribe of Levi, not the royal line.

(Some Christians desperately suggest that the word "cousin" might allowably be translated "countrywoman," just as believers might call each other "brother" or "sister," but this is *ad hoc*.)

Since Jesus was not the son of Joseph, and since Jesus himself appears to deny his Davidic ancestry (Matthew 22:41-46), the whole genealogy is pointless. Instead of rooting Jesus in history, it provides critics with an open window on the myth-making process. The Gospel writers wanted to make of their hero nothing less than what was claimed of saviors of other religions: a king born of a virgin.

The earliest Gospel written was Mark. Matthew and Luke based their stories on Mark, editing according to their own purposes. All scholars agree that the last 12 verses of Mark, in modern translations, are highly dubious. Most agree that they do not belong in the bible. The earliest ancient documents of Mark end right after the women find the empty tomb. This means that in the first biography, on which the others based their reports, there is no post-resurrection appearance or ascension of Jesus. Noticing the problem, a Christian scribe at a much later time inserted verses 9-20. The Gospel accounts cannot be considered historical, but even if they were, they tell us that the earliest biography of Jesus contains no resurrection! They tell us that the Gospels were edited, adapted, altered and appended at later times to make them fit the particular sectarian theology of the writers.

The Gospels themselves are admittedly propagandistic: "And many other signs truly did Jesus in the presence of his disciples, which are not written in this book: But these are written that ye might believe that Jesus is the Christ, the Son of God; and that believing ye might have life through his name." (John 20:30-31) This hardly sounds like the stuff of objective historical reporting. This verse sends up a red flag that what we are reading should be taken with a very large grain of salt.

HOW DID THE MYTH ORIGINATE?

If Jesus is a myth or a legend, how did the story originate? How did there come to be a worldwide following of billions of Christians spanning two millennia if the story is not true? An idea does not need to be true in order to be believed, and the same could be asked about any other myth: Santa Claus, William Tell or Zeus. Nevertheless, it is not unfair to ask skeptics to suggest an alternative to historicity.

There are a number of plausible explanations for a natural origin of the Jesus myth, none of which can be proved with certainty. Unbelievers are not in agreement, nor need they be. Some skeptics think that Jesus never existed at all and that the myth came into being through a literary process. Other skeptics deny that the Jesus character portrayed in the New Testament existed, but feel that there could have been a first-century personality after whom the exaggerated myth was patterned. Others believe that Jesus did exist, and that some parts of the New Testament are accurate, although the miracles and the claim to deity are due to later editing of the original story. Still others claim that the New Testament is basically true in all of its accounts except that there are natural explanations for the miracle stories. (It is not just atheists who possess these views. Many liberal Christians, such as Paul Tillich, have "de-mythologized" the New Testament.)

None of these views can be proved, any more than the orthodox position can be proved. What they demonstrate is that since there do exist plausible natural alternatives, it is irrational to jump to a supernatural conclusion.

1) One of the views, held by J. M. Robertson and others, is that the Jesus myth was patterned after a story found in the Jewish Talmudic literature about the illegitimate son of a woman named Miriam (Mary) and a Roman soldier named Pandera, sometimes called Joseph Pandera. In *Christianity and Mythology*, Robertson writes: "...we see cause to suspect that the movement really originated with the Talmudic Jesus Ben Pandera, who was stoned to death and hanged on a tree, for blasphemy or heresy, on the eve of a Passover in the reign of Alexander Jannaeus (106-79 B.C.E.)." Dr. Low, an accomplished Hebraist, is satisfied that this Jesus was the founder of the Essene sect, whose resemblance to the legendary early Christians has so greatly exercised Christian speculation.

2) Another view is that the Jesus myth grew out of a pre-Christian cult of Joshua. Some suggest that the New Testament story about swapping Jesus for Barabbas (meaning "son of the father") arose from the tension between two different Joshua factions. Origen mentioned a "Jesus Barabbas." The name "Jesus" is the Greek for Joshua ("Yeshua" in Hebrew). In Mark 9:38 the disciples of Jesus saw another man who was casting out devils in the name of Jesus (Joshua). The Sibyllene Oracles identify Jesus with Joshua, regarding the sun standing still.

3) Other scholars suggest that the Jesus story is simply a fanciful patchwork of pieces borrowed from other religions. Pagan mythical parallels can be found for almost every item in the New Testament: the Last Supper, Peter's denial, Pilate's wife's dream, the crown of thorns, the vinegar and gall at the crucifixion, the mocking inscription over the cross, the Passion, the trial, Pilate's washing of hands, the carrying of the cross, the talk between the two thieves hanging beside Jesus, and so on. There were many crucified sun gods before Jesus. There was the crucifixion of Antigonus, the "King of the Jews," and Cyrus, a Messianic figure. Prometheus and Heracles wear mock crowns, and in some versions of the story Prometheus is executed by crucifixion. Babylonian prisoners dressed as kings for five days, then they were stripped, scourged and crucified.

Attis was a self-castrated god-man who was born of a virgin, worshipped between March 22 and March 27 (vernal equinox) and hanged on a cut pine tree. He escaped, fled, descended into a cave, died, rose again and was later called "Father God." The Greek god Dionysus was a man-god said to be the "Son of Zeus." He was killed, buried, descended into hell, and rose from the dead to sit at the right hand of the father. His empty tomb at Delphi was long preserved and venerated by believers. The Egyptian Osiris, two millennia earlier, was said to have been slain by Typhon, rose again and became ruler of the dead. There is the story about Simon the Cyrenian sun God who carried pillars to his death. (Compare with Simon the Cyrene who carried the cross of Jesus in the New Testament.) Before Jesus there were many ascension myths. Adonis and Attis also suffered and died to rise again. So did Enoch, Elijah, Krishna, Heracles, Dionysus and, later, Mary.

Mithra was a virgin-born Persian god. In 307 C.E. (just before Constantine institutionalized Christianity), the Roman emperor officially designated that Mithra was to be the "Protector of the Empire." Historian Barbara Walker records this about Mithra:

"Mithra was born on the 25th of December...which was finally taken over by Christians in the 4th century as the birthday of Christ. Some say Mithra sprang from an incestuous union between the sun god and his own mother... Some claimed Mithra's mother was a mortal virgin. Others said Mithra had no mother, but was miraculously born of a female Rock, the *petra genetrix*, fertilized by the Heavenly Father's phallic lightning.

"Mithra's birth was witnessed by shepherds and by Magi who brought gifts to his sacred birth-cave of the Rock. Mithra performed the usual assortment of miracles: raising the dead, healing the sick, making the blind see and the lame walk, casting out devils. As a Peter, son of the *petra*, he carried the keys of the kingdom of heaven... His triumph and ascension to heaven were celebrated at the spring equinox (Easter)...

"Before returning to heaven, Mithra celebrated a Last Supper with his twelve disciples, who represented the twelve signs of the zodiac. In memory of this, his worshippers partook of a sacramental meal of bread marked with a cross. This was one of seven Mithraic sacraments, the models for the Christians' seven sacraments. It was called *mizd,* Latin *missa,* English *mass.* Mithra's image was buried in a rock tomb... He was withdrawn from it and said to live again.

"Like early Christianity, Mithraism was an ascetic, anti-female religion. Its priesthood consisted of celibate men only...

"What began in water would end in fire, according to Mithraic eschatology. The great battle between the forces of light and darkness in the Last Days would destroy the earth with its upheavals and burnings. Virtuous ones...would be saved. Sinful ones...would be cast into hell... The Christian notion of salvation was almost wholly a product of this Persian eschatology, adopted by Semitic eremites and sun-cultists like the Essenes, and by Roman military men who thought the rigid discipline and vivid battle-imagery of Mithraism appropriate for warriors.

"After extensive contact with Mithraism, Christians also began to describe themselves as soldiers for Christ;... to celebrate their feasts on Sun-day rather than the Jewish sabbath... Like Mithraists, Christians practiced baptism to ascend after death through the planetary spheres to the highest heaven, while the wicked (unbaptized) would be dragged down to darkness." (*The Woman's Encyclopedia Of Myths And Secrets,* pages 663-665)

The name "Mary" is common to names given to mothers of other gods: the Syrian Myrrha, the Greek Maia and the Hindu Maya all derived from the familiar "Ma" for mother. The phrases "Word of God" and "Lamb of God" are probably connected, due to a misunderstanding of words that are similar in different languages. The Greek word "logos," which means "word," was used originally by the gnostics and is translated as "imerah" in Hebrew. The word "immera" in Aramaic means "lamb." It is easy to see how some Jews, living at the intersection of so many cultures and languages, could be confused and influenced by so many competing religious ideas.

Christianity appears to have been cut from the same fabric as pagan mythology, and early Christians admitted it. Arguing with pagans around 150 C.E., Justin Martyr said: "When we say that the Word, who is the first born of God, was produced without sexual union, and that he, Jesus Christ, our teacher, was crucified and died, and rose again, and ascended into heaven; we propound nothing different from what you believe regarding those whom you esteem sons of Jupiter (Zeus)."

In the fourth century a Christian scholar named Fermicus attempted to establish the uniqueness of Christianity, but he was met at every turn by pagan precedents to the story of Jesus. He is reported to have said: "Habet Diabolus Christos sous!" ("The Devil has *his* Christs!") If early Christians, who were closer to the events than we are, said the story of Jesus is "nothing different" from paganism, can modern skeptics be faulted for suspecting the same thing?

4) W. B. Smith thinks there was a pre-Christian Jesus cult of Gnosticism. There is an ancient papyrus that has these words: "I adjure thee by the God of the Hebrews, Jesus." *The Jesus Mysteries: Was the Original Jesus a Pagan God?* makes a compelling case that the original Christians were indeed gnostics and that the story of Jesus was invented by Hellenistic Jews in Alexandria as a mystery play patterned after the Osiris/Dionysus mystery cults, and was not to be taken literally. The play depicted a god-man who died and came back to life. It was only after Constantine in the fourth century decreed that the story should be literal and suppressed Gnosticism that the life of Jesus became suddenly "historical."

5) G. A. Wells is another scholar who believes Jesus never existed as a historical person. He and others see Jesus as the personification of Old Testament "wisdom." The Dead Sea Scrolls have Essene commentary on the Old Testament wisdom literature, and Wells has found many parallels with the life of Jesus. The book of Proverbs depicts "Wisdom" as having been created by God first, before heaven and earth. Wisdom mediates in creation and leads humans into truth. Wisdom is the governor and sustainer of the universe. Wisdom comes to dwell among men and bestows gifts. Most people reject Wisdom and it returns to heaven. Solomon's idea of a just man is one who is persecuted and

condemned to a shameful death, but then God gives him eternal life, counting him as one of the "sons of God," giving him a crown and calling him the "servant of the Lord." He is despised and rejected. In *The Jesus of History and Myth*, R. J. Hoffman writes: "In sum, musing on the Wisdom and on other Jewish literature could have prompted the earliest Christians to suppose that a preexistent redeemer had suffered crucifixion, the most shameful death of all, before being exalted to God's right hand."

6) Randall Helms in the article "Fiction in the Gospels" in *Jesus in History and Myth* presents another view. Helms notices that there are many literary parallels between Old Testament and New Testament stories. He calls this "self-reflexive fiction." It is as if there are some skeletal templates into which the Jews placed their stories. One example is the comparison between the raising of the son of the widow of Nain in Luke 7:11-16 and the raising of the son of a widow of Zarephath in I Kings 17. Not only is the content similar, but the structure of the tale is almost identical. Other examples are the storm stories in Psalms and Jonah compared with the New Testament storm story in Mark 4:37-41, and the story of Elijah's food multiplication with that of Jesus. The first-century Jews were simply rewriting old stories, like a movie remake. This view, in and of itself, does not completely account for the entire Jesus myth, but it does show how literary parallels can play a part in the elaboration of a fable.

7) John Allegro suggested that the Jesus character was patterned after the Essene Teacher of Righteousness, who was crucified in 88 B.C.E. He wrote that the Dead Sea Scrolls prove that the Essenes interpreted the Old Testament in a way to make it fit their own messiah. Allegro writes: "When Josephus speaks of the Essene's reverence for their 'Lawgiver'…we may assume reasonably that he speaks of their Teacher, the 'Joshua/Jesus' of the Last Days. By the first century, therefore, it seems that he was being accorded semi-divine status, and that his role of Messiah, or Christ, was fully appreciated." (*The Dead Sea Scrolls and the Christian Myth*)

8) An example of one of the many naturalistic attempts to explain the miracles is the "swoon theory" found in *The Passover Plot* by Dr. Hugh J. Schonfield. This is the idea that the resurrection story is basically historically accurate but that Jesus merely fainted, and was presumed to be dead, coming back to consciousness later.

Some of these explanations turn out to be just as difficult to believe as the miracle reports themselves, in my opinion. But they are, nevertheless, viable hypotheses that show that even if the documents are entirely reliable, the story itself can be explained in other ways. If it is possible for part of a story to be misunderstood or exaggerated, then why not the whole thing?

Prudent history demands that until all natural explanations for the origin of an outrageous tale are completely ruled out, it is irresponsible to hold to the literal, historical truth of what appears to be just another myth.

ARE THE MIRACLES HISTORICAL?

During a debate at the University of Northern Iowa, I asked my opponent, "Do you believe that a donkey spoke human language?"

"Yes, I do," he responded.

"Yesterday, I visited the zoo," I continued, "and a donkey spoke to me in perfect Spanish, saying, 'Alá es el único Dios verdadero.' Do you believe that?"

"No, I don't," he answered without hesitation.

"How can you be so quick to doubt my story and yet criticize me for being skeptical of yours?"

"Because I believe what Jesus tells me, not what you tell me."

In other words, miracles are true if the bible says so, but they are not true if they appear in any other source. When questioning the miracle reports of the New Testament, this becomes circular reasoning.

The presence of miracle stories in the New Testament makes the legend highly suspect. But it is important to understand what skeptics are saying about miracles. Skeptics do not say that the miracle reports should be automatically dismissed, *a priori*. After all, there might be future explanations for the stories, perhaps something that we yet do not understand about nature.

What skeptics say is that if a miracle is defined as some kind of violation, suspension, overriding or punctuation of natural law, then miracles cannot be *historical*. Of all of the legitimate sciences, history is the weakest. History, at best, produces only an approximation of truth. In order for history to have any strength at all, it must adhere to a very strict assumption: that natural law is regular over time.

Without the assumption of natural regularity, no history can be done. There would be no criteria for discarding fantastic stories. Everything that has ever been recorded would have to be taken as literal truth.

Therefore, if a miracle did happen, it would pull the rug out from history. The very basis of the historical method would have to be discarded. You can have miracles, or you can have history, but you can't have both.

However, if a miracle is defined as a "highly unlikely" or "wonderful" event, then it is fair game for history, but with an important caveat: outrageous claims require outrageous proof. (This does not mean we need a miracle to prove a miracle. It means we need *more* proof for an outrageous claim than we do for a more credible claim.) A skeptic who does allow for the remote possibility of accurate miracle reporting in the Gospels nevertheless must relegate it to a very low probability.

Since the New Testament contains numerous stories of events that are either outrageous (such as the resurrection of thousands of dead bodies on Good Friday) or impossible, the story must be considered more mythical than historical.

CONCLUSION

Either in ignorance or in defiance of scholarship, preachers such as televangelist Pat Robertson continue to rattle off the list of Christian "evidences," but most bible scholars, including most non-fundamentalist Christians, admit that the documentation is very weak. In *The Quest of the Historical Jesus*, Albert Schweitzer wrote: "There is nothing more negative than the result of the critical study of the life of Jesus... The historical Jesus will be to our time a stranger and an enigma..."

To sum up: 1) There is no external historical confirmation for the Jesus story outside of the New Testament. 2) The New Testament accounts are internally contradictory. 3) There are many other plausible explanations for the origin of the myth that do not require us to distort or destroy the natural worldview. 4) The miracle reports make the story highly suspect. (In the next chapter I will discuss another argument against historicity: evidence of legendary growth.)

The Gospel stories are no more historic than the Genesis creation accounts are scientific. They are filled with exaggerations, miracles and admitted propaganda. They were written during a context of time when myths were being born, exchanged, elaborated and corrupted, and they were written to an audience susceptible to such fables. They are cut from the same cloth as other religions and fables of the time. Taking all of this into account, it is rational to conclude that the New Testament Jesus is a myth.

Chapter Sixteen
Did Jesus Really Rise From the Dead?

During the 19 years I preached the Gospel, the resurrection of Jesus was the keystone of my ministry. Every Easter I affirmed the Apostle Paul's admonition: "If Christ has not been raised, then our proclamation has been in vain and your faith has been in vain."[1] I wrote a popular Easter musical called *His Fleece Was White as Snow* with the joyous finale proclaiming: "Sing Hosanna! Christ is risen! The Son has risen to shine on me!"[2]

But now I no longer believe it. Many bible scholars[3] and ministers—including one third of the clergy in the Church of England[4]—reject the idea that Jesus bodily came back to life. So do 30 percent of born-again American Christians![5] Why? When the Gospel of John portrays the postmortem Jesus on a fishing trip with his buddies and the writer of Matthew shows him giving his team a mountaintop pep talk two days after he died, how can there be any doubt that the original believers were convinced he had bodily risen from the grave?

There have been many reasons for doubting the claim, but many critical scholars today agree that the story is a "legend." During the 60 to 70 years it took for the Gospels to be composed, the original story went through a growth period that began with the unadorned idea that Jesus, like Grandma, had "died and gone to heaven." It ended with a fantastic narrative produced by a later generation of believers

---

1   I Corinthians 15:17.

2   *His Fleece Was White As Snow*, by Dan Barker, Manna Music, Inc., 1978.

3   Including the Westar Institute, Santa Rosa, California, with 70+ bible scholars and many books and publications.

4   *The Daily Telegraph*, London, July 31, 2002.

5   "Americans' Bible Knowledge Is in the Ballpark, But Often Off Base," July 12, 2000, Barna Research Group.

that included earthquakes, angels, an eclipse, a resuscitated corpse and a spectacular bodily ascension into the clouds.

The earliest Christians believed in the "spiritual" resurrection of Jesus. The story evolved over time into a "bodily" resurrection.

As we saw in the previous chapter, the Jesus of history is not the Jesus of the New Testament. Some scholars believe the whole story is a myth, and others feel it is a legend based on some simple core facts that grew over time. This chapter will show that at least the resurrection part of Jesus' story is legend. A tale can be both myth and legend because all you need for a legend to start is a *belief* in a historical fact, whether that belief is true or not. But to most true believers, especially to fundamentalist inerrantists, there is no difference between whether the Jesus story is a complete myth or a legend based on some early facts. Either way, the New Testament loses reliability.

Before discussing the legend hypothesis in detail, let's look briefly at some of the other reasons for skepticism.

CAN HISTORY PROVE A MIRACLE?

If the resurrection happened, it was a miracle. Philosopher Antony Flew, in a 1985 debate on the resurrection[6], pointed out that history is the wrong tool for proving miracle reports. (It doesn't matter that Flew, once an atheist, later devolved into deism. He did not change his opinion on miracles or the resurrection of Jesus.) "The heart of the matter," said Flew, "is that the criteria by which we must assess historical testimony, and the general presumptions that make it possible for us to construe leftovers from the past as historical evidence, are such that the possibility of establishing, on purely historical grounds, that some genuinely miraculous event has occurred is ruled out."

When examining artifacts from the past, historians assume that nature worked back then as it does today; otherwise, anything goes. American patriot Thomas Paine, in *The Age of Reason,* asked: "Is it more probable that nature should go out of her course, or that a man should tell a lie? We have never seen, in our time, nature go out of her course; but we have good reason to believe that millions of lies have

---

6   *Did Jesus Rise From The Dead? The Resurrection Debate,* Gary Habermas and
     Antony Flew, ed. Terry L. Miethe, Harper & Row, 1987. Flew's remarks were
     inspired by David Hume's *First Enquiry.*

been told in the same time; it is, therefore, at least millions to one, that the reporter of a miracle tells a lie."

It is a fact of history and of current events that human beings exaggerate, misinterpret or wrongly remember events. Humans have also fabricated pious fraud. Most believers in a religion understand this when examining the claims of *other* religions.

A messiah figure coming back to life—appearing out of thin air and disappearing—is a fantastic story by anyone's standard, and that is what *makes* it a miracle claim. If dead people today routinely crawled out of their graves and went back to work, a resurrection would have little value as proof of God's power. The fact that it is impossible or highly unlikely is what makes it a miracle.

And that is what removes it from the reach of history.

History is limited; it can only confirm events that conform to natural regularity. This is not an anti-supernaturalistic bias against miracles, as is sometimes claimed by believers. The miracles may have happened, but in order to *know* they happened, we need a different tool of knowledge. Yet except for faith (which is not a science), history is the only tool Christians have to make a case for the resurrection of Jesus.

Examining a miracle with history is like searching for a planet with a microscope.

David Hume wrote: "No testimony is sufficient to establish a miracle unless that testimony be of such a kind that its falsehood would be more miraculous than the fact which it endeavours to establish."[7] As I'll mention more than once, Carl Sagan liked to say, "Extraordinary claims require extraordinary evidence." Such evidence is exactly what we do not have with the resurrection of Jesus.

Protestants and Catholics seem to have no trouble applying healthy skepticism to the miracles of Islam, or to the "historical" visit between Joseph Smith and the angel Moroni. Why should Christians treat their own outrageous claims any differently? Why should someone who was not there be any more eager to believe than doubting Thomas, who lived during that time, or the other disciples who said that the women's news from the tomb "seemed to them as idle tales, and they believed them not?" (Luke 24:11)

---

7   *Of Miracles*, pp.115-116.

Thomas Paine points out that everything in the bible is *hearsay*. For example, the message at the tomb (if it happened at all) took this path, at minimum, before it got to our eyes: God, angel(s), Mary, disciples, Gospel writers, copyists and translators. (The Gospels are all anonymous and we have no original versions.) If history cannot prove a miracle, then certainly secondhand hearsay cannot either.

At best (or worst), this should convince us not that the resurrection is disproved, but that disbelief in the resurrection is rationally justified. The incompatibility of miracles with the historical method is persuasive, especially to those not committed *a priori* to the truth of religious scripture, but we still need something more than this if we are to say with confidence that the bodily resurrection did not happen.

NATURALISTIC EXPLANATIONS

Some critics have offered naturalistic explanations for the New Testament stories of the empty tomb. Maybe Jesus didn't actually die on the cross; he just passed out, and woke up later—the "swoon theory"[8]. Or perhaps the disciples hallucinated the risen Jesus. (They and "five hundred" others, Paul reported.) Or Mary went to the wrong tomb, finding it empty, mistaking the "young man" for an angel. Or perhaps the body was stolen—the "conspiracy theory." This is an idea that boasts a hint of biblical support in that the only eyewitnesses (the Roman soldiers) said that was exactly what happened.[9] Or perhaps Jesus' body was only temporarily stored in the tomb of Joseph of Arimathea (possibly with the two thieves) and was later reburied in a common grave, the usual fate of executed criminals.[10] Or perhaps someone else, such as Thomas, was crucified in Jesus' place.[11]

---

8   See for example *The Passover Plot: A New Interpretation of the Life and Death of Jesus,* by Hugh Schonfield.

9   Matthew 28:11-15.

10 See "Historical Evidence and the Empty Tomb Story: A Reply to William Lane Craig," by Jeffery Jay Lowder, 2001. www.infidels.org/library/modern/jeff_lowder/empty.html.

11 "Thomas" and "Didymus" both mean "twin." Many early Christians believed Jesus had an identical twin brother. See *The Jesus Mysteries: Was the "Original Jesus" a Pagan God?* by Timothy Freke and Peter Gandy, pages 117-118. Although some early Christians and modern scholars conclude that Thomas must have been crucified in Jesus' place, the authors say no, "the Gnostics invented the tradition of Jesus' twin brother as an allegory for the ancient Daemon/eidolon doctrine."

These hypotheses have various degrees of plausibility. In my opinion, none of them seem overly likely, but they are at *least* as credible as a corpse coming back to life and they do fit the biblical facts.

"Why have you ruled out the supernatural?" is a question believers sometimes ask. I answer that I have not ruled it out: I have simply given it the low probability it deserves along with the other possibilities. I might equally ask them, "Why have you ruled out the natural?"

The problem I have with some of the natural explanations is that they give the text too much credit. They tend to require almost as much faith as the orthodox interpretation. Combined with the historical objection and the mythicists' arguments, the existence of a number of plausible natural alternatives can bolster the confidence of skeptics, but they can't *positively* disprove the bodily resurrection of Jesus.

INTERNAL DISCREPANCIES

The resurrection of Jesus is one of the few stories that is told repeatedly in the bible—more than five times—so it provides an excellent test for the orthodox claim of scriptural inerrancy and reliability. When we compare the accounts, we see they don't agree. An easy way to prove this is to issue this challenge to Christians: Tell me what happened on Easter. I am not asking for proof at this stage. Before we can investigate the truth of what happened, we have to know what is being claimed to have happened. My straightforward request is merely that Christians tell me exactly what happened on the day that their most important doctrine was born. Believers should eagerly take up this challenge, since without the resurrection there is no Christianity. Paul wrote, "If Christ be not risen... we are found false witnesses of God; because we have testified of God that he raised up Christ: whom he raised not up, if so be that the dead rise not." (I Corinthians 15:14-15)

The conditions of the challenge are simple and reasonable. In each of the four Gospels, begin at Easter morning and read to the end of the book: Matthew 28, Mark 16, Luke 24 and John 20-21. Also read Acts 1:3-12 and Paul's tiny version of the story in I Corinthians 15:3-8. These 165 verses can be read in a few moments. Then, without omitting a single detail from these separate accounts, write a simple, chronological narrative of the events between the resurrection and the ascension: what happened first, second and so on; who said what and when; and where these things happened.

The narrative does not have to strive to present a perfect picture—it only needs to give at least one plausible account of all of the facts. *The important condition to the challenge, however, is that not one single biblical detail be omitted.* Of course, the words have to be accurately translated and the ordering of events has to follow the biblical ordering. Fair enough?

Many bible stories are given only once or twice, and are therefore hard to confirm. The author of Matthew, for example, was the only one to mention that at the crucifixion dead people emerged from the graves of Jerusalem to walk around and show themselves to everyone—an amazing event that would hardly have escaped the notice of the other Gospel writers, or any other historians of the period. But though the silence of other writers weakens the likelihood of this story—because if they did repeat it, believers would certainly tout the existence of such confirmation—it does not disprove it. Disconfirmation comes with contradictions.

Thomas Paine tackled this matter 200 years ago in *The Age of Reason,* stumbling across dozens of New Testament discrepancies: "I lay it down as a position which cannot be controverted," he wrote, "first, that the agreement of all the parts of a story does not prove that story to be true, because the parts may agree and the whole may be false; secondly, that the disagreement of the parts of a story proves the whole cannot be true."

I tried to solve the discrepancies myself, and failed. One of the first problems I found is in Matthew 28:2, after two women arrived at the tomb: "And, behold, there was a great earthquake: for the angel of the Lord descended from heaven, and came and rolled back the stone from the door, and sat upon it." (Let's ignore the fact that no other writer mentioned this "great earthquake.") This story says that the stone was rolled away after the women arrived, in their presence. Yet Mark's Gospel says it happened *before* the women arrived: "And they said among themselves, Who shall roll away the stone from the door of the sepulchre? And when they looked, they saw that the stone was rolled away: for it was very great." Luke writes: "And they found the stone rolled away from the sepulchre." John agrees. No earthquake, no rolling stone. It is a three-to-one vote: Matthew loses. (Or else the other three are wrong.) The event cannot have happened both before and after they arrived. Some bible defenders assert that Matthew 28:2

was intended to be understood in the past perfect, showing what had happened before the women arrived. But the entire passage is in the aorist (past) tense and it reads, in context, like a simple chronological account. Matthew 28:2 begins, "And, behold," not "For, behold." If this verse can be so easily shuffled around, then what is to keep us from putting the flood before the ark, or the crucifixion before the nativity?

Another glaring problem is the fact that in Matthew the first post-resurrection appearance of Jesus to the disciples happened on a mountain in Galilee (not in Jerusalem, as most Christians believe), as predicted by the angel sitting on the newly moved rock: "And go quickly, and tell his disciples that he is risen from the dead; and, behold, he goeth before you into Galilee; there shall ye see him." This must have been of supreme importance, since this was *the* message of God via the angel(s) at the tomb. Jesus had even predicted this himself 60 hours earlier, during the Last Supper (Matthew 26:32). After receiving this angelic message, "Then the eleven disciples went away into Galilee, into a mountain where Jesus had appointed them. And when they saw him, they worshipped him: but some doubted." (Matthew 28:16-17) Reading this at face value, and in context, it is clear that Matthew intends this to have been the *first* appearance. Otherwise, if Jesus had been seen before this time, why did some doubt? Mark agrees with Matthew's account of the angel's Galilee message, but gives a different story about the first appearance. Luke and John give different angel messages and then radically contradict Matthew. Luke shows the first appearance on the road to Emmaus and then in a room in Jerusalem. John says it happened later than evening in a room, minus Thomas. These angel messages, locations and travels during the day are impossible to reconcile.

Believers sometimes use the analogy of the five blind men examining an elephant, all coming away with a different definition: tree trunk (leg), rope (tail), hose (trunk), wall (side) and fabric (ear). People who use this argument forget that each of the blind men was *wrong:* an elephant is not a rope or a tree. You can put the five parts together to arrive at a noncontradictory aggregate of the entire animal. This hasn't been done with the resurrection.

Apologists sometimes compare the resurrection variations to differing accounts given by witnesses of an auto accident. If one witness says the vehicle was green and the other says it was blue, that could be accounted for by different angles, lighting, perception or definitions of words. The important thing, the apologists claim, is that they do agree on the basic story—there was an accident (there *was* a resurrection). I am not a fundamentalist inerrantist. I'm not demanding that the evangelists must have been expert, infallible witnesses. (None of them claims to have witnessed the actual resurrection.) But what if one person said the auto accident happened in Chicago and the other said it happened in Milwaukee? At least one of these witnesses has serious problems with the truth.

Luke says the post-resurrection appearance happened in Jerusalem, but Matthew says it happened in Galilee, *sixty to 100 miles away!* Could they all have traveled 150 miles that day, by foot, trudging up to Galilee for the first appearance, then back to Jerusalem for the evening meal? There is no mention of any horses, but 12 well-conditioned thoroughbreds racing at breakneck speed as the crow flies would need about five hours for the trip, without a rest. And during this madcap scenario, could Jesus have found time for a leisurely stroll to Emmaus, accepting "toward evening" an invitation to dinner? Something is very wrong here.

This is just the tip of the iceberg. Of course, none of these contradictions prove that the resurrection did *not* happen, but they do throw considerable doubt on the reliability of the supposed reporters. Some of them were wrong. Maybe they were all wrong.

I say to Christians: Either tell me exactly what happened on Easter Sunday or let's leave the Jesus myth buried next to Eastre (Ishtar, Astarte), the pagan Goddess of Spring after whom your holiday was named.

CONSISTENTLY INCONSISTENT
(KJV=King James Version; NRSV=New Revised Standard Version; NIV=New International Version)

What time did the women visit the tomb?

- Matthew: "as it began to dawn" (28:1)

- Mark: "very early in the morning . . . at the rising of the sun" (16:2, KJV); "when the sun had risen" (NRSV); "just after sunrise" (NIV)

- Luke: "very early in the morning" (24:1, KJV) "at early dawn" (NRSV)

- John: "when it was yet dark" (20:1)

Who were the women?

- Matthew: Mary Magdalene and the other Mary (28:1)

- Mark: Mary Magdalene, the mother of James, and Salome (16:1)

- Luke: Mary Magdalene, Joanna, Mary the mother of James and other women (24:10)

- John: Mary Magdalene (20:1)

What was their purpose?

- Matthew: to see the tomb (28:1)

- Mark: had already seen the tomb (15:47), brought spices (16:1)

- Luke: had already seen the tomb (23:55), brought spices (24:1)

- John: the body had already been spiced before they arrived (19:39, 40)

Was the tomb open when they arrived?

- Matthew: No (28:2)

- Mark: Yes (16:4)

- Luke: Yes (24:2)

- John: Yes (20:1)

Who was at the tomb when they arrived?

- Matthew: One angel (28:2-7)

- Mark: One young man (16:5)

- Luke: Two men (24:4)

- John: Two angels (20:12)

Where were these messengers situated?

- Matthew: Angel sitting on the stone (28:2)

- Mark: Young man sitting inside, on the right (16:5)

- Luke: Two men standing inside (24:4)

- John: Two angels sitting on each end of the bed (20:12)

What did the messenger(s) say?

- Matthew: "Fear not ye: for I know that ye seek Jesus, which was crucified. He is not here for he is risen, as he said. Come, see the place where the Lord lay. And go quickly, and tell his disciples that he is risen from the dead: and, behold, he goeth before you into Galilee; there shall ye see him: lo, I have told you." (28:5-7)

- Mark: "Be not afrighted: Ye seek Jesus of Nazareth, which was crucified: he is risen; he is not here: behold the place where they laid him. But go your way, tell his disciples and Peter that he goeth before you into Galilee: there shall ye see him, as he said unto you." (16:6-7)

- Luke: "Why seek ye the living among the dead? He is not here, but is risen: remember how he spake unto you when he was yet in Galilee, saying, The Son of man must be delivered into the hands of sinful men, and be crucified, and the third day rise again." (24:5-7)

- John: "Woman, why weepest thou?" (20:13)

Did the women tell what happened?

- Matthew: Yes (28:8)

- Mark: No. "Neither said they any thing to any man." (16:8)

- Luke: Yes. "And they returned from the tomb and told all these things to the eleven, and to all the rest." (24:9, 22-24)

- John: Yes (20:18)

When Mary returned from the tomb, did she know Jesus had been resurrected?

- Matthew: Yes (28:7-8)

- Mark: Yes (16:10, 11[12])

- Luke: Yes (24:6-9, 23)

- John: No (20:2)

When did Mary first see Jesus?

- Matthew: Before she returned to the disciples (28:9)

- Mark: Before she returned to the disciples (16:9, 10[12])

- John: After she returned to the disciples (20:2, 14)

---

12 The verses from Mark 16:9-20 are included here for those who think Mark's finale is authentic. Even though they are not authentic, they do show a contradictory story from whoever added them, most likely a Christian.

Could Jesus be touched after the resurrection?

> • Matthew: Yes (28:9)

> • John: No (20:17) *and* Yes (20:27)

After the women, to whom did Jesus first appear?

> • Matthew: Eleven disciples (28:16)

> • Mark: Two disciples in the country, later to 11 (16:12, 14[12])

> • Luke: Two disciples in Emmaus, later to 11 (24:13, 36)

> • John: Ten disciples (Judas and Thomas were absent) (20:19, 24)

> • Paul: First to Cephas (Peter), then to the 12. (Twelve? Judas was dead). (I Corinthians 15:5)

Where did Jesus first appear to the disciples?

> • Matthew: On a mountain in Galilee (60-100 miles away) (28:16-17)

> • Mark: To two in the country, to 11 "as they sat at meat" (16:12,14[12])

> • Luke: In Emmaus (about seven miles away) at evening, to the rest in a room in Jerusalem later that night. (24:31, 36)

> • John: In a room, at evening (20:19)

Did the disciples believe the two men?

> • Mark: No (16:13[12])

> • Luke: Yes (24:34—it is the group speaking here, not the two)

What happened at that first appearance?

- Matthew: Disciples worshipped, some doubted, "Go preach." (28:17-20)

- Mark: Jesus reprimanded them, said, "Go preach" (16:14-19¹²)

- Luke: Christ incognito, vanishing act, materialized out of thin air, reprimand, supper (24:13-51)

- John: Passed through solid door, disciples happy, Jesus blesses them, no reprimand (21:19-23)

Did Jesus stay on earth for more than a day?

- Mark: No (16:19¹²) Compare 16:14 with John 20:19 to show that this was all done on Sunday

- Luke: No (24:50-52) It all happened on Sunday

- John: Yes, at least eight days (20:26, 21:1-22)

- Acts: Yes, at least 40 days (1:3)

Where did the ascension take place?

- Matthew: No ascension. Book ends on mountain in Galilee

- Mark: In or near Jerusalem, after supper (16:19¹²)

- Luke: In Bethany, very close to Jerusalem, after supper (24:50-51)

- John: No ascension

- Paul: No ascension

- Acts: Ascended from Mount of Olives (1:9-12)

It is not just atheist critics who notice these problems. Christian scholars agree that the stories are discrepant. Culver H. Nelson: "In any such reading, it should become glaringly obvious that these materials often contradict one another egregiously. No matter how eagerly one may wish to do so, there is simply no way the various accounts of Jesus' postmortem activities can be harmonized."[13]

A. E. Harvey: "All the Gospels, after having run closely together in their accounts of the trial and execution, diverge markedly when they come to the circumstance of the Resurrection. It's impossible to fit their accounts together into a single coherent scheme."[14]

Thomas Sheehan agrees: "Despite our best efforts, the Gospel accounts of Jesus' post-mortem activities, in fact, cannot be harmonized into a consistent Easter chronology."[15]

The religiously independent (though primarily Christian) scholars at the Westar Institute, which includes more than 70 bible scholars with a Ph.D. or the equivalent, conclude: "The five gospels that report appearances (Matthew, Luke, John, Peter, Gospel of the Hebrews) go their separate ways when they are not rewriting Mark; their reports cannot be reconciled to each other. Hard historical evidence is sparse."[16]

I have challenged believers to provide a simple non-contradictory chronological narrative of the events between Easter Sunday and the ascension, without omitting a single biblical detail. Some have tried but, without misinterpreting words or drastically rearranging passages, no one has given a coherent account. Some have offered "harmonies" (apparently not wondering why the work of a perfect deity should have to be harmonized), but none have met the reasonable request to simply tell the story.

LEGEND

C. S. Lewis and Christian apologist Josh McDowell offer three choices in urging us to consider who Jesus was: "Liar, Lunatic, or Lord."[17] But

---

13 Culver H. Nelson was founding minister of the Church of the Beatitudes, Phoenix, Arizona.

14 *New English Bible Companion to the New Testament,* Oxford University Press, 1988.

15 *The First Coming: How the Kingdom of God Became Christianity,* by Thomas Sheehan, Random House, 1986, p. 97.

16 *The Acts of Jesus: What Did Jesus Really Do?* by Robert W. Funk and The Jesus Seminar, Polebridge Press, 1998.

17 *Mere Christianity,* by C. S. Lewis (1943, MacMillan) and *More Than A Carpenter,* by Josh McDowell (1987, Tyndale House).

this completely ignores a fourth option: Legend. If the Jesus character is a literary creation—whether partially or completely—then it was others who put words in his mouth, and it is grossly simplistic to take these words at face value.

A legend begins with a basic story (true or false) that grows into something more embellished and exaggerated as the years pass. When we look at the documents of the resurrection of Jesus, we see that the earliest accounts are very simple, later retellings are more complex and the latest tales are fantastic. In other words, it looks exactly like a legend.

The documents that contain a resurrection story[18] are usually dated like this: Paul: 50-55 (I Cor. 15:3-8); Mark: 70 (Mark 16); Matthew: 80 (Matthew 28); Luke: 85 (Luke 24); Gospel of Peter: 85-90 (Fragment); John: 95 (John 20-21). This is the general dating agreed upon by most scholars, including scholars at the Westar Institute. Some conservative scholars prefer to date them earlier, and others have moved some of them later, but this would not change the *order* of the writing[19], which is more important than the actual dates when considering legendary growth. Shifting the dates changes the shape but not the fact of the growth curve.

I made a list of things I consider "extraordinary" (natural and supernatural) in the stories between the crucifixion and ascension of Jesus. These include: earthquakes, angel(s), rolling stone, dead bodies crawling from Jerusalem graves ("Halloween"[20]), Jesus appearing out of thin air (now you see him) and disappearing (now you don't), the "fish story" miracle,[21] Peter's noncanonical "extravaganza" exit from the tomb (see below), a giant Jesus with head in the clouds, a talking cross and a bodily ascension into heaven.

---

18   There was also an appearance story in a lost book known as the Gospel of the Hebrews, probably written in the mid second century. We find a few quotes from this book in the writings of others. Jerome quoted the appearance story. Since it is not a complete resurrection account, it can't be compared with the others.

19   Except perhaps for Peter, which might have been later than John.

20   Matthew 27:52-53. "And the graves were opened; and many bodies of the saints which slept arose, And came out of the graves after his resurrection, and went into the holy city, and appeared unto many."

21   John 21:1-14.

Perhaps others would choose a slightly different list, but I'm certain it would include most of the same events. I do not consider events that are surprising to be extraordinary. For example, seeing a man whom you thought was dead is indeed surprising, but not extraordinary. Neither is it extraordinary to have a vision of a person who is dead or presumed dead. (My dad heard the voice of my mother for a long time after she died, and though it seemed quite real and "spooky," he knew it was just in his mind. After a period of time those hallucinations abated. That is not extraordinary.) Then I counted the number of extraordinary events that appear in each resurrection account. In the order in which the accounts were written, Paul has zero, Mark has one, Matthew has four, Luke has five, Peter has six and John has at least six. (John wrote, "And many other signs truly did Jesus in the presence of his disciples, which are not written in this book." 20:30) Putting these on a time graph produces a curve that goes up as the years pass. The later resurrection reports contain more extraordinary events than the earlier ones, so it is clear that the story, at least in the telling, has evolved and expanded over time.

In finer detail, we can count the number of messengers at the tomb, which also grows over time, as well as the certainty of the claim that they were angels. Paul: 0 angels. Mark: 1 young man sitting. Matthew: 1 angel sitting. Luke: 2 men standing. Peter: 2 men/angels walking. John: 2 angels sitting. Other items fit the pattern. Bodily appearances are absent from the first two accounts, but show up in the last four accounts, starting in the year 80 C.E. The bodily ascension is absent from the first three stories, but appears in the last three starting in the year 85 C.E. This ballooning of details reveals the footprints of legend.

The mistake many modern Christians make is to view 30 C.E. backward through the distorted lens of 80-100 C.E., more than a half century later. They forcibly superimpose the extraordinary tales of the late Gospels anachronistically upon the plainer views of the first Christians, pretending naively that all Christians believed exactly the same thing across the entire first century.

PAUL (YEAR 55 C.E.)

How can we say that Paul reported no extraordinary events? Doesn't his account include an empty tomb and appearances of a dead man?

Here is what Paul said in I Corinthians 15:3-8, around the year 55 C.E., the earliest written account of the resurrection:

> "For I delivered unto you first of all that which I also
> received, how that
> Christ died for our sins
> in accordance with the Scriptures,
> and was buried. [*etaphe*]
> And he was raised [*egeiro*] on the third day
> in accordance with the Scriptures
> and he appeared [*ophthe*] to Cephas [Peter]
> and then to the twelve.
> Afterward, he appeared to more than 500 brethren,
> most of whom are still alive,
> though some have fallen asleep.
> Afterward he appeared to James,
> and then to all the missionaries [apostles].
> Last of all, as to one untimely born,
> he appeared also to me."

This is a formula, or hymn, in poetic style that Paul claims he "received" from a believer reciting an earlier oral tradition. He edited the end of it, obviously. It is possible that this passage originated just a few years after Jesus lived, although notice that Paul does not call him "Jesus" here. It is interesting that one of the arguments some apologists give for the authenticity of the New Testament is that it is written in a simple narrative style, unlike the poetic style of other myths and legends—yet the very first account of the resurrection is written in a poetic, legendary style.

This letter to the Corinthians was written at least a quarter of a century after the events to people far removed from the scene—Corinth is about 1,500 miles away by land. None of the readers, many or most not even born when Jesus supposedly died, would have been able to confirm the story. They had to take Paul's word alone that there were "500 brethren" who saw Jesus alive. Who were these 500 nameless people, and why didn't they or any of the thousands who heard their stories write about it? And isn't 500 a suspiciously round number? And why didn't Jesus appear to anyone who was not part of the in-crowd of believers? In any event, what Paul actually wrote here does not support a bodily resurrection. It supports legend.

First, notice how simple it is, this earliest resurrection story. No angelic messages, no mourning women, no earthquakes, no miracles and no spectacular bodily ascension into the clouds. Nor is there an empty tomb. The word "buried" is the ambiguous *etaphe*, which simply means "put in a grave (*taphos*)." Although a *taphos* could be a common dirt grave (the most likely destination of executed criminals) or a stone sepulchre (such as the one owned by Joseph of Arimathea), it is important to note that this passage does not use the word "sepulchre" (*mnemeion*) that first appears in Mark's later account. Since Paul does not mention a tomb, we can hardly conclude with confidence he was thinking of an "empty tomb." Those who think he was talking of a tomb are shoehorning Mark's Gospel back into this plain hymn.

Neither is there a resurrection in this passage. The word "raised" is *egeiro*, which means to "wake up" or "come to." Paul did not use the word resurrection (*anastasis, anistemi*) here, though he certainly knew it. *Egeiro* is used throughout the New Testament to mean something simpler. "Now it is high time to awaken [*egeiro*] out of sleep"[22] was not written to corpses. "Awake [*egeiro*] thou that sleepest, and arise [*anistemi*] from the dead, and Christ shall give thee light"[23] was also written to breathing people. So, Paul obviously means something nonphysical here, even with his use of "resurrect," contrasted with *egeiro* (before you get up, you have to wake up). Matthew uses *egeiro* like this: "There arose a great tempest in the sea, insomuch that the ship was covered with waves: but he was asleep. And his disciples came to him and awoke [*egeiro*] him, saying, Lord, save us: we perish."[24] No one thinks Jesus resurrected from a boat.

Whatever Paul may have believed happened to Jesus, he did not say that his revived body came out of a tomb. It is perfectly consistent with Christian theology to think that the *spirit* of Jesus, not his body, was awakened from the grave, as Christians today believe that the *spirit* of Grandpa has gone to heaven while his body rots in the ground. In fact, just a few verses later, Paul confirms this: "Flesh and blood cannot

---

22 Romans 13:11.

23 Ephesians 5:14.

24 Matthew 8:24-2.

inherit the kingdom of God."[25] The physical body is not important to Christian theology.

But what about the postmortem appearances Paul mentions? Don't they suggest a risen body? Actually, the word "appeared" in this passage is also ambiguous and does not require a physical presence. The word *ophthe*, from the verb *horao*, is used for both physical sight as well as spiritual visions. For example: "And a vision appeared [*ophthe*] to Paul in the night; there stood a man of Macedonia... And after he had seen the vision [*horama*], immediately we endeavored to go into Macedonia..."[26] No one thinks the Macedonian was standing bodily in front of Paul when he "appeared" to him.

Paul includes Peter in his list of "appearances" by Christ, yet at the Transfiguration described in Matthew we find the same word used for an "appearance" to Peter that was *not* physical: "And after six days Jesus takes Peter, James, and John his brother, and brings them up into a high mountain apart, and was transfigured before them: and his face did shine as the sun, and his raiment was white as the light. And behold there appeared [*ophthe*] Moses and Elijah talking with him."[27] Did Moses and Elijah appear *physically* to Peter? Shall we start looking for their empty tombs? This is obviously some kind of *spiritual* appearance.

Besides, if we believe Mark and Matthew, Paul's first witness to the resurrection appearances was an admitted liar. In a court of law, Peter's reliability would be seriously compromised since he had repeatedly denied knowing Jesus just a couple of days earlier, after he had promised Jesus he would be loyal.[28] Paul himself was not above using a lie if it furthered his message: "Let God be true, but every man a liar... For if the truth of God hath more abounded through my lie unto his glory; why yet am I also judged a sinner?"[29]

Paul, needing to establish credentials with his readers, tacks onto the list that Christ "appeared also to me," so if we look at the description of that appearance, we can see what he means. Paul claimed that he had met Jesus on the road to Damascus, but notice that Jesus did

---

25   I Corinthians 15:50.

26   Acts 16:9-10. *Horama* is from the same verb as *ophthe*.

27   Matthew 17:1-3.

28   Matthew 26:69-75, Mark 14:66-72.

29   Romans 3:4, 7.

not *physically* appear to Paul there. He was knocked off his horse and blinded. (I know there is no horse in the story, but for some reason I picture a horse—an example of legend making!) How could Jesus appear physically to a blind man? Paul's men admit they did not see anyone, but just heard a voice (Acts 9:7) or did not hear a voice (Acts 22:9). Take your pick[30]. This "appearance" to Paul was supposedly years after Jesus ascended into heaven, which raises a good question: Where was Jesus all those years? Was his physical body hanging around in the clouds, hovering over the road to Damascus? Did he need a haircut? What did he eat up there? How did he bathe?

Clearly, Paul did not shake hands with Jesus, yet he includes this "appearance" in the list with the others in I Corinthians 15. Elsewhere Paul elaborates on his roadside encounter: "For I neither received it of man, neither was I taught it, but . . . when it pleased God...to reveal his Son in me, that I might preach him among the heathen, immediately I conferred not with flesh and blood."[31] Notice he does not say "I met Jesus physically" or "I saw Jesus." He says God "revealed his son *in* me." This was an *inner* experience, not a face-to-face meeting. This is exactly how many modern Christians talk about their own "personal relationship" with Jesus.

All of the "appearances" in I Corinthians 15:3-8 must be viewed as psychological "spiritual experiences," not physiological encounters with a revived corpse. If they really happened they are unusual, but they are not extraordinary. Such hallucinating, daydreaming or imagining happens in most religions. In Paul, we have no empty tomb, no resurrection and no bodily appearances.

MARK (YEAR 70 C.E.)

About 15 years later, the next account of the resurrection appears in Mark, the first Gospel, written at least 40 years after the events. Almost all adults who were alive in the year 30 C.E. were dead by then[32]. No one knows who wrote Mark—the Gospels are all anonymous and names

---

30 See "Understanding Discrepancy" chapter 14.

31 Galatians 1:12-16.

32 *Regional Model Life Tables and Stable Populations*, A. Coale and P. Demeny, 2nd ed., 1983. This represents statistically exact results for third world countries in the 19th/early 20th century with living conditions essentially the same as those in ancient Rome. Thanks to Richard Carrier for this data.

were formally attached to them much later, around the year 180 C.E.[33] Whoever wrote Mark is speaking from the historical perspective of a second generation of believers, not as an eyewitness.

His account of the resurrection (16:1-8) is only eight verses long. The 12 succeeding verses that appear in some translations (with snake handling and poison drinking) were a later addition by someone else (evidence that Christian tampering began early).

Mark's story is more elaborate than Paul's, but still very simple, almost blunt. If we consider the young man at the sepulchre "clothed in a long white garment" to be an angel, then we have one extraordinary event. Just one.

There are no earthquakes or postmortem appearances, and there is no ascension. In fact, there is *no belief* in the resurrection, and no preaching of a risen Christ. The book ends with the women running away: "...neither said they any thing to any man; for they were afraid," a rather limp finish considering the supposed import of the event.

Notice that the young man says, "he is risen (*egeiro*)." Like Paul, he avoids the word "resurrection." Such words can be uttered in the presence of a dead body, as they are at many funerals.

MATTHEW (YEAR 80 C.E.)

In Matthew, a half century after the events, we finally get some of the fantastic stories of which modern Christians are so fond. The earthquake, rolling stone and "Halloween" story[20] appear for the first (and only) time. We also have a bonafide angel and postmortem appearances.

LUKE (YEAR 85 C.E.)

Matthew and Luke were based to some degree on Mark, but they each added their own wrinkles. In Luke, we have the "now you see him, now you don't" appearance and disappearance of Jesus, and a bodily ascension. We also have two angels, if we consider the men "in shining garments" to be angels.

GOSPEL OF PETER (YEAR 85 C.E.)

This is a fragment of an extracanonical Gospel, purportedly authored by Simon Peter (which means it was composed by another creative

---

33 Although names of various Gospels had been loosely assigned to the books by tradition in the early and mid 2nd-century, they were first formally attached to all of them by Irenaeus in 180.

Christian), that begins in the middle of what appears to be a resurrection story. The dating is controversial, but it certainly was composed no earlier than the 80s C.E.

A crowd from Jerusalem visited the sealed tomb on the Sabbath. On Easter morning, the soldiers observed the actual resurrection after the stone rolled by itself away from the entrance (no earthquake). In an extravaganza of light, two young men descended from the sky and went inside the tomb, then the two men whose heads reached to the sky carried out a third man who was taller, followed by a cross. A voice from heaven asked, "Have you preached to those who sleep?" The cross answered, "Yes!" Then someone else entered the tomb. Later the women found a young man inside saying something similar to what was said in Mark. "Then the women fled in fear." This is fantastic stuff.

GOSPEL OF JOHN (YEAR 90-95 C.E.)

The last of the canonical Gospels appears to be mainly independent of the others in style and content, which is why Mark, Matthew and Luke, but not John, are called the "synoptic Gospels." (Maybe we can call John the "myopic Gospel." Myopia affects vision at a distance.) John's resurrection story has real angels, bodily appearances (including a "now you see him" manifestation through shut doors), the "fish story" miracle and an ascension. By now the legend has become—legendary.

The anonymous writer ends his Gospel with the claim that there were "many other things which Jesus did, the which, if they should be written every one, I suppose that even the world itself could not contain the books that should be written."[34] John is obviously exaggerating, but this is no surprise since he admits that his agenda is not simply to tell the facts: "And many other signs truly did Jesus in the presence of his disciples, which are not written in this book: But these are written, that ye might believe that Jesus is the Christ, the Son of God; and that believing ye might have life through his name."[35] This is not the work of a historian; it is propaganda written "that you might believe." Authors like this should be read with a grain of salt.

---

34   John 21:25.

35   John 20:30-31.

DID THE DISCIPLES DIE FOR A LIE?

We often hear that the resurrection *must* have happened because the disciples were so confident they endured torture and death for their faith (though there is no first-century evidence for this claim). But think about this. The Gospels were written between the years 70 C.E. and 100 C.E. The authors were most certainly not Matthew, Mark, Luke or John, but let's assume (for the sake of argument) that the writers (whoever they were) were young men who knew Jesus and were perhaps 20 or 25 years old when he died. (Matthew the tax collector and Luke the physician were maybe older?) The life expectancy in that century was 45 years,[36] so people in their 60s would have been *ancient*. (As recently as the 1900 U.S. Census, people 55 and older were counted as "elderly.") Mark would have been 65, Matthew at least 70, Luke at least 75 and John almost 90 when they sat down to write.

How did the disciples survive the alleged persecution and torture to live long enough to write those books? Being martyred is no way to double your life expectancy. It makes more sense to think those anonymous documents were composed by a later generation of believers. They were not eyewitnesses.

WHY DO SO MANY BELIEVE IN THE RESURRECTION?

In any open question, we should argue from what we do know to what we do not know. We do know that fervent legends and stubborn myths arise easily and naturally. We do not know that dead people rise from the grave. We do know that human memory is imperfect. We do not know that angels exist.

Some Christians argue that the period of time between the events and the writing was too short for a legend to have evolved; however, we know this is not true. The 1981 legend of the Virgin Mary appearance at Medjugorge spread across Yugoslavia in just *two days,* confirmed by repeated corroborative testimony of real witnesses who are still alive. International pilgrims visited the place almost immediately, some claiming they were healed at the spot. Yet few Protestants believe the story. Shall we start looking for the empty tomb of Mary?

---

36   See note 32.

The legend of Elian Gonzales, the young Cuban refugee who was rescued off the coast of Florida in 1999, developed into an organized cult within a couple of weeks. There were claims that he was the "Cuban Messiah" who would set his oppressed people free from the Castro Devil, sightings of the Virgin Mary in downtown Miami, and tales of his protection by angels and dolphins (actually dolphin fish).[37] The extraordinary 19th-century stories of Mormon founder Joseph Smith were accepted as gospel fact within a few short years.

There was plenty of time for the legend of the resurrection of Jesus to evolve.

We do know that people regularly see deceased relatives and friends in dreams and visions. My own grandmother swore to me that she regularly saw my dead grandfather entering the house, smiling and waving at her, often accompanied by other dead relatives who were opening and closing drawers. Should I have dug up my grandfather's grave to prove she was only dreaming or hallucinating in her grief? Would that have made any difference?

Yet some Christians insist that this is exactly what would have happened if the story of Jesus were false. If the tomb were not empty, detractors could have easily silenced the rumors by producing the body. But this assumes that they cared enough to do such a thing—they didn't do it when Herod heard rumors that John the Baptist had been raised from the dead.[38] It was a crime to rob a grave, and who would have known where to find it? (Early Christians never venerated Jesus' empty tomb, which is another evidence it did not exist.) Also, it was at least seven weeks after the burial before the resurrection was first preached during Pentecost. By the time anyone might have cared to squelch the story, two or three months would have passed—and what happens to a dead body in that climate for that period of time? The body of Lazarus was "stinking" after only four days.[39] If someone had had the gumption to locate and illegally dig up the decayed body of Jesus and parade it through the streets, would the disciples have believed the unrecognizable rotting skeleton was really their Lord and

---

37 For one source, see "The 'Elian Gonzalez' Religious Movement" at www.religioustolerance.org/elian.htm.

38 Matthew 14:1-2.

39 John 11:17, 39.

Savior? I don't think so, any more than my grandmother would have been convinced she was deluded.

During one of my debates, Greg Boyd offered the simple argument that the resurrection *must* have happened because otherwise we have no explanation for the birth and the tremendous growth of the Christian Church. Where there's smoke, there's fire, he insisted. But this argument can be equally applied to the "smoke" of other religions, such as Islam, with hundreds of millions of good people believing that the illiterate Muhammad miraculously wrote the Koran.

It can be applied to the "smoke" of Mormonism, with millions of moral and intelligent individuals believing the angel Moroni gave Joseph Smith gold tablets inscribed with the *Book of Mormon*. "Why should non-Mormons find the story hard to believe?" Robert J. Miller asks. "After all, it is no more plausible than dozens of stories in the bible (for example, Jonah and the whale) that many Christians believe with no difficulty at all. The difference has very little to do with the stories themselves and a great deal to do with whether one approaches them as an insider or an outsider. Putting it a bit crudely perhaps, stories about *our* miracles are easy to believe because they're true; stories about *their* miracles are easy to dismiss because they're far-fetched and fictitious."[40]

It could also be applied to the Moonies, Jehovah's Witnesses and many other successful religious movements. If smoke is evidence of fire, are they all true?

SO WHAT DID HAPPEN?

If the story is not true, then how did it originate? We don't really know but we can make some good guesses, based on what happened with other legends and religious movements and what we know about human nature.

Assuming that the New Testament is somewhat reliable, Robert Price offers one sensible scenario. Peter's state of mind is the key. The disciples had expected Jesus to set up a kingdom on earth, and this did not happen. He was killed. They then expected Jesus to return, and this did not happen. Nothing was going right and this created a cognitive dissonance. Peter, who had promised loyalty to Jesus and then denied

---

40 *The Jesus Seminar and its Critics,* Robert J. Miller, Polebridge Press, 1999, p. 134.

him publicly a few hours before the crucifixion, must have been feeling horrible. (The day after "Good Friday" is called "Black Sabbath," the day the disciples were in mourning and shock.)

Imagine you had a horrible argument with a spouse or loved one where you said some unpleasant things you later regretted, but before you had a chance to apologize and make up the person died. Picture your state of mind: grief, regret, shock, embarrassment, sadness, and a desperate wish to bring the person back and make things right. That's how Peter must have felt.

Believing in God and the survival of the soul, Peter prays to Jesus: "I'm sorry. Forgive me." (Or something like that.) Then Peter gets an answer: "I'm here. I forgive you." (Or something like that.) Then Peter triumphantly tells his friends, "I talked with Jesus! He is not dead! I am forgiven!" His friends say, "Peter talked with Jesus? Peter met Jesus? He's alive! It's a *spiritual* kingdom!" (Or something like that.) Paul then lists Peter as the first person to whom Christ "appeared."

We don't need to know exactly what happened, only that things like this do happen. Look at the 19th-century Millerites, who evolved into the Seventh Day Adventists when the world did not end as they had predicted. Or the Jehovah's Witnesses, whose church rebounded after the failed prophecies of Charles Russell and Joseph Rutherford that the world would end in 1914. Oops, they meant 1925. (They got creative and said Jesus actually returned to earth "spiritually.") After the 21st-century death of Rulon Jeffs, the Prophet of the Fundamentalist Latter Day Saints church who was predicted to rise from the dead, his son Warren Jeffs declared that his father had, in fact, been resurrected "spiritually" and was now directing the church from another dimension. Warren then took his father's many young wives, the ones that did not run off. (See *Stolen Innocence* by Elissa Wall.)

Robert Price elaborates: "When a group has staked everything on a religious belief, and 'burned their bridges behind them,' only to find this belief disconfirmed by events, they may find disillusionment too painful to endure. They soon come up with some explanatory rationalization, the plausibility of which will be reinforced by the mutual encouragement of fellow believers in the group. In order to increase further the plausibility of their threatened belief, they may engage in a massive new effort at proselytizing. The more people who can be convinced, the truer it will seem. In the final analysis, then, a radical disconfirmation of belief may be just what a religious movement needs to get off the ground."[41]

There have been other plausible scenarios explaining the origin of the legend, but we don't need to describe them all. The fact that they exist shows that the historicity of the bodily resurrection of Jesus cannot be taken as a given.

THE LEGEND IDEA IS RESPECTFUL

The idea of a legend is respectful of the humanity of the early Christians. We do know that the human race possesses an immense propensity to create, believe and propagate falsehood. So, what makes the early Christians exempt? Weren't they just people? Did they never make mistakes? Were they so superhuman that they always resisted the temptations of exaggeration and rhetoric? Did they have perfect memories? Given the discrepancies in their accounts, why not treat those early believers like ourselves, not as cartoon characters but as real human beings with normal human fears, desires and limitations? The fact that my grandmother was hallucinating did not make me love or respect her any less.

The legend idea is respectful of the historical method. We are not required to jettison the natural regularity that makes history work. We can take the New Testament accounts as reports of what people sincerely *believed* to be true, not what is necessarily true. We can honor the question, "Do you believe everything you read?"

The legend idea is respectful of theology. If Jesus bodily ascended into physical clouds, then we are presented with a spatially limited flat-earth God sitting on a material throne of human size, with a right and left hand. If Jesus physically levitated into the sky, where is his body now? Does he sometimes need a haircut? If the bodily resurrection is viewed as a legendary embellishment, then believers are free to view their god as a boundless spiritual being, not defined in human dimensions as the pagan gods were.

---

41 *Beyond Born Again,* by Robert M. Price. Section II—The Evangelical Apologists: Are They Reliable? Chapter 6: "Guarding An Empty Tomb." (www.infidels.org/library/modern/robert_price/beyond_born_again/chap6.html) See also *When Prophecy Fails: A Social and Psychological Study,* by Leon Festinger, HarperCollins College Div, 1964.

Bible scholars conclude: "On the basis of a close analysis of all the resurrection reports, [we] decided that the resurrection of Jesus was not perceived initially to depend on what happened to his body. The body of Jesus probably decayed, as do all corpses. The resurrection of Jesus was not an event that happened on the first Easter Sunday; it was not an event that could have been captured by a video camera... [We] conclude that it does not seem necessary for Christians to believe the literal veracity of any of the later appearance narratives."[42]

Finally, the legend idea is respectful of the freedom to believe. If the resurrection of Jesus were proved as a blunt fact of history, then we would have no choice, no room for faith. You can't have the freedom to believe if you do not have the freedom not to believe.

---

42   *The Acts of Jesus: What Did Jesus Really Do?* by Robert W. Funk and The Jesus Seminar, Polebridge Press, 1998, p. 533.

PART 4

Life Is Good!

Chapter Seventeen
We Go to Washington

"When a religion is good, I conceive it will support itself; and when it does not support itself, and God does not take care to support it so that its professors are obliged to call for help of the civil power, 'tis a sign, I apprehend, of its being a bad one."
— **Benjamin Franklin**

During the presidential campaign of 2000, George W. Bush visited Milwaukee and posed for a photo op at Faith Works, a publicly funded faith-based agency housed in a convent. He promised that when he became president, programs like this would receive billions more in public aid. He pledged to "level the playing field," to allow overtly religious organizations with religious agendas to compete for public dollars to provide social services.

Of course, many religious groups were already receiving vast infusions of public money. Prior to the Welfare Reform Act, however, these groups were required to form a different "secular" arm and keep separate books. If they took down their crosses and religious symbols and did not preach or proselytize, they could use tax dollars to feed the hungry, provide housing for the homeless and perform other useful social services. We at the Freedom From Religion Foundation had been uncomfortable with that arrangement because money that tax-exempt religious organizations would have used for social work could be spent on ministry. But we had never sued over such subsidies, since the government could claim a purely secular agenda in granting such money and the religious organizations ostensibly were using the tax dollars for "secular" purposes.

While many religious people and organizations have done truly good work, using their faith as a vehicle for charity, what is often ignored is the fact that, while their church gets the credit, the taxpayers often get the bill. Groups such as Catholic Charities USA, Lutheran Social Services and Jewish Social Services have provided community services for decades with little apparent proselytizing (although not without occasional scandal, such as when audits revealed that Catholic Charities took free U.S. government surplus grain and sold it to famine victims).

George W. Bush changed that dynamic. He turned the tentative "charitable choice" provisions into a major federal faith-based bureaucracy. His "faith-based initiative" erased the line between church and state, encouraging all religious groups to apply for federal money without the need to set up a separate organization or pretend to be secular. One of his first acts as president was to set up the Office of Faith-Based and Community Initiatives in the White House, headed by John DiIulio. Offices in other departments followed. Since 2001, thousands of religious "charities" have sprung up, all attracted by the promise of public dollars. Many had no previous track record. Billions of tax dollars have freely flowed to undisguised religious organizations that openly laud faith to accomplish their mission. For many of these groups, social work is secondary to their primary mission of saving souls and promoting their gospel. Far too often, the provision of social services is just an excuse to proselytize to students, prisoners, patients and other needy people.

Faith Works was an explicitly Christian organization whose purpose was "to bring homeless addicts to Christ." It ministered to recently paroled inmates, ostensibly trying to reconnect them with the outside world and find them employment. This is a worthy goal, but Faith Works' only tools were prayer, bible study and church attendance, with the hope that the participants might meet someone in church who would give them a job. It had no certified counselors; indeed, Faith Works had no track record of accomplishment in Milwaukee. The organization's only claim to effectiveness was that it was "faith-based." Wisconsin's Republican governor, Tommy Thompson, diverted hundreds of thousands of dollars of "discretionary" funds to jump-start Faith Works—funds that were given to the state via the federal

Temporary Assistance for Needy Families program. Faith Works did not open its doors until after it had received huge taxpayer grants. After finding out about the program, thanks to Bush's campaign endorsement, we sued.

I was a taxpayer plaintiff in that case, along with Annie Laurie and Anne Gaylor, as staff members of the Freedom From Religion Foundation. Gov. Thompson, a Roman Catholic, was outraged that we would challenge the program—especially since President Bush endorsed it. He vowed to resist our attempt to stop it. But Wisconsin Attorney General James Doyle (a Democrat who later became governor) advised him not to fight us. Doyle pointed out that spending public money on a private religious ministry is unconstitutional. The governor ignored his attorney general's advice and hired expensive outside counsel to defend the state from our lawsuit. Thompson had reacted identically to two previous cases by the Foundation: our "Good Friday" and "Marriage Savers" lawsuits. Both times he lost. Doyle was right: where public money goes, public accountability should follow. Faith Works, a private religious organization, was not responsible to the government or to the people.

When we got into discovery in the Faith Works lawsuit, it became clear that this would be a slam-dunk. Scratching beneath the surface revealed that this fly-by-night religious outfit was taking tax dollars for purely sectarian purposes. Although Faith Works claimed after the fact that it was segregating public money from private donations, restricting tax dollars to the "secular" part of its work, the judge saw through this ploy.

A pitiful number of men had "graduated" from the expensive program, and trying to get figures from Faith Works on its effectiveness was like fishing in a dry lake. The group had no way to separate the funds or the program. Money is fungible. It all went to enhance ministry. We won a strong decision from the federal court. (We eventually lost a lesser complaint tacked onto that lawsuit challenging a smaller allocation through the Department of Corrections. The courts, invoking a lamentable school-voucher reasoning, decided this was "voluntary.") Since our main victory staunched the major flow of funds, Faith Works dried up and went out of business. Without tax dollars, it was nothing.

Our Faith Works lawsuit was the first fully adjudicated victory of a challenge to George W. Bush's faith-based initiative. Since that time, the Freedom From Religion Foundation has taken the lead in this arena, filing and winning more cases around the nation than any other state-church group.

Another memorable case involved MentorKids USA of Phoenix, Arizona, an offshoot of Watergate felon Chuck Colson's Prison Ministry. Its stated purpose is to mentor the children of inmates, which sounds like a reasonable goal. Who would not want to help these needy kids? But it turns out that its mandatory activities included bible reading, prayer and proselytizing. The ministry was taking public money in order to bring these children and their families to Jesus Christ. MentorKids restricted its volunteer mentors to church-going evangelical Christians who signed a fundamentalist religious mission statement. A Roman Catholic contacted us, complaining that his application to become a mentor with the group was turned down because he could not in good conscience sign a statement of faith avowing that he believed in the literal six days of creation described in the book of Genesis. "Even the pope knows the earth is more than 6,000 years old!" he said.

We won this case easily. Not only was the grant to MentorKids not renewed, but this was the first time promised funds were withheld from a faith-based charity. Maddeningly, in reply to one of our motions, an attorney for the United States wrote that it is up to watchdog groups such as ours to monitor the "faith-based initiative."

Why is there no governmental oversight of how public money is spent by these organizations and churches? Probably because there is an assumption that if it is religious, it must be good. It is assumed that we must simply trust the faith-based groups to be honest and responsible. Ironically, the separation of church and state makes the government reluctant to interfere with private religious groups. In reality, no church or religious school in the country is responsible to the public. Churches pay no taxes and file no IRS 990 forms—while all other nonprofit groups, including the Freedom From Religion Foundation, are required to provide these forms to the government to show where the money comes from and how it is spent. (Those annual 990 forms are cumbersome and time-consuming. Every penny is tracked. The forms are available to the public so you can examine what happens with the money you donate to any other nonprofit group. The Freedom From Religion Foundation has received top marks for consecutive years by Charity Navigator, which tracks and analyzes 990 forms.)

"Faith-based" religious groups want it both ways. They want public money—which includes some of *my* taxes—but they don't want to provide public accountability. But they *should* be accountable. Why would they not want to be? Can you see the potential for abuse that such a system allows? Yes, many religious groups are honest—a few of them even refuse to take public money—but many are not and it is lawsuits like ours that prove it.

By 2004, we had won faith-based lawsuits in Montana, Arizona, Alaska and Minnesota and had cases pending in other states. We were starting to wonder why the burden for policing these religious groups had to fall on the shoulders of small organizations like ours. Wasn't that the government's job? Why should we be running around the country putting out fires? Why were there any fires in the first place?

We had originally hoped that our victories would be a lesson to Bush and others in the government that they should back off from throwing tax dollars at religious organizations. But the president's faith-based program just got stronger, larger and more expensive.

Like planaria flatworms that can regrow their heads or video game warriors that never die, faith-based offices began popping up in many departments of the federal government. Education, Health and Human Services (led for a while by former governor Tommy Thompson), Housing and Urban Development, Labor, Justice, Agriculture, International Development, Homeland Security, Commerce, Small Business and Veterans Affairs all had a faith-based office. They also started appearing in many governors' offices and even within city governments. Encouraged by the Bush administration's active courting, they were raking in millions of dollars.

The White House and Cabinet-level faith-based offices don't actually hand out money, but they provide services to religious organizations and sponsor massive conferences and workshops, some of which were described by the press as tantamount to religious revival services that included prayer and Christian music. Our government actively invites faith organizations to the tax-supported conferences, even offering a proverbial "free lunch" by encouraging them to apply for money and teaching them how to fill out the grant applications. Bush told the faith-based groups that there was a pile of government money and here is how you can get it. We think this is unconstitutional. Our secular government should not be promoting or funding religion.

We are not opposed to the freedom of private, tax-exempt religious groups to do their ministry. They are welcome to advertise, to appeal to supporters, to raise funds and to attempt to earn the respect that will attract donations toward their mission—but they should do it with private funding, not with the tax dollars that belong to all of us. They should figure out how to raise money with no special handholding by the government. That is what the separation of church and state should mean. None of us should be compelled to support someone else's religion. In fact, if I were running a religious charity I would be embarrassed to admit that my god was not big enough to provide for my needs or direct my activities. If my religion were so ineffectual that I had to go begging from the public till for tax dollars, that would be a bald admission of failure or, at the very least, of ineptitude, as Benjamin Franklin suggested in the quote at the top of this chapter.

In 2004, after a string of victories, we decided to strike higher up. We sued the White House itself. We thought it was wrong for a president to abuse the secular office by actively promoting religion. Anne, Annie Laurie and I, as federal taxpayers and Foundation figureheads, joined by the Freedom From Religion Foundation (representing all taxpayers), filed suit in federal court challenging the formation of an internal faith-based bureaucracy in the Executive Branch (the faith-based offices in the White House and at the Cabinet level). Diligent Madison attorney Rich Bolton, who by now had become the nation's leading expert on faith-based challenges, represented us. By that time, Jim Towey had become the new "faith-based czar" at the White House. (DiIulio had resigned, citing dissatisfaction with the program.)

The federal judge soon dismissed our case, not on the merits, but on the question of our "standing" to sue. He ruled that we taxpayers do not have the right to challenge the creation of the federal faith-based offices. It is true that taxpayers ordinarily do not possess such a right. I can't sue the vice president over what brand of photocopier he purchases, or the president over what country he chooses to invade. But the Supreme Court, in *Flast v. Cohen* (1968), had previously carved out a narrow exception for violations of the Establishment Clause of the First Amendment ("Congress shall make no law respecting an establishment of religion...") when it involves activities funded by Congress under the Congressional Tax and Spending clause. We were convinced that the *Flast* precedent gave us the right to sue. How else could citizens get at the violation? If we did not possess "standing" to sue, no one did. How could that be right?

The judge argued that taxpayer standing under *Flast* applies only to money that Congress specifically allocates to the Executive Branch, not to discretionary dollars that the president uses from general appropriation. If Congress tells the administration to spend the money on religion, then we Americans can challenge it. Otherwise there is no "nexus," no taxpayer connection, no injury, no case. Such reasoning provides a loophole that allows a president—especially a theocratic or imperial president—to get away with violating the Constitution. In fact, Bush had been trying to get Congress to fund the faith-based initiative, and failed (generally). So he simply did an end-run around Congress, created the faith-based initiative and spent the money anyway.

We appealed our loss of standing to sue to the 7th Circuit Court of Appeals in Chicago. To our great satisfaction, a panel of judges overturned the district judge's opinion, siding with us. Judge Richard Posner, a generally conservative judge who declared that the president should not be insulated from judicial scrutiny on religious matters, wrote the strong decision. "Suppose the Secretary of Homeland Security," Posner wrote, "who has unearmarked funds in his budget, decided to build a mosque and pay an Imam a salary to preach in it because the Secretary believed that federal financial assistance to Islam would reduce the likelihood of Islamist terrorism in the United States... It would be too much of a paradox to recognize taxpayer standing only in cases in which the violation of the establishment clause was so slight or furtive that no other basis of standing could be found, and to deny it in the more serious cases."

We were pleased with that decision—it is always nice to win—and were prepared to go back into district court to try the case on its merits. But the United States government was not happy. It petitioned the U.S. Supreme Court to overturn the appeals court decision. In late January 2006, only two weeks after our appeals court victory, a Bush right-wing nominee, Samuel Alito, replaced Supreme Court Justice Sandra Day O'Connor. By that time, Jay Hein had become the new head of the White House Office of Faith-Based and Community Initiatives, so the case was called *Hein v. Freedom From Religion Foundation*. The U.S. Supreme Court does not take many cases, and we did not want them to take ours. We were winning.

In December 2006, the Supreme Court announced that it would hear the government's appeal. The justices would not have taken the case unless at least four of them wanted to decide it. Some observers thought the high court took the case to clear up conflicting circuit court precedent on the standing issue (as some of the appeals court judges recommended), but others were convinced it simply wanted to keep us out of court. Annie Laurie was horrified. Her quick head count of justices gave us only four sure votes. I was hoping Anthony Kennedy might be a swing vote, giving us a 5–4 victory. We would have to wait more than six months to know the outcome.

We flew to Washington, D.C., to witness the oral arguments before the Supreme Court in February 2007. Rich Bolton sat before the bench with D.C. attorney Andy Pincus, who volunteered to do the oral arguments for us *pro bono*, assisted in preparation by students at Yale Law School. It was admittedly exciting to be in the Supreme Court as plaintiffs in a significant lawsuit. Although somewhat esoteric in that it dealt with standing rather than the actual First Amendment complaint, the litigation was nevertheless being carefully watched by civil liberties groups around the nation. We knew a victory would send a strong message that the White House is not immune from judicial scrutiny over religious activities conducted by the government. But we also knew we could lose, with an outcome that would possibly make things worse than they had been before. The justices could simply overturn the appeals court and deny our standing to sue in this particular case, claiming there was no direct Congressional appropriation, or the court could go further and shut the door completely, overturning the *Flast* precedent. We were all nervous over the possibilities.

Major newspapers were on our side. On February 28, the day of the oral arguments, *The New York Times* opined: "The Bush administration is pushing an incorrect view of standing as it tries to stop the courts from reaching the First Amendment issue... Procedural issues like standing can have an enormous impact on the administration of justice if they close the courthouse door on people with valid legal claims. The Supreme Court has made it clear that taxpayers may challenge government assistance to religion. The justices should affirm Judge Posner's ruling so the courts can move on to the important question: Do the Bush administration's faith-based policies violate the Constitution?"

Many state-church and civil liberties groups filed friend-of-the-court briefs on our behalf, including the American Civil Liberties Union, Americans United for the Separation of Church and State, the Baptist Joint Convention for Religious Liberty, People for the American Way, the Anti-Defamation League, Center for Free Inquiry/Center for Secular Humanism, American Atheists, American Jewish Congress & American Jewish Committee, and a group of prominent "historians and legal scholars" who detailed the history of sectarian divisiveness and intolerance that led to the religion clauses of the First Amendment. The United States' friend-of-the-court briefs most notably included one from the ousted "Ten Commandments Judge," Roy Moore, and another from televangelist Pat Robertson's law school. (The briefs and media stories can be read at the Freedom From Religion Foundation's Web page at www.ffrf.org.)

During oral arguments, we were initially surprised to hear Justice Antonin Scalia interrupt the U.S. Solicitor General to ask why the same action by the Executive Branch would be considered unconstitutional *with* Congressional appropriation but constitutional *without* it. "Yeah," I thought. "Good question!" But we later realized that Scalia wants to eliminate *all* taxpayer standing over federal Establishment Clause violations. He and Justice Clarence Thomas want to overturn the *Flast* precedent. Some of the other questions hinged on trivial issues, such as exactly how many tax-funded bagels at the faith-based conferences would be unconstitutional. If the president has the intention to promote religion, it doesn't matter *how* much money is spent—even "Three Pence" was too much, according to James Madison.

Ours was the only case heard that day. After the oral arguments, it was quite fun to walk down the broad steps of the Supreme Court. ABC News filmed me and Annie Laurie stepping down to the bank of microphones and cameras to talk with the national media. The publicity generated so many hits to our Web site that it not only crashed our server but dozens of others as well. (Sorry, whoever you were!) The Freedom From Religion Foundation signed up 800 new members in just two weeks alone!

On June 25, my birthday, we got news that we had lost the case, by a vote of five to four. Annie Laurie was right (she usually is). Three justices—Roberts, Kennedy and Alito—insisted that *Flast* did not give us standing and denied our right to sue due solely to the fact that

Bush used discretionary funds. Their three votes, combined with Scalia and Thomas, who vociferously urged the overturning of *Flast,* meant there was no way we could win. We couldn't help noticing that the five justices who ruled against us were all practicing, conservative Roman Catholics. We now have a conservative majority on the Supreme Court that pledges a part of its allegiance to the Vatican. *The Los Angeles Times* opined the next day: "Two generations' worth of common sense went by the wayside as the court, in a mere plurality opinion, allowed taxpayers to challenge such spending if it is done by Congress but barred them from seeking redress if it is the president who authorizes the money. The court's reasoning was satisfying to no one and resulted in a strange fragmentation of the justices, with the chief leading two other colleagues in the main opinion, joined in concurrence by the bench's two most conservative members. The largest group of justices speaking with one voice actually was in dissent, in which Justices David H. Souter, John Paul Stevens, Ruth Bader Ginsburg and Stephen G. Breyer all joined."

In his dissenting opinion, Justice Souter wrote: "Here, the controlling, plurality opinion declares that *Flast* does not apply, but a search of that opinion for a suggestion that these taxpayers have any less stake in the outcome than the taxpayers in *Flast* will come up empty: the plurality makes no such finding, nor could it. Instead, the controlling opinion closes the door on these taxpayers because the Executive Branch, and not the Legislative Branch, caused their injury. I see no basis for this distinction in either logic or precedent, and respectfully dissent."

Justice O'Connor had been the court's true swing vote. Our lawsuit was Samuel Alito's first case dealing with religion, and many were watching to see how the new court would shape up. O'Connor's replacement by Alito—one of the lasting legacies of the Bush presidency—not only tipped the court but also appears to have stuck it in the wrong direction, like a broken compass. (The only defense we can muster for Kennedy was his concurring opinion's firm refusal to go along with Scalia and Thomas in overturning *Flast.*) As a protest, on Freethought Radio the week after the decision, we played the song, "It don't mean a thing if it ain't got that swing."

Since the decision in *Hein v. Freedom From Religion Foundation* dealt only with standing, not with the merits of our complaint, our loss does not mean that what President Bush did is constitutional.

Nor does it mean that we cannot continue challenging violations of the First Amendment. It does mean none of us can challenge *this* particular violation. No American taxpayer, religious or not, has the right to challenge, on purely taxpayer grounds, a discretionary action that violates the Establishment Clause by the Executive. The religious right may have got more than it bargained for. If a future president or governor wants to use general funds to insult Christianity (as unlikely at that prospect may be), the *Hein* decision means that no Baptist, Methodist or Catholic taxpayer can stop it as a taxpayer. The bar has been raised. Shortly after the June 25 decision, the Freedom From Religion Foundation reluctantly had to back out of a strong lawsuit challenging a "God pod" at the women's prison in Grants, New Mexico. The judge had indicated that if we lost the *Hein* case he would dismiss the lawsuit on standing, so we withdrew. We will revisit the violation with a stronger challenge in the future.

There are three ways, at least, to continue challenging the faith-based initiative. First, if we can connect the program to a direct legislative appropriation, then taxpayer standing is solid. (We actually did establish in our Supreme Court brief that Congress for years had debated and voted on the faith-based appropriations we were challenging, but we had a stacked Court.) Second, we can sue with a plaintiff who has direct injury—not just a taxpayer, but someone who is personally affected by the program itself. This could be a prisoner, student, patient or recipient of service. Third, our favorite solution: Congress can stop the unconstitutional funding stream. Even the majority opinion agreed that "Congress can quickly step in" if it wants to.

The best hope for the world is secular government. There are enough real causes of social conflict on this planet without the manufactured cause of religious divisiveness. In a democratic, egalitarian society, we should embrace the freedom to disagree about religious opinions, which also means we should denounce the freedom to ask our government to settle the argument. The government, at all levels, must diligently remain neutral. Working to keep state and church separate is a task that is crucial to preserving tolerance and peace, and the only way to have a "heaven on earth." It is certainly a more practical mission than what I was doing for 19 years: trying to usher people into an imaginary heaven.

Chapter Eighteen
Adventures in Atheism

In February 2008 I stood on the Brazilian coast at Cabo Branco, looking out across the Atlantic Ocean toward Africa. I had been invited to represent atheism at the annual Nova Consciência conference, a huge multi-cultural, interfaith "anti-Carnival" that promotes tolerance in the northeastern city of Campina Grande. After the five-day meeting, I especially wanted to visit Cabo Branco, the easternmost point of the Americas. Some of my new friends drove me there so that I could stand facing east with my arms stretched out and my back to the entire American continents. I can now literally say that I have taken atheism to the ends of the earth.

A year earlier, I was at the exact opposite spot in Africa, near Kribi, Cameroon, which corresponds to the point where Cabo Branco would have been connected with Africa 150 million years ago. I had stood on the African continent with my arms stretched out, facing west across the ocean that is being formed by the Mid-Atlantic Ridge. The geographical points are not due east-west because the continents have drifted somewhat southwest-northeast of each other. (As "proof" of continental drift, I did notice that Cabo Branco, a year later, seemed to be an inch further away, and I found the other half of a broken rock that I had spotted in Africa. Just kidding!)

There I stood, a medium-sized mammal on a spinning, evolving planet, orienting myself with a physical sense of place and geography, knowing how immensely long it took for all this to happen, and smiling at my earlier fundamentalist self who used to believe that the world was (at most) 10,000 years old.

As a child in Sunday School, I put pennies in a plastic bread loaf to help missionaries travel to "deep, dark Africa" to convert poor, lost souls to Jesus. I had wondered what it would be like to do something so grandiose and exotic, so whole-heartedly obedient to Christ. Fifty years later, I got to travel to Africa for the first time, but not as a Christian missionary. If going on a mission means spreading the "good news," then that's exactly what I did.

The Cameroon Freethought Association invited me to speak at the first international French-African conference of nonbelievers and humanists. I didn't see any "poor lost souls" on the continent. I saw a people drenched in religion, from Protestants, Catholics and Muslims to local tribal believers. I saw an enterprising nation of hard-working people, though I did get robbed by the police while riding in a taxi ($70 for the gendarme beer fund is a small price to pay for a good story to tell). And while the standard of living is lower than in the U.S. and corruption is pervasive, I saw few beggars and no abject poverty. (I told them I think the only difference between Africa and the United States is that we Americans know how to hide our corruption better.) I met some wonderful freethinking university students and other enlightened nonbelievers who told me that the last thing their continent needs is more religion! It is encouraging to see how freedom of conscience is cherished all over the world. For me, it was a real adventure to play a small part in bringing the good news of atheism to Africa.

The same religious dynamic is true in Brazil. Although 90 percent of the population claims to be Catholic, in reality most of the people practice a syncretism of Afro-Brazilian religions mixed in with Christianity, plus Pentecostalism, Islam, Buddhism, Hare Krishna and dozens of other faiths. They don't need any more missionaries. They need freethought. They need fair economic opportunities. I noticed that although many Brazilians struggle to put milk on the table, they all seemed to have enough money for Carnival, the lottery, beer and church. ("Beer" and "church" happen to rhyme in Portuguese: *cerveja* and *igreja*. It would make a good song!) Getting rid of the church would give everyone a 10 percent raise, for starters.

As I was standing at Cabo Branco looking out across the vast blue Atlantic, thinking about the continental plates drifting apart, my mind drifted back, naturally enough, to my visit to Iceland two years earlier to attend an atheist/humanist conference. Iceland was formed—is still being formed—by lava flowing up from the Mid-Atlantic Ridge as the plates are separating. Half of Iceland is on the trailing edge of the North American Plate (San Francisco is on the leading edge), and the other half of Iceland is on the trailing edge of the Eurasian

Plate. A small busload of us atheist and humanist visitors stood at the location the Icelanders claim is exactly over the Mid-Atlantic Ridge, with one plate to the east and the other to the west of the valley at Thingvellir. At this spot, the Althing, one of the world's oldest parliaments, a pagan government, was formed in the year 930. Annie Laurie and I had joined an international roster of speakers in Reykjavik, the world's northernmost capital. It was our first visit to the country, and the first time fellow participants Richard Dawkins and Julia Sweeney had seen Iceland. It was great fun to tour the exotic, varied land with such insightful people, all of us wide-eyed at the strange and beautiful scenery. We got to stand at the top of the Godafoss, the waterfall into which the pagans were forced to throw their wooden gods in the year 1,000 when the invading Christians from Norway gave them a choice: convert or die. (I wonder if that happened on a Thursday, the day we still honor their god Thor.) If I had had a wooden cross and a statue of the Virgin Mary, I would have lobbed them into the falls, too. Naturally, I stood there also with my arms spread apart: "I claim this land in the name of reason." The greatest pleasure of that trip was meeting the local atheists and humanists, and learning that fundamentalism is virtually nonexistent in a culture that descended from the pagan Vikings. The annual Atheist Picnic in July was freezing cold, but it was a hoot!

Representing the Freedom From Religion Foundation, I get to engage in similar atheist "missionizing" all across the American continent—although most of the people I meet are already freethinkers doing their own brave work. I am not the Great American Prophet bestowing blessings from afar. I am a peer and a coworker, joining with other enlightened non-souls to bring reason, science and humanism to a faith-soaked planet.

In one memorable trip, I was invited to represent atheism at the 2005 World Religions Conference in Kitchener, Ontario. I had told the organizers I would love to participate but that atheism is not a religion, so they changed the program to "World Religions and Philosophies" in order to accommodate me. I think it is fantastic that atheism is starting to be recognized as a legitimate point of view, that atheists are no longer automatically seen as evil and immoral, and that we are occasionally invited to sit down at the table with everyone else.

As recently as the 1960s and 1970s, atheists were not even considered part of the fabric of society. You had to be religious—any kind of religious, even cultish or nutty—to be considered a good person.

Provincial and municipal dignitaries and hundreds of registrants, including many freethinkers from the local humanist society, attended the huge conference in Kitchener. I sat on the stage alongside a Sikh, Muslim, Roman Catholic, Jew, Buddhist and Native American spiritualist. We all disagreed, of course, but we did so civilly, with a spirit of understanding and tolerance. We looked for areas of agreement and overlap.

In the United States, the fastest growing religious identification is "nonreligion." Today, there is a whole generation of young people for whom the phrase "godless Communist" is dusty ancient history. Americans between the ages of 15 and 30 are currently the least believing demographic in the nation, with as many as 30 percent being nonreligious. Speaking at college campuses is especially rewarding for me. I am often invited by a secular campus organization for a debate, lecture or concert.

The kinds of students who take the initiative to run a freethought (atheist, agnostic, humanist, skeptic) group are cream-of-the-crop. Considering that students are very busy, and usually very poor, and that becoming involved with campus activism is completely discretionary, they have to be highly motivated to go to the trouble of engaging in such activism. I often ask the leaders why they formed the group, and they usually respond that it's because they want to socialize with like-minded nonbelievers, and because they want to "fight back." Religious groups on campuses are often very pushy and obnoxious, and the nonbelieving students want to counter their proselytizing to promote reason, science and human ethics over faith, superstition and orthodoxy. Some of the most fun moments of my life have been *after* these campus events when we all go out for pizza and debate the hours away. I learn a lot from these bright, caring students. Many of them are studying on the cutting edge of science, history, philosophy, language and law, and I get to pick their brains and bask in their enthusiasm. The future of freethought looks bright.

In Dublin, I learned from students at University College that the current generation of Irish youth sees itself as completely separate from the past, as their parents were from their grandparents, although to an even greater degree. They are trying to catch up with the rest of secularized Europe. The young Irish are embarrassed at their history of religious divisiveness and intolerance. Some of them mentioned that the scandals of sexual impropriety among the priests have lowered the country's respect for religion and weakened the church's influence. It appeared that about half of the students involved with that 2007 debate were atheists, so they were not bothered by my outspoken views. But they wanted to know, "Are you a Catholic atheist or a Protestant atheist?" (Richard Dawkins later told me that this is an old joke, but it was new to me.)

Something significant is happening in the United States. The number of campus secular clubs is growing rapidly. I remember 15 or 20 years ago counting about a half dozen groups, but today there are hundreds. The Freedom From Religion Foundation has been working with the Secular Student Alliance (SSA) in a joint outreach project to college campuses, and the SSA is very busy just trying to keep up with the increase in affiliates. That is encouraging. If we can divert just one young mind from going into the ministry or from wasting time and money on religion, we have made the world a better place.

We have suffered enough from the divisive malignancy of belief. Our planet needs a faithectomy.

I gave up the religion, but I kept the music. As atheist conductor David Randolph, a Lifetime member of the Freedom From Religion Foundation, writes in his book, *This is Music*, there is no such thing as religious music. Music is just music, and it is the lyrics that make a song "religious" or "freethought." As an atheist, I have written a number of freethought and humanist songs that I am eager to perform to any willing audience. I have also discovered a treasure of historical freethought music, including Tom Lehrer's crowd-pleasing "Vatican Rag," the traditional English ballad "The Vicar of Bray" and Irving Berlin's rebuke to censors, "Pack Up Your Sins and Go To The Devil in Hades." It was pleasing to walk into London's Conway Hall a few years ago and see myself billed as "Dan Barker: The Singing Atheist."

But the most satisfying production I have been involved with is *Tunes 'n Toons* with Steve Benson. Steve is the Pulitzer Prize-winning editorial cartoonist of the *Arizona Republic*, a former Mormon and a grandson of Ezra Taft Benson, who was once president of the Mormon Church and President Dwight Eisenhower's secretary of agriculture.

When Steve made a very public break with Mormonism in the early 1990s, it embarrassed his family and the Church. Since that time, the once-conservative artist has transformed himself (he's "born again!") into one of the funniest and sharpest nationally syndicated editorial cartoonists in the country. (His editor complains, "A picture is worth a thousand phone calls.")

Steve and I do a timely show looking at religion in the news that combines my tunes with his cartoons. It is one of the most challenging projects I have ever worked on and one of the most rewarding. We now have about four hours of material, but each show has to be updated with fresh cartoons and whittled down to 60–90 minutes. We work feverishly up to the last minute inserting new dialogue (such as "Do televangelists do more than lay people?") and songs (such as "Godless America, Land That We Love") before going on stage, tailoring each performance for the occasion. We have played in Las Vegas, the District of Columbia, California, Washington, Texas, Wisconsin and other states, but most deliciously in Salt Lake City, where we did our Mormon version of the show. The first time we presented the show in Utah was for a group of ex-Mos (former Mormons) during General Conference Week of the Mormon Church. It was there that we were "inspired" at the last minute to write the "Salt Lake City Blues."

Atheist "evangelism" doesn't just happen in front of an audience. Driving back to Phoenix after that show in Salt Lake City, Steve and I stopped at a vista in northern Arizona. I walked to a stand where a Navajo named Bobby was selling jewelry.

"I'm also a Native American," I said. "Lenape tribe. Delaware Indian."

Bobby nodded.

Pointing to an array of silver necklaces, I asked, "Why are you selling Christian crosses?"

"People buy them," he replied.

"But don't we have any pride?" I asked. "The European invaders took our land, our buffalo, our history, our freedom and, obviously, our dignity, or else we wouldn't be so eager to embrace the religion of our oppressors."

I imagined I had scored a point, until he said, "They gave us hope." Yes. He was hoping tourists would purchase his crafts. Tourists living on stolen land.

"So you're a Christian?"

"I'm a Mormon," he replied slowly.

"A Mormon?" Steve was walking toward us, so I raised my voice. "Here's someone I think you should meet."

"I used to be a Mormon," Steve said. "I'm an atheist now. My grandfather was president of the Mormon Church."

"The Mormon religion has been a great blessing to our people," Bobby said.

"But it is demeaning," Steve replied. "*The Book of Mormon* says that the Indians are descendants of the wicked Lamanites, who were cursed with a dark skin for their disobedience to God."

Bobby looked up at Steve's white face.

"How does that make you feel?" Steve asked.

"We deserved it," Bobby replied.

My mouth froze open.

"*The Book of Mormon* says the Indians will become 'white and delightsome' if they convert," Steve continued.

"But that's true," Bobby replied, claiming that when the Indians converted, they started getting lighter. "My skin will change color."

"That's not going to happen," Steve responded.

"Well, the church has done a lot for me," Bobby replied, "because I strayed as a youth."

We encouraged Bobby to actually read the *Book of Mormon* and the bible, to learn something about the history of his faith and the oppression of Christianity. To be friendly, I bought one of his necklaces, but it was one without a cross. Although it was sad to see Bobby's self-debasement, it was actually a memorable moment for us both. Steve had been a missionary to Japan (trying to turn Buddhists into Mormons) and I had been a missionary to Mexico (trying to turn Catholics into Christians), and now here we were, doing reverse penance, bringing the good news of atheism to poor lost America.

Reaching out to the unmassed masses, the FFRF has a national weekly show, *Freethought Radio*, with "slightly irreverent views, news and interviews." It debuted in April 2006 on The Mic 92.1, a progressive talk radio station in Madison, Wisconsin. The hour-long weekly program, hosted by Annie Laurie and me and produced by Brian Turany (with help from former FFRF staffer Lynn Lau), went national on Air America Radio in October 2007 and is broadcast on weekends by affiliates in the United States. It is also podcast to listeners around the world. Our first guest was Ernie Harburg, son of the famous American lyricist Yip Harburg, a nonbeliever who wrote "Somewhere, Over the Rainbow." Since that time we have had the immense pleasure of interviewing atheist and agnostic movers and shakers and state/church litigants and activists from all over the country and the world. We interviewed Ron Reagan about how he knew he was an atheist as a child, even as his parents, Nancy and Ronald Reagan, were taking him to Sunday School. We had evolutionary biologist Richard Dawkins on the show just before his blockbuster book, *The God Delusion,* was published, and then had him again the following year to exult in the international success of the book.

We talked with Sam Harris about *The End of Faith* and Daniel Dennett told us about *Breaking the Spell* (of religion). It has been exciting to speak with such luminaries as authors Steven Pinker (*The Blank Slate*), Susan Jacoby (*Freethinkers* and *The Age of American Unreason*), mathematician John Allen Paulos (*Innumeracy* and *Irreligion*) and Matthew Chapman (great-grandson of Charles Darwin, who wrote *40 Days and 40 Nights* about the Dover, Pennsylvania, "intelligent design" trial).

We have also talked with *The Nation* columnist and author Katha Pollitt (*Learning to Drive*), Scott Dikkers of *The Onion*, scientist/activist Eugenie C. Scott of the pro-evolution National Center for Science Education, children's author Philip Pullman (the week *The Golden Compass* movie was released), Pledge of Allegiance attorney/plaintiff Michael Newdow and actress/comedian Julia Sweeney (whose hilarious play and movie, *Letting Go of God*, is quite moving and, to borrow a phrase from the play, "scathingly brilliant").

Other guests include *God is Not Great* (another blockbuster atheist book) author Christopher Hitchens, Nebraska senator Ernie Chambers, state/church plaintiffs Ellery Schempp and Jim McCollum, abortion-clinic bombing victim Emily Lyons (who barely survived and is now half blind with nails still embedded in her body), NBC correspondent Betty Rollin, editorial cartoonist Steve Benson, atheist and actress Janeane Garofalo, 90-year-old Nobel Laureate Paul D. Boyer and 93-year-old Carnegie Hall conductor David Randolph (both Lifetime members of the FFRF), scientist/author Robert Sapolsky (*Primate's Memoir*), *The Progressive* editor Matt Rothschild, journalist William Lobdell (author of *Losing My Religion: How I Lost My Faith Reporting on Religion in America*), *New York Times* science writer Natalie Angier (author of *The Canon*), author Ann Druyan (Carl Sagan's widow and co-author of *Contact, Comet,* and *Shadows of Forgotten Ancestors*), *Kingdom Coming* author Michelle Goldberg, poet and Darwin scholar Philip Appleman, feminist author Ellie Smeal, feminist author Robin Morgan, feminist author Barbara G. Walker, feminist songwriter Kristin Lems, skeptics Michael Shermer and the "Amazing" James Randi, as well as dozens of other fascinating national and local activists and authors.

We have interviewed FFRF founder Anne Nicol Gaylor, who as a volunteer runs The Women's Medical Fund, the nation's longest-running abortion charity. The Fund has helped tens of thousands of indigent women exercise their constitutional rights. (Who said atheists don't do good deeds?) Instead of preaching religion, I get to do a radio sermon called "Pagan Pulpit" in which I analyze the bible and current events from a freethought perspective. Other segments on Freethought Radio include "Theocracy Alert," "Ask an Atheist" and "Freethinkers' Almanac," in which we profile the lives and accomplishments of famous nonbelievers in history. We also discuss our current lawsuits and state/church complaints and play historical and contemporary freethought music.

We have met many of the *Freethought Radio* guests in person, since some have been speakers at the annual national conventions of the Freedom From Religion Foundation, where atheists and agnostics around the country come for freethought fellowship, camaraderie and music. For me, the greatest adventure of atheism is getting to know all of these smart, empathetic activists. Author Oliver Sacks, describing himself as "an old Jewish atheist," gave his first talk on rejecting religion at our 2005 convention in Florida. We also got to meet Nobel Prize-winning physicist Steven Weinberg, White House correspondent Helen Thomas, author Taslima Nasrin (who is under threat of a death fatwa), ethicist Peter Singer (it is interesting that the world's leading ethicist is an atheist), political cartoonist Edward Sorel, editorial cartoonist Don Addis, attorney Alan Dershowitz and many other fascinating thinkers and shakers.

Meeting these people in person is, for me, almost like dining with royalty. When I took Oliver Sacks to lunch in Orlando before his talk, he showed me his journals in which he was working on his latest book

about music (which became *Musicophilia: Tales of Music and the Brain*).
He is a delightful person, like a child wide-eyed with wonder at the
marvels of the universe and the weird intricacies of the brain, still carrying the periodic table in his wallet. He is somewhat hard of hearing
and the restaurant was a bit noisy, and this provided the occasion for a
humorous moment. I asked him what he thought about the hypothesis
that music is a result of the brain's need to perceive vowel sounds. He
stopped and looked at me like I was crazy. Then he laughed and said,
"Oh. I thought you said 'bowel' sounds!" (Well, I *have* heard some
music like that.)

Since then, Annie Laurie and I have twice had the pleasure of
accompanying Oliver Sacks to Carnegie Hall to hear David Randolph
conduct the exquisite St. Cecilia Chorus (a completely secular group,
David reminds us, with perfect vowel sounds) perform Mendelssohn,
Orff and Verdi. Hearing Verdi's *Requiem* while sitting in the center
of the first balcony in the box next to 93-year-old David's engaging
93-year-old wife Mildred was a freethought triple-header: the atheist David Randolph conducted the atheist Giuseppe Verdi in the hall
named for the freethinker Andrew Carnegie. David Randolph, by the
way, is the oldest person to have conducted at Carnegie Hall. He also
holds the world record for complete performances of Handel's *Messiah*:
more than 170 times with full orchestra and chorus. (How's that for
being a tolerant atheist?)

That Verdi performance was May 2, 2008. The next morning we
caught a direct flight from New York to Los Angeles, arriving just in
time to change into "black tie" attire for Julia Sweeney's wedding to
Michael Blum. What a show! (They should have charged admission.)
Julia, looking gorgeous (*nothing* like the Androgynous Pat character
she used to play on *Saturday Night Live*), and Michael were married by
Father Guido Sarducci (comedian Don Novello), who used the hotel
menu and Wikipedia as his source texts and only referred to the bible
to criticize Jesus' handling of the water-to-wine incident (calling it a
"frivolous miracle.")

The atheist/agnostic culture is still so rarefied that it seems possible to meet just about every freethought dignitary in the world. As
co-president of the FFRF, it has been my lucky lot to make many
of the award presentations at our annual conventions. Handing the
Foundation's "Emperor Has No Clothes" award to Julia Sweeney,

Christopher Hitchens, Steven Weinberg, Steven Pinker, Robert Sapolsky, Oliver Sacks, Alan Dershowitz and Peter Singer, among many other notables, has been an immense pleasure.

I was interviewed by NBC News correspondent and author Betty Rollin at Lake Hypatia (where she pronounced Alabama a "bad hair state") for a *Religion & Ethics News Weekly* television segment on atheism.

I was taken to lunch at the Bowery Bar in New York City by Deena Rosenberg (author of *Fascinating Rhythm: The Collaboration of George and Ira Gershwin*) and her husband, Ernie Harburg, who picked up the check and said, "Let's let 'Somewhere, Over the Rainbow' pay for the meal."

We got to take Richard Dawkins to lunch before he gave his Distinguished Lectures talk at the University of Wisconsin, a talk that "sold out" like a rock concert with people showing up begging for tickets. (By the way, the Richard Dawkins Foundation produces a scarlet letter "A" pin and I wear one almost wherever I travel. So far, I have only met one other person wearing such a pin: Richard Dawkins. Who wants to be next?)

Atheism has no hierarchy, no clergy and no chosen people more "holy" than anyone else. The members of the Foundation are just as important as the speakers and guests. We are all part of the same species, using our individual talents to make the world a better place, in our own way. Many of the bravest people are those who need to remain anonymous, local residents complaining about a violation of state/church separation in their town, risking retribution to their families if the people in their superstitious county learned their identities. This was especially true of the courageous family that challenged bible classes being conducted in the public schools in Rhea County, Tennessee. Not even their own children knew it was their parents who complained! When the FFRF filed suit with that family as plaintiffs, the Chattanooga judge granted a federal protective order after learning that many conservative Christians in the city of Dayton (famous for the 1925 Scopes Trial) were demanding to know their identity, threatening to run them out of town. They were able to file anonymously as "John Doe," "Jane Doe" and "Doe Child 1," etc.

It was a real adventure for me to fly down there and meet secretly with the father to talk through the process. I sensed both his palpable fear of the local bigots and his intense devotion to the principle of keeping religion and government separate. Although it was a long fight—the school board and county board would not budge an inch—we won that case easily. Our lawsuit (which we nicknamed "Scopes II") stopped a 50-plus-year violation that had students from the fundamentalist Bryan College (a legacy of William Jennings Bryan, the creationist attorney who debated Clarence Darrow in the Scopes Trial) entering the public schools during class hours to teach the bible to fifth graders. To this day, no one (other than the attorneys, who are under a federal order) knows the identity of that family, which doesn't want any recognition. *These* intelligent, ethical, working class people are my real heroes. They are much more courageous than any Christians I have ever known.

Another real adventure is finding other former clergy, like myself, who are now atheists or agnostics. Richard Hewetson, an Episcopal priest whose bishop knew he was gay when he was ordained, says that the reason he entered the ministry was that, at the time, he considered the church to be the best vehicle for helping people. Dick, who is one of the funniest guys I know, says another reason he became a priest was so that he could be around men who wore dresses. He left the ministry because he could "no longer pretend to believe the church's teachings or practices." Today he is retired, living in San Francisco on a pension from the church, volunteering for progressive causes and speaking out as an atheist, finally able to help people without the fog of superstition.

Patrick Maguire was formerly a Roman Catholic priest. He and I were once guests on the national *Sally Jessy Raphael Show*, talking about our respective deconversions. He *looked* just like an Irish priest, with his twinkle and hint of a brogue. "I realized that in the origins of Christianity there was nothing really unusual about Catholicism," he said. "They had taken all kinds of things from other religions (such as Mithraism), even the title 'Father.' Those religions believed in a God who was born of a woman, very often a virgin… For these reasons, and much more, I came to the conclusion that I simply could not believe." He left the priesthood and the faith, while his brother, Daniel, left the priesthood but remained a liberal believer, teaching at a Catholic university.

Patrick very soon fell in love with a woman, but they decided to wait for five years to get married. "The crazy reason was that I didn't want my colleagues to get the idea that I left for anything except my conviction, which is rather silly, really." When they finally did get married, his wife became ill and, tragically, died within a few months. "Was it worth it?" he asked. Religion denied them those years of happiness. Patrick taught philosophy at a California college, where he was once asked by the students to give an atheist invocation at graduation.

Jim O'Brien is another one-time Catholic priest who didn't realize what he actually believed until it was too late. He was teaching a class of high school girls and a box with random questions was being passed around the room. He drew the card asking, "Do you believe in God?" The girls all laughed when they heard such a ridiculous question for a priest to answer. "I laugh, too," Jim reports. "But I can't think of an answer. In fact, I can't think of anything to say. The room goes very, very quiet. I am still a blank, but a tiny voice in the back of my head says, terrifyingly, 'You're out of a job.'"

Delos McKown was a Baptist preacher who left the ministry and became head of the philosophy department at Auburn University. Reading Corliss Lamont's *Illusion of Immortality* had a profound influence on his thinking. Charles French was another Baptist minister who was more concerned with the "social" in the "social Gospel" than he was with the "Gospel," so he left the church and the faith but continued to work for social betterment.

Ed Wilson was a Seventh Day Adventist minister who abandoned the religion and is now an agnostic: "I have come to believe that the doctrine of self-abnegation is one of the more damaging tenets of Christianity. This degrading of the self in the exaltation of Jesus... the 'I am nothing, Christ is all' teaching is a stultifying approach to life which I believe has crippled the psyches of millions. Good sense humility is healthy, but the self-abnegation which is taught as a central idea in Christianity is sick."

Farrell Till was a Church of Christ minister and missionary who made the mistake of studying the bible too closely. "Once my faith in inerrancy was shaken," he wrote, "I was able to see the folly of stupid attempts to justify the despicable conduct of the Hebrew god. When I crossed that line, I had gone too far ever to turn back again." Adrian Swindler (what a great name for a minister!) was also a Church of Christ minister who saw the light and left the faith.

Hector Avalos was a child preacher who became so obsessed with the bible that he immersed himself in Hebrew. He was the first Mexican-American to get a Ph.D. in biblical languages from Harvard. I used to preach on the very hillside in Nogales, Mexico, where Hector was born, and it is not impossible that he was one of the little children who came to listen to me playing the accordion and preaching in that city when I was a teenager. He also knew the Christian records of Manuel Bonilla that I had produced in Spanish. Now Hector and I can smile and compare notes about what we used to believe and preach (in two languages). He is currently a professor of religious studies, teaching the bible as an open atheist, at Iowa State University and is author of *Fighting Words: The Origins of Religious Violence* and *The End of Biblical Studies*. He is one of the experts whose brain I often get to pick when it comes to biblical questions.

Mitch Modisett was a Methodist minister who read more of the liberal theologians than was healthy for his faith. "I realized that I could not go through life explaining to people that I really did not believe all the things that they think I am supposed to believe. I did not want to go through life deceiving people."

Thomas Vernon was a Baptist minister who lost his faith but tried to stay in the pulpit for a while. "My disenchantment with organized religion was the result more of moral than intellectual difficulties," he said, in reference to the immorality of the church. He later taught philosophy at the University of Arkansas.

Tom Reed was a Mississippi Roman Catholic priest who realized that the church was hindering civil rights, so he left the ministry for a life of social work. Bob Semes, a former Episcopal priest, left the ministry and started the Jefferson Center in Ashland, Oregon, promoting reason and science over faith and orthodoxy.

Lee Salisbury, a former Pentecostal minister and missionary, now works with Minnesota Atheists as a kind of resident biblical scholar. Paul Heffron is a former Congregationalist–UCC minister, now a nonbeliever, who plays jazz piano in the Minneapolis area (and we love to compare notes, literally!). Richard Pope was ordained by the Evangelical Church Alliance and spent 13 years on the staff of the Young Life Campaign. He is now an atheist who says, "I was, for all those years, unknowingly living and preaching a lie."

Levi Fragell, formerly a fundamentalist minister, is now an outgoing atheist working with the Human-Etisk Forbund, the Norwegian Humanists. Maureen Hart was a Roman Catholic nun but lost her faith while working as a nurse in a mental hospital. She realized there simply cannot be a god who would allow such pointless suffering. Rabbi Sherwin Wine left the faith but not the culture of Judaism, and, as an atheist, started the completely nontheistic Society for Humanistic Judaism.

I recently talked with a former imam of more than 20 years, from an Arabic country now living in the United Kingdom, who asked me not to divulge his name. (He is not afraid for himself, but for his family.) He says it was learning the lies, hypocrisy and fabrication in the translations of the Koran that started him on his path to atheism—to anti-theism, he says, in the case of Islam. We spoke on the phone about the book he is writing. "When I left Islam," he told me, "I became more human. I used to care what people thought about me, as a religious leader, but now I just want to be an ordinary person, not looking at other people as infidels to save." He sounded so relieved to be talking friend-to-friend with a former clergyman from another religion that he used to hate. "When you dig a little deeper," he said, "you learn that Islam is a very fragile religion." Maybe that's why it needs to be bolstered with such fanaticism.

I know many more former clergy, representing a cross section of faith from conservative to liberal, from Pentecostals to mainline ministers, but their stories are too numerous to tell here. In 2007, I got a series of e-mails from a Mennonite minister who had lost his faith and told his superiors that he wanted to leave the pulpit. But they asked him if he would stick it out until the end of the year (until they could find a replacement!) This man was torturing himself. He was getting up to preach as an atheist—I know the feeling—and trying not to talk about "God." Instead, he talked about "love" and "helping others," as he was counting the weeks until he could be free at last. I also heard from a minister's wife who has given up her faith, and it seems that her husband may not be too far behind. I told her that I sympathized with their predicament and that it might help them to know that I will not be praying for them.

Of course, the ongoing adventure has been working for more than 20 years with the FFRF. When I first met Foundation founder Anne Gaylor I knew I was in the presence of a gracious genius. I had no idea I would eventually get to work side-by-side with Anne and her daughter, Annie Laurie, trying to keep state and church separate and educating the public about the views of nontheists.

Freethought Today, published since 1983, is the nation's only freethought newspaper. We also publish books, including our best-selling *Born Again Skeptic's Guide to the Bible* by Ruth Hurmence Green, Yip Harburg's *Rhymes For The Irreverent* (illustrated by Seymour Chwast), *One Woman's Fight* by victorious 1948 Supreme Court litigant Vashti McCollum, my book *Just Pretend: A Freethought Book for Children*, a biography of the illustrious 19-century freethinker Robert G. Ingersoll (*American Infidel*, by Orvin Larson), Anne Gaylor's *Lead Us Not Into Penn Station* and Annie Laurie's books *Woe To The Women: the Bible Tells Me So* and *Women Without Superstition: No Gods–No Masters*.

In the past two decades, we've had a lot of adventures and worked many long hours to try to counter the din of America's growing religious right. Some of the most glowing moments have been filing important lawsuits to protect the American principle of the separation between church and state. When we win one of those lawsuits—and we usually do win—that is heaven on earth!

Among recent forays, we started a national Wake Up America campaign in 2006, placing billboards along highways saying "Beware of Dogma" and "Imagine No Religion," with the goal of having at least one erected in every state (or just about every state, since Hawaii outlaws billboards).

We erect an annual atheistic winter solstice sign at the Wisconsin capitol, protesting religious holiday messages on government property. Anne Gaylor wrote the inscription: "At this season of the Winter Solstice, may reason prevail. There are no gods, no devils, no angels, no heaven or hell. There is only our natural world. Religion is but myth and superstition that hardens hearts and enslaves minds."

We sponsor annual student essay contests with cash awards, one for high school seniors and another for college students. Our Alabama chapter hosts an annual July 4th weekend for southern freethinkers at the Foundation's southern Freethought Hall on Lake Hypatia (which also boasts the nation's only Atheists in Foxholes monument, honoring nonbelievers in the military).

We bestow the "Emperor Has No Clothes Award" to public figures who speak plainly on religion. The "Freethinker of the Year Award" is awarded to people who make significant contributions to keep state and church separate. The "Student Activist Award" is self-explanatory. The "Freethought Heroine Award" honors the contributions of women to freethought and state/church separation, and the "Tell It Like It Is Award" goes to brave members of the media who are unafraid to critique religion.

We produce educational products, such as bumper stickers, T-shirts and greeting cards, to publicize freethought views.

The Foundation has also produced a number of freethought music CDs, including *Friendly, Neighborhood Atheist* and *Beware of Dogma* with more than 50 historic and contemporary, irreverent songs. One of my favorite irreverent joys is performing live piano/vocal concerts, singing "You Can't Win With Original Sin" and "Nothing Fails Like Prayer" in front of an audience of unsanctimonious nonbelievers.

It's a dad's place to give advice to his children, and over the years I have repeated two mottos to my kids. The first is "If you stop learning, you stop living." The second is "Life is to be enjoyed." I'm glad to brag that I have great kids, and that they have a dad who lives up to the advice he gives them. As an atheist, I have *learned* so much, and I have enjoyed life much more than when I was a believer constrained by orthodoxy. Life is a great adventure!

Chapter Nineteen
Life and Death Matters

It was 5:30 in the morning on Monday, Labor Day 1989, when I heard a thump. I was asleep in bed, or half-asleep, during those early hours when time makes no sense, when you shut off the alarm and close your eyes for just a few more seconds and suddenly an hour has gone by. I might have blinked and wondered, "What was that?" We lived in a four-unit apartment building and often heard muffled noises from the neighbors. I drifted back to sleep.

Annie Laurie was pregnant, early in her eighth month, and we were excited that we were going to have a baby in about seven weeks. She was fretting that the apartment was not ready—no crib or decorations yet in the tiny spare room. We were attending natural birth classes, going through lists of names, not yet knowing if it was a boy or a girl. Her pregnancy was normal. She went to work and lived like always, with some prudent precautions. Two weeks earlier she had "passed" a checkup with her doctor, although she was told her blood pressure was slightly elevated, which was attributed to a rare cup of coffee she had had that day. Two days before she had shown up for another checkup, but her doctor was doing a delivery so Annie Laurie made an appointment for after the three-day Labor Day weekend holiday. On Sunday her fingers and toes seemed slightly swollen and she complained of a headache, so I went to the store to get her some Tylenol. That evening she asked for a back rub, but after that I didn't realize she was having a restless night or that she had woken up with a bad headache and had gotten out of bed early Monday morning, feeling like something was very wrong.

Then a strange thing happened. As I was falling back asleep after hearing that thump, I noticed that my legs were running down the hallway. I don't think I was quite awake when I found myself outside the bathroom. I pushed on the door and realized there was a body wedged between it and the wall. Some adrenaline must have kicked in, because time slowed *way* down. Annie Laurie had passed out and fallen back against the wall, her head and neck wedged in the corner with the door. She was unresponsive, convulsing violently, and was not breathing. I sat her up and moved her toward the bathtub where she could lean more upright, and she started gasping for air. I knew I had to call 911 immediately but the closest phone was in the living room, and she kept collapsing and falling back down. I propped her up a second time, then dashed to the phone. It felt like slow motion, but I must have been moving at fast-forward speed. The 911 operator was talking so slowly! I ran back to the bathroom in time to catch Annie Laurie again, still unconscious, shaking, gulping. I remember telling myself, "Think clearly. Don't goof this up. Do the right thing." I was so calm that I didn't have to tell myself not to panic.

The paramedics got there in a quick four minutes (which seemed like half an hour), pronounced that she was having a seizure and whisked her into the ambulance, telling me not to follow them but to drive to the hospital separately. Even though I thought my wife might be dying, I decided that I would wait to leave until I could methodically collect her purse with her insurance card and identification. I also put some of her belongings in a bag—change of clothes, robe, brush, slippers, the book she had been reading. Then I drove quietly down the nearly deserted, early morning holiday streets of Madison, not knowing what I would find at the hospital.

They didn't tell me anything, only that she was in the emergency room. I spent an hour making phone calls to relatives and getting her checked in, not knowing how much time she would be spending there. If any. When I reached Annie Laurie's mother on the phone, she asked me, "She's not going to die, is she?" I had no idea—she might have already been dead—but I replied, "No, of course not." Finally, the doctors all came rushing out of emergency with her body on a gurney. Annie Laurie was semiconscious, writhing. They told me she was having an eclamptic seizure. Eclampsia (from the Greek word for "lightning") is pregnancy-induced hypertension. With most women, there is usually a period of pre-eclampsia during which the condition can be monitored and handled, avoiding full-fledged eclampsia. With Annie Laurie it had come on like, well, lightning. (She had probably been having undiagnosed pre-eclamptic symptoms for about two weeks, but we did not know it.) Without treatment, she would die.

The doctors asked me to follow them to the maternity ward, because the only cure for eclampsia is immediate delivery. Annie Laurie was conscious enough to hear the medical staff say they were taking her to the birthing room, and she tried to get off the gurney, saying, "No! It's too soon for delivery." Two young male interns were walking down the halls with us, and one of them blurted out, "Wow. A real pre-eclamptic seizure!" in a tone of amazement. The other intern said, "This is not pre-eclamptic. This is full eclampsia!" Apparently eclampsia is now very rare in our country. Although the interns' detached comments during our emergency seemed a bit undiplomatic—"Wow, look, she's actually dying!"—I guess we should be glad that we provided future doctors with a real-life learning experience.

The maternity ward, when we arrived, seemed like a scene in a movie. Eleven people descended out of nowhere with tubes and monitoring gadgets and a gas mask, leaving and entering the room, calmly and efficiently administering their services. There was about an hour's wait until Annie Laurie became stabilized. Amazingly, even though she was drifting in and out of consciousness, she was cognizant enough to joke that after all, "It *is* Labor Day." There was nothing I could do but sit off to the side and watch them work as a woman giving birth in the next room was screaming full-throated profanity—well, as Annie Laurie noted, *somebody* should be in labor that day.

Annie Laurie's parents, Anne and Paul, and her twin brother, Ian, drove to the hospital. Family members were permitted to talk to Annie Laurie calmly for a few minutes. Ian asked me the same question: "Is she going to die?" This time I said, "I don't know. I don't think so." Annie Laurie's pediatrician when she was young, Dr. Hania Ris, also arrived. That was a comfort. She was a close family friend and a highly respected physician.

They wheeled Annie Laurie into the operation room around 9 a.m. for an emergency C-section. When our daughter was born, three women greeted her: two female physicians (the surgeon and Annie Laurie's doctor) and Dr. Ris, who had been allowed to monitor. Our baby weighed two pounds, 15 ounces. Tiny! (I used to joke that we could mail her by book rate at that weight.)

Post-surgery, it was not a good sign that Annie Laurie immediately swelled up like the Michelin tire man, due to edema. No one—not even our landlady, a nurse who happened to be on a hospital elevator with us on the way to ICU—recognized her marshmallow face. She didn't have any elbows! She was in danger of organ failure and many other horrible things and stayed in intensive care for two full days.

Our baby was taken immediately to the intensive care section of the Special Care Nursery (the preemie ward), where she was placed in an incubator, hooked up to tubes and put under a sun lamp to combat jaundice. Hospital policy was to keep all premature babies at least 24 hours in intensive care before moving them to the medium care and then regular care sections. I went in to see what our new daughter looked like and when I touched her little palm, she grabbed onto my finger and held real tight—poor little thing. She looked like a half-baked chicken with a large Martian head, but was so impossibly beautiful.

Later that morning I called my parents in Arizona to tell them what had happened, and it was at that point that I fell apart. After the immediate crisis was over, my brain must have exited the survival mode and allowed the emotions to tumble in. I could barely speak a word to my mother on the phone.

Our baby, through it all, was just fine. The doctors and nurses were not worried about her, although it turns out there had been a problem that only came to light the morning she was born. During the C-section they noticed that the placenta was half separated and would have progressed to placenta abruptio, which can starve the fetus and result in a still birth. Our daughter was tinier than expected—she would have been small anyway—but her lungs were much more developed than they should have been, due to the fact that she had been struggling for oxygen. Although the eclampsia almost killed them both, it actually may have saved our daughter's life.

Annie Laurie did not see the baby for more than a day, and she confesses that although we kept reassuring her that everything was fine she was nonetheless irrationally convinced that something was horribly wrong with our daughter. On the second day, we wheeled the incubator to her ICU room to try to reassure her. Annie Laurie was still too sick, however, to make much of the historic occasion of bonding with her new daughter. Annie Laurie's face, neck, chest and arms were covered with lurid bruises. Our baby was only 16 inches long, all head and skinny arms and legs. Her skin was baked red from the sun lamp; a needle was taped on her scalp. Annie Laurie was not impressed, but she humored us and allowed the nurse to snap a Polaroid moment of a swollen, dopey mother looking even more like an alien than her scrawny infant! That photograph is hidden carefully in one of the baby albums.

Annie Laurie was out of it for many days, so when the birth certificate was ready to be signed I decided to pick a name. We liked Elizabeth (from *Pride and Prejudice*, not from the bible) and some variant of Anne (like her mother's and grandmother's names), but the most recent name we had discussed and agreed on was Sabrina. So, I figured that our daughter wanted to be named Sabrina and was born at just the right moment, before we changed our minds. I picked her middle name from the language of my Lenape (Delaware Indian) tribe. "Delatah" means "thought," so instead of naming our godless daughter Faith or Grace, we have a thinking child named Sabrina Delata Gaylor. (There was no question she would take Annie Laurie's last name. We did think about forming a combined name, but Sabrina Gaybar just doesn't work. I'm not sure why.)

Annie Laurie likes to brag that she lost 30 pounds in two days, but that just shows the extent of her post-birth edema. Her blood pressure was fluctuating so much that the attendants brought back the "eclampsia kit." During the fifth and sixth nights in the hospital, when she was graduated to the "birthing suite," she asked me to stay with her on the couch provided for new dads. She was now aware of her narrow escape and was briefly terrified of the dark, afraid of dying alone.

During this entire traumatic experience we never once thought of invoking a god for help. We never prayed, never even considered it. What we did invoke was some of the best medical care in the Midwest. Religion was not only the furthest thing from our minds, it was totally nonexistent. In fact, if a chaplain had come into the room while Annie Laurie was recuperating her blood pressure would have shot up! (Annie Laurie was the first person to write a nonfiction book, *Betrayal of Trust*, about the scandal of pedophilia and sex abuse in the clergy.) We invoked not a supernatural deity, but the love and support of our community, mostly caring, nonbelieving friends and relatives.

Annie Laurie came home after 10 days, without Sabrina. Before Sabrina came home, we were both able to attend the baby shower that turned into a post-baby shower. Sabrina was released about two weeks after that, weighing just under four pounds. That week I took a photograph of her tiny hand on the piano next to my hand, her hand covering just one key. It was scary having such a tiny creature in the house. We had to take infant CPR classes at the hospital, and we remember walking past the nursery with the "monster babies" (those with normal birth weights).

The Special Care Nursery continued to monitor Sabrina's development. After a grueling cognitive examination at a year and a half, one staffer pronounced Sabrina a "genius baby." Her incredible focus and attention span put her clear off the bell curve they were using. Unsurprisingly, her gross motor skills were a little behind, but that presented no problem. "Sabrina will jump when she wants to," they reassured us. Although always in the fifth percentile for weight and height over the years, Sabrina gradually caught up. Today, a still tiny 91 pounds, she stands five feet tall, the same height as my mother and only two inches shorter than Annie Laurie. A fourth-generation freethinker (on her mother's side), Sabrina "the thinker" has graduated from high school with honors and is looking forward to studying creative writing in college.

Annie Laurie escaped the ordeal with no lasting damage. She can't recall much about the first few days in the hospital, including many things she told us. The last thing she remembers that Labor Day morning is feeling sick in the bathroom, trying to call out to me, realizing she could not speak or move, and then blacking out. If I hadn't heard that thump, she would have died and that would have been her last memory. When I asked her what it feels like to die, she said, "It's not fun."

Woody Allen said, "I'm not afraid of death. I just don't want to be there when it happens." Annie Laurie was there when it happened, and you would think that if she had had even the slightest inclination to religious feelings, that's when it would have come out. There *are* atheists in foxholes. Annie Laurie never thought to pray at any point when she knew she was in trouble. She did not cry out to a god at the last moment, and why would she? She was not raised religious. Millions of good people get through life without superstition.

Woody Allen also said, "I do not believe in an afterlife, although I am bringing a change of underwear." We nonbelievers have to face mortality just like everyone else. Although we would all like to stay healthy and postpone the end as long as possible, we know that none of us are getting out of this alive. Rationalists don't like it, but as realists we accept death as a natural part of life. None of us would be alive if other things did not die.

We atheists believe in life *before* death. Before we were born, there was a very long time, perhaps an eternity, when we did not exist, and it did not bother us one bit. The same will be true after we are dead. What matters is that we are alive now. These living, breathing, hurting, singing, laughing bodies are *worth* something, for their own sake. Since there is no life after death—how could there be when the body and the brain decay?—we have to make the most of it now, before it is too late. Suppose you knew you were going to die a week from Tuesday. How would you spend your final days? Would you ignore your friends and family? Would you walk past a bed of tulips without stopping? Would you take things for granted? If you knew you were going to die for good—as we atheists know—then you would be hypersensitive to every joy, every tragic beauty. "This is the last time I will hug my nephew," you might say. "This is the final autumn I will see the leaves changing." You would stop and take notice, just as we do with a garden of flowers, knowing that in a few days those blossoms will be gone.

Atheism actually enhances the value of life. We tend to give greater value to things that are rare: gold, diamonds, honesty. The air we breathe is important, but it is plentiful and we get it for free. (We only pay for it underwater or on Mount Everest.) The scarcity and brevity of life is what enlarges its value. We mourn the deaths of older people, but we consider it a greater loss when a young child dies. The fact that we are going to die is what makes life precious.

If life is eternal, then life is cheap.

If we waste any moment of our precious lives on the hope of an afterlife, we rob ourselves of real joy and value in the here and now. Our lives are all we have, and we should enjoy them to the fullest, minute by fragile minute. Bertrand Russell wrote: "I believe that when I die I shall rot, and nothing of my ego will survive. I am not young and I love life. But I should scorn to shiver with terror at the thought of annihilation. Happiness is nonetheless true happiness because it must come to an end, nor do thought and love lose their value because they are not everlasting."

Even if there were an "afterlife," why would it be eternal? (Headline: "Scientists Find the Afterlife and It Is Six Minutes Long.") As an atheist, I actually think there is an afterlife, and it lasts exactly as long as my own life, and I am living it right now. During my "previous life," beginning on that deserted beach near Santa Monica just before my mother's egg was fertilized, I was merely one of many sperm, all striving to reach the goal. Millions of my potential brothers and sisters were swimming and fighting, directed by an inner drive to survive that was no less eager than mine, with no less potential for a future existence. But out of all those countless throngs of little bodies who strove for the prize, I am the one that made it. I reached the goal, the "afterlife" of the egg. My body, the sperm, died and disappeared, and only the information in the little packet of DNA "passed on" to the "other side" and united with my maker. I got to live on, and the others did not. I got to develop and be born and learn to walk and go to school and take piano lessons and taste chocolate. I get to die. Many are called, but few are chosen.

"If there is no hope of eternal life, then what is the purpose of life?" is a question we atheists often hear. My response is that there is indeed no purpose of life. There is purpose *in* life. If there were a purpose *of* life, then that would cheapen life. It would make us tools or slaves of someone else's purpose. Like a hammer that hangs on the garage wall waiting for someone to build something, if we humans were designed for a purpose then we would be subservient in the universe. Our value would not be in ourselves. It would exist in our submission to the will of the toolmaker. That is slavery to a master, or infant dependency on a father figure. Besides, if there is a god, what is the purpose of *his* life? If he doesn't need a purpose, why do we? Doesn't a father need to have had a father? A true father does not want the child to remain forever subservient, finding purpose in pleasing the will of the parent. A true father expects the child to become a peer, with its own purpose, even if it disagrees with the parent. If I raise a child who is eternally dependent on me for meaning, then I am an inept parent.

There is no purpose of life. Life is its own reward. But as long as there are problems to solve, there will be purpose *in* life. When there is hunger to lessen, illness to cure, pain to minimize, inequality to eradicate, oppression to resist, knowledge to gain and beauty to create, there is meaning in life. A college student once asked Carl Sagan:

"What meaning is left, if everything I've been taught since I was a child turns out to be untrue?" Carl looked at him and said, "Do something meaningful."

Who would dare say that Elizabeth Cady Stanton, a nonbeliever, had no purpose in life? She fought for 50 years for women's equality. Or, what about Margaret Sanger? Many of those who demonize Sanger still choose to practice birth control, which is now prevalent due to her tireless and brave efforts. Or Bertrand Russell? Or any of a huge number of nonbelievers who have enhanced life by focusing on practical matters. If you can find a problem to solve, an issue to work on, then you have purpose in life.

What do the following pieces of beloved music have in common?

> Brahms' "Lullaby"
> "Moonlight Sonata"
> "Somewhere, Over the Rainbow"
> "Pomp and Circumstances"
> "Do, Re, Mi"
> "Imagine"
> "Over the River and Through the Woods"
> "It's Only a Paper Moon"
> "Rhapsody in Blue"
> "Lark Ascending"
> "Maple Leaf Rag"
> "My Old Kentucky Home"
> Ravel's *Bolero*
> "The Barber of Seville"
> *Missa Solemnis*
> "Blue Moon"
> "Scenes From Childhood"
> Verdi's *Requiem*
> *Symphonie Fantastique*
> *Appalachian Spring*
> "God Bless America"

"There's No Business Like Show Business"
Shostakovich's *Eighth Symphony*
"Summertime"
"Old Man River"
"The Way You Look Tonight"
"Peter and the Wolf"
"Brother, Can You Spare a Dime?"
"Send in the Clowns"
"Night and Day"
"Anything Goes"
Also Sprach Zarathustra
Bizet's *Carmen*

These were all composed by (or had the lyrics written by) atheists and agnostics. Yes, Irving Berlin, the man who wrote "God Bless America" and "White Christmas," did not believe in a god and actually hated Christmas. Some of these composers, such as Edward Elgar ("Pomp and Circumstances") and Mozart, started out as believers and later became unbelievers or skeptics. The list above includes the work of Yip Harburg (lyricist of "Over the Rainbow" and "Paper Moon"), Ludwig Von Beethoven, Richard Rodgers, Maria Lydia Child (lyricist of "Over the River"), George Gershwin, Ira Gershwin, Johannes Brahms, Ralph Vaughan Williams (who as an atheist composed hymns for the *English Hymnal*), Maurice Ravel, Giaochino Rossini, Hector Berlioz, Robert Schumann, Georges Bizet, Richard Strauss, Sergei Prokofiev, Giuseppe Verdi (an altar boy who grew up to say "Stay away from priests!"), Stephen Foster, Scott Joplin, Aaron Copland, Dmitry Shostakovich, Jerome Kern, Cole Porter, Jay Gorney (composer of "Brother, Can You Spare a Dime,") and Stephen Sondheim. Other nonbelieving composers include Fritz Delius, Niccolo Paganini, James Taylor and Björk. Who would dare say these creative people had no meaning in life?[1]

The FFRF has compiled a list (constantly being updated) of hundreds of atheists, agnostics and doubters who have made significant contributions to the world, including abolitionists, actors, artists, athletes, attorneys, authors, civil libertarians, entertainers, composers, dancers,

---

[1] For documentation of most of these composers and songwriters, see my article "It Ain't Necessarily So: Music's Debt to Nonbelievers" in *Everything You Know About God is Wrong: The Disinformation Guide to Religion*, edited by Russ Kick, (2007, The Disinformation Company).

directors, economists, educators, environmentalists, explorers, feminists, historians, humanitarians, inventors, journalists, judges, mathematicians, philanthropists, philosophers, physicians, playwrights, poets, politicians, psychologists, reformers, revolutionaries, scholars and scientists.[2] These are people with real purpose in life.

In 2006, I was on the national Christian *Total Living Network* television program with philosopher and author William Lane Craig for a very informal "God in America" debate in talk-show format. He is a good debater, one of the best. After the show, he handed me a booklet he wrote called *God, Are You There? Five Reasons God Exists and Three Reasons It Makes a Difference.* (I address one of his "reasons" in Chapter 8).

In the booklet, Craig writes that belief in God makes a difference because "If God does not exist, then life is ultimately meaningless." Well, yes, Bill, life *is* ultimately meaningless, and we should not want it any other way if we value life. If you have to resort to the rhetorical device of appealing to the reader's dissatisfaction with reality, fear of mortality and a desire for something "ultimate," simply assuming that such wishful thinking confers automatic credibility or dignity to the larger question, then you are admitting that your basic evidences for a God are not strong enough to stand on their own. You don't need any reasons at all, with that logic. You can simply say, "Being a mere mortal mammal makes me feel unimportant, so I'm going to believe in God."

Truth is truth. It shouldn't matter what any of us wants to believe. The fact that life is *ultimately* meaningless does not mean it is not *immediately* meaningful.

"But my personal religious experience of knowing and loving God is so special," believers will often say, "that I feel sorry for you atheists who have nothing like that." Oh, really? I play jazz piano. When I am performing with the right musicians at the right place, there is a kind of "magic" that often happens when we players are hearing the beauty and looking at each other with big smiles, knowing we are creating something special and unique. It gives an illusion of transcendence, as if "The Song" were out there, above and around us, wrapping us in the moment. This ecstasy doesn't happen on every gig, but when it does we

---

2   See http://ffrf.org/day/daybytopic.php.

know it is just an illusion. And we don't care. It is an illusion to live for. Suppose I were to say, "Oh, you poor non-jazz-musicians; you don't know what you are missing. I can't describe it to you, and even if you listen to us you are not going to understand what is happening in our minds. It's very real and you'll just have to take our word for it." You would understand that I am talking about something that is happening to *me*, not to you, and the fact that you lack my inner experience is no threat to your own self-worth or worldview. What if I were to say that the only way you can have true meaning in *your* life is if *you* practice piano for four hours a day for 20 years and learn to play jazz, like *I* did? You would think I was joking, or seriously deluded.

I do not deny that spiritual experiences are real. They happen all over the world, in most religions. I deny that they point to anything outside of the mind. I had many religious experiences, and I can still have them if I want. As an atheist, I can still speak in tongues and "feel the presence of God." It is peaceful and integrative and "meaningful" in some strange way. I'm sure Buddhists and followers of Hare Krishna have similar experiences when they chant. As a Christian, of course, I interpreted the feelings from meditating on Christ or speaking in tongues as a direct proof of the Holy Spirit. Even without speaking in tongues, I used to feel the presence of Jesus, my imaginary friend. It seems rather silly now, since there is no God—and I only speak in tongues once every few years just to see if I still have the touch—but this does tell me something about the human mind. We are very creative, imaginative and "mystical." Well, most of us. There are many atheists as well as believers who have never felt a thing. I think across the bell curve of susceptibility to "mysticism," most of us fall somewhere in the middle and I fall way over to the right side. (Pun intended.)

I know some atheists who pooh-pooh religious experiences, thinking they are all made up, purely psychological tricks of an unsophisticated mind. But they are wrong. Religious experiences are very real. I had them as a believer, and I can duplicate them as a nonbeliever. Most of us have had convincing dreams. Suppose you had a horrible nightmare that a bogeyman was crawling in your bedroom window. You sit up screaming, waking up the rest of the house. Your hands are sweating and your heart is pounding and your breath is shallow. No one would deny that you just had a very real experience. That nightmare was a powerful moment, with physical consequences. Based on your behavior alone, we would conclude that *something* happened to you.

But there is no bogeyman crawling through the window. Once you realize it is a dream, you can relax and go back to sleep. That's how it is with me. I have realized that those religious experiences that I had, and can still duplicate if I should desire, are all in the mind. Of course, why would I want a phony religious experience—especially the nightmare of hell?—when I can have something more beautiful playing the piano?

I often play piano in big bands composed of musicians representing a diversity of political, philosophical and religious opinions. Most of the players are creative and open-minded, but there are sometimes ultra-religious and reactionary musicians in the group with whom I would not want to live in the same neighborhood. Yet when the music starts, we forget all that and form a band, looking at each other with mutual enjoyment and respect, exulting in the harmony we are creating. In a sense, the inner experience of music is truly transcendent and can bring us all together in the especially human "universal language." Religion divides; art unites. If only the countries of the world would come together to make music, think of the harmony that would result. Pastor and Christian author Greg Boyd told me he plays drums and that he would love to jam with me on the piano sometime. If we could find a Jewish bassist, a Hindu flautist, a Muslim percussionist, a Native American Spiritualist guitarist and a Buddhist singer—imagine!

"If there is no God, why do so many people believe in God?" That is a question I am often asked. "If there is a god-shaped hole in us, doesn't that mean there is something to fill that hole?" There are many scientific hypotheses about the origin of religious belief. Some think the fear of death, the desire for meaning, the need for moral structure or community, the ambition to control the masses and other conscious feelings all contribute to our "nature" to be religious. But I think this is backwards. Why religion as opposed to something else?

Scientists are now approaching the brain as the result of selectionist adaptations that happened as our species evolved. Obviously, in the trivial, reductionist sense, everything comes down to genetics, although this may not tell us much at the level of the individual, tribe or culture. Some think there may be a "God gene" (or collection of genes) that conferred a survival advantage to our ancestors but is no longer necessary, although we are stuck with it by inheritance, like goosebumps. (Our ancestors were very hairy apes who would fluff up their fur to keep warm or to appear larger to an attacker. Whenever you see your apparently useless goosebumps you are looking at a proof of evolution, at something you inherited from earlier primates.) If this is true, we still have to ask why we have that gene or instinct rather than something else.

I can't answer the question definitively here, since the science of the origin of religion and the susceptibility to belief is still being explored, but I will offer my two favorite hypotheses, either of which is plausible and either (or both) of which may be part of a fuller understanding in the future. Perhaps there will be better answers, but these are presented as examples of how we can think about the question in a naturalistic, evolutionary way.

I was walking in the woods some years ago when I saw a snake on the trail. I stopped and stared at it. Then as I moved carefully closer, I saw that it was just part of a tree root, not a snake. Even then, I cautiously stepped over it. Why did I do that? Why would I make such a mistake? I think it is because my ancestors who made *that* mistake were more likely to survive than their contemporaries who made the opposite mistake. Obviously, being bitten by a snake lowers your chances of having offspring, so the "snake as stick" tendency would not be passed on to future generations as frequently as the "stick as snake" tendency.

Some scientists and philosophers, including Pascal Boyer, call this the "agency detector." An agency is a person, animal, creature, intelligence or something else with a mind and internal purposes. The agency can act: it may want to eat you, compete with you, mate with you or otherwise gain an advantage over you. You are better off knowing an agency is there than not knowing it. It is an advantageous survival tactic to approach such agencies carefully, or to avoid them altogether. Little children wake up in the middle of the night screaming because they think there is a monster crawling out from under the bed. Often it is a false alarm, but on average it was better for a family to have such sensitive children because the danger of predation was (is) real. Even today, in the safety of our modern homes, if you are awakened at night by a scratching sound on the window, is your first thought to rationally conclude it is just a tree branch, or does your mind automatically think the worst? The fear is real, buried in the instincts formed by the genes inherited from our ancestors. If you are walking down a dark alley and see a looming shape in front of you, don't you automatically assume it is a threat or potential danger? Like the goosebumps that rise unbidden, you have no choice. We are naturally self-protective. It is in our nature to see "agency" out there, even when it is not there. It happened to me last winter when I was shoveling snow off the driveway one night and was startled to see a person standing next to me. The "person" turned out to be the large trash bin on the curb. Those things happen to all of us, and we can't help it.

When our ancestors, who carried those same genes, heard rumbling noises in the clouds, they couldn't help picturing agency. They automatically assumed it was a large animal or person, like an angry father—a very large and potent agency—and they called it Zeus or Thor. When they felt earthquakes and saw volcanoes erupt, they "knew" it was a powerful mother. (Why was the sky male and the earth female? Maybe because the rain "impregnates" the soil?) The environment was imbued with "personality." Natural forces and random processes of fertility and weather and all the jumble of unpredictable, frightening occurrences were automatically thought to be "agents" out there—gods, devils, angels, demons, ghosts, witches, orixás. This was not because there was any practical or immediate reason, but simply because we inherited the tendency to make that mistake for very good evolutionary reasons. Those who did not make that mistake were less likely to survive to become ancestors. Today, even though we still possess the instinct to err on the side of caution, we know that it is indeed a mistake we are making. (Most of us.)

However, evolution also needs variety. We can't all be the same, otherwise something that wiped out one of us would wipe out all of us. That's why we have sexual reproduction, with each sibling different from the parents and from each other, to increase the odds that some of our offspring will survive whatever pathogens, invaders or "acts of God" nature throws at us.

Thousands of physical and behavioral variations make all of us different. Some of us, by nature, are going to wake up in the middle of the night screaming more than others. Some of us are more likely than others to "detect agency"—to be religious. In my case, it seemed automatic: God existed without a doubt in my mind. In the case of Annie

Laurie's father, Paul Gaylor, it was the opposite. As a very small child, he knew that religious teachings were phony. At first he thought his parents and community were just faking it, then later he was convinced they were all crazy. The "Amazing" James Randi says it was the same with him: he never believed, not even as a small child. Most of us fall somewhere in the middle of that bell curve, and some more to one side than the other. This means that some of us have to work harder than others to overcome the natural tendency to assume a "presence" out there. Some people are so far to one side that if they also have mental health issues, they think *they* are God and we have to lock them up.

The other hypothesis that I find attractive is articulated by Richard Dawkins and seems to complement the agency detector. The human species evolved with two conflicting advantages: an upright structure and a large brain. As we stood erect the pelvis opening became smaller, making it even more difficult to give birth to an enlarging skull. As a result, Homo sapiens are born prematurely compared to other mammals, some of which stand up and walk into the forest when they are only minutes old. The human infant is half-baked, and needs at least a full year of complete dependency on its parents or adult community in order to have the slightest chance at survival. (Imagine leaving a month-old baby out in the woods.)

As the human child is growing and learning, it is crucial during the early years that it unquestioningly obey the instructions of the parents. It would do no good for the child to say, "I am skeptical about my Mom's warning to stay out of the street. I'm going to try it for myself." Our species would never get off the ground with such an attitude. None of us would live long enough to breed. Dawkins suggests that dependency on a father figure during childhood may be hard-wired into our genes, a necessary survival tactic of a premature primate. But as we mature, we eventually become parents ourselves with instincts and knowledge that we acquire on our own, as well as knowledge passed on to us from the previous generation. We then have less need for the care and protection of adults. (This may have been especially true during the first hundred thousand years or so of human existence, when the average life expectancy was only 25-30 years.) Yet even so, the tendency to "obey the parent" and "find comfort in the mother or the father" lingers on, and the length of time it lingers varies from person to person. Many of us grow up to adulthood still feeling a need for the security of the father figure. This need is a result of our prematurity and is a kind of longing for the simpler days of childhood when we did not have to think for ourselves.

Combine this longing for a dependent and sheltered childhood with both the tendency to detect agency in nature and the evolutionary advantage of variation, and you can see how the human mind would possess a variable tendency to naturally "reach out" to an external father or mother figure. Since in the past our parents died on average younger than they do today (due to much shorter life expectancy), and since we still needed them—indeed, we dreamed about dead ancestors—we created god(s) to fill that gap. God belief is a kind of delayed development. Again, there will be a variation in intensity of these tendencies among humans, as some will be more religious than others. But combine the tendency with cultural and social pressure and it is not difficult to see how belief is embraced and coddled. Getting rid of the "father-figure agency" is a part of maturing. It is a sign of mental health, and the only way to truly grow up.

The fact that we possess genes that were good for the survival of our ancestors does not mean our inherited instincts are naturally "good" for us today. They aren't good or bad; they happened to be the fittest, and like it or not, they are what made us what we are today. Providing an evolutionary explanation for religion does not require that we submit to our superstitious nature. The same could be said about our tendencies toward sexism, racism and xenophobia, which we are trying to combat in the modern world. We have evolved a neocortex (where we get reason) on top of our animal instincts, and we can override those tendencies. Violence is also a part of our inheritance, and any one of us can act violently if we are pushed hard enough. (Some need less pushing than others.) We have these sharp canine teeth that were used to tear into the flesh of other living creatures, but we don't need to use them for that. We now have a frontal lobe in the brain that stops us, that checks our instincts. Using judgment, we can stem racism, sexism and violence. Using reason, we can rise above religion.

Even though everything reduces to genetics, it doesn't follow that love loses its meaning. I wrote a song in 2007, "inspired" (if I can borrow a word) by something Richard Dawkins wrote in *Unweaving the Rainbow* calling for an integration of art and science. It's a love song, a jazz ballad that simply assumes the underlying fact of evolution.

"It's Only Natural"
by Dan Barker

Thanks to Galileo
for showing us our humble place in outer space.
And thanks to Mister Darwin
for showing us the origin of the human race.
Which means that our precious romance
Is mainly the product of chance,
And these feelings of love so frenetic
Are just genetic.
It's only natural that I would want you.
It's only natural that you want me.
A million years of evolution had its way,
So we can blame it on our parents' DNA.
I move instinctively in your direction.
Somehow you signal me to turn and see.
You will always be my natural selection,
As a voluntary choice, naturally.

"Isn't atheism just another religion?" No, it isn't. Atheism has no creeds, rituals, holy book, absolute moral code, origin myth, sacred spaces or shrines. It has no sin, divine judgment, forbidden words, prayer, worship, prophecy, group privileges or anointed "holy" leaders. Atheists don't believe in a transcendent world or supernatural afterlife. Most important, there is no orthodoxy in atheism. We don't have to think or act alike. Allowing for differences of opinion is a sign of health. *Montreal Gazette* cartoonist Terry Mosher drew an editorial cartoon that said: "Here's a headline we never see: Agnostics slaughter Atheists!"

"What about hope? What about salvation? If atheism is not a religion, what do atheists have to look forward to? Is there an atheist salvation?" In many religious traditions, "salvation" is a deliverance from danger, disease and death. Most believers see this alliterative trio of troubles in both natural and supernatural ways. Danger can arise from an occupying conqueror, or from the threat to morality and order by evil spirits or devils. Disease and death can be feared both physically and spiritually. Atheists, with the same human desires and fears, also care about deliverance, but only as *natural* concerns. We see deliverance coming, if it is to come at all, in the real world, from our own human efforts.

Sometimes no deliverance is needed at all. The New Testament Jesus reportedly said, "They that are whole have no need of a physician, but they that are sick" (Matthew 9:12). We atheists consider ourselves whole, thank you. We are not sick. We don't need the doctor. Suppose you were convicted of a horrible crime and sentenced to life in prison, but after a few years behind bars you are surprised to hear you are being released. This "salvation" would be a wonderful experience. But which would make you feel better: learning you were released because you were pardoned by the good graces of the governor, or because you were found to be innocent of the crime? Which would give you more dignity?

We atheists possess "salvation" not because we are released from a sentence, but because we don't deserve the punishment in the first place. We have committed no "sin." Sin is a religious concept, and in some religions salvation is the deliverance from the "wages of sin"— which is death or eternal punishment. Sin has been defined as "missing the mark" of God's expectations or holiness, or "offending God," so it follows that since there is no god, there is no sin, therefore no need of salvation. How much respect should you have for a doctor who cuts you with a knife in order to sell you a bandage? Only those who consider themselves sinners need this kind of deliverance—it is a religious solution to a religious problem.

If salvation is the cure, then atheism is the prevention.

Canadian physician Dr. Marian Sherman, a prominent atheist from Victoria, B.C., in an article titled "What Makes an Atheist Tick?" in the September 11, 1965, issue of the *Toronto Star Weekly*, is quoted as saying:

"Humanism seeks the fullest development of the human being... Humanists acknowledge no Supreme Being and we approach all life from the point of view of science and reason. Ours is not a coldly clinical view, for we believe that if human beings will but practice love of one another and use their wonderful faculty of speech, we can make a better world, happy for all. But there must be no dogma."

When asked about death, Dr. Sherman replied: "It is the end of the organism. All we can hope is that we have found some sort of happiness in this life and that we have left the world as a little better place."

Those with a negative view of human nature might seek help in solving problems from outside humanity. But those with a positive view of human nature—a true hope—will work for "salvation" from within the human race, using the tools of reason and kindness.

If you want to be a good, kind person, then be a good, kind person.

If salvation is the freedom from sin, then we atheists already have it. If salvation is deliverance from oppression and disease in the real world, then there is work to do. In this ongoing effort to make our planet a better place—to have true peace on earth—we atheists and humanists are happy to work shoulder-to-shoulder with the truly good religious people who also strive for a future with less violence and more understanding.

Selected Bibliography

This is a partial list of writings I found useful (in all, or in part) in writing this book. I include it here as a convenience for readers who want to study further.

Why I Am an Atheist

Angeles, Peter, ed. *Critiques of God*. New York: Prometheus Books, 1976.

Angier, Natalie. "Confessions of a Lonely Atheist." *The New York Times Magazine*, January 14, 2001.

Antony, Louise M., ed. *Philosophers Without Gods: Meditations on Atheism and the Secular Life*. Oxford: Oxford University Press, 2007.

Avalos, Hector. *¿Se Puede Saber si Dios Existe?* (Can We Know If God Exists?) New York: Prometheus Books, 2003.

Davies, Paul. *Cosmic Jackpot: Why Our Universe Is Just Right for Life*. New York: Houghton Mifflin, 2007.

Dawkins, Richard. *The God Delusion*. Boston: Houghton Mifflin, 2006.

Edis, Taner. *The Ghost in the Universe: God in Light of Modern Science*. New York: Prometheus, 2002.

Edis, Taner. *Science and Nonbelief*. New York: Prometheus Books, 2008.

Everitt, Nicholas. *The Non-existence of God*. New York: Routledge, 2004.

Flynn, Tom, ed. *The New Encyclopedia of Unbelief.* New York: Prometheus Books, 2007.

Hitchens, Christopher. *God Is Not Great: How Religion Poisons Everything.* New York: Twelve, 2007.

Hitchens, Christopher, ed. *The Portable Atheist: Essential Readings for the Nonbeliever.* Philadelphia: Da Capo, 2007.

Harris, Sam. *The End of Faith: Religion, Terror, and the Future of Reason.* New York: W. W. Norton, 2004.

Jacoby, Susan. *Freethinkers: A History of American Secularism.* New York: Metropolitan Books, 2004.

Kick, Russ, ed. *Everything You Know About God Is Wrong: The Disinformation Guide to Religion.* New York: The Disinformation Company, 2007.

Krueger, Douglas E. *What Is Atheism? A Short Introduction.* New York: Prometheus Books, 1998.

Lalli, Nica. *Nothing: Something to Believe In.* New York: Prometheus Books, 2007.

Lamont, Corliss. *The Illusion of Immortality.* Fourth Edition. New York: Frederick Ungar Publishing, 1965.

Le Poivedin, Robin. *Arguing for Atheism: An Introduction to the Philosophy of Religion.* New York: Routledge, 1996.

Martin, Michael. *Atheism: A Philosophical Justification.* Philadelphia: Temple University Press, 1991.

Martin, Michael. *The Cambridge Companion to Atheism.* New York: Cambridge University Press, 2007.

Mills, David. *Atheist Universe: The Thinking Person's Answer to Christian Fundamentalism.* Berkeley: Ulysses Press, 2006

Paine, Thomas. *The Age of Reason.* Citadel Press, 1794. First published in 1794.

Paulos, John Allen. *Irreligion: A Mathematician Explains Why the Arguments for God Just Don't Add Up.* New York: Hill and Wang, 2008.

Rees, Martin. *Before the Beginning: Our Universe and Others.*
Reading, Massachusetts: Helix Books, 1997.

Sagan, Carl. *The Demon-Haunted World: Science as a Candle in the
Dark.* New York: Random House, 1995.

Sagan, Carl. *The Varieties of Scientific Experience: A Personal View of
the Search for God.* Edited by Ann Druyan. New York: Penguin
Press, 2006.

Seckel, Al, ed. *Bertrand Russell on God and Religion.* New York:
Prometheus Books, 1986.

Smith, George H. *Atheism: The Case Against God.* New York:
Prometheus Books, 1979.

Smith, George H. *Why Atheism?* New York: Prometheus Books,
2000.

Stein, Gordon, ed. *An Anthology of Atheism and Rationalism.*
Prometheus Books, New York, 1980.

Stein, Gordon, ed. *A Second Anthology of Atheism and Rationalism.*
New York: Prometheus Books, 1987.

Stenger, Victor J. *God: The Failed Hypothesis; How Science Shows That
God Does Not Exist.* New York: Prometheus Books, 2008.

Weinberg, Steven. *Facing Up: Science and Its Cultural Adversaries.*
Cambridge: Harvard University Press, 2001.

What's Wrong with Christianity

Avalos, Hector. *The End of Biblical Studies.* New York: Prometheus
Books, 2007.

Avalos, Hector. *Fighting Words: The Origins of Religious Violence.*
New York: Prometheus Books, 2005.

Ehrman, Bart D. *God's Problem: How the Bible Fails to Answer
Our Most Important Question—Why We Suffer.* San Francisco:
HarperCollins, 2008.

Ehrman, Bart D. *Misquoting Jesus: The Story Behind Who Changed
the Bible and Why.* San Francisco: HarperCollins, 2005.

Ehrman, Bart D. *The New Testament: A Historical Introduction to the Early Christian Writings*. New York: Oxford University Press. 1997.

Finkelstein, Israel, and Neil Asher Silberman. *The Bible Unearthed: Archaeology's New Vision of Ancient Israel and the Origin of Its Sacred Texts*. New York: The Free Press, 2001.

Funk, Robert W. *The Five Gospels: The Search for the Authentic Words of Jesus*. New York: Polebridge Press, 1993.

Funk, Robert W. and The Jesus Seminar. *The Acts of Jesus: The Search for the Authentic Deeds of Jesus*. San Francisco: Harper San Francisco, 1998.

Gaylor, Annie Laurie. *Woe to the Women: The Bible Tells Me So*. Revised edition. Madison, Wisconsin: FFRF, Inc., 2004.

Green, Ruth Hurmence. *The Born Again Skeptic's Guide to the Bible*. Madison, Wisconsin: FFRF, Inc., 1979.

Leedom, Tim, and Maria Murdy, eds. *The Book Your Church Doesn't Want You to Read*. New York: Cambridge House Press, 2007.

Russell, Bertrand. *Why I Am Not a Christian*. New York: Touchstone, 1957.

White, Andrew D. *A History of the Warfare of Science with Theology in Christendom*. 2 vols. New York: Prometheus Books, 1993.

Morality (Chapter 12)

Branden, Nathaniel. *The Psychology of Self-Esteem*. Los Angeles: Nash, 1969.

Buckman, Robert. *Can We Be Good Without God? Biology, Behavior, and the Need to Believe*. New York: Prometheus Books, 2002.

Carrier, Richard. *Sense and Goodness Without God: A Defense of Metaphysical Naturalism*. Bloomington, Indiana: Author House, 2005.

Dawkins, Richard. *Unweaving the Rainbow: Science, Delusion and the Appetite for Wonder*. Boston: Houghton Mifflin, 1998.

Dennett, Daniel C. *Freedom Evolves.* New York: Viking, 2003.

De Waal, Frans, Stephen Macedo, and Josiah Ober. *Primates and Philosophers: How Morality Evolved.* Princeton: Princeton University Press, 2006.

Gazzaniga, Michael S. *The Ethical Brain.* New York: Dana Press, 2005.

Jefferson, Thomas. *The Jefferson Bible: The Life and Morals of Jesus of Nazareth.* Boston: Beacon Press, 1989.

McCabe, Joseph. *Sources of the Morality of the Gospels.* London: Watts, 1914.

McGowan, Dale, ed. *Parenting Beyond Belief: On Raising Ethical, Caring Kids Without Religion.* New York: Amacom, 2007.

Nielsen, Kai. *Ethics Without God.* New York: Prometheus Books, 1990.

Ridley, Matt. *The Origins of Virtue: Human Instincts and the Evolution of Cooperation.* New York: Penguin Books, 1996.

Russell, Bertrand. *Bertrand Russell's Dictionary of Mind, Matter & Morals.* New York: Citadel, 1952.

Shermer, Michael. *The Science of Good and Evil: Why People Cheat, Gossip, Care, Share, and Follow the Golden Rule.* Times Books, 2004.

Smith, Tara. *Viable Values: A Study of Life as the Root and Reward of Morality.* Oxford: Rowman & Littlefield, 2000.

Wielenberg, Erik J. *Value and Virtue in a Godless Universe.* Cambridge: Cambridge University Press, 2005.

Did Jesus Exist? (Chapter 15)

Allegro, J. M. *The Dead Sea Scrolls and the Christian Myth.* New York: Prometheus Books, 1984.

Arnheim, M. A. *Is Christianity True?* New York: Prometheus Books, 1984.

Baigent, Michael, and Richard Leigh. *The Dead Sea Scrolls Deception.* New York: Summit Books, 1991.

Brandon, S. G. F. *The Trial of Jesus of Nazareth.* New York: Scarborough, 1979.

Carmichael, J. *The Death of Jesus.* New York: Horizon, 1982.

Doherty, Earl. *Challenging the Verdict: A Cross-Examination of Lee Strobel's "The Case for Christ."* Ottawa, Canada: Age of Reason Publications, 2001.

Doherty, Earl. *The Jesus Puzzle: Did Christianity Begin with a Mythical Christ? Challenging the Existence of an Historical Jesus.* Age of Reason Publications, 2005.

Frazer, Sir James G. *The Golden Bough.* MacMillan, 1956.

Freke, and Gandy. *The Jesus Mysteries: Was the "Original Jesus" a Pagan God?* New York: Three Rivers Press (Crown), 2001.

Gratus, J. *The False Messiahs.* Taplinger, 1975.

Hoffman, R. Joseph. *Jesus Outside the Gospels.* New York: Prometheus Books, 1984.

Hoffman, R. Joseph, ed. *The Origins of Christianity.* New York: Prometheus Books, 1985.

Hoffman, R. Joseph, and G. A. Larue, editors. *Jesus in History and Myth.* New York: Prometheus Books, 1986.

Martin, Michael. *The Case Against Christianity.* Philadelphia: Temple University Press, 1990.

Miller, Robert J. *The Jesus Seminar and Its Critics.* Santa Rosa, California: Polebridge Press, 1999.

Price, Robert M. *Deconstructing Jesus.* New York: Prometheus Books, 2000.

Price, Robert M. *The Incredible Shrinking Son of Man: How Reliable Is the Gospel Tradition?* New York: Prometheus Books, 2003.

Remsburg, John E. *The Christ.* New York: The Truth Seeker Company, 1909.

Robertson, A. *Jesus: Myth or History?* London: Watts, 1949.

Robertson, J. M. *Pagan Christs*. New York: University Books, 1967.

Schonfield, Hugh J. *The Passover Plot: A New Interpretation of the Life and Death of Jesus*. New York: Bernard Geiss Associates, 1965.

Schweitzer, Albert. *The Mysticism of Paul the Apostle*. New York: MacMillan, 1955.

Schweitzer, Albert. *The Quest of the Historical Jesus*. New York: MacMillan, 1954.

Sheehan, Thomas. *The First Coming: How the Kingdom of God Became Christianity*. New York: Random House, 1986.

Smith, Morton. *Jesus the Magician*. San Francisco: Harper & Row, 1978.

Talbert, Charles H. *Reimarus: Fragments*. Lives of Jesus series. Philadelphia: Fortress Press, 1970.

Walker, Barbara G. *The Woman's Encyclopedia of Myths and Secrets*. San Francisco: Harper & Row, 1983.

Wells, G. A. *Did Jesus Exist?* London: Pemberton, 1975.

Wells, G. A. *The Historical Evidence for Jesus*. New York: Prometheus Books, 1982.

Wells, G. A. *The Jesus of the Early Christians*. London: Pemberton Books, 1971.

Wells, G. A. *The Jesus Legend*. Peru, Illinois: Open Court Publishing, 1996.

Zindler, Frank. *The Jesus the Jews Never Knew*. Cranford, New Jersey: American Atheist Press, 2003.

Did Jesus Rise From the Dead? (Chapter 16)

Crossan, John Dominic. *The Birth of Christianity: Discovering What Happened in the Years Immediately After the Execution of Jesus*. San Francisco: Harper San Francisco, 1989.

Festinger, Leon. *When Prophecy Fails: A Social and Psychological Study*. San Francisco: HarperCollins, 1964.

Flew, Antony, and Gary Habermas. *Did Jesus Rise from the Dead?* San Francisco: Harper & Row, 1987.

Lüdemann, Gerd. *The Resurrection of Christ: A Historical Inquiry.* New York: Prometheus, 2004.

Lüdemann, Gerd, and Alf Ozen. *What Really Happened to Jesus: A Historical Approach to the Resurrection.* Westminster John Knox Press, 1996.

Price, Robert M., and Jeffery Jay Lowder, eds. *The Empty Tomb: Jesus Beyond the Grave.* New York: Prometheus Books, 2005.

Wall, Elissa. *Stolen Innocence: My Story of Growing Up in a Polygamous Sect, Becoming a Teenage Bride, and Breaking Free of Warren Jeffs.* New York: William Morrow, 2008.

Former Believers (Chapter 18)

Ali, Ayaan Hirsi. *Infidel.* New York: Free Press, 2007.

Babinski, Edward T. *Leaving the Fold: Testimonies of Former Fundamentalists.* New York: Prometheus Books, 1995.

Cooke, Bill. *A Rebel to His Last Breath: Joseph McCabe and Rationalism.* New York: Prometheus Books, 2001.

Grierson, Bruce. "An Atheist in the Pulpit: What Happens When Religious Leaders Lose Their Faith?" *Psychology Today,* January/February 2008.

Hewetson, Richard. "From Christian to Human Being." *Freethought Today,* June/July 2000. http://ffrf.org/fttoday/2000/june_july2000/hewetson.php.

Ketter, Vern. *Think About It! From Priest to Peace.* Bloomington, Indiana: Authorhouse, 2006.

Lobdell, William. *Losing My Religion: How I Lost My Faith Reporting on Religion in America.* New York: HarperCollins, 2009.

Loftus, John W. *Why I Rejected Christianity: A Former Apologist Explains.* Victoria, B.C.: Trafford Publishing, 2007.

McLoughlin, Emmett. *Famous Ex-Priests.* New York: Lyle Stuart, 1968.

O'Brien, James M. *Confessions of a Sixties Priest: But Probably Not What You're Thinking.* iUniverse, Inc., 2008

O'Brien, James M. *Making a Priest in the Fifties: Memoir of a Nervous Seminarian.* iUniverse, Inc., 2006.

Reed, Tom. "From Roman Catholic Priest to Atheist." *Freethought Today,* June/July 2002. http://ffrf.org/fttoday/2002/june-july02/reed.php.

Runyon, G. Vincent. *Why I Left the Ministry and Became an Atheist.* San Diego: Superior Books, 1959. http://www.infidels.org/library/historical/vincent_runyon/left_ministry.html.

Templeton, Charles. *Farewell to God: My Reasons for Rejecting the Christian Faith.* Toronto: McClellan and Stuart, Inc., 1996.

Warraq, Ibn. *Why I Am Not a Muslim.* New York: Prometheus, 1995.

Origin of Religion (Chapter 19)

Boyer, Pascal. *Religion Explained: The Evolutionary Origins of Religious Thought.* New York: Basic Books, 2001.

Dennett, Daniel C. *Breaking the Spell: Religion as a Natural Phenomenon.* New York: Viking, 2006.

Pinker, Steven. *The Blank Slate: The Modern Denial of Human Nature.* New York: Viking, 2002.

Sapolsky, Robert M. "Circling the Blanket for God." Chap. 17 in *The Trouble with Testosterone.* New York: Scribner, 1998.

Shermer, Michael. *How We Believe: The Search for God in an Age of Science.* New York: W. H. Freeman & Company, 1999.

Shermer, Michael. *Why People Believe Weird Things: Pseudoscience, Superstition, and Other Confusions of Our Time.* New York: W. H. Freeman, 1997.

Wilson, David Sloan. *Darwin's Cathedral: Evolution, Religion, and the Nature of Society.* Chicago: University of Chicago Press, 2002.

Wolpert, Lewis. *Six Impossible Things Before Breakfast: The Evolutionary Origins of Belief.* New York: W. W. Norton, 2006.

Wright, Robert. *The Moral Animal: Why We Are the Way We Are; The New Science of Evolutionary Psychology.* New York: Vintage Books, 1994.

Index

A

Ad hominem arguments, 53, 54, 71, 87–89, 93, 249

Adam, 3, 34, 124; and biblical contradictions, 237

Adultery, and seventh commandment, 188

Afterlife, 342–44; atheist concept, 344–45

"Agency detector" theory, 350–54

Agnosticism, 96–97; definition, 96, 119

Ahaziah, and biblical contradictions, 235

Allegro, John, 273

Allen, Woody, 342

Anaheim Christian Center, 3, 8

Anger, 89–90

Animals on ark, and biblical contradictions, 237

"Anti-theists," 98

Arcadia Friends Church, 20–21

Archer, Gleason, 246

Archko Volume, 262

Argument from Incredulity, 50, 105–106

Ark, and biblical contradictions, 237

Atheism, 87–103; definitions, 97–98, 118, 120; vs. Christianity (author's debates), 68–82, 185–86. *See also specific issues*

Atheist afterlife, 344–45

Atheists: musical composers, 346–47; well-known, 327–36, 347–48. *See also specific names*

Atheists United, 61

Avalos, Hector, 77, 199, 333

Azusa Pacific College (later University), 18, 19, 20, 53–54, 251

B

Bar-Serapion, Mara, 261

Barfoot, Milton, 56

Barker, Carol (first wife), 20, 24, 41, 63

Barker, Dan (author): atheist beliefs, 40–41, 87–103; call to the ministry, 3–4, 5, 13–14; children, 20, 24, 65–66, 337–42; college years, 18–20; debates, as atheist, 68–82, 185–86; deconversion letter, 44–45, 46–48; deconversion, reactions to, 48–66; and FFRF, 309–19, 322–36; as minister, 23–44; missionary work in Mexico, 5–6, 14; musical work, 5, 8, 9, 14–15, 20, 21, 24, 25–29, 35, 44–50, 66; ordination, 23–24; personal religious experience, 3–4, 5, 10–11, 30–31, 36, 37–38; questions about Christianity, 33–45; religious work, after college, 20–44; religious work, early, 5–18; travels, as atheist, 68, 320–36; as "true Christian," 31–32; youth, 3, 5–18, 60

Barker, Darrell (brother), 5, 56, 60–61, 108

Barker, Keith (uncle), 62–63

Barker, Norman (father), 4–5, 57, 59–60, 102

Barker, Pat (mother), 5, 57–59

Barker, Tom (brother), 5, 61

BE/NBE sets (existence/nonexistence), 131–34, 142

Beatitudes, 197–201

Behavioral dilemmas. *See* Morality

Belief, religious, origin of, 111, 349–53

Benson, Steve, 324–26

Berry, Joy, 20, 28

Bible, 40, 92–93, 115–16; contradictions and discrepancies, 56, 116, 222–50, 265, 281–89; ethics, 201–202; "good" teachings, 184–202; and human rights, 171–72; metaphors/parables, 33, 34, 39, 131; and "might makes right," 167–70; and moral examples, 172–77; and morality, 69–70, 112–13, 161–202, 203–207; Old Testament/New Testament parallels, 195, 273; translations/versions, 241–42, 248–49, 250

Big Bang and Big Bang cosmology, 74–75, 107, 108, 131, 133, 135, 136–37

Birth of Jesus. *See* Jesus, birth

Blind men and elephant analogy, 283

Blindness analogy, and faith, 112

Bolton, Rich, 314, 316

Bonilla, Manuel, 14–15, 27, 54

Book of Mormon, 264, 301, 326

Boone, Pat, 29

Bova, Ben, 38

Boyd, Greg, 73, 124, 301, 349

Boyer, Pascal, 350

Buddhism: "Golden Rule" version, 193; Ten Precepts, 192

Burckhardt, Jacob, 254

Bush, George W., 309, 310, 311, 313, 315, 318

C

Calvin, John, 70

Capital punishment, and bible, 183; Fourth Commandment, 164, 187

Carrier, Richard, 78, 232

Castration, and Jesus, 180

Catholic Church, and Second Commandment, 187

Causality and cause/effect arguments, 114, 130–44

Character attacks, 88–89

Charismatic Movement, 3, 21, 22

Christianity vs. atheism (author's debates), 68–82, 185–86

Christians in Action (CIA), 61

Church of Jesus Christ of Latter Day Saints. *See* Mormons

Clergy, former, becoming atheists, 331–34

Colson, Chuck, 312

Compassion, 215–16

Confucianism, "Golden Rule" version, 193

Copleston, Frederick, 141, 143

Corey, Michael, 78

Cosmos and cosmological arguments, 107–109, 125, 130–44

Cox, Shirley and Verlin, 52

Craig, William Lane, 131, 132–35, 136, 141, 142, 347

Creation, 105–10, 130–44; and biblical contradictions, 237

Creationism, 38, 106, 220

Crucifixion. *See* Jesus, crucifixion

Cummins, Ted, 20–21

D

D'Souza, Dinesh, 82–83

Daniels, Edwin (pseudonym), 49

David and the Shewbread story, and biblical contradictions, 231

Davies, Paul, 107

Dawkins, Richard, 50, 105, 324, 330, 352, 353–54

Dead Sea Scrolls, 272, 273

Death, 342–43, 355

Decalogue. *See* Ten Commandments

Deceit, and God, 176

Declaration of Independence, 216, 218

Deism, definition, 118

DiIulio, John, 310, 314

Disabled, and God, 176

Dispensationalists, and Old Testament, 165

Domeij, Scoti, 51–52

Doyle, James, 311

E

Edwards, James, 11–14

Ehrman, Bart, 263

Elohim, 186

K

Kalam Cosmological Argument, 130–44
Khalfan, Ali, 80–81
Killing; and biblical contradictions,
   222–23; and God, 172–77, 217; and
   Sixth Commandment, 188, 203–207
King, Martin Luther, 200
Koran. *See* Islam
Kuhlman, Kathryn, 8–10

L

Law of Reciprocity, 194
Laws of nature, 71–72, 82, 109–10
Laws of thermodynamics, 71–72; defini-
   tion, 109–10
Laziness, in bible, 201
Lewis, C. S., 290
Liberals, 33–34, 37
Life after death, 342–44; atheist concept,
   344–45
Life, meaning and purpose, 148–52,
   344–45, 347
Lord and Master concept, in bible, 184
Love, 195–96; understanding of, 89,
   150, 151
"Love thy neighbor" concept, 194–97
Lowe, Walter, 185–86
Lucian, 261
Lueders, Bill, 58
Luke. *See* Gospels
Lying, biblical contradictions, 223–24

M

Maguire, Patrick, 331–32
Manna Music, 25, 26, 35, 50
Mark. *See* Gospels
Martin, Michael, 97, 132
Matthew. *See* Gospels
McBain, Loren, 51
McDowell, Josh, 262–63, 290
McKown, Delos, 332
Meekness; in Beatitudes, 197–98; in
   Christian history, 198
MentorKids USA, 312
Metaphors/parables, of bible, 33, 34,
   39, 231

Michal, and biblical contradictions, 238
Miller, Robert J., 301
Millerites, 302
Ministers, "qualifications" of, 95–96
Miracles, 94, 117, 274–75, 278–80
Mithra and Mithraism, 270–71
Modisett, Mitch, 333
Moore, Roy, 317
Moral relativism, 213
Morality, 152–55, 208–21; and
   bible, 69–70, 112–13, 161–202,
   203–207; definition, 214; and Ten
   Commandments, 187–90
Morehead, John, 81
Mormons, 260, 264, 278, 300, 301, 326
Mortality, 342–43
Moses, 173–74; and biblical contradic-
   tions, 229; and Ten Commandments,
   190–91
Mother Teresa, 178, 215
Multiverse concept, 107–109
Murder; and biblical contradictions,
   222–23; and God, 172–74, 177,
   217; and Sixth Commandment, 188,
   203–207
Music, composed by atheists/agnostics,
   345–46

N

Name calling, and biblical contradictions,
   233
Natural (descriptive) laws, 71–72, 82,
   109–10
Natural rights, 216, 218
Natural selection, 110, 220
Nature, definition, 154
NBE/BE sets (nonexistence/existence),
   131–34, 142
Nelson, Culver H., 289–90
Nero, 260

O

O'Brien, Jim, 332
Oath swearing, and biblical contradictions, 235–36

Obedience to law, and biblical contradictions, 236–37
Occam's Razor, 91
Office of Faith-Based and Community Initiatives, 310
Olson, Roxanne, 53
Ontological arguments, 115
Origen, 255, 256, 269
Original sin, 183. *See also* Sin and sinners

P

Pagan mythical parallels to Jesus story, 269–72
Paine, Thomas, 116, 278–79, 280, 282
Pandera, Joseph, 269
Parable/metaphors, of bible, 33, 34, 39, 231
Paradise Remembered, 62, 63
Parascientific claims, 117–18
Parental sins, and biblical contradictions, 228–29
Pascal, Blaise, 114, 115
Pascal's Wager, 114–15
Paul: and commandments, 195; and Jesus, 243–50, 264–65; and resurrection, 292–96
Paul's men, and biblical contradictions, 238, 243–50, 265, 296
Paulos, John Allen, 82
Payne, Peter, 70–71
"Peace," use in bible, 199
Peralta, Eli, 50–51
Perfection, definition, 154
Personal religious experiences, 72, 110–11, 112, 347–49
Petry, Fred, 27, 28
Pfeiffer, Gary, 19
Philo-Judaeus (Philo of Alexandria), 253–54
Phlegon, 262
Photius, 254
Pincus, Andy, 316
Pliny (the younger), 259
Pontius Pilate, 256, 260
Pope, Richard, 333
Posner, Richard, 315
Poverty, and Jesus, 178–79
Price, Robert, 301–302

Psychic powers, 117–18
Punishment for parents' sins, and biblical contradictions, 228–29

Q

Qibla (directional prayer wall), 80
Quantum physics, 117

R

Racism, and God, 177
Rajabali, Hassanain, 78–80, 92
Randi, James, 352
Randolph, David, 324
Rationalism, definition, 119
Reality, definition, 119
Reason, definition, 119
Receiver-transmitter argument, 111
Reed, Tom, 333
Reincarnation, 117–18
Relativism, 209–21
Religion, definition, 118
Religious belief, origin, 111, 349–53
Religious experiences. *See* Personal religious experiences
Remsburg, John E., 253–54, 258
Resurrection. *See* Jesus, resurrection
Revelation, 116
Richard Dawkins Foundation, 330
Robertson, J. M., 269
Robertson, Pat, 275
Russell, Bertrand, 88, 115, 141, 143, 172, 343, 345
Russell, Charles, 302
Rutherford, Joseph, 302

S

Sabbath, 153, 163–64, 167, 174–75, 187, 217; and biblical contradictions, 224–25
Sacks, Oliver, 328–29
Sagan, Carl, 279, 344–45
St. Anselm, 115
St. Augustine, 138
Salisbury, Lee, 333
"Salvation," 354, 355